An Idea, and Bullets

An Idea, and Bullets

A Rice Roots Exploration of Why No French,
American, or South Vietnamese General Could
Ever Have Brought Victory in Vietnam

An AUSA Book

* * *

William Haponski

ISBN: 1499622236
ISBN 13: 9781499622232
Library of Congress Control Number: 2016900636
CreateSpace Independent Publishing Platform, North Charleston, SC

Combatant Books
8284 SE 176th Lawson Loop
The Villages, FL 32162

Cover photo: Rice paddy near Thu Dau Mot (Phu Cuong), courtesy Major (Ret)
James C. Pitts

Dedicated to

General of the Army (Ret--French) Jean Delaunay
Geneviève (de Galard) de Heaulme, "The Angel of Dien Bien Phu"
Colonel (Ret--French) Jean de Heaulme
Lieutenant Colonel Nguyen Minh Chau (Former Marine Corps,
Republic of Vietnam)
Dr. Charles Lamb
Sandra Haponski
Maura and Stephen Cornell
Colonel (Ret—USA) Jerry J. Burcham
Troopers and Soldiers of 11th Armored Cavalry Regiment,
Vietnam and Cambodia
Troopers and Soldiers of Task Force 1-4 Cavalry,
1st Infantry Division, Vietnam

"You cannot kill an idea with bullets"

General Jacques Philippe Leclerc
Commander, French Expeditionary Corps entering Vietnam 1945

Contents

Foreword

∗   ∗   ∗

IN THE EIGHT YEARS FROM 1775 to 1783, American revolutionaries astounded observers in capitals all across Europe by defeating—against all odds—mighty Great Britain. They did so on the wings of a supremely motivating dream: to gain independence and to create a single nation united.

Nearly two centuries later, in the 30 years from 1945 to 1975, Vietnamese revolutionaries, driven by that very same dream, shocked the world by defeating, one after the other, three powerful foes: France, the United States, and their fellow countrymen in the southern half of Vietnam.

That is more than a coincidental similarity of aspirational ideas and surprising outcomes. Ho Chi Minh, the revered Communist and Nationalist leader of Vietnam's revolutionaries from well before WW II, dramatically proclaimed his movement's basis to a huge cheering Throng in Hanoi in 1945. "All men are created equal," he said. "The Creator has given us certain inviolable Rights; the right to Life, the right to be Free, and the right to achieve Happiness." After pausing for effect, he continued, "These immortal words are taken from the Declaration of Independence of the United States of America in 1776. In a larger sense, this means that: All the people on earth are born equal; All the people have the right to live, to be happy, to be free." He then invoked a second declaration, the one guiding the French Revolution in 1791, saying,

"Men are born and must remain free and have equal rights. Those are undeniable truths."

In the light of that animating vision--the unwavering idea of a united Vietnam free of foreign influence--William Haponski holds that no French or American or South Vietnamese general could have gained a victory in Vietnam. That is his central theme as he tells the story of those three decades of war.

His telling is as unique as his thesis. Although the book itself is solid history, Haponski's style is far from that of the traditional historian. While he writes often in the first person and does not shy away from placing himself in the story where appropriate, the tone is not that of a memoir. That out-of-the-ordinary approach reflects the author himself. Haponski has examined the war exhaustively for half a century, at every level from reflections on his first-hand experiences to post-doctoral research. The result is an absorbing blend ranging from the deeply personal to the academically professional. He has created a multi-dimensional narrative, at once alive and lucid.

A most valuable facet of the book is its focus on events *inside* Vietnam, placed in the clarifying framework of the four distinct phases of the long war. First, from 1945 to 1954, was the fight against the French. Next came a decade of transition, 1954 to 1964, as American military elements gradually took the place of French forces. Then, from 1965 to 1972, was the ill-fated American effort to defend South Vietnam. And finally, 1973 to 1975, the conquest of South Vietnam. To understand the Vietnam War, to really understand it, one must know the essence of all four phases.

Ever since North Vietnamese tanks rolled into Saigon in April 1975, journalists and generals and politicians and historians have debated heatedly over why America lost. Conclusions abound.... It was a default, not a defeat. It was lost in Washington, not in Vietnam. Poor generalship is to blame. And on and on.

This book might not stop the debate, but it deftly rearranges the arguments. Haponski contends no general—no general—could have mustered military forces to defeat the enduring idea of a free and uni-fied Vietnam. That idea, so fervently held, provided the Vietnamese the will to persevere unto victory no matter how long it took or how painful the cost.

In the end, willpower trumped firepower.

--Lieutenant General (Ret) Dave R. Palmer

Preface

*   *   *

"THE POLITICIANS, MEDIA, AND HIPPIES lost that war for us!" Since the 30 April 1975 fall of Saigon how many times have we heard it, or something like it? Especially from veterans who sacrificed so much, having buddies killed, getting wounded themselves, getting Dear John letters, acquiring cancers from toxins, trying to deal with their physical wounds and PTSD?

Many vets have expressed their feelings more colorfully: "The ******* *politicians*, ******* *media*, and ******* *hippies* lost that******* war for us!"

Can the vets who fought close in—down in the jungles and rice paddies, on the inland waterways, or overhead engaging the enemy—be faulted for such a view when it also came as a post-war assessment from the very top? The senior American commander in charge of prosecuting the war during its buildup and peak of fighting was Admiral U.S.G. Sharp, Commander in Chief Pacific. As such, he was in overall charge of U.S. operations in the war—on land, on water, and in the air. He concluded his memoir, saying: "The real tragedy of Vietnam is that this war was not won by the other side, by Hanoi or Moscow or Peiping. It was lost in Washington, D. C."[1]

This remains an all too common belief. The stark facts, though, are that the Vietnam War was lost before our first American shot was fired. In fact, it was lost before the first French Expeditionary Corps shot, almost two decades before us, and was finally lost when the South Vietnamese after us fought partly, then entirely, on their own. It was not a war in which the generals of France, America, or South Vietnam could have led to victory.

It is important for Americans to understand why.

America's inability to win in Vietnam cannot be just dumped conveniently onto the laps of the Washington politicians who established the rules of engagement within which the war could be fought. In essence those parameters boiled down to restrictions on crossing borders during the ground war in South Vietnam, blockading North Vietnamese ports, and conducting the air war over North Vietnam. Washington rejected the "kick ass and take names" approach of tough-talking men such as General Curtis LeMay and Senator Barry Goldwater—LeMay who in World War II courageously had shown he could fight and destroy, and Goldwater who had performed often dangerous service in that war. Their utterances on how to win the Vietnam War—bomb them back to the Stone Age; make that place a mud puddle—were roundly rejected by the American people and decision makers in Washington, and rightly so.[2]

The ultimate American intention after the 1954 Geneva Accords was to enable Republic of Vietnam (South Vietnam) to remain a sovereign nation. After commitment of ground combat units in 1965, the commander of Military Assistance Command Vietnam (MACV), General William C. Westmoreland, was given authority to fight the ground war within South Vietnam as he saw fit and was afforded enormous resources to do so. This same authority was passed on to his successor, General Creighton W. Abrams, who had still substantial but steadily diminishing resources. History shows that despite great odds and burdensome limitations, victory had sometimes been snatched from the jaws of defeat. Why that was not to be the case in Vietnam needs exploration.

Shortly after World War II ended, a hero of that war, General Jacques Philippe Leclerc,[3] commanded the French Expeditionary Corps entering Vietnam. De Gaulle gave him the mission of restoring the status quo, that is, returning Indochina to its prewar colonial condition.

Quickly Leclerc committed French Union troops to action in this hostile environment and soon began to discover what an enormous task it would be. He concluded, "You cannot kill an idea with bullets."[4]

He urged his government to negotiate.

France chose bullets.

The rest is tragic history.

Causes of American failure stemming from high level politics and policies have been profusely dissected, analyzed, and argued, and there is little need to go there again except to provide background. This book, rather, is the story of the conflict of the 30-year war *within Vietnam*, 1945-1975. It is by a person who was a combatant not only in six violent, large battles and many smaller firefights, but a leader with a full range of pacification duties, a commander who lost 43 wonderful young men killed and many more wounded, men who were doing what their country asked of them. This story is the result of a quest for answers by one who, after decades of wondering what it was about—*what was it all about?*—turned to a years-long search of French, American, and Vietnamese sources and conducted a multitude of queries of participants.

It is a story of success on the one hand, defeat on the other, and the ingredients of both, inspirational or sordid as they may be.

It is a story mostly lived and revealed by the people *inside Vietnam* who were directly involved in the war: from French, American, and Vietnamese leaders in high positions, down to the jungle boots and sandals level of the fighters, and among the Vietnamese people who were living the war. Because of what was happening *inside Vietnam itself*, no matter what policies and directives came out of Paris or Washington, or the influences in Moscow or Beijing, it is about a *Vietnamese idea* which would eventually triumph over bullets.

Hal Moore, Twelve Inches, and Another Couple Inches

Our story of an idea is perhaps best opened by Hal Moore. As a lieutenant colonel, Harold G. (Hal) Moore commanded his battalion of 1st

Cavalry Division in what many recognize as the first major battle of the American war, fought at LZ X-Ray in the Ia Drang Valley, 14-16 November 1965. His book, written with reporter Joe Galloway, *We Were Soldiers Once . . . and Young*, and the resulting movie, *We Were Soldiers*, powerfully depict the very best that America had to offer: its soldiers locked in mortal combat with highly capable, determined soldiers of North Vietnam.

Lieutenant General Harold G. "Hal" Moore, 27 May 1975. (NARA)

Hal Moore is one of the greatest American soldiers to come out of Vietnam alive. Certainly he is one of the most highly respected – even loved – by not just his veterans of that battle, but by many other soldiers who in one way or another have known him, either personally, through his writing, or through his continuing efforts to help all veterans and their families. Retired Lieutenant General Moore and Joe Galloway, the journalist who was at Hal's side during the fierce fighting, made trips back to Vietnam beginning in 1990 and ending in 1999. Their first trip was to meet commanders who had fought against them in those hellish days in the Ia Drang Valley. They were unsuccessful in their first attempts to meet Hal's counterpart or other commanders. On a following trip, though, because of his book in which he fully accorded the North Vietnamese the respect they deserved as formidable opponents, he and his party were granted permission to tour the battlefield itself, accompanied by the lieutenant general who as a lieutenant colonel had commanded the forces Hal had fought.

In a book which resulted from those return trips, again with Galloway as coauthor, *We Are Soldiers Still*, Hal said, "When my soldiers spoke harshly, with anger, of our enemies, I told them to remember that these men had mothers who would be shattered by the news of their deaths; that they, like us, had been caught up in great power politics and were doing their duty as we were."[5]

Across the years I have tried to tell my veterans much the same thing. Like Moore's veterans, some of my men understand and accept this and feel compassion for our former enemies and their families, and some don't.

In his 1990 trip to Hanoi, Moore met an official in the Ministry of Foreign Affairs, a tough old soldier who had fought the French. Moore said, "He seemed bemused by our total focus on our war in Vietnam and suggested that we might profit from a visit to the Vietnam Historical Museum nearby. . . . The high point for us was not the exhibits but finding a huge mural that stretched across one long wall that was both a timeline and a map of Vietnam's unhappy history dating back well over a thousand years. There on the wall we saw thick red arrows dropping down into Vietnam from the north, depicting half a dozen invasions and occupations of Vietnam by neighboring China, and some of those occupations lasted hundreds of years before Vietnamese patriots and rebels drove them out, again and again and again. The Chinese section of the timeline stretched out for fifty feet or so. The section devoted to the French and their 150 years of colonial occupation was depicted in about twelve inches. The miniscule part that marked the U.S. war was only a couple inches."[6]

A couple inches!
Moore said, "It put everything into a perspective few Westerners seemingly had ever considered before marching their soldiers off into the jungles of a nation full of ardent nationalists who had demonstrated that they were fully prepared to fight for generations until the foreign occupier got tired of war, or choked on his own blood."[7]

I have never seen the map, confining my 2005 and 2010 visits back to Vietnam to the boondocks north of Saigon where as a lieutenant colonel I commanded the armored cavalry task force of 1st Infantry Division. But anyone who can envision the mural that Moore described has gone a long way toward understanding why no French or American general could ever have "won" the wars France and the U.S. fought in Vietnam.

Neither could any South Vietnamese general have defeated his opponents. Not necessarily because he was a bad general – there were some good South Vietnamese generals, and many heroic and dedicated South Vietnamese soldiers and civilians – but because of what so many North Vietnamese and Viet Cong had and too many South Vietnamese lacked—*fire in the belly*!

That fire started way back on the left edge of the mural. It blazed at times, fell back into glowing embers, then grew bright again, fell back and blazed again, and again. Without forgetting the huge portion of early invasions and domination that forged Vietnamese spirit, we can focus on the "twelve inches" that was the French portion and the "couple inches" of American. Such small segments. Such huge tragedies.

The French failed. Subsequently no American general, regardless of how skilled or how good his strategy and tactics, could have led to victory in that war. Not General Westmoreland. Not General Abrams. Not General Weyand who followed Abrams. And not any American generals who might otherwise have been selected to command the effort instead of them. And most definitely not any of the South Vietnamese generals who carried on the war to its conclusion in 1975.

Why?

The essence of the answer lies in an idea expressed by these closely related words: *Independence* and *union*, or *unification* as it came to be called. The idea was a *Vietnamese* idea that was virtually the lifeblood of the Vietnamese people.

Acknowledgments

✳   ✳   ✳

MERLE L. PRIBBENOW, JR., FOR translations from Vietnamese histories and documents, and sharing his insights to the nature of South and North Vietnamese and their conduct of the war.

Colonel (Ret) Jerry J. Burcham, for insightful editing, assisting in acquiring and processing illustrations, and generously aiding the publication process.

Anne Le Dimna Marsilio, for ensuring the accuracy of my French translations.

Lieutenant General (Ret) Dave R. Palmer for his contribution of the Foreword.

Roger Cirillo, PhD, Director of AUSA book program for his years of encouragement and continuous support.

Research team of 1-4 Cavalry, especially Ronald M. Halicki for getting research started, Colonel (Ret) Carl H. "Skip" Bell III, for heading the team; archivists (former) Sergeant Michael T. O'Connor, and Sergeant First Class (Ret) Terry L. Valentine, for their years of efforts and insights; Major (Ret) James C. Pitts, for his significant input; Lieutenant Colonel (Ret) James A. "Jay" Ward, for map research and production; Major (Ret) Thomas C. Witter, for insights to the nature of civil affairs and pacification efforts.

Indochina

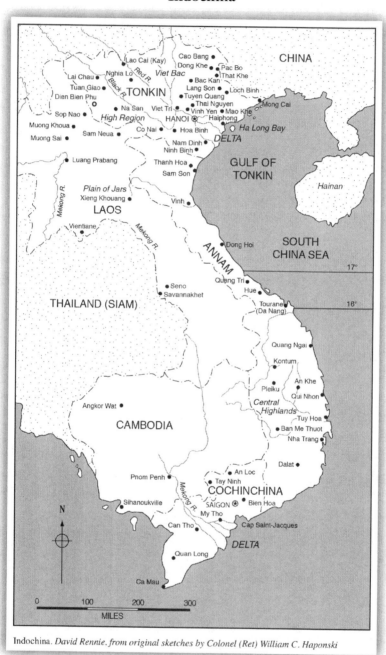

Indochina. *David Rennie. from original sketches by Colonel (Ret) William C. Haponski*

North Vietnam

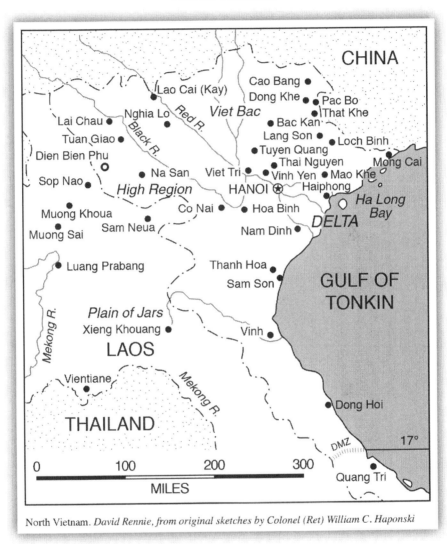

North Vietnam. *David Rennie, from original sketches by Colonel (Ret) William C. Haponski*

South Vietnam

South Vietnam. *David Rennie, from original sketches by Colonel (Ret) William C. Haponski*

1st Infantry Division Area of Operations

Area of Operations 1st Infantry Division. *David Rennie. from original sketches by Colonel (Ret) William C. Haponski*

Part One: The French War - The Idea, and Bullets

*   *   *

General Vo Nguyen Giap:
"*C'est fini*. It's over. We will yield no longer."
Hanoi, 18 December 1946

*   *   *

CHAPTER 1

Independence, Union

*   *   *

THOSE WORDS—*INDEPENDENCE, UNION*—CAME TO ILLUMINATE the aspirations of millions of Vietnamese, North and, yes, South.

The consuming desire for independence had been imbedded in the Vietnamese for two thousand years. They hated foreign domination, whether Chinese, Mongol, Champa, French, Japanese, French again, or American. Independence and union of their country became a passionate credo of not just the 20th century Vietnamese Communists, but of other independence-minded Vietnamese nationalists as well. It was the Communists, however, who organized early and well, and from a slow beginning spread this desire to a sufficiently large core of adherents that ultimately it became the driving force of the North as well as many in the South throughout thirty years of Indochina wars. In Saigon on 30 April 1975, after decades of enormous sacrifices and losses on both sides, the gates of the Diem-named Independence Palace were smashed down, and a new government took charge. From all the tragic waste emerged a new Vietnam. That it was deeply flawed then, and to a large degree still is, does not seem as important to most Vietnamese as the fact that after desperate struggle, Vietnam since 1975 has been one nation, independent, unified.

*   *   *

I served as a lieutenant colonel in two combat units in Vietnam – 11th Armored Cavalry Regiment, and 1st Squadron, 4th Cavalry, 1st Infantry

Division. In 11th Cav in 1968 I was first the plans and operations officer, then executive officer, the two top staff roles. In 1-4 Cav in 1969 I was the commander. In these assignments I was deeply into pacification and violent combat against our enemy's guerrilla, local and regional, and main forces. I reacted to their attacks and planned and directed a variety of actions against them. I was with my men, many times shot at on the ground and in the air, mortared and rocketed. I narrowly missed mines and being hit, and like them I unknowingly sucked in the defoliant toxins that have killed, or is killing many of us. I had direct or indirect responsibility in the killing of over one thousand enemy. And at very close range I killed one man, perhaps three men, who came near to killing me. I knew from fighting the enemy and interrogating prisoners that, like my soldiers, most of my enemy were incredibly dedicated, courageous young men.

In 11th Cav we lost 64 troopers KIA while I was with the regiment, not counting the soldiers from our Vietnamese Ranger battalions or U.S. infantry battalions under our operational control. In Task Force QuarterCav I lost 36 task force soldiers killed and seven others I had responsibility for protecting. Around 100 of my soldiers were evacuated from the battlefield with serious wounds, and many others were patched up and returned to duty. These soldiers were wonderful young men, called to perform tasks well beyond their 18, 19, 20 or so years, day after day, night after endless terrible night, to the end of their tours, medical evacuations, or deaths. I have experienced agonizing sorrow for those men killed and dreadfully wounded, and for their families and loved ones. Those great guys served their country magnificently. They were the best.

For years afterward I found myself pondering the enormous tragedy, wondering what it was about. *What in hell was it all about?*

In 1998, 29 years after I had come home, I was cleaning my storage shed and found myself looking at my old GI footlocker. I do not know why, but I opened it. The footlocker still smelled of Vietnam, an unmistakable musty smell of jungle and earth. I pulled out my journals, maps, letters, audiotapes, and other memorabilia, then put everything back except the journals: three large notebooks full of entries. I placed the journals on a shelf in my bedroom. On the Internet I came across a reference to my old unit. That led to contact with Mike O'Connor, who, I discovered, as a young sergeant had commanded a tank in my B Troop during our fierce QuarterCav battle in the Michelin Plantation, and we began corresponding. But for another year I could not bring myself to read my journals. When I finally looked into the first of them I knew I had to revisit that fantastically agonizing – and compelling—experience.

Mike had developed a unit website, and with his help I began contacting former soldiers of my task force and, my curiosity piqued by what they told me, I began researching in earnest. Having committed so much of myself to this war, I had arrived at the point of wanting to know what it was about – not for our president and national leaders who committed us to a war to contain Communism, citing the domino theory—not even so much for our nation which had seemed to come apart as a result of that war—I wanted to know what it was about for *me*, for *my men*.

Soon I established a research team of over a dozen of my veterans, and we met and recovered thousands of pages of original documents from National Archives. A few were in my handwriting; some others were typed operation orders bearing my signature. I began studying the war in earnest, doing Internet research, buying books, making several more trips to National Archives, corresponding with Frenchmen who had fought in the Indochina war, querying my troopers and other veterans. Within a year I had collected copies of all unit records from squadron and battalion and higher units up to MACV which related to our 1968-69 11th Cav and 1-4 Cav experiences, and I added to this collection in the next several months and years.

During the war in Vietnam I had been profoundly curious about our enemy. I took every opportunity to root out and absorb information. Through my interpreters I extensively interviewed many prisoners. I probed intelligence personnel in my headquarters, adjacent and higher headquarters and in district and province advisory staffs. I had many conversations with a Vietnamese district chief and his village chiefs, all with long experience in fighting our common enemy. I talked with residents of hamlets about the Viet Cong and NVA. At scenes of our small contacts and large battles I tried to discover how our enemy lived and fought. What did they believe? Why did they do the things they did? I tried also to learn as much as possible about the South Vietnamese with whom I came into contact, soldiers and civilians.

From my decades-later research, I learned much more than I knew when I served in Vietnam, particularly about the enemy – the fighters themselves, their units, their terrain, and especially their motivations. Much of the enemy story was contained in our records, in particular, interrogation of prisoner of war reports and other intelligence reports. I collected hundreds of books and articles, and thousands of original documents in French and English. Also of great interest were translations of books and other material that had been written by our former enemy. One such book was the official history of the People's Army of Vietnam, *Victory in Vietnam*, translated by Merle Pribbenow. I contacted him and learned that he was an Indochina expert, retired from the CIA. After countless exchanges of information by mail and email, I found that Merle had given me a unique opportunity to discover much more about the actual enemy who had faced my units. His keen insights into our former enemy's order of battle, personnel, combat practices, mannerisms, and motivations have been invaluable.

Some of the sources for this book are the same as for my earlier books, *One Hell of a Ride*, and *Danger's Dragoons*, an updated, more comprehensive edition of *One Hell*. My sources are:

1) My Vietnam journals. 2) Letters and audio tapes to and from my wife, daughter, friends and family, and many photos and films I took in Vietnam. 3) A multitude of interviews, letters, e-mails, personal conversations, recorded and unrecorded phone calls with former members of my task force. 4) Original records of participating U.S. and South Vietnamese units from squadron/battalion through Army levels

(over 15,000 pages of documents, most from National Archives, some from other repositories). 5) Original North Vietnamese unit histories and articles, some translated specifically for me by Merle Pribbenow. 6) Endless queries of an important South Vietnamese official, Lieutenant Colonel Nguyen Minh Chau. 7) Original materials from French colonial times, supplemented by personal accounts sent to me by French combatants in the Indochina war. 8) All the books, articles and other secondary sources I could find on American, South Vietnamese, North Vietnamese, French, and British units in our area of operations,[1] their commanders and methods, especially those written by combatants. (9) A trip to Vietnam in 2005 to study the scenes of our actions, talk with Vietnamese participants on both sides in the war, and meet one of my "adopted" daughters from the hamlet that was the center of our 11th Cav pacification operations. (10) Additionally, for this current book I made another trip to Vietnam in 2010 to get more information and meet the remainder of my "adopted" Vietnamese family. Also I added substantially to my secondary sources of books and articles.

My experiences in Vietnam combat and my subsequent studies led me to conclude that:

1) The Vietnam War was lost before French expeditionary corps or American combat units came ashore. Said another way, there was never a war there which could be won. The reasons lie in the history of Vietnam and the character of its people going back more than 2,000 years.

2) From about 1930 forward, the desire for independence from foreign domination was so strong among the Vietnamese that it would sustain its growing number of adherents no matter how long the effort, no matter what the sacrifice. From about 1944, the desire for unification of their nation began to coalesce with the desire for independence. From 1945 to 1954 the Viet Minh fought and ultimately defeated the French Expeditionary Corps. The bulk of the Vietnamese people, North and South, so much

resented French domination that no French high commissioner(s) or general(s) could have brought victory in Vietnam.

3) Following the 1954 Geneva Accords, the Communists were able to reenergize the North and many Vietnamese in the South to fight the Southern government and military. They would outlast any other power which threatened their view of independence and unification.

4) By mid 1964 the intensive U.S. military and economic aid program in South Vietnam had failed. It would have failed under any MAAG/MACV commanding general or American ambassador because so many South Vietnamese people would not support their government. The North could govern and harness the will of the people; the South could not.

5) After the March 1965 insertion of U.S. ground combat forces, the People's War strategy of Ho Chi Minh and Vo Nguyen Giap proved flexible in adapting to changed circumstances, just as it had during the French war. They were able to fight using guerrillas, local and regional forces, and main forces simultaneously, with some pauses in intensity which enabled them to regroup and go at it again. They were aided by an extensive intelligence and espionage network which persisted despite vigorous attempts to counter it. No American generals, followed after 1971 by South Vietnamese generals, could permanently diminish the recuperative powers of their enemy.

6) The one chance for success—pacification—could never succeed in the South, no matter how promising, for two basic reasons. First, the South Vietnamese government could not gain the loyalty of a sufficient number of its people. Second, virtually every pacification effort was planned and supported by Americans instead of South Vietnamese. Even had the South Vietnamese planned and conducted the operations, they could not have succeeded because the efforts, almost always corrupted by an inbred manner of doing business, came from the top down and

not the village up. Importantly, South Vietnam's regular army, ARVN, was widely despised by the people. While I was with my "adopted" Vietnamese family in 2010 I asked them many questions about their experiences as children and young adults during the war. They had lived in a tiny agricultural hamlet up against the jungle of War Zone D. Among my questions, I asked if they were afraid of the VC? Of the Americans? No, they were not afraid of either. But they didn't like and were afraid of the ARVN.

*   *   *

One commentator said, "To begin the story of America's 'longest war' in the Johnson years---or even in the Kennedy Thousand Days---is like coming into a darkened theater in the middle of the picture. You can gather what has happened after awhile, but the relationship between what you are seeing happen on the screen and what had gone before remains fuzzy."[2] Yet that is what not just many historians but also key players in the war itself have done. William Colby, one of the most important among them in his role as America's Vietnam pacification manager, entitled his book, *Lost Victory: A Firsthand Account of America's Sixteen –Year Involvement in Vietnam.* He said we must investigate "the 'dilemma of defeat' . . . . from the perspective of the War on the ground and in the villages, jungles, mountains, and rice paddies of South Vietnam. We must review the long span of the years from 1959, when the Vietnamese Communists decided to open the 'Second Indochinese War' against the 'American-Diem' Government of South Vietnam, to their final victory in 1975."[3]

His book, based on his experiences from then forward, provides much-needed insights into the later stages of pacification as he built toward his conclusion that we lost a war which should have been a victory. This dedicated American who sacrificed much to serve our country went on to become the director of the CIA. He investigated well, and he

pulled together many pieces from his research, contacts, and own experiences. But by starting in 1959 "in the middle of the picture" without
considering the long Vietnamese history of struggle against foreigners,
without understanding the Confucian nature of Vietnamese character,
without considering the French war, compounded by gravely misunderstanding the American war despite his close involvement in it, he came
to the wrong conclusion. There was no Lost Victory. There was never a
victory to be won.

*　　*　　*

Kennedy's Secretary of State, Dean Rusk, said that of the president's
advisers, in 1961 only Under Secretary of State George W. Ball opposed
a gradual increase in military support of President Diem's South
Vietnam, believing it would lead inevitably into commitment of ground
troops. Rusk said of those advisers, "We knew that tough days lay ahead,
although none of us except George Ball guessed how tough indeed they
would be."[4] Ball told Kennedy during the dark days of 1963 that "To
commit American [ground combat] forces to South Vietnam would, in
my view, be a tragic error. Once that process started, I said, there would
be no end to it. 'Within five years we'll have three hundred thousand
men in the paddies and jungles and never find them again.' . . . To my
surprise, the President seemed quite unwilling to discuss the matter,
responding with an overtone of asperity: 'George, you're just crazier
than hell. That just isn't going to happen.'"[5]

Reflecting on Kennedy's assassination, General Bruce Palmer said,
"Since that day I have often asked myself what would have happened
with respect to South Vietnam if President Kennedy had lived. It is
a fascinating question on which to speculate. My own view is that he
would not have committed major U. S. combat forces, and that quite a
different story would have unfolded, although the ultimate fate of South
Vietnam might well have been the same."[6] However, Secretary Rusk "in
a news conference in September 1963, two months before his death . . .

summed up what he called 'a very simple policy' in regard to Vietnam: 'We want the war to be won, the Communists to be contained, and the Americans to go home. That is our policy. I am sure it is the policy of the people of Vietnam. We are not there to see a war lost.'"[7]

It is tempting but ultimately fruitless to indulge in what might-have-been, could-have-been, shoulda-coulda. "History" has a multitude of definitions, depending on the source. Common to most of them, however, is the word *events*. In this book I attempt to present *events* as they *were*, events which show that neither the French nor the American nor the South Vietnamese governments and military could ever have won a war in Vietnam regardless of who led the efforts.

The thinking, planning, and efforts in Paris, Washington, Beijing, and Moscow of course were important to the conduct and outcome of the war—important in just that order, with Paris leading (for without the tragic mistakes in Paris, the Vietnamese struggles for independence and unity would inevitably have had a profoundly different character, (though probably the same outcome—an independent, unified, Communist Vietnam). But that is matter for speculation. This book deals with what actually happened.

Many authors have set forth "Lessons Learned." Unfortunately, as our wars in Afghanistan, Iraq, Syria, and engagements elsewhere in our ongoing counter-war on terror have so well demonstrated, many of those "lessons" were not indeed "learned," or if they were, were ignored. In this book I try to present as succinctly as possible *the essence of the contest itself inside the political and social framework that constrained and guided it on both sides—that is, <u>within Vietnam</u>*—and leave it to the reader as to what lessons could have been learned. There are several, crucial to our approach to current and future wars. For example, the search into what makes Islamic State so powerful is increasingly focusing on ideas rather than bullets. The commander of U.S. Special Operations in the Middle East said, "We do not understand the movement, and until we do, we are not going to defeat it. . . .We have not defeated the idea. We do not even understand the idea."[8]

I have long been deeply interested in what the Vietnam combatants revealed about their experiences. I consider the term "combatants" to include all those who planned and fought within Vietnam—from Ho Chi Minh and Le Duan down to the Viet Minh and Viet Cong guerrillas; from Ngo Dinh Diem and Nguyen Van Thieu down to the ARVN sergeant who was my interpreter; from General Westmoreland and General Abrams down to the American sergeant who was my radioman. Writings of the highest level combatants and information about them of course are crucial to an understanding of the war. But interesting, and in many respects, the most revealing, stories were written by combatants who at the time thought and fought at the mid- and lower-levels. Their stories are usually unburdened by high level politics. Crucial matters were being debated and decided in Paris and Washington. But it was the matters in Hanoi and Saigon and throughout Vietnam, *among the combatants themselves which ultimately decided the war.* It is what the combatants believed, what they felt, what they *did,* that made all the difference.

CHAPTER 2

Indochina to September 1945

*   *   *

THE RECORDED HISTORY OF VIETNAM is nearly 3,000 years old. From 207 BC for about 1,100 of those years, Chinese dynasties either ruled directly or dominated the Vietnamese. A revolt in 40 AD led by two Vietnamese sisters named Trung succeeded in recapturing a significant portion of Vietnam from the hated Chinese, but it was crushed within two years. Another woman, Ba Trieu, in 225 AD led a revolt that was longer lasting, almost a quarter century. In later years, Vietnamese children learned the stories of these heroic women whose courage, patriotism, and martial skills explain to a large degree why women have historically been so highly regarded in Vietnamese society, not just within the family, but in important public leadership roles.

In 938 AD a naval battle on the Bach Dang River near Halong Bay in Northern Vietnam brought the Vietnamese a period of independence. This was later challenged and at times usurped by periodic Mongol and Chinese invasions until the early 15ᵗʰ century when the Vietnamese again regained power.

The hate for foreign rule resulted in inherent resentment of the Chinese specifically, and any type of foreign domination generally. The fact that for some periods the Vietnamese were able to gain independence gave much later Vietnamese hope they could do it again.

Pham Van Dong, Premier of the Democratic Republic of Vietnam (DRV)—North Vietnam—then of the Socialist Republic of Vietnam (SRV) during and after the Vietnam War, said, "Our history, from the time of the Hung kings and the Trung sisters, to the era of President Ho Chi Minh and beyond has been a history of great struggle. Throughout history, the Vietnamese people have always done their best to defend the country and to build the nation."[1]

French Colonialism

The arrival of Roman merchants in 166 BC seems to have been the earliest contact with Westerners. Many centuries were then to pass before Marco Polo came to trade in 1292. The first modern Europeans appeared in the early 16th century. French colonialism in Indochina then arose from the compulsion to spread Catholicism and the perceived need to keep up with the British and Dutch in economically exploiting Southeast Asia. For over 200 years, the various Vietnamese rulers generally tolerated Catholicism. By 1800, when French presence in Indochina now predominated over other European nations, there were an estimated 300,000 Vietnamese Catholics with about 200 Vietnamese priests and three bishops. In the next three decades, tensions between Catholics and basically Confucian rulers erupted into violence, and Catholics were persecuted. In the 1830s, Catholic missionaries were hunted down and executed.

In 1847 the emperor Tu Duc "ordered execution of all foreign missionaries, the exiling of Vietnamese Catholic leaders, and prohibition of trade with Westerners. Tu Duc's harsh policy toward his approximately 400,000 Christian subjects was the single most important factor in Vietnam's coming loss of independence. To pro-colonial Frenchmen, it provided moral justification for their encroachments."[2]

The depredations of Vietnamese rulers against French Catholic missionaries and their Vietnamese converts gave France excuse for outright conquest. Napoleon III ordered the French navy into action. In 1858 gunships bombarded the port of Tourane (Da Nang) and then moved south to enable capture of what became Saigon. The French annexed three provinces around Saigon and in 1867 three more in an effort to quell the bands of armed guerrillas who were making life intolerable for the French.

The earliest French military forces were naval with their usual component of marine infantry on board for shore action. Later, small ground units were introduced and based ashore as the need arose. Supplementing the white French forces since 1859 were the *Jaunes* – Yellows – Indochinese troops in French service. Troops employed in Indochina were of four types: Regular French Forces (all white); Coloniale (most from North Africa, dark-skinned with mostly white officers); Nationale (Vietnamese and some Cambodian and Lao—again with a predominance of white officers); and French Foreign Legion, the famed *Légion Etrangère* (of many nationalities with French and German constituting the majority, and mostly French leaders).

By 1893 five regions of Indochina emerged, each with somewhat different means of French governance. Cambodia and Laos lay to the west of Vietnam, which consisted of Tonkin in the north, Annam in the center, and Cochinchina in the south. Cochinchina was linked closest of all to Paris, having been designated as a colony and sending a delegate (French of course) to the French National Assembly in Paris. A French Governor General (sometimes called High Commissioner) of all five parts of Indochina established himself at Hanoi in Tonkin, and for decades thereafter the capital migrated semiannually between Hanoi (in the summer) and Saigon (winter) to take advantage of differing seasonal weather. Many Vietnamese resented not just their loss of independence but, with the codified division of Vietnam into three regions, their unity.

Jules Ferry, twice prime minister of France in the period 1880-1885, expressed the views of the fervent pro-colonialists in a speech to the Chamber of Deputies:

Gentlemen, we must speak more loudly and more honestly! We must say openly that indeed the higher races have a right over the lower races. . . .

"I repeat, that the superior races have a right because they have a duty. They have the duty to civilize the inferior races. . . . In the history of earlier centuries these duties, gentlemen, have often been misunderstood; and certainly when the Spanish soldiers and explorers introduced slavery into Central America, they did not fulfill their duty as men of a higher race. . . . But, in our time, I maintain that European nations acquit themselves with generosity, with grandeur, and with sincerity of this superior civilizing duty. . . . A navy such as ours cannot do without safe harbors, defenses, supply centers on the high seas. . . . And that is why we needed Tunisia; that is why we needed Saigon and Indochina. . . and why we shall never leave them!"[3]

On the positive side, the *mission civilisatrice,* civilizing mission, of the French showed itself in many improvements: suppression of malaria, building of roads, railroads, docks, canals, hospitals, schools, construction projects of all kinds. Saigon, with its magnificent French colonial style buildings and beautiful parks and landscaping, became known as "The Pearl of the Orient" or "Paris of the Orient." Critics could argue that all were for the benefit of the French, but in fact a large segment of the Vietnamese people began to live a lifestyle more like that of the progressive nations of the West, and they readily saw its advantages. Many, perhaps most, Vietnamese were caught in a love-hate relationship with the French, admiring and emulating their western culture and hating them for their domination. From the beginning of French colonization, the stage was set for a Vietnamese struggle once again to throw off the foreign yoke and gain independence.

Ho Chi Minh and Early Indochinese Communism

The Russo-Japanese War of 1904-05 had profound consequences for Vietnam. Fought over Russia's attempt to ensure a year-around port on the Pacific at Port Arthur in Manchuria, the war ended in a surprising, humiliating defeat for the Russians. The fact that an Oriental power was able to defeat a European nation was not lost on Vietnamese groups gearing up to move for independence from the French, least of all on Nguyen Sinh Cung, if in fact that was his name.[4] The details of his early life are sketchy, with conflicting accounts. Later, among other aliases, he was known as Nguyen Ai Quoc (Nguyen the Patriot), and later still as Ho Chi Minh (The Enlightened One).

Ho was born in Nghe An Province of Annam on 19 May 1890. His father, Nguyen Sinh Sac, was a minor mandarin-style official and teacher, educated but impoverished. Ho's father disdained both the French and the imperial court of Annam at Hue and imbued his son with patriotic deeds of heroes who struggled against oppression. Sac guided him too in studying the "inner ethical content of Confucian philosophy."[5] The Confucian values of patience, perseverance, and patriotism were ingrained in Vietnamese culture, and young Cung would make them tenets of his life. Pointing to mandarin-influenced upbringing also of Pham Van Dong, Carlyle A. Thayer correctly highlighted the importance of Confucianism in the values of Ho and his adherents: "These individuals combined the traditional value system inculcated by Confucianism-----loyalty and service to the national community based on moral and ethical values-----with the new revolutionary and scientific values of Marxism-Leninism."[6]

A former South Vietnamese lieutenant general, Dong Van Khuyen, highlighted the Confucian ethic which historically so shaped Vietnamese culture: "For many generations Vietnamese rulers had been taught to hold the general populace in high esteem and respect. Almost all leaders of Vietnamese history upheld the Confucian principle of 'People First, Government Second.' The people were a major force that enabled Vietnam to survive as a nation despite foreign invasions and domination. It was the Vietnamese people who helped the Viet Minh win the War of Resistance against the French. In fact, their strategy was built on a popular base and, with the solid backing of this base, guerrilla warfare thrived and developed until conditions for victory were finally attained in 1954. . . . For the South Vietnamese government soldiers, winning popular sympathy was an uphill task because, in the people's eyes, they were the successors of the French Union forces."[7]

Ho understood the people, and he never stopped telling his adherents that in the revolution, the people had to come first—and he meant it. The people responded in massive numbers not just by following and admiring him, but loving him. To many he was 'Uncle,' a most affectionate term in Vietnamese culture.

Ho became a teacher of Chinese and the Vietnamese quoc ngu, the Romanized writing which took the place of Chinese characters. He advocated independence and had to move quickly at times to keep out of the reach of French authorities. From 1911, Ho spent some time at sea as a kitchen helper, then in New York and Boston restaurants as a helper and pastry chef.

After the outbreak of the First World War in 1914 "some 50,000 Vietnamese troops and 50,000 Vietnamese workers were sent to Europe. . . . 80,000 Vietnamese were either fighting for the French Army or working in French factories side by side with French women."[8] The Vietnamese "also endured additional heavy taxes to help pay for France's war efforts."[9] What, Ho certainly wondered, would the Vietnamese receive in return?

The 1917 Russian Revolution provided impetus to social movements worldwide, especially in underdeveloped countries. After some time in London, Ho had gone to France and become a spirited speaker among French socialists and labor groups. He was particularly enamored of Lenin, much more than Communist theorists who spoke of Communist utopia. Lenin knew that revolution would take organization, hard work, and force. By the time of the Versailles Peace Conference of 1919 Ho was trying to see the leaders of France, Great Britain, and the United States to get their support, but failed. He seems to have had to settle for passing out his flyer, a petition demanding political autonomy and traditional freedoms of a democratic society—freedom of religion, assembly, press, and equality with the French in Vietnam. Up to this time he was much more a nationalist proselytizing for independence than a Communist, but it was the Communists who were disrupting the comfortable world order of nations, and Ho joined others as a founding member of the

French Communist Party. He saw that the French Communists generally were not much interested in the Indochinese situation, having quite enough problems of their own to occupy them. Ho tried to educate them, and at the same time reach the Vietnamese in France. "Ho . . . traveled extensively throughout France in 1919-21, addressing large crowds of Vietnamese war workers and soldiers awaiting repatriation to the Far East. Thus, tens of thousands of Vietnamese who had come into contact with the white man's world and seen its failings from close up, were for the first time given an interpretation of what they were seeing and how it could affect their future. That interpretation was both nationalist and Communist, and its seeds matured slowly over the next two decades."[10] His work caught the attention of some Russian Communists, and in 1924 Ho was invited to Moscow. Surreptitiously he left France, successfully evading the Sûreté. In Russia Ho studied Marxist and Leninist thought, and participated in and addressed an early Comintern Congress. He had passed from relatively unknown revolutionary into one who was acquiring international respect.

In 1924 Ho went on to China and organized revolutionary gatherings while beginning to be recognized as an important figure in the worldwide Communist movement. "Vietnamese Communism was born, if so amorphous a development as a modern mass movement has a fixed time and place of birth, in Canton in 1925."[11] While there, he created a Vietnamese Revolutionary Youth League based on Confucian teachings, emphasizing patriotism.

At first Ho got support from Sun Yat-sen's nationalist Kuomintang Party (KMT), presumably because he and those around him were fiercely nationalist. Chiang Kai-shek, then commandant of the Whampoa Military Academy where Ho occasionally lectured, succeeded to leadership of the KMT. Some of Ho's adherents were trained at Whampoa until the KMT realized that Ho and those around him were not only nationalists who would fight for Indochinese independence, but also Communists.

It was in Canton that the person who eventually was to become known as a nation's kindly Uncle first revealed the cruel lengths he would go to in order to ensure the success of the revolution he envisioned. Ho had sent cadre back into Indochina to conduct subversive works. Some among them had proven unreliable or refused to follow Communist orders, so "Their names were leaked by the Communists to French Intelligence, and the Sûreté in Vietnam was only too glad to pick them up on arrival."[12]

By 1927 the KMT were convinced that most of the Vietnamese nationalists in Canton were indeed Communists, and Ho left quickly for Moscow.

Rubber Plantations, Hotbeds of Communist Recruitment

In Vietnam the terrible conditions for workers in the mines of the North and rubber plantations of the South provided hotbeds for early Communist recruitment. The French had trouble attracting Vietnamese laborers in the areas around the plantations in the South, largely because these people knew what life on the plantations was all about. Nor could the French entice the nearby minority Stieng, Moïs or others of the Montagnard tribes onto the plantations and keep them there. These indigenous people loved their comfortable, lackadaisical lifestyle in their deep jungle settlements too much to do the grueling work necessary to make a plantation run. But in Tonkin there was starvation and incredible hardship which killed hundreds of thousands.[13] Unscrupulous French and Vietnamese recruiters exploited the situation, signing up hordes of desperate people and transporting them in slave-like conditions for labor in the southern plantations. Many of them would die there of disease brought on by overwork, mistreatment, and unhealthy conditions that were part and parcel of jungle life as they cleared the primeval forest, planted rubber trees, maintained the plantations, and harvested the latex.

Tran Tu Binh, in his book, *The Red Earth: A Vietnamese Memoir of Life on a Colonial Rubber Plantation*,[14] tells what it was like to be a young Tonkinese rubber worker in 1927. "The French colonialists had a shortage of workers for their plan of exploitation, so the advertisements were overflowing with words of sugar and honey: [that the workers] would go for a period of three years, and at the end of that period they could return home with all their transportation expenses paid; that there would be three square meals a day, with beef and fish; that there would be seven kilograms of rice a month, and two suits of work clothes a year; that in case of illness workers would be cared for and would not have to pay for their medicines; that before they left each person would receive ten piasters to pay for their immediate needs, and so on."[15]

After a miserable journey south aboard a French ship, when it docked in Saigon, "the overseers, both French and Vietnamese, sprang noisily aboard. They used canes on the heads of recruits, counting us like animals. . . . Every time new recruit workers arrived, they had to be divided among the various companies to see to it that each company received a fair share. . . . At that time we did not imagine that the number of people who would escape death would be so small. Nor could we imagine the kinds of lives we would lead at the rubber plantations. It is fortunate that someone lived through it all to recount the horrible scenes of those hells on earth."[16]

Tran Tu Binh's hilly plantation at Phu Rieng was 60 air miles northeast of Saigon. Forty years after Binh toiled there, from my helicopter I found the abandoned, overgrown plantation to look hellish, partially because of the war and the imagined as well as actual enemy under the dense jungle canopy that surrounded it, but mostly because of the dreadful isolation. Off the few dirt roads euphemistically labeled as "routes" on our maps, the forest went on and on and on forever. We insensitively called it "Indian Country."[17]

The Michelin Company's huge plantation 40 miles northwest of Saigon would seem to have been more hospitable, flat as it was, with more than one road running through it, and on the bank of the Saigon River. But the work conditions were terrible. In clearing the jungle and planting the rubber trees, workers weakened by malnutrition contracted malaria and died by the dozens from lack of medicine and proper health care. In addition to fierce ants and scorpions and deadly mosquitoes, the workers sometimes encountered terrifying pythons and tigers. The Communist *History* of the Michelin rubber workers reported, "Right up to the nine-year war against the French, tigers still walked around in broad daylight, killing people."[18]

The *History* continued, "The workday was long, from ten to twelve hours [six days a week]. . . . On Sunday [the coolies] had to work half a day. . . . Every village [of 22 within the plantation] had its own counting field – the place where the workers gathered for a head count by their assigned contract numbers (workers were assigned numbers – names were not used). It became regular practice that each day this place was used to administer punishment to the contract workers. Every possible excuse, even minor things like arriving late, being too slow to answer, or forgetting one's assigned number, were enough for them to administer physical punishment. At the counting field they beat people very brutally. . . . The foremen and bosses were all evil. Aside from a few who still had a conscience and were only working as foremen to make enough to eat, most of them wanted to demonstrate their loyalty to the owners in order to get salary increases. The foremen were Vietnamese, and the bosses were French [or half-French]."[19]

In 1927, soon after the *Companie Michelin* began developing its second plantation at Thuan Loi near Phu Rieng, a worker killed a French foreman, the first instance of serious revolt by the workers. Growing unrest was followed by the worldwide Great Depression which had a devastating effect on workers everywhere. The French reacted harshly against striking workers, exacerbating the hatred. By 1930, rubber prices had plummeted to less than one-fourth their 1928 value. So it is not surprising that Thuan Loi was hit by a general uprising on 3 February 1930, suppressed by the French military, gendarmes, and provincial Vietnamese security units. This event naturally affected the Dau Tieng workers and they too rose in protest, calling out to the plantation manager just transferred down from Thuan Loi, "Soumagnac, get out. You will not be allowed to make the workers eat spoiled rice and rotten fish, you will not be allowed to beat the workers."[20] Security troops at Dau Tieng fired on and killed two of the demonstrators.

Ho as Communist Party Organizer

Only a week before, now in Hong Kong, Ho Chi Minh had been instrumental in drawing together bitterly divided Communist organizations. A few days later he addressed them and all countrymen:

"Workers, peasants, soldiers, youth, and pupils!

"Oppressed and exploited compatriots!

"Sisters and brothers! Comrades! . . . .

"The Vietnamese Communists, formerly working separately, have now united into a single party, the Communist Party of Indochina [ICP] to lead our entire people in their revolution. . . . From now on we must join the Party, help it and follow it in order to implement the following slogans:

1. To overthrow French imperialism, feudalism, and the reactionary Vietnamese capitalist class.
2. To make Indochina completely independent. . . . "[21]

Although it was not apparent at the time, here at age 40 was Ho, the leader of a movement in a small area of the world largely dismissed by the West, Soviet Union, and China alike as inconsequential. From this unlikely beginning, Vietnamese Communism would grow to have enormous global consequences.

Communists and Nationalists

Plantation violence plus unrest and disobedience among mineworkers were only part of the problems for French colonial authorities. Nationalist, non-Communist independence groups had been developing since the last half of the 19th century. In fact by the 1920s and 1930s they were stronger than the Communists. One of these independence groups, the Viet Nam Quoc Dan Dang (VNQDD, Vietnamese Nationalist Party) had directed its recruiting efforts toward not just civilians but also Vietnamese members of the French colonial forces. Shortly after the February 1930 uprising at the Michelin's Thuan Loi plantation, the VNQDD incited a mutiny of over 50 soldiers at Yen Bai garrison northwest of Hanoi, supported by a large number of civilians who had forced their way inside the compound. The mutiny failed when other Vietnamese soldiers in their units refused to follow the mutineers. Shortly afterward the guillotine was busy dealing with soldier and civilian nationalists.

After the plantation violence of 1930, despite some concessions by the French, worker discontent increased as disruptions and violence continued for the next few years, spreading to several other plantations and other industries in the Saigon area. All the while, the Communists grew in number, starting with a handful, and spreading through the plantations. The Dau Tieng Communist Party Chapter, which was directly subordinate to the Saigon City Party Committee, was formed in late 1936. In 1937 there was another large worker strike in Dau Tieng in which four workers were killed and 41 arrested. And so it went. The French struck back hard, and "as 1939 began, because of the savage suppressions by the enemy, the Dau Tieng Party Chapter was shattered."[22]

Both the so-called many "nationalist" parties and the Communists were nationalists—that is, patriotic independence organizations. In terms of parties, however, the various groups were properly termed Nationalist or Communist. They locked in mortal combat, intellectual and often physical, out of which one would emerge as the much more powerful party—the Communist. The Nationalists believed that the Communists were too ideological and closely linked to the international interests of Communism directed from Moscow and far too little concerned with Vietnamese independence goals and methods. That they were basically wrong in this belief did not deter them from pursuing their objectives. The VNQDD was modeled after the Chinese KMT from whom they got support. Their organization was loose, often fractured, inefficient, in comparison to the more tightly knit, efficient and disciplined Communist organization. The Nationalists were impetuous and wanted independence now. The Communists planned for the long haul and chose their targets and methods far more carefully.

In 1939 the French had outlawed the ICP, and its leaders fled to China or went underground, mostly in the Viet Bac, the mountainous region north of Hanoi where Communist recruiting had been quite successful. Many unlucky ones were caught and sent to the notorious prison, Poulo Condor, on an island in the South China Sea. Later, Vietnamese who survived the horrible prison experience took it as a badge of honor in their fight against the French.

Indochina in World War II

World War II broke out on 1 Sevptember 1939 with the German invasion of Poland. Then in 1940 the Germans invaded France. Colonel Charles de Gaulle had commanded his armored regiment well, was promoted to brigadier general and given command of the 4th Armored Division. After de Gaulle attacked to relieve pressure on the British evacuation of Dunkirk, on 5 June Prime Minister Paul Reynaud appointed him Under Secretary of State for National Defence and War, a position in which he headed coordination with British forces. De Gaulle wanted to set up a resistance government in North Africa, the complications of which led to Reynaud's resignation, the rise of Marshal Philippe Pétain to head a collaborationist government (the Vichy regime), and the flight on 17 June of de Gaulle to England where he later in absentia was condemned to death for treason by the Petain government. De Gaulle made the famous 18 June 1940 radio call on BBC to all Frenchmen to resist and fight the enemy until once again France was free. "France is not alone! She is not alone! She is not alone! She has a vast Empire behind her. She can align with the British Empire that holds the sea and continues the fight. She can, like England, use without limit the immense industry of the United States." His impassioned plea was heard at the time by relatively few Frenchmen, but its later response was huge. The French Resistance was created, and this heretofore little-known brigadier general set to work to create a Free French government. By September 1941 he had established the *Comité National Français* (CNF), the French National Committee, the Free French government-in-exile.

At the time of the German invasion of France, French Indochina was in a pitifully weak condition. There were less than 40,000 French people in the five parts of Indochina with only about 30,000 troops of all kinds in the ground forces, 17,500 of whom were Indochinese; 800 in the naval forces, half of whom were Indochinese; and 1,500 in the air forces, of whom 1,000 were Indochinese.[23] De Gaulle was in no position to provide support, Britain was fighting for its very survival, and America was trying to stay out of the active fighting while it supplied arms and other support to Allied forces.

The mighty Japanese military had invaded China, were set on conquering all of Asia, and now were at the northern border of Vietnam. The French in Indochina, ill-equipped and cut off from their support base half a world away, were faced with the prospect of defending against mighty Japan. Sailing out of Vietnamese ports, the French navy had only one cruiser and four cutters to defend a 1,500 mile coastline against the powerful Japanese Navy. The French air force had about 100 outdated planes, mostly observation and utility or transport, whereas "sleek Japanese bombers and fighter aircraft made prewar French biplanes and Potez transports look quaint indeed."[24]

General Georges Catroux, Governor General of Indochina, was in a tough spot. He had no respect for a Vichy regime but felt it was his duty to keep Indochina French as long as possible. The Japanese began pressuring him for concessions in order to make Indochina an asset in their plan for domination of east and southeast Asia. The immediate problem for the Japanese was the rail line and the roads from northern Vietnam running across the border with China. American weapons and other military equipment and supplies were making their way from the harbor at Haiphong to Chiang Kai-shek's forces in southern China. The Japanese demanded that Catroux cut off this supply line. Washington said it could give no support to Catroux who then was forced to acquiesce. Back in France, Vichy thought Catroux had given in too easily and sent Admiral Jean Decoux to replace him. This well suited the general who flew to join the Free French and eventually become commander of French forces in the mid-East.

In September of 1940 the Japanese were coercing the Vichy French administration of Indochina, now under Decoux, into transit agreements, and when negotiations seemed to be too slow, Japanese troops came across the Chinese border and overran border posts, fiercely resisted by the French defenders who took heavy casualties. The Japanese said it had been a misunderstanding and then pressured Decoux into turning over three airfields in Tonkin, followed in July 1941 by eight more in southern Indochina, accompanied by withdrawal of the French garrisons from those places. On 28 July 1941, four months before Pearl Harbor, the Japanese marched into Saigon and established their complete supremacy by occupying key positions throughout Vietnam. An eye-opener for the Americans was the Japanese takeover of Cam Ranh Bay, a marvelous deep water port for the Japanese Navy. Only 800 miles east across the South China Sea was the Philippines, defended by American and Filipino troops.

The Japanese saw it to their advantage to leave the Vichy French administrators largely in place. For the next nearly four years Admiral Decoux tried to preserve as much as he could of Indochina from Japanese encroachment but was forced by circumstances largely to cooperate with them. The dreaded Japanese Kempeitai kept the French Sûreté and the rest of Decoux's government under close surveillance.

Ho Chi Minh saw the war as a marvelous opportunity. In his 1941 "Letter from Abroad," he wrote:

"Elder citizens!

"Sages and heroes!

"Scholars, farmers, workers, merchants, and soldiers!

"France has been lost to the Germans, French strength here is dissipated, yet still they raise our taxes to loot us, still they mount white terror against the people. In foreign dealings they hold their breath fearfully, giving some land to Siam, kneeling down in surrender to Japan. Meanwhile our people have to wear two yokes, continuing to serve as buffaloes and horses for the French, but now also being slaves of the Japanese. In such painful, tormenting conditions shall we simply fold our arms and wait to die? No, absolutely not! More than twenty million descendants of Lac and Hung [ancient heroes] are determined not to be perpetual slaves without a country!"[25]

Despite Ho's optimism, the combination of the Japanese and the French Vichy government caused the Communists serious problems. The worker's *History* said, "These two fascist, colonialist powers worked together to oppress and exploit our people."[26] The Michelin Plantation became a refuge for Party members and sympathizers in surrounding provinces.

Fearful though the times were, and wary of the Japanese, independence-minded Vietnamese were nevertheless heartened by recognition that once again Oriental troops had vanquished Westerners, this time the French in Indochina. Although Vietnamese Communists were hunted and persecuted by Decoux, the Communists had no love for the Japanese either, and in time would come to resist them. Despite the unfavorable odds, Ho was determined that the Indochinese Communist Party would take advantage of the times to strengthen themselves, enlarge their ranks, and when circumstances were right, defeat both the Japanese and the French.

Ho's Early Work in Tonkin

Ho had not set foot in his homeland since 1912. Twenty-nine years later, in February 1941, he crossed the border from China into northern Tonkin and set up his headquarters in a cave at Pac Bo, a small hamlet near the border in the Viet Bac. From the 1930s a small number of Vietnamese Communists had done well in this region in propagandizing their *doc lap* – independence – theme, and as the years passed, more of the locals became not just willing listeners and sympathizers, but proponents of the cause. In 1940 and 1941, Ho's close follower and later general, Vo Nguyen Giap, made trips to the Viet Bac to contact committed and potential recruits. Many of these were from various Montagnard tribes. A local Nung tribesman, Chu Van Tan, became a close friend of Giap, and he later became a general and the first Viet Minh defense minister.

At Pac Bo, Ho conferred with Giap, Truong Chinh, Pham Van Dong, and other early leaders on the course to take. A young revolutionary asked, "How can we have a revolution without arms and where are we going to find guns?' . . . Ho replied, 'We must rely on our own force with some outside help. When the people absorb this beautiful idea of revolution, they will create the strongest of forces. Everything because of the people; everything for the people. People first, guns last. If we have the people on our side, then we will have guns. If we have the people, we will have everything.'"[27] This belief became the heart and soul of the long Communist-led wars against the French and Americans: politics aimed at gaining popular support were much more important than military force.

In May, in a hut near the cave while sitting on a block of wood at a wooden table, Ho convened the Eighth Plenum of the Indochinese Communist Party. It established the League for the Independence of Vietnam: *Việt Nam Độc Lập Đồng Minh Hội*, or Viet Minh, that provided the armed element of the Party. A decision which was to guide their war policy from then until the end in 1975 was "that the demands of ideology and class war must be subordinated to those of the anti-imperialistic struggle for national independence."[28] This was a crucial concept. Ho would strongly express Communist views, only later to amend them, abandon them temporarily, deny them, adapt to any change in circumstances so long as by doing so the struggle could continue and eventually succeed. At one point he would even disband the Indochinese Communist Party in order to give the impression that the independence movement was not controlled by Communists, but by revolutionaries, all of whom were nationalists.

Ho's Privations

In August 1942 Ho set out once more for China, headed for Chungking, the provisional capital of the Chinese Nationalist government. Located there were the headquarters of a sizable Soviet delegation, the command post of U.S. operations in the China-Burma-India theater, and a detachment of the OSS, forerunner of the CIA. The Chinese Nationalists and Communists were bound by a temporary, uneasy cooperative arrangement with the common purpose of driving the Japanese out of China. Thus, if Ho was lucky, he could make contact with high level people in the Chinese, Soviet, and U.S. governments, seeking information on operations that would affect Indochina, and hoping for support of his cause.

Ho and his Vietnamese companion walked through dangerous country of southern China to reach a safe house for a bit of welcome rest. Then with a different Vietnamese as his guide, they set out and were stopped by police. Suspected of being a spy, Ho was arrested. This began a period of incredible hardship during which he somehow managed to get some writing materials and wrote poems, recording his experiences and thoughts. He estimated he had passed through 18 prisons. He was "led from one prison to the other on foot, usually with hands and arms tied, on an exhausting march covering dozens of miles." When he was transported by boat his feet were tied to the roof of the junk, and he described himself as a "torture victim from another age." When they traveled by train he was "tied up in the tender on a pile of coal." The final prison was a den of thieves, cutthroats, and miscellaneous unfortunates, and the only place he could find to rest at all was next to the filthy latrines. "Ho spent time with men who had fallen into ruin and suffered both social and moral ostracism, which taught him more about mankind than he could have learned from a course in psychology."[29] A biographer described his condition: "By now his body was emaciated and covered with sores, his hair had begun to turn gray, and his teeth were falling out."[30]

After months of such inhumane conditions, while the Chinese authorities were assessing his potential usefulness, Ho was treated better. No longer shackled at night, fed better, he was even allowed to read books and write to comrades in China and Vietnam. In September 1943 he was released from jail but not allowed to travel. He spent his time in political activities among Chinese and Vietnamese. Then when the Chinese had decided Ho was the best person to lead a Vietnamese resistance movement against the Japanese, restrictions were further eased, and he traveled, lectured, and continued political work in southern China.

*   *   *

In November 1942 the Allies landed in North Africa and caused the collapse of Vichy there, resulting in large numbers of Vichy units going over to the Allies. The Germans quickly took over Vichy southern France, and the Vichy government became a shadow of its former self. The question now for Indochina was whether Decoux could continue to maintain administrative control. The Kempeitai began keeping an even closer eye on his government.

Events in Pac Bo

In September 1944 Ho was granted freedom by the Chinese, and after arduous travel he arrived back in Pac Bo. While he had been gone, his Communist colleagues had done a considerable amount of proselytizing throughout Vietnam and had gained significant support among the people. Especially in the Viet Bac stronghold, called the "Liberated Zone," the Party leadership had notably improved in recruiting and organizing civilians for resistance, and in training men and women for military service.

Ho Chi Minh, 1944. (NARA)

For two years the war had been going badly for the Axis Powers both in the Pacific and North Africa, and getting progressively worse. In June 1944 the Allies had landed in Normandy. In the Pacific, the Japanese were being relentlessly pushed back. Relative to colonialism, in July 1944, de Gaulle said, "The aim of French policy is and will remain to raise all these territories to as high a level as possible, so that every one is able to look out for its own interests and to be represented within a federal system. This is the policy France will pursue, in particular for Indochina."[31]

De Gaulle's words rang hollow. In Vietnam the Communists believed in independence, not continued subjugation within a French system. The time for decisive action was drawing near.

In Pac Bo, Ho held a meeting of comrades at which Giap said, "Uncle put forth the question of organizing the National Liberation Army. Turning to me, he said in conclusion, 'This you should carry out. Can you do that? We are still weak, the enemy is strong. But we must not let them annihilate us, must we?'

"I answered, 'Yes, I'll do it.'"

Ho insisted, "The first battle must be successful."[32]

Later, Ho had a stroke of good luck. On 11 November 1944 a U.S. reconnaissance plane over mountainous terrain along the Chinese-Vietnamese border had an engine failure and the pilot, Lieutenant Rudolph Shaw, bailed out. Viet Minh got to him just ahead of both a Japanese and a French patrol. Ho Chi Minh soon heard of this and directed that the pilot be delivered to him at Pac Bo. After nearly a month of negotiating virtually impassable terrain with guides whose only English was "America! Roosevelt!", the weak, despairing Shaw was greeted in English by Ho, who also spoke fluent French and Chinese: "'How do you do, pilot! Where are you from?' Shaw was reportedly so excited that he hugged Ho and later said to him, 'When I heard your voice, I felt as if I were hearing the voice of my father in the United States.'"[33]

Ho and his small party set out walking, headed for Kunming to deliver Shaw back to the Americans. Just across the border, Chinese authorities sent Shaw on ahead by air to Kunming, leaving Ho's group to get there the best way they could, which initially was by foot. Some days into the journey Ho was ill and they had to stop to rest in a small Chinese town. A Vietnamese comrade who lived there "recalled that Ho Chi Minh looked sickly and emaciated, and ate little. His uniform was patched and worn, and his thin canvas shoes were full of holes. . . . Ho had recently caught a fever from another traveler, and he seemed uncharacteristically depressed. Yet his mind was still focused on his cause."[34]

Giap's Early Leadership

During Ho's absence, at Pac Bo Giap prepared for a military strike. Finally, in early December instructions came in a letter from Ho. A unit was to be formed, The Vietnam Propaganda Unit for National Liberation. The letter said, "It shows by its name that greater importance should be attached to the political side than to the military side. . . . At first its size is small; however, its prospect is brilliant. It is the embryo of the Liberation Army and can move from north to south, throughout Vietnam."[35]

Giap had no formal military study or training. He had a baccalaureate in political science from the University of Hanoi, followed by one year teaching history in a private school before his revolutionary activities consumed him. But from his teens, Giap had avidly studied military history, especially that of Napoleon, and he knew the intricacies of numerous historical battles so well that in his teaching he left students spellbound. In December 1944 at Pac Bo, instant "General" Giap gathered an "army" of 34 comrades to go forth to battle, 31 men and three women. He sent a 12- or 13-year old boy into the nearby garrison of Phai Kat to spy. The young fellow performed useful tasks for the French in the garrison while gathering information on their layout, personnel, and daily activities. This tactic of careful acquisition of advance information before attack was to persist throughout the 30-year war.[36]

Giap's group was armed with "two revolvers, seventeen rifles, fourteen flintlocks, and one light machine gun [actually, probably a submachine gun]."[37] Giap three decades later wrote, "We forgot that we were only 34 human beings equipped with rudimentary weapons. We imagined ourselves to be an army of steel, not to be defeated by any force, ready to destroy the enemy. Confidence, eagerness prevailed."[38]

On Christmas Eve his small force assembled around their red flag with gold star. They took a ten-point pledge, the first of which was "To sacrifice everything for their fatherland so as to make Vietnam independent."[39] They set off, dressed as a mandarin patrol with fake authorization papers, talked their way into the Phai Khat outpost and quickly overcame the defenders. When the French commander rode up shortly after, they killed him and his horse. During that night they then marched 20 miles to the Na Ngan post, disguised by uniforms captured at Phai Khat, posing as a patrol which had captured some Communists. Again they gained entrance, and this time shooting broke out within the post, killing five occupants. The others were taken prisoner (and by some accounts were killed, as were the Phai Khat defenders – the accounts are murky). The 9th Colonial Infantry Regiment of the Tonkin Division retaliated with a powerful sweep of the area, rounding up suspects, seizing some arms, killing 75. No one could possibly recognize the tremendous significance of this first direct combat of Giap's Viet Minh unit against French, that it would be precursor to an all-out, thirty-year war.

From Phai Khat, Giap went to other bases in the Viet Bac, significantly adding to his military strength. Caves near Cao Bang became his first headquarters, and there in addition to his main forces he created regional and district armed militias and village self-defense forces. The latter were 30-man platoons poorly armed but trained in putting out mines, booby traps and punji pits. In all types of forces more time was spent on political indoctrination than military training.

The Communist official book, *The 30-Year War, 1945 – 1975*, Vol.1, published in Hanoi in 2002, describes the build-up. "At first, everything was lacking: food, weapons, coverlets, medicine. The troops often had nothing to eat, yet they remained in an eager and joyful mood. . . . Not long afterward our strength increased from a few dozen to several hundred. Young people came in great numbers to enlist into the army. The Viet Bac people extended eager assistance in all fields. Some people even sold their buffaloes and lands to help, and people in other places also extended all-out assistance. . . . Not only did the liberated zone [northwest, north and northeast of Hanoi] come into existence, but base areas were built up everywhere."[40]

Among Merle Pribbenow's many translations of Vietnamese Communist histories which he shared with me are several relating to Giap recruiting Montagnards, a general name for the many mountain tribes such as found in the Viet Bac. Pribbenow said, "The Communists probably had some success with the Montagnards because they paid attention to them, sent out cadres to proselytize and recruit them, to live and work with them (like U.S. Special Forces did). They promised the Montagnards a degree of autonomy, just as did French intelligence. . . . The initial guerrilla group that General Giap formed in 1944 that is officially viewed as the founding unit of the People's Army of Vietnam [PAVN, familiarly NVA—North Vietnamese Army—in American jargon] was made up primarily of Montagnards. [And later] a number of Viet Minh units, especially the 316th Division, were made up largely of ethnic minority tribesmen. A substantial number of Montagnards also supported the Viet Cong in the South, especially in the mountains of western I Corps (Eye Corps) and in portions of the Central Highlands."[41]

Nationalist or Communist?

About at the time in 1944 when Giap was forming the nucleus of his army, in a military academy just north of Hanoi two young Vietnamese cadets were preparing for regular commissions in the French Army. One of them, Tran Van Don, wrote, "One afternoon the bugle sounded, calling us to fall in ranks for a special ceremony. The symbol of the foreign country we were serving, the French tricolor, flapped in the gentle evening breeze. The flagstaff flew no other; nothing of our own to honor as we stood at rigid attention. The ceremony came to an end and we were dismissed. Xuong and I faced each other, evidently moved by the same thoughts. There were tears in our eyes. At that moment, in the splendid effusiveness of youth, we swore that we would from now on dedicate our whole lives to serve only one country, Vietnam, and to defend only our own national colors in independence and freedom." Xuong kept his oath. Under the red flag with yellow star in the middle he went on to become a reputed guerrilla fighter and province chief in the North. Tran Van Don also kept his oath. Under the yellow flag with three horizontal red stripes, in the South he rose to become a lieutenant general and finally, Defense Minister in President Thieu's cabinet.[42] Independence and unity. Both wanted it desperately, each in his own way. Only one, Xuong, would see his aspirations realized.

Also about then, other young men and women were graduating from the high schools of Hanoi and the University of Hanoi with a burning nationalist spirit. Many of them, such as the young man Bui Diem, would oppose the Communists not as soldiers of the government but as members of secret non-Communist nationalist parties. He was not related to the later President Ngo Dinh Diem of the Republic of Vietnam (South Vietnam). Rather, he came from a prominent mandarin family and had been one of Giap's history students at the high school Lycée Thang Long in Hanoi. He said, "Giap's history course was supposed to cover France from 1789 to the middle of the nineteenth century. . . . 'Look,' Giap said, pacing back and forth at the front of the room, 'there are a lot of books about this stuff. If you want to know about it, you can look it up. I'm only going to tell you about two things: the French Revolution and Napoleon.' . . . [Giap's] admiration for the Revolution and its leading figures glowed in these lectures, and Giap spoke not as a mere historian but as a passionate advocate. . . .We students felt that our country was on the verge of striking out for its freedom, and there wasn't a soul who didn't want to be part of that. . . . New nationalist groups were forming a number of different parties under the name Dai Viet (Great Vietnam)."

When Giap disappeared from the Lycée, rumor had it that he had gone to the Viet Bac to train revolutionaries. Bui Diem, a bit later a University of Hanoi student in mathematics, was intrigued by nationalistic youth groups. The students bicycled on weekends to historic sites honoring past heroes. "The French authorities could hardly object to such orderly excursions. Sitting around campfires, we would discuss how the Trung sisters had overthrown the Chinese occupiers of the first century. . . . Afterward we would sing, so loudly the woods seemed to reverberate: 'Brothers, students, stand up! Answer the call from rivers and mountains. Go forward, always forward. Have no regrets ever about sacrificing your lives.'"

"In public the students were united. In private it was a different story. Gradually, each of us joined one or another of the parties that promised to mold a reality from the desire for freedom. At that time, in 1943 and 1944, few had any idea of the distinctions between these parties, or even a good concept of which was which. They all said they were fighting for independence. That was enough. . . . It was not generally known . . . that the Viet Minh was Communist controlled. Ho Chi Minh was not a name anyone had yet heard of."

Diem joined one of the parties, the Dai Viet. Unfortunately for these non-Communist, fervidly nationalist parties they had a mortal flaw: "Lack of a well-formulated political program." Bui Diem said, "[It] was a weakness the Dai Viet Quoc Dan Dang [DVQDD] shared with all the other parties but one. The Viet Minh, founded and controlled by a core of trained, clear-sighted, and committed Communists, brought to the struggle for independence qualities the nationalists were never able to match."[43]

The Communists were much more organized than the various nationalist groups who were plagued by infighting. The Communists had a broad-based strategy of appealing to the people on many levels—personal, societal, economic, political; the nationalists were much more single-mindedly focused on getting the French out, without a strategy as to what would then happen to the people. The Communists were much better trained, with many of their leaders having close ties to Moscow or Beijing or both, and they were more disciplined, insisting on adherence to Party guidance. And they began early to build a spirited, disciplined armed force.

The Japanese Coup

The 1944/45 fall-winter harvest of rice in Tonkin had been greatly impeded by Japanese crop-planting restrictions, confiscation of crops, drought, and then flood. Famine resulted in deaths estimated from the hundreds of thousands to two million Vietnamese. The Communists gained considerable support when they worked assiduously to try to get food to the masses.

By early March 1945, the Japanese in Indochina were in an increasingly precarious position. Advancing American forces across the Pacific had placed them in a stranglehold. Burma, Iwo Jima, the Philippines— all had been lost. The possibility of the Vichy French forces within Indochina suddenly taking the side of their enemy was real and immediate. The Japanese had long been concerned with pro-Allied sentiments, though necessarily subdued, within this French Indochina army. Throughout his tenure Admiral Decoux had surreptitiously maintained some contact with de Gaulle's men, and Decoux's commander in the North, General Eugène Mordant, had direct contact and had been named by de Gaulle as Supreme Commander of the Free French forces of Indochina, effective upon order. The Japanese could not be sure that Decoux, whose goal was to preserve what he could of French interests in Indochina, would not, when the time was ripe, suddenly go over to the Allies and take his troops with him. The time had come to act.

In Saigon, in the late afternoon of 9 March 1945 the Japanese secretly gave Decoux an ultimatum: turn over administrative control of all Indochina to the Japanese and disarm and confine French troops to barracks. Decoux refused. Under arrest, the admiral could not get an order out to his forces to resist. Pre-positioned Japanese troops swept down upon startled French garrisons throughout Indochina, and in most cases the confused French, not hearing from their command in Saigon as to what they were expected to do, had no choice but to obey the Japanese. Some got word, though, of what had happened and managed to retain their arms and fiercely fight back. A Vietnamese-owned newspaper in Saigon on the morning following the coup carried the headline, "Liberation Day for our Country of Vietnam has arrived."[44] Had the coup not occurred, quite certainly Admiral Decoux would have delivered Indochina back to de Gaulle's new Provisional Government at the end of the war. Instead, he was taken up to the Loc Ninh rubber plantation north of Saigon to be confined and contemplate his fate until war's end.

Taking advantage of the confusion, Vietnamese prisoners all over the country escaped as French jail guards abandoned their posts and tried themselves to escape from the Japanese. At Lang Son in Tonkin, General Emile-René Lemonnier was ordered to surrender his entire command or face death. He refused, and he and Résident Camille Auphalle were ordered to dig their graves. Upon continued refusal they were beheaded.

A large contingent of mixed stragglers from various French military units in Tonkin was able to fight its way out of encirclement and head toward China. As days turned into weeks they desperately fought off the pursuing Japanese. One large segment of them even made their way to Dien Bien Phu and held there for awhile but then had to move on. While there at an airstrip built in 1939, they seem to have received some supplies, landed by Americans from southern China. However, other elements of the pathetic French stragglers claim to have received no such help. In fact, they said, on higher command orders the Americans were not only forbidden to come to their aid with nearby Chinese forces but not even allowed to drop supplies or other assistance until much too late. This decision seems to have been based, among other considerations, on the American command's knowledge that President Roosevelt, because of an anticolonial attitude, was not anxious to do anything to help the French in Indochina. A significant number of French troops eventually escaped into China but hundreds of them died fighting or were hideously tortured and massacred upon capture. The ones who did make it across the border were rounded up and confined by the Chinese. The Americans seemed indifferent, too busy with their own war. Some French in Indochina had risked their lives sheltering downed American airmen and aiding in their escape. Also, teams of de Gaulle's Free French fighters had been parachuted into Indochina to aid in the fight against the Japanese. The French were dismayed that their forces had received such American treatment in return during their hour of need.

The Japanese coup caused considerable consternation in U.S. intelligence circles. The Americans needed information on Indochina, and it was possible that the small bands of French Resistance there would no longer be able to communicate with Ceylon and Kunming. An OSS officer in China, Lieutenant Charles Feng, wanted to meet Ho, which would be a wonderful opportunity for Ho. OSS Major Archimedes Patti wrote of this encounter. "Feng described their first meeting [on 17 March 1945 in China]: 'I asked [Ho] what he wanted. . . . He said—only recognition of his group . . . . ' They met again three days later and worked out details for Ho to return to Indochina where intelligence listening posts would be set up with OSS radios and OSS-trained Vietnamese operators."[45] Soon Ho was to meet Patti, the newly appointed head of the OSS mission to Indochina who wrote: "A slender, short, man fifty or sixty years old, approached me with a warm smile and extended hand. Perfectly at ease and in English he said, 'Welcome, my good friend.' I took Ho's thin, almost fragile hand and expressed my pleasure in meeting a man who had so many American friends in Kunming."[46]

The OSS was not unaware of President Roosevelt's attitude about France and Indochina. FDR had an unfavorable impression of de Gaulle from the very beginning, and he had been critical of France's poor showing against the Germans. Roosevelt was turned off by colonialism, and he tried to put out of mind that his closest ally, Winston Churchill, was at the head of a colonial empire, bigger than that of France. Roosevelt and Churchill had met in August 1941 and issued a joint declaration which came to be called "The Atlantic Charter," later affirmed by the Allies. One of the principal points stated was that they "respect the right of all peoples to choose the form of Government under which they will live." Did this not apply to Indochina? Whereas Roosevelt could, and would, make rationalizations for Churchill and colonial Great Britain, he would not do the same for de Gaulle and France. He basically did not want to do anything to assist France in regaining its colonies, but of course he also did not want to help Communists. The OSS in China, well out of earshot of the head shed in the U.S., felt that Ho could be of use in the war against Japan. Also by 1944 they were turned off by the Chinese Nationalists whom they saw as corrupt and not committed enough to fight the Japanese. Ho seemed eager to do so.

On 24 March 1945 the French government in Paris announced an Indochinese Federation of Allied States, covering the five Indochinese areas: Laos, Cambodia, and the three parts of Vietnam. While it offered much broader privileges within a French Union than had been the case with pre-war Indochina, Ho and other nationalist leaders denounced the Federation decree as falling far short of true independence.

Post-coup, in April the Japanese formally gave Indochina its independence (while they still of course pulled the strings). The Vietnamese Communists began making full use of five months of total Japanese control of the French by strengthening themselves for the struggle they felt sure was soon to come. By May, working out of the Viet Bac, they had "liberated" nine Tonkin provinces and parts of two others, and Giap proclaimed the formation of the People's Liberation Army. He also was named a member of the Central Committee of the Indochinese Communist Party, an important formal juncture of his military and political duties.[47]

In July one of Patti's OSS teams in southern China parachuted into the Viet Bac and contacted Viet Minh, with the eventual mission to raid a Japanese position. The OSS team leader was taken to a hut with a banner over the entrance in English: "Welcome to our American friends." The team members gave the Viet Minh some weapons, but their greatest gift was perhaps to save Ho's life. He was trembling and had a high fever, so they gave him "quinine, sulfa drugs, and vitamin capsules," and within a few days he was "well on his way back to health."[48] Patti said that the team "spent four weeks in training about two hundred handpicked future leaders of the armies of Generals Chu Van Tan and Vo Nguyen Giap in the use of the latest American weapons and guerrilla tactics."[49] The raid for which the OSS team had prepared never happened. Astonishingly, on 6 August an atom bomb was dropped on

Hiroshima, and on 9 August another on Nagasaki. On 15 August Japan gave notice of unconditional surrender.

* * *

De Gaulle had long been planning for an expeditionary force of two divisions to fight the Japanese in the Pacific arena, which included Indochina. When in 1944 he had offered this idea to the Americans and British he was given the cold shoulder. FDR saw the plan as a way for French colonialism to regain a toehold. De Gaulle nevertheless had gone ahead with plans, and two early units, the 5th Régiment d'Infanterie Coloniale (5th RIC) and a Commando naval air parachute detachment, were already in Ceylon. De Gaulle felt that Free French blood spilled on Indochinese soil could make an impressive claim for reestablishment of control in Indochina. At the Yalta Conference in February 1945, to which de Gaulle pointedly was not invited, a very ill FDR was said to have told Stalin that no U.S. ships would carry French troops to Indochina (a policy which Truman initially would continue).

Ho's Provisional Government

With Japanese announcement of intended surrender, the Viet Minh were ecstatic. At least one enemy had been taken care of, and the way now seemed clear to go after the French. On 16 August 1945 in Hanoi, having taken over the French Résident Supérieur's mansion as the seat of a new government, the Viet Minh People's Congress proclaimed a provisional government under President Ho Chi Minh. On 19 August, in celebration as part of the famed "August Revolution," the Viet Minh orchestrated a huge demonstration in Hanoi.

Ever since the Japanese coup, Emperor Bao Dai at the imperial capital of Hue had been propped up on his throne by the Japanese as the nominal ruler of Vietnam. He sensed what would lie ahead for France and Vietnam if de Gaulle's France was to reassert its rule over Indochina. On that same day of 19 August the emperor sent a message to de Gaulle:

Emperor Bao Dai. (Corbis)

"I address myself to the people of France, to the country of my youth. I address myself as well to its chief and liberator [de Gaulle], and I wish to speak as a friend rather than as Chief of State."

"You have suffered too much during four deadly years [of World War II] not to understand that the Vietnamese people, who have a history of twenty centuries and an often glorious past, no longer desire and can no longer endure any foreign domination or governments."

"You will understand still better if you could see what is happening here, if you could feel the will for independence which has been smoldering in the hearts of all and which no human force can hold in check any longer. Even if you were to come to re-establish French government here it would not be obeyed: each village would be a nest of resistance, each former collaborator an enemy, and your officials and your colonists themselves would ask to leave that unbreathable atmosphere."

"I beg you to understand that the only means of safeguarding French interests and the spiritual influence of France in Indochina is to recognize unreservedly the independence of Viet-Nam and to renounce any idea of reestablishing French sovereignty or French administration here in any form."

"We would be able to understand each other so easily and to become friends if you would stop hoping to become our masters again."

"In making this appeal to the well known idealism of the French people and to the great wisdom of their leader, we hope that the peace and the joy which has come for all the peoples of the world will be equally ensured to all the inhabitants of Indochina, native as well as foreign."[50]

If de Gaulle had heeded this sage advice, France, America, and the people of Vietnam—North and South—might have been spared many long years of agony. But he could not. The colonial concept was imbedded in French politics and culture. It would have taken almost superhuman sensitivity and courage for de Gaulle or any leader of the French nation to make decisions that would entirely upset that order. So de Gaulle remained determined that France should first reestablish the status quo before he took up the idea of independence for Vietnam, a form of which he preferred but, as events took their tragic turns, he was later powerless to negotiate.

On 20 August Giap attacked a French garrison in Thai Nguyen just north of Hanoi, and the French provincial governor quickly capitulated, resulting in seizure of 160 Vietnamese troops of the French forces, along with their arms and ammunition. The Japanese garrison in the village likewise was deemed a wonderful source of weapons. However, no matter that the Japanese emperor had announced surrender days earlier, the garrison put up a stiff fight until 26 August when they finally surrendered. Giap directed this battle dressed in a white suit, tie, and brimmed dress hat, the "uniform" he chose to wear for the first months of the war.[51]

Contrary to the experience at Thai Nguyen, after the Emperor's surrender announcement the Japanese in Vietnam basically tried to help the Viet Minh and impede French efforts to regain control. In several places they opened their arms depots to the Viet Minh. Additionally, they continued to hold their French prisoners for another month and in some instances provided training for the Viet Minh. Many, especially Kempeitai, deserted, joined, and led Viet Minh units. A few Japanese were still fighting the French in Indochina until the war with Ho's government ended nine years later.

The immediate problem for the French in Paris after the Japanese surrender announcement was to establish the new French Indochina administration before the Communists grew any stronger. De Gaulle's forces had long planned on first entering Saigon with military units to ensure the security of their administration rather than entering Hanoi. This was for two main reasons.

First, Cochinchina had long been an actual colony, not just a protectorate. It had representation in the National Assembly in Paris, and it had the most colons – French colonial residents. It was the most modern and economically developed of the five areas of Indochina. When Frenchmen thought of Indochina, they thought first and foremost of Saigon.

Second, the strongest nationalist movement was in the North. The Viet Minh and other independence groups had been developing both political and military strength there that could pose a serious problem for French troops from the exterior if they tried to land in the North. Considering the strength of Communists and non-Communists in the North, every faction being nationalists and vying for dominance, and all fiercely committed to freedom from French rule, it was better for the French to gain a solid foothold in the South before turning militarily to the North.

The "Return" of the French to Indochina

By late August 1945, in Paris the French Fourth Republic was on the way to being constituted with de Gaulle as its provisional president. Although of course "the French" had never left Indochina, several historians refer to the early post-World War II period in Indochina as the "return" of the French. The problem now was to get French troops into Indochina quickly enough to prevent a Communist takeover and to establish conditions for a federal union of Indochina states. These events are presented in some detail because the early French experience provided the foundation from which the French war would progress, and then morph into the American war.

On the evening of 22 August, Captain (soon Colonel) Jean Cédile, recently appointed Commissioner of the French Republic for Cochinchina, parachuted with three others into a rice paddy of Tay Ninh Province. It was Cédile's first and only jump. The team was surrounded by Cao Dai[52] farmers who backed off when a Japanese detachment arrived. Stripped of clothes, hands tightly bound behind their backs, and thrust into the back of a truck, Cédile and his men were driven a bumpy, humiliating 50 miles south to Saigon. There a Japanese colonel gave them back their clothes and put them in detention with little to eat or drink.[53] Within a few days Cédile was allowed to meet with Viet Minh representatives, who refused to negotiate. Then he was driven north to Loc Ninh by a Japanese captain to meet with Admiral Decoux who, on a sickbed, was still under Japanese guard at the plantation. Decoux was astonished to learn that according to the Allied Southeast Asia Command (SEAC) agreement, Chinese and British troops, not French, were to receive the Japanese surrender in Indochina, and he berated Cédile and the French Resistance "idiots" who, he was convinced, by their subversive activities had brought on the 9 March Japanese coup de force. Cédile did not take kindly to the tongue-lashing and left Decoux under Japanese guard.[54]

Also on 22 August, Pierre Messmer, the newly appointed Commissioner of the French Republic for Tonkin,[55] parachuted in with two other team members 30 kilometers northwest of Hanoi where they were immediately taken prisoner by the Viet Minh. Soon after, all became seriously ill, perhaps from poison, and one died.[56] Messmer and the other surviving member were later rescued by Chinese troops and finally made it to Hanoi in late October, much too late to influence the course of events. Both Cédile and Messmer were de Gaulle men with no experience in Indochina.

The OSS and the DRV

On that same day of 22 August, Major Patti flew into Hanoi to establish a second OSS headquarters there and soon was visited by Giap. Patti wrote, "In impeccable French, Giap conveyed President Ho's personal welcome. . . . We were to consider ourselves guests of the Vietnamese government." After formal pleasantries, over coffee Giap wanted to know, "Would the French be allowed to occupy Vietnam?" Patti replied, "We should all understand that France had been an ally, had suffered greatly in the war. . . that France could not be denied our friendship, even though we might disagree with her colonial policies."

Giap led Patti and his staff outside where there seemed to be a ceremony of some kind awaiting them. "A fifty-piece military band had been formed directly across the street facing us. Waving in the breeze were five huge flags representing the United States, Great Britain, the Soviet Union, China, and the Democratic Republic of Vietnam. To our left was a military unit of about a hundred men standing at 'present arms.' . . . To our right were smaller units of unarmed youths in sparkling white uniforms. . . . Giap pointed with pride to 'my troops who have just arrived from the mountains.' . . . Within seconds all flags were dipped except the Stars and Stripes, and the band struck up the 'Star Spangled Banner.'"

Then the units passed in review, followed by a large crowd of civilians carrying placards of welcoming and political messages, then teens and adults singing their national anthem accompanied by the band.

When all was done, Giap said, "This is the first time in the history of Vietnam that our flag has been displayed in an international ceremony and our national anthem played in honor of a foreign guest. I will long remember this occasion."[57]

Then Giap took Patti to see Ho. Patti wrote, "A wisp of a man came forward. I was pleased to see him again but thoroughly shocked. Ho was only a shadow of the man I had met . . . four months earlier. Ho introduced me as 'our American friend from Washington.' Somewhat embarrassed and not wanting a false impression regarding my official status, I corrected, 'From Kunming, please!' Everyone laughed, and Ho repeated, 'From Kunming.'"[58] The position of the OSS had been not to side openly with either the French or Viet Minh. As a professional, Patti gathered, processed, and analyzed information from all sides but tried to avoid giving the impression of supporting one or the other. Above all he was wary of any word or action which implied that the United States supported Communism. One cannot read Patti, though, without detecting his obvious admiration, even personal liking, for the little man who had persevered through such strenuous circumstances in his attempt to forge an independent nation.

The pressure of events on Bao Dai had been too great. His tenuous rule as emperor ended on 25 August when he abdicated in favor of Ho's provisional government. Although Ho appointed him as "Supreme Advisor" to his government, the former emperor soon left for France. Bao Dai was not pro-French politically, just culturally with his fondness for wine, women, and song. In Hanoi and Hue the matter seemed to be settled, and by 25 August in Saigon the Viet Minh more than any other liberation group was in control of what government existed, nearly completing the "August Revolution" of the Communist Party.

All the world knew that on 2 September 1945 General MacArthur would receive the formal surrender of Japan aboard the battleship *Missouri*. Ho Chi Minh chose that same day to announce the independence of Vietnam under the new government, the Democratic Republic of Vietnam (DRV). On the eve of Independence Day in Hanoi, Patti had dinner with Ho and Giap at the Bac Bo Palace, formerly the Résidence Supérieur and now the headquarters of Ho's new government. During dinner conversation, Ho told Patti "his people aspired to travel outside Viet Nam, 'particularly to America, as I did long ago.' They looked forward to the day when France was not the only place to study, when study was not limited to the privileged, when students could also study in the United States."[59] Ho invited Patti to be on the official platform the next day during the announcement.

That next day broke bright and clear. General Leclerc, the highly respected commander of the French 2nd Armored Division which had been chosen to liberate Paris, had been on his way to Indochina when he was detoured north to sign the Japanese Instrument of Surrender for the French. On the USS *Missouri*, General MacArthur, well aware of the difficulties of fighting Orientals in jungle conditions, gave Leclerc some advice: "*Amenez des troupes, des troupes, encore des troupes.*" Bring troops, troops, and more troops.[60]

Ho's Democratic Republic of Vietnam

Meanwhile, on that same day in Hanoi, Ho Chi Minh would proclaim the founding of the Democratic Republic of Vietnam (DRV). Patti had declined Ho's invitation to be on the platform, no doubt concerned that his appearance might be taken as an official U.S. endorsement of Ho's DRV. He chose instead to stand in the crowd to observe reactions. The preparations in the days preceding the ceremony had been elaborate. Armed groups, both Communists and non-Communists, and civilians alike had thronged into the capital, carrying their flags, crying out slogans, singing patriotic songs, chanting *doc lap* over and over.

The crowd had begun arriving early in the morning, but they had a long wait. After several hours, troops were called to attention and a hush came over the crowd, by some estimates, a half million.[61]

Patti wrote, "The suspense was broken by a voice at the microphone introducing Ho as the 'liberator and savior of the nation.' The crowd, led by well-placed party members, intoned the chant, *Doc-Lap* (Independence), repeated over and over for several minutes. Ho stood smiling, diminutive in size, but gigantic in the adulation of his people.

Raising his hands in a paternal gesture, he called for silence and began his now-famous proclamation with the words:

"'All men are created equal. The Creator has given us certain inviolable Rights; the right to Life, the right to be Free, and the right to achieve Happiness.'

"Ho stopped short and asked his listeners: 'Do you hear me distinctly, fellow countrymen?' The crowd roared back: 'YES!' . . . .

Ho continued, "These immortal words are taken from the Declaration of Independence of the United States of America in 1776. In a larger sense, this means that: All the people on earth are born equal; All the people have the right to live, to be happy, to be free.

"Then turning to the Declaration of the French Revolution in 1791 on the Rights of Man and the Citizen, Ho said 'it also states: Men are born and must remain free and have equal rights. Those are undeniable truths.'"[62]

Chaos in Saigon, and British Intervention

World War II had dealt an all but fatal blow to colonialism. The United States led the way before the war by positioning the Philippines for independence, a move interrupted by the war, then granted after war's end. The breakup of the British Empire began with withdrawal from India in 1947, followed by widespread decolonization by European powers. France was the holdout.

Since the Japanese surrender two weeks earlier, Hanoi had been generally in a hopeful, celebratory mood, but elsewhere tensions were building. The Indochinese Communist Party (ICP) was inciting demonstrations not just in Hanoi, but all over the country. North of Saigon "rubber plantation workers gravitated toward the Loc Ninh--Saigon railway line, then walked south to Ben Cat and the provincial seat [Thu

Dau Mot village (Phu Cuong)], where they joined with Vanguard Youth groups, townspeople, farmers, and a sprinkling of Stieng minority members [Montagnards] to sing revolutionary songs, salute the Viet Minh flag, listen to speeches, yell 'Long Live the ICP!' and eventually occupy government facilities."[63] Mandarins had been killed in Hue, and murders of Frenchmen and those Vietnamese who opposed the Viet Minh had begun in earnest.

SEAC reported as of 1 September 1945: "Events have taken a grave turn and the revolutionaries have proclaimed a state of siege. Great confusion reigns at Saigon. The Communists have seized crossroads and strategic points and have cut off electricity. Newspapers have been suspended."[64] On 2 September in Saigon, simultaneously with the Hanoi celebration, a rally of a quarter million people of various independence groups paraded under banners that read: "Down with fascism and colonialism!" "Vietnam has suffered and bled under the French yoke!" "Long live the USSR and the USA!" "Long live Vietnamese independence!" Vietnamese youths taunted French soldiers still imprisoned under Japanese guard in a Saigon prison whereupon the soldiers draped the tricolor from their cell windows, sang the "Marseillaise" and traded insults with the crowd. By mid-afternoon the crowd in the center of Saigon became frenzied and shots were fired. Father Tricoire, a Catholic priest who was watching the demonstration, was dragged from the steps of the Saigon Cathedral and murdered. "Five other French people were killed, and many were beaten and dragged off to prison."[65]

Major General Douglas Gracey, commander of the excellent 20th Indian Division, had been tasked by SEAC with getting quickly to Saigon to restore order and disarm and repatriate the Japanese troops in Indochina south of the 16th Parallel. This amounted to the southern half of Annam, some of Laos, and all of Cambodia and Cochinchina. The Nationalist Chinese were to do the same with the Japanese north of that line, which included the northern half of Annam, most of Laos, and all of Tonkin. Ho had already gotten the upper hand in the North. If the Viet Minh were not to do likewise in the South, immediate action was needed.

On 5 September 1945 a British medical team parachuted into Saigon, and the next day, the first British troops began arriving at Tan Son Nhut airfield. The first French detachment from the exterior arrived on 12 September. Gracey himself landed at Tan Son Nhut on 13 September. On hand was a guard of Japanese soldiers surrounding the airfield to provide security, a small group of the most senior Japanese officers to greet him, and a large crowd of French civilians. The crowd cheered as each arriving aircraft loaded with soldiers taxied to a stop on the tarmac. A roar went up for Gracey as finally he exited. After brief salutes and exchange of words with the Japanese officers, Gracey moved to his car, past a smaller crowd of Vietnamese whom no one seemed to recognize but were later said to be Viet Minh wanting to petition him. He was driven off toward his new headquarters. "The road to Saigon was lined with Union Jacks and a cheering throng; most of the French population were in the streets to greet the senior Allied officers."[66]

Soon the Nationalist Chinese troops of Chiang Kai-shek would plunder their way from the border, enter Hanoi, and thus begin a period of uneasy coexistence. Ho's government occupied the former Resident Superior's mansion, but the Chinese general wielded the supreme authority by virtue of having almost 150,000 troops in Tonkin.

In Saigon, other than the single company of Frenchmen that had been flown in on the 12th, the only other French troops were what was left of the 11th Colonial Infantry Regiment (11th RIC), the unit that for decades had been stationed in Saigon and Thu Dau Mot and since the Japanese coup had been decimated and imprisoned in Saigon under severe conditions for six months. Only perhaps 1,000 were anywhere near fit for service. Most of the survivors were still suffering from starvation, mistreatment, and disease. With what forces could be mustered, on 17 September the French took control of two munitions supply points in the Saigon area, an important development since when the 11th Colonial men were first released from confinement they had only bamboo staves and a few old firearms to protect themselves and French citizens from hostile Vietnamese. The 11th RIC men, many of them embittered by the treatment they had received from Vietnamese jailers, began taking out their resentment on any Vietnamese they encountered, and Gracey had to order them back to barracks.

"Before 1940, a force of only 10,776 regular French troops, 16,218 men of the indigenous militia, and 507 French police agents [gendarmes and Sûreté] was sufficient to keep order among 19,000,000 Vietnamese."[67] But now the situation in Saigon had become increasingly dangerous for the Allied forces and colons, and many more troops were needed. Viet Minh and other revolutionaries had taken over key positions in the civil administration to include the police headquarters, Radio Saigon, and some of the most powerful financial institutions. Gracey knew that big trouble was ahead if he allowed this to continue, so he quietly retook control of a few of these critical positions and then, on the night of 22/23 September accomplished what some describe as a coup, sweeping aside weak resistance and seizing critical points to include bridges that controlled access to the city. By evening of the 23rd the Viet Minh had been largely evicted and the French government reinstalled in Saigon, but, as events were soon to show, at great cost. Some of the bitter French former prisoners treated their Vietnamese jailers and others brutally, and other Vietnamese scrambled to strike back.

Street fighting erupted and many on both sides were killed and wounded. By the following night, the Saigon area had exploded in violence. "On 24/25 September 1945, the Viet Minh began their long war. Troung Chinh [member of the National Liberation Committee, later First Secretary of the Communist Party] wrote not long after those events: 'People's power had scarcely been founded in Viet Nam when the British forces . . . landed in Indo-China. . . . On September 23, armed and protected by the British forces, the French colonialists launched their attack and occupied Saigon. Our people replied by force of arms, *and from that moment, our heroic resistance began.*'"[68]

On the night of the 25th in the northern outskirts of the city, the resistance did not seem so heroic when "[Vietnamese] broke into the Cité Heraud, a residential area outside the perimeter controlled by the British forces, where mostly minor French administrators of modest income lived, as well as non-commissioned officers and mixed-breed families. The slaughter which followed was violent and the killers retreated carrying 64 hostages with them, few of which were to be recovered alive. The Japanese who were in charge of the sector participated complicitly in the crime, not intervening at any time to come to the aid of the victims."[69] By some accounts, as many as 150 men, women, and children were horribly slaughtered. If anyone had any doubts as to what kind of war would result from the French "return" to Indochina, the question was settled in those days and nights of 23-25 September 1945. This would be *une guerre sans merci*, a war without mercy, fought by men on both sides who often resembled crazed beasts tearing at one another, exacting the maximum of pain and suffering to the last drop of blood.

The editors of *The 30-Year War, 1945-1975*, published in Hanoi in 2000, state that it is a book researched by Army men under the direction of General of the Army Hoang Van Thai and other generals, and "the men were either direct participants in the events presented or witnesses to them." The book states that beginning on 24 September 1945, "weapons, money, medicines from North and Central Vietnam were urgently sent to the South. Young people volunteered to enlist in the army and various units urgently left for the South."[70] Despite denials by the North, often repeated throughout the war, this statement acknowledged what the leaders of South Vietnam, the French, and the American authorities well knew: the North under Ho and his compatriots was in charge of the war. The North soon designated a commander of forces in the South. In many instances, leaders of the Viet Minh, and later the Viet Cong, had some latitude in the South, but from earliest times it was the North which would direct the war, in North, Central, and South Vietnam.

CHAPTER 3

General Leclerc, October 1945 - June 1946

* * *

The First French General

Philippe François Marie de Hauteclocque was born in 1902, descendent of a noted family which included a knight of the Crusades in the 12th century. A distinguished Saint Cyr cadet, upon commissioning he joined the cavalry. After North African assignments, as a captain in 1935 he was appointed to the coveted post of commandant of cavalry at Saint Cyr. On a maneuver, his horse suddenly bolted from an auto, fell, and crushed his rider's leg under him. In extreme pain, Philippe remounted, led his squadron back to campus and passed them in review. Thereafter, because of the seriously broken leg he habitually used a cane. During the German occupation of World War II Hauteclocque took the nom de guerre, Philippe Leclerc, to protect his family in occupied France.

Among the French generals of World War II, Leclerc stood out. At war's end, he was chosen to head Corps Expéditionnaire Français en Extrême-Orient (CEFEO), the overall French military command in Indochina. Leclerc's military experience had been in North Africa, France, and Germany. He had none in Indochina.

The general landed in Saigon on 5 October 1945. Following the brief ceremony Leclerc was driven through the streets of Saigon and welcomed by a deliriously joyful French population. "We have come," he told them, "to reclaim our inheritance." (Not good news to Vietnamese.) Two days later in a tropical downpour he spoke to a mostly French crowd of 10,000 assembled near the steps of the Governor General's

Palace. Thinking of the road ahead, he said to them, "The Indochinese, lost momentarily in a disastrous [Communist] propaganda, are not our enemies. They will soon also play their role in the French community [of nations]. . . . *They are not our enemies!*"[1]

General Philippe Leclerc troops the line of General Douglas Gracey's 20th Indian Division honor guard at Tan Son Nhut airbase on 5 October 1945, with Gracey behind Leclerc. (NARA)

According to General Adolphe Vézinet, Leclerc's chief of staff, Leclerc had been instructed that, before the anticipated arrival a few weeks later of Vice Admiral Thierry d'Argenlieu, High Commissioner for Indochina, he was also to assume that higher role which was principally to reestablish French sovereignty in Indochina. "Tonkin and Annam," Vézinet said, "already under the authority of the national government [of Ho Chi Minh] in Hanoi, were in open revolt [against the French]. The two realms of Cambodia and Laos expressed their friendship for France but asked that it recognize their independence in the French Union. As for Cochinchina, it seemed still little affected by the Viet Minh revolution except for Saigon. . . Practically speaking, the means for certain operations in the Center [Annam] and in the North [Tonkin], already solidly held by the Viet Minh, would exceed the possibilities of the French army forces – only Cochinchina might be suitable for a military pacification operation of the classic type."[2]

"Pacification" to the French meant something different from what it came to mean to the Americans. Although the French attempted to provide security for villages and work with local officials to enable a better life for the people, too often "pacification" meant simply establishing fortified areas and eliminating any opposition within or outside them.

General Leclerc, deeply religious, was as good as they came—in any army. General George S. Patton's diary extracts reveal the spunky Leclerc to be not unlike Patton himself. General of the Army Omar Bradley, in discussing the liberation of Paris said, "The French 2nd Armored had fought gallantly at Argentan [in the Falaise pocket of France] where it held Patton's shoulder for two weeks. Its respected and celebrated commander, . . . Leclerc, had escaped from the Germans after having been captured in 1940. In 1943 during the Libyan campaign, he led a desert striking force across the Sahara . . . to join Montgomery's Eighth Army in Tripoli. . . . A magnificent tank commander, Leclerc had already made an unscheduled bid for the liberation of Paris. . . . Any number of American divisions could more easily have spearheaded our march into Paris. But to help the French recapture their pride after four years of occupation, I chose a French force with the tricolor on their Shermans." Bradley tells the humorous story of Leclerc's advance being brought to a standstill at the edge of Paris by the point column joining the delirious crowds of welcoming citizenry in "wine and celebration." Thereupon Bradley, probably with tongue in cheek, ordered the American 4th Infantry Division to take the city, and when the word got leaked, no doubt intentionally, "Leclerc's troopers mounted their tanks and burned up the brick roads, and liberated Paris."[3]

At that time Leclerc was 41 years old. The French troops who knew him best held him in the highest professional regard and, moreover, liked him. He was at once hard taskmaster and nice man, able to smile and laugh easily among his troops. Many pictures show him, cane in hand, talking with his men, and they are obviously enjoying the encounter, well at ease.

When Leclerc arrived in Saigon on 5 October he should have had his 9ᵗʰ Colonial Infantry Division (9ᵗʰ DIC) ashore, but they had repeatedly been held up for months due to lack of ships. Only the Americans had them available. At first Truman seemed noncommittal, but then expressed his support for the French. Eight American ships were finally made available to the French and the 9th DIC set sail. Leclerc, his commanders and their men were to learn quickly what a formidable foe they faced. Most of the basic features characterizing the entire nine-year French war were played out in these early days, thus are an important part of our story.

Leclerc, although a four-star general—equivalent to three stars in the U.S. Army—wisely chose to place himself and all arriving French forces under Gracey's (two-star) command until he could get enough troops on the ground to ensure that he himself could exercise control of the French units. Even before he had begun to fight, Leclerc recognized that this war would be unlike anything he had encountered in North Africa and Europe. Vézinet said that when Leclerc gained experience in Indochina he made it known he wanted at all costs to keep the war generalized because there was no military solution. It was in this frame of mind that Leclerc would come to say, *"You cannot kill an idea with bullets."*[4]

By "generalized," knowing that ultimately there needed to be a political solution, he meant that, in the interim, political and civil actions had to go hand-in-glove with military. The "idea" that could not be killed by military force was Vietnamese, their yearning for independence within a country they could call their own.

Ponchardier

Because the Free French had played a minor role in the Pacific war, at the time of the Japanese surrender there were few troops under the French flag in the Far East. In southern China, northern Laos, and Tonkin were scant remnants of the poorly-equipped French Regular, Colonial, and Foreign Legion troops who had barely escaped the Japanese coup of 9 March 1945. The French military within Indochina who had been imprisoned by the Japanese were in no shape to receive a Japanese surrender within Indochina or to combat the Viet Minh. After more than five months of brutal imprisonment or fighting a rear guard action, many of them resembled Auschwitz survivors. A brigade at far-off Madagascar was not combat ready to be sent to Indochina, and they had no shipping. However, in relatively nearby Ceylon was Commando du Special Air Service Bataillon (SASB) with available ship transport. This unit had been trained by the British and usually was called "Commando" or "SAS Ponchardier" after its colorful leader, Lieutenant Commander Pierre Ponchardier. It was almost battalion-size, a three-company unit, one of elite naval paratroops and two of colonial infantry. Because of his exploits in the French underground, Ponchardier was already a legend, and he was soon to become even more famous.

Ponchardier's unit was destined to be fed quickly into a war unlike that which French and other Allied troops had fought in Africa, the Middle East, or Europe. Even though the Allies had gained considerable experience in jungle warfare in the Pacific and Southeast Asia, it was in locations where the indigenous populations largely were with them or neutral, and not against them – a huge difference. Even in that war the French participation had been minimal. Facing the early French fighters arriving in Indochina and all later French units was a war in which Maoist People's War principles would be used first to frustrate and ultimately to defeat them in an alien terrain, culture, and language.

With gruff affection Ponchardier's men called him "le Ponch," or "Pompon" – loosely translated, "He takes the cake!"[5] Of medium height, he was built like a blockhouse with a head that thrust up almost without a neck from his broad shoulders. Barrel-chested, strong-bodied, he was imposing, an original. "To be modest was not in his character. Always the first to set the example of fearlessness in combat, he found it natural to savor the laurels of victory. He liked to earn glory and did not hide it."[6] His men loved it and took courage from him. Superbly intelligent, unconventional, high-spirited, he was a quick but careful planner. Not trusting only to a radio for communication in a fight, he carried an auto horn to signal his troops with such calls as "rally on me." All in all a remarkable character.

As a Naval College graduate, Ponchardier was first a line officer aboard ships, then a submariner, then a naval aviator. When the Germans took northern France in 1940 he and other aviators without planes to fly went to Morocco. But wanting to fight Germans, he made his way back to Paris to join his younger brother Dominique who was setting up a Resistance network. The brothers narrowly escaped death or capture by the Gestapo on several occasions. In the autumn of 1944, with Paris back in the hands of the French, the Germans sure to be defeated, but with the war in the Pacific still going on, the admiral commanding the naval air arm – who was one of the former Resistance leaders – had asked Pierre what he now wanted to do.

"I would like to form a commando of aeronaval parachutists. Along the lines of the British SAS, against the Japanese."

Ponchardier's Resistance buddies scoffed at the idea – *sailor* parachutists! But three of them rallied to le Ponch and would later accompany him to the Far East. As it turned out, the French war in Indochina, like World War II, was a war *par excellence* for parachutists, running the gamut from a jump by a single clandestine person to several hundred dropped for specific missions that could not be accomplished otherwise.

Beginning in February 1945, le Ponch and his men were in England for parachute and commando training. One of his men created the SASB insignia: *"À la vie, à la mort"* – to life, to death.[7] On 2 August 1945, only days before the first atom bomb, the sailors had disembarked at Ceylon where Ponchardier was given two additional companies, colonial infantry parachutists. This created a furor among the soldiers of those two companies who had trained with their infantry regiment comrades and now were being split off to be led by – of all things – a *sailor*! But the soldiers were soon to sing the praises of *their* sailor—when they were not cussing him.

On 23 September in Ceylon, SAS Ponchardier had passed in review before General Leclerc. The general seemed pleased but, when asked what he thought, replied, "I'll wait until I see you at work."[8]

A few days later, aboard the French destroyer *Triomphant*, SAS Ponchardier watched, fascinated, as their ship threaded its way slowly up river from Cap St Jacques (Vung Tau) through a maze of Japanese ships sunk by American air attacks. The ship docked at Saigon, greeted by a joyful crowd of Europeans. Among them, "A detachment of skeleton-like sailors, survivors of the Japanese prisons, was lined up to render honors."[9]

That night, as Ponchardier's unit was quartered at a hospital between Saigon and Cholon, some of his anxious sentries opened fire with rifles and machine guns in the direction of uncertain noises. In the morning, le Ponch was furious and told his men that henceforth, "for each bullet fired he wanted to see the body of a Viet."[10]

On the 8th of October, Ponchardier was summoned to Leclerc's headquarters. He had now been in country six days, three more than the general, and he was in ill humor, waiting for a mission. General Gracey, Colonel Cédile, and the Viet Minh had arranged a cease fire some days earlier, but in minor ways it was being violated daily. Ponchardier's big mouth often got him into trouble with senior officers. Today this lieutenant commander bluntly asked the four-star general if he (Ponchardier) had been brought to Indochina to fight or be a tourist. Leclerc raised his eyebrows, took a breath, and told Ponchardier he had received three complaints from the Japanese about gangsters in commando uniforms who had hijacked their cars. Ponchardier lowered his eyes, not responding to the accusation, and in a non sequitur replied that the Viets were mocking them with their "truce." Leclerc, no doubt with a sigh, tacitly agreed when he told him that the Brits could not act offensively right now due to the truce until such time as the enemy made a big mistake. Then he brought Ponchardier to a map on the wall, pointed, and told him that he wanted his unit to reconnoiter that area in conjunction with the 11th RIC. It was the wetlands on the northeast edge of Saigon, including the Botanical Gardens beyond which the Saigon River made a big loop.

On the 9th le Ponch reconnoitered in daylight by boat on the river and made plans. On the 11th, the Viet Minh made the big mistake, assassinating a British officer and a Gurkha. The normally good-natured and now incensed Gracey thundered, "We'll give them hell!"[11]

The next day the British and French launched their joint operation at the eastern edge of Saigon. Ponchardier with the bulk of his command went by LCI (Landing Craft Infantry) on the Saigon River as the remainder of his commando and other units started their sweep through the wetlands on foot. This would be the first of many "brown water" operations for the French in Vietnam, in many cases the only way to reach points at which they could disembark and engage enemy with their rifles and machine guns while their river craft provided supporting fires. By daylight Ponchardier's men on foot had engaged the enemy and killed several. Shortly thereafter, those aboard the LCI disembarked, killed or chased off enemy, and took their initial objectives. But le Ponch was riled. Many of his men had far too much equipment and personal gear hung on them for this kind of work. He said that next time they would take mess gear, extra shoes and underwear to change, period!

Before long, the troops were in among a large nest of Japanese-trained snipers up in trees and taking casualties, two killed, four wounded. Aspirant (cadet) Bussières, the first to be killed, was later buried in Saigon, a sad reflection of what was to be the fate in nine years of war for so many other French, French Union, and Vietnamese incorporated into French units: 77,333 dead, wounded, or missing.[12]

Ponchardier, hurting from taking casualties, had seen the group of houses where the fire was coming from and ordered them burned as the only way to drive out the enemy. Some of his commandos objected: "We are not going to cause problems everywhere like the colonials did."

Then they saw the large explosions coming from the munitions caches hidden within the burning houses and changed their minds.[13]

With Ponchardier's men going about their business, at midday Leclerc appeared on the scene to see how things were going. After the general left, Ponchardier heard that the Viets had taken several dozen French civilians as hostages, then killed them and thrown their bodies into the river. However, a prisoner told them that about 40 other hostages were still alive. Ponchardier's men raced to the site, drove off the guards and rescued the hostages, their hands tied behind their backs, crying hysterically with relief.

This twelve-day operation had been a good shakedown for SAS Ponchardier, and Leclerc said now that he had seen them at work he could tell them he liked what he saw. Ponchardier's Commando had been tested by both land and river operations, and this was to benefit them well during the more rigorous challenges ahead. The first major French unit from the exterior had killed enemy and had its men killed in return. On the other side, many locals were further embittered and joined the Viet Minh.

In order not to waste precious time, Leclerc was committing piecemeal what small forces he could get as soon as he could lay hands on them. Even the French sailors from the ships that had just debarked troops were not spared. If they had had any visions of shore leave with glorious nights of revelry with Oriental beauties in Saigon, that imagined glamorous, mysterious Paris of the East, they were soon dispelled. Leclerc was going to use every man he could get. He asked for and got several hundred volunteers from those ship crews. They formed into "battalions," some not larger actually than companies, and they would fill in for awhile as grunts.

The turmoil in and around Saigon continued. British engineers were attacked near Tan Son Nhut, Japanese handed over tons of munitions to the Viet Minh from several ammunition dumps around Saigon, and French military and civilians continued to be killed. The French executed some Japanese officers who had defected and were leading Viet

Minh units. Meanwhile, British Spitfire reconnaissance missions were reporting large units of Viet Minh north of Saigon.

Brigadier General Raoul Salan, assigned to command in the North, arrived in Saigon in late October. One evening Major Raymond Dronne, the man who had commanded the lead unit of Leclerc's 2nd Armored in liberating Paris, dined with Salan and Leclerc. Salan said, "Dronne . . . stated his concept of pacification: 'It cannot be the business of the regular army, it needs intelligent cadre, very flexible, mindful of their responsibility. Very quickly the military must be replaced with the administration (with a little 'a'), the man who first handles the reorganization of the village, the [central] market, the [communal] garden, the rice paddies. The country has been smothered by the Japanese, veritable bloodsuckers. It must be given back some pure air.'"[14] Leclerc agreed.

Unfortunately, Dronne's idea was not to be much carried out by the French, and even if it had been, it would have suffered from the same malaise that doomed the later huge American pacification program—to be planned and led by foreigners, not Vietnamese.

Massu

When Leclerc was appointed Supreme Commander in June 1945 he had naturally turned to his former command, the 2nd Armored, to supply an advance fighting force for Indochina. He appeared in front of assembled veterans and asked them to raise their hands, all who wanted to go with him. Hands had shot up, among them that of Jacques Massu. This soldier said, "Out of instinct, without even reflecting, I brandished high my arm. The idea of leaving such a leader never occurred to me."[15]

An infantry officer with a nose that led to his moniker *Roi des Nases* – King of Noses – 37-year-old Lieutenant Colonel Jacques Massu had been one of Leclerc's finest commanders, the leader of 2e Bataillon de Marche du Tchad. Chad, a predominantly Muslim nation, was among the territories of French Equatorial Africa which during World War II produced some highly capable warriors for France. Major Dronne, a 2ⁿᵈ Armored veteran, took command of this battalion mounted on M5 half-tracks which, as with all other vehicles, were American. Massu added a reconnaissance squadron (company-size) of Spahis (Moroccans) equipped with M8 Greyhound armored cars. A tank company of M5A1 Stuart light tanks, an engineer company, a medical company, and two other companies were created for administrative, logistical, and maintenance support. A medical evacuation unit mounted in 3/4 ton Dodge ambulances was part of the supporting troops. The two-person teams of each ambulance were the famous Rochambelles, women who had performed heroically as part of Leclerc's division. All the men and women of this new task force, Groupement Massu, were volunteers.[16]

Massu chose fellow veterans of 2ⁿᵈ armored, Major Maurice Sarazac as second in command, and Major Jean Julien Fonde as his chief of staff (executive officer). Altogether, Massu had four majors, 12 captains, 90 first and second lieutenants, and about 1,800 or so lower ranks for a total of around 2,000 personnel. He said of Groupement Massu, "It was a magnificent instrument of war which I inherited."[17]

Massu landed at Tan Son Nhut on 19 October and went immediately to meet Leclerc at headquarters in Saigon. He found Ponchardier already there.

Massu learned that under British command, forces had reasonably well secured Saigon and the immediate environs, but getting rice transported from the Mekong Delta was a problem. The area around Go Cong, My Tho, and Can Tho in the Delta was rife with what Leclerc and his staff were calling, variously, rebels, revolutionaries, insurgents, terrorists. They were the problem, and the general told Massu he needed to take and then control these principal villages. My Tho and the surrounding area was key to unlocking road and rail movement to Cholon/Saigon, and water transport to Saigon, and up the Bassac River to Phnom Penh.

Opération Moussac, the first all-French military action, was a late October thrust, a pincer movement directed at My Tho on the Mekong River south of Saigon. Commander Francois Jaubert of the French navy was in Saigon ahead of Leclerc, and from headquarters in the old Saigon Yacht Club Jaubert had begun to develop a riverine force from whatever resources were at hand: Japanese junks, barges, private boats now pressed into war service—anything that could float, had a motor that could be made operable, and carry troops. Initially Leclerc had been only moderately interested in the prospect of naval involvement. But while they were planning the operation, Jaubert quietly had said to him, "*Mon général, Cochinchine n'etait pas le Sahara.*" Cochinchina indeed was not the Sahara where Leclerc had operated in wide-open, sweeping armored movements.

Groupement Massu with its tanks, scout cars, and infantry in half-tracks, would move south out of Saigon by a main road bordered by swampy land. Ponchardier's Commandos and a detachment of sailors-now-soldiers would move down rivers and canals on Jaubert's makeshift vessels.

No time was to be wasted. With only four days to debark, get into temporary quarters, receive orders and plan for action, Massu would become the first French commander to launch operations outside the Saigon/Cholon area. He would employ all his troops except Sarazac's 200 men who were still on the passenger ship *Pasteur* that would not arrive until almost a month later. Under his command he would have his own groupement, Ponchardier and his commandos, Company A/5th RIC, and a unit of sailors from the battleship *Richelieu*.

Massu put one of his officers up in a two-seater Japanese Zero to reconnoiter the route. Leclerc listened to the man's report of many impassable cuts the enemy had made in the road and told him, "You are a pessimist." If the report was correct, though, this would mean big trouble for Massu.

The Mekong Delta south of Saigon is a wet lowland only a few meters above sea level, cut up by many natural rivers and streams as well as hundreds of canals, small and large. To put it mildly, it was not very inviting territory for Massu's armored force.

Two months after the operation, Massu's headquarters began publishing periodic booklets, *Coups de Massu—Massu's Strikes*—which documented the unit's experiences:

"At dawn on the 25th, Groupement Massu went to war. At 4 A.M. one felt the excitement of these days of attack. . . the tank engines roaring, the grating of the half-tracks, the clicks of the machine guns being armed and the bands of cartridges as they unrolled, the jeeps which passed by the column, the shouted orders, the blaring radios. Dronne ['s unit] marched at the front, followed by [that of] Fonde at a heady speed until the first cut in the road."[18]

Massu's column had not gotten far before they discovered the truth of the aerial reconnaissance report. His engineers passed to the head of the column with their bulldozer and trucks carrying girders and began filling in the first of 24 large cuts in the road. These obstacles came to be called "piano keys" because from the air they resembled the black keys of a piano, taking up most, but not all, of the space between the edges of the road. The Viet Minh, knowing that the French would be coming, had pressed into service, either by force or voluntarily, hundreds of local inhabitants. Using hand tools and small dredging sleds pulled by oxen or water buffaloes, a cut would be started at one edge of the roadway and excavated several feet wide and deep going about two-thirds the distance perpendicularly across the road surface. Then about ten feet from the first cut, and starting at the other edge of the road, another parallel cut would be made two-thirds the distance back toward the opposite side. This pattern would be continued several times. The Vietnamese could use the road on their bicycles or oxcarts simply by taking their time and winding around each cut on the undisturbed surface that remained. Jeeps sometimes could also make the passage. However, a column of trucks or armored vehicles could not navigate it.[19]

The unaccustomed heat and oppressive humidity were tough on Massu's men, so newly arrived in country, and now they were stopped on the road. Even with their bulldozer, much of the work facing the engineer company was back-breaking hand labor under the full sun, and with adrenalin pumping, the urgency of the situation caused more sweat. When Massu's engineers and lead unit filled in the obstacles, one by one, enough so the column could pass, they came finally to a blown bridge. It was evident they would not be able to enter My Tho on the 25th as planned, but would have to work all night long on a passage and continue the advance the next day. Leclerc appeared and spurred the men on, but, annoyed, he ultimately had to give up the idea of Massu's ground unit taking My Tho on the first day of the campaign.

Massu said, "Around us, indifferent to our tribulations, the peasants worked in the rice paddies."[20] (They were doing the same type of thing two decades later. When one of our armored vehicles would hit a mine the people often would go on with their field work, seeming not even to notice us, while we suspected with good cause that among them was the person who planted or detonated it.)

Leclerc had been highly frustrated at Massu's slow pace in his attack on My Tho, and Ponchardier's ad hoc waterborne force had easily beaten Massu to the objective. The lesson had not been lost on Leclerc and he later gave Jaubert all the support he could in fashioning a more professional "brown water" navy. That early use in the Mekong Delta would prove how important a waterborne component would be to the overall French military effort.

Leroy

Books by those who served in Indochina as admirals or generals in the highest French military and government positions, such as those of Admiral Jean Decoux, Admiral Thierry d'Argenlieu, General Raoul Salan, or General Henri Navarre of course are essential for understanding the Indochina War. But books written by lower ranking officers, NCOs, and soldiers or seamen are no less important. They provide rice roots views of the conflict. Most of them are intriguing, real page-turners. Such is the book by Colonel Jean Leroy, *Fils de la Rizière* (*Son of the Rice Paddy*). This astonishing man was born in 1920 to a French colonial father and a fervently Buddhist mother on the island of An Hoa near My Tho in the Mekong Delta. Despite meager means, the father was able to send Jean to a My Tho Catholic school where the Brothers baptized him, which he later recognized was of "capital importance" in his life.[21]

An aspirant (officer cadet) in the l'Infanterie Coloniale from 1940, Leroy had been a lieutenant in Ban Me Thuot, 170 miles northeast of Saigon, on 10 March 1945, the day after the Japanese coup. The Japanese attack there came at 0100 hours but the post had gotten no warning and it fell in a matter of minutes. As it happened, one company of 80 men was out in the jungle on a mission to gather firewood and kill game to supply the garrison when Jean, commanding it, was suddenly stopped on a trail by his father and warned. Jean led his men back to the post and attacked the Japanese, only to be beaten back into the jungle. The detachment made their escape with only the little ammunition left in their pouches, water in their canteens, and rations for a short period in their packs, pursued by the Japanese. Week by week, day by day, in horrible jungle conditions his little troop dwindled, some dying, some slipping away to try to make their way home. The small remainder was finally reduced to a handful wracked with disease, nearly starving, buying a little rice from Moïs Montagnards deep in the jungle. The survivors were afflicted with genital crabs, ticks, and leeches, and some had contracted malaria.

For awhile this little band successfully conducted ambush operations against the Japanese. Then one night in the jungle, Leroy was startled awake by two Japanese soldiers who bound him and took him back to Ban Me Thuot. He learned that two Moïs who had sold him rice in the jungle had informed the Japanese. The Kempeitai then brutally tortured him for days. Finally he was to be transferred to Saigon, and on the way the news came of the atom bombs and end of the war. Nevertheless his captors threw him into the Saigon prison where he was to witness the horrible consequences of the Japanese treatment of European prisoners.

After several austere days, employing a ruse, he was released and made contact with the French underground intelligence service. Shortly Leclerc's headquarters heard of him and wanted him for Operation Moussac. Fluent in French and Vietnamese and knowledgeable as a resident of the area around My Tho, he could prove highly useful. Leroy was placed under command of Ponchardier as an intelligence officer.

Ponchardier's Waterborne Assault

Ponchardier's force consisted of his own men, the converted sailors from the battleship *Richelieu*'s "battalion," and the gunboat *Gazelle* which would escort three Japanese invasion barges, each with a Japanese crew of helmsman and engineer in the uniform of the Imperial Navy.[22] Inside the barges were the rest of the *Richelieu's* men. The main force with Ponchardier aboard had as objective My Tho. The gunboat flotilla would assault the nearby hamlet of My Loi then advance 15 kilometers south to take Go Cong.

Late in the afternoon of 24 October, Ponchardier's small flotilla had headed south. Aboard an American LCI left over from World War II were about 400 men consisting of 300 of Ponchardier's SASB and a company of 100 from the *Richelieu*. The gunboat and barges loaded with the other *Richelieu* men would use an alternate water route.

The LCI men were packed in like sardines. Leroy was aboard, headed toward his birthplace. Early evening rains hit, and he and the others hunched their backs under a downpour. At 1930 hours, almost two hours after sunset, they came to the entrance of the canal that led directly upstream to My Tho. It was in an area held by the Binh Xuyen, an extensive gang of murderers, extortionists, and thieves which plagued Saigon and environs. Ponchardier found the canal blocked across its entire width with large junks linked together with a heavy chain. Bullets from both banks of the canal began striking the sheet metal of the LCI and ricocheting off. The captain of the boat, a very young British ensign who that night performed like a seasoned veteran, called for full speed ahead, steered directly into a junk and smashed it. The chain made a sinister noise scraping the bow of the LCI and snapped. The enemy fire redoubled, and the LCI opened up with its 40 mm cannon. Gasoline-powered junks burst into flames and in a matter of minutes the LCI was upstream. The night fell silent. When Leroy raised his head he could see beautiful rubber plantations on both sides of the canal – but also a Japanese guard post. The LCI slowed so that a French captain who spoke Japanese could yell out and negotiate with the guard, telling them that aboard were British troops of General Gracey, charged to go disarm Japanese garrisons according to terms of the armistice. The Japanese sentinel presented arms in salute, and the LCI proceeded upstream, slowing to repeat the procedure with other sentinels every two or three kilometers.

The rain had stopped, and the troops drank from their canteens and smoked. Leroy was overjoyed at being back in the land of his youth. My Tho lay directly ahead. The LCI slowed and idled, maintaining its position, and in a few minutes had put out men both up and downstream from the village to lie under the trees in ambush positions. Ponchardier called for LeRoy and asked him if he thought they could take My Tho without waiting for Massu's armored column to arrive by road.

"According to my information," Leroy replied, "it is only weakly defended."

In telling the story, Leroy wrote that Ponchardier, this "loud-mouthed corsair of a bygone era," leader of a "troop of scrawny wolves" nodded, and at 0300 the LCI slid quietly up to the wharf of My Tho. Three Vietnamese sentinels armed with lances were on guard. One they shot dead, and the other two fled. Leroy jumped onto the wharf in chase, caught one and slapped him hard across the face, demanding to know where other defenders of the post were. His prisoner turned out to be a terrified 16- or 17-year old kid who fell on his knees and begged for his life.

Leaving him, Leroy continued on with three men to the public works building, kicking the butts of the startled inhabitants who then, mouths open and arms raised, fearfully watched as his party quickly searched the premises. A phone rang. Leroy answered. It was the Viet Minh at the command post of My Tho wanting to know what was going on and, by the way, who was he? Leroy barked he was the chief of police of Tan An making an inspection, and hung up.

He went on to enter the postal station, and there the phone was also ringing. This time he told them that the LCI was just a junk going to Phnom-Penh. The next time the phone rang the situation was more problematic. The Viet Minh on the other end told him that French sailors from the *Richelieu* had debarked. How they gotten that information Leroy did not know. He testily responded that they were on a harmless night exercise and ended the conversation, shouting a Viet Minh slogan. Going on to the local jail he found confused guards who complained they had not been paid in two months. Leroy went into the director's office, removed money from a chest, paid the guards for past service and contracted with them to lock up some captured Viet Minh and guard them.[23]

As Ponchardier's men were quickly getting My Tho under control, encountering only light resistance, the experience of the *Richelieu* detachment with the gunboat turned out to be not nearly so pleasant as they debarked to attack the nearby village of My Loi.

Guiberteau

Ensign Yannick Guiberteau from the *Richelieu*'s crew described how everything had gone according to plan as their barges rendezvoused with the gunboat *Gazelle* during the darkness of the 25th. But then as some of the 80 men on his barge were put ashore at My Loi they received heavy fire from the underbrush along a frontage of 100 meters. He said, "Our inexperienced troop was incapable of surviving night combat against a large well-armed enemy force." The barges piloted by the terrified Japanese helmsmen backed off rapidly to a safe position behind the *Gazelle* which with its 90 mm cannon laid down a barrage along the riverbank. The men ashore were in a bad spot but managed to position themselves for rescue. Guiberteau's friend, Ensign Gamblin, had been mortally wounded and died after finally being taken aboard a boat. Three others were dead and a dozen wounded, including two other officers who were narrowly saved by medics on the *Gazelle*. A salient trait of the enemy which was to persist throughout thirty years of war was demonstrated in this early action. Whereas Ponchardier's enemy had largely melted from his superior force at My Tho, those facing the many fewer Richelieu men inflicted heavy casualties. In accordance with Ho's and Giap's plan for People's War, when their enemy was perceived to be weaker they would attack them fiercely; when stronger they would withdraw and wait for another day.

At daybreak, still aided by fire from the gunboat and using additional troops to assault, the second attempt to land succeeded without opposition. The enemy had disappeared. On the afternoon of the next day, the landing party assembled and rendered honors to their four comrades, buried not more than 100 meters from where they had fallen. The men of the *Richelieu*, with some bitterness, talked about why the intelligence had depicted an unoccupied hamlet for them to assault, and why such an inexperienced group, sailors turned instantly into infantrymen, was chosen in the first place for such a mission. The realities of the war had begun to set in.[24] Young, eager Frenchmen, anxious to perform their duties well, had many more such realities to face in the months and years to come.

Casualties of War

In Ponchardier's group there was only one man wounded on the night of the 25th, and that may have been from friendly fire. As his men swept through the village, firing at Viets fleeing them, they came upon a Japanese sentinel standing guard at his post who earned their great respect by simply remaining there calmly as the bullets were flying around him, and each time a commando passed by he would salute. Putting up little resistance, several Vietnamese were prisoners, and among the dead were some village inhabitants who had been hit in the firing. By 0500 the sweep of My Tho was complete and all critical points outposted. Two French soldiers indulged their macabre humor by putting a Viet corpse in a rocking chair and setting it to rocking on the veranda of a house.

After daylight, several Annamite nuns came from the vicinity of the church to welcome the Frenchmen, bringing them a breakfast of coffee and delicious biscuits made of rice and manioc. This was nice, but Ponchardier went among his men reminding them over and over, "Attack or be attacked. To take a village is good, to hold it is better."[25] From his command post in a house, he quickly dispatched his units in all directions to enlarge the area they held.

During the day, Ponchardier heard by radio of the slow progress of Massu and was amused. On this day, the 26th, as darkness fell, the lead unit of Massu's column finally got into My Tho. Major Dronne, known for his great sense of humor, called out to one of Ponchardier's cadet-officers who was bare-chested, Japanese helmet on his head, and a red bandana around his neck: "What is it with the disguise? Couldn't you get a proper uniform?"

The cadet answered, "We left with what we had on our backs. We don't have trucks to transport our dining halls."

Dronne cracked up laughing and continued on his way without another word.[26]

Massu, though, was in understandably ill humor. The next morning he was welcomed to town by a grinning Ponchardier, bare-chested, submachine gun in hand, wearing khaki shorts and with his auto horn hung on his belt. He had invested and taken My Tho totally by surprise on the first night. The enemy, they found, had put virtually all of their resources into defending against Massu's attack by land, a mistake they would not repeat in this vast Mekong Delta where movement by water was much more certain than by land.

Meanwhile, Leroy and his men made a gruesome discovery, mutilated cadavers floating in a stream. Their bodies were recovered and buried in a mass grave. These were civil servants and leading citizens of the region that the Viet Minh had tortured, then killed. Later, along the route to nearby Go Cong, they found large puddles of blood congealed at the base of poles where the red flag with yellow star still hung. Leroy said that according to the intelligence they got, "the Viets had tied men and women to these poles."[27]

The ordeal of the *Richelieu* men was not over with My Loi. The mission of those men with the gunboat was to continue on to Go Cong to link up with Massu's force. As Guiberteau and his company progressed, he lost an 18-year old sailor killed, and the advance became quite strange indeed. They found some Japanese bicycles which proved handy for road use, and they commandeered a dozen horses which enabled them to traverse rice paddies. Here they were, sailors fighting as soldiers, wearing caps sporting *Richelieu* ribbons, aboard bicycles and horses!

They came upon a small post of Japanese soldiers who had been forgotten but were continuing their service in this remote place. They made themselves useful to Guiberteau. While the Japanese stood guard at night, some Moïs tribesmen in the woods beyond their perimeter were keeping watch on all this activity, and one of them shot an arrow into a Japanese sentinel, not knowing, probably, that the war with the Japanese had ended. And a few nights later the Japanese helped beat off a Viet Minh attack that left a dozen wounded among the sailor-infantrymen. The total casualties from the "battalion" of 250 men from the Richelieu were heavy: six dead, 33 wounded, and several others ill.[28]

In the next few days after having taken My Tho, Ponchardier and his men quickly took the important villages of Vinh Long, Can Tho, and Cai Rang in waterborne operations and, for the time being, these actions reasonably well reestablished French control over the Mekong.

Pacification, and Atrocities

Leclerc needed Groupement Massu for another mission, but he knew from the beginning that for any overall success in regaining Indochina he would have to not just take key villages but then provide security for the people in them. He knew that his war could not be search and destroy in an area, then departure. Whereas many of Massu's men would leave shortly on a new mission, for the time being, Dronne's colonial infantry would be left behind along with Ponchardier's commandos and the *Richelieu* contingent. They were to remain in the area for a few weeks until relieved of their pacification mission.

Jean Leroy tells how in those first few days of November the French expanded their operations and divided the zone into three subsectors for pacification. He said it was, however, by no means pacified. The French troops were far too few, and the Viets would lie low during the day, reappear at night, put out their ambushes, and menace and assassinate inhabitants in the villages. Families scattered by the fighting could be returned to their homes, but they needed to be protected. How and with what? Leroy said an idea came to him in a flash of intuition. To fight effectively against the Viet Minh who were indigenous to the Delta he would have to raise a group of men from this same area to combat them – partisans. *Catholic* partisans. The subsector commander, Major Dronne, liked the idea and put it to Leclerc who approved. The first group of twenty was formed from the prisoners Leroy had rescued that first night at My Tho. Each man was outfitted with sneakers and a rifle taken from My Tho's Japanese garrison. From this nucleus Leroy was to develop a regional force that would be first a source of amazement and later consternation at the highest government levels.

During this time in November 1945, incidents happened that brought home even more forcefully that this would be a war unlike any these Frenchmen could have imagined. Ensign Guiberteau told how two soldiers from a unit that relieved them had gone out on a foraging mission to steal chickens. They were surprised by a Viet Minh patrol who captured one of them while the other managed to hide himself under a bush. As the latter watched in utter horror, frozen in place with fear, the Viet Minh cut off his friend's head with a machete.[29]

Warrant Officer Guinet of 5th RIC also had a horror story to report. His unit had found a shed containing the tortured corpses of French sailors hung on hooks. Even at this early date in the war, atrocities committed by both sides were old news.

Serge Jacquemond was with the civil services detachment sent in to reestablish administrative control. He observed Ponchardier's methods in pacifying the area. Ponchardier called it "cleansing." Jacquemond said it was sometimes "heavy-handed, ineffective, and politically incorrect, too brutal in my opinion. What is clean for the military, is it not sometimes filthy for the civilian?" The Viet Minh with good cause quickly came to name Ponchardier's unit, "Les Tigres," partly because of their striped camouflage uniforms, but also because of their ferocity and tenacity. This was understandably a source of pride among these tough troops who had been trained to fight fiercely and without pity, accurately observing that their enemy did the same.[30]

Little or no quarter given, none expected. On both sides: Viet Minh and French – men who could weep over the tragedies brought upon their own troops and innocent civilians by war, they were themselves the cause of those tragedies. Such was the nature of this *guerre sans merci*. God help any combatant captured by the other side. For the remainder of the French war, many on both sides would submerge themselves in unspeakable bloody atrocities.[31]

The Rochambelles

Suzanne Torrès had been with the 2nd Armored Division since North Africa as head of the Rochambelles, and when Leclerc needed a woman to head *le Corps feminine* in Indochina, 1,200 strong, she was his choice. She had been delighted to accompany Groupement Massu on the aircraft carrier from France and took every opportunity now that she was headquartered in Saigon to go visit "her" 2nd Armored men and "her" Rochambelles. A gutsy gal whom her women called "Toto," she had driven down to My Tho in one of the resupply convoys. She learned that the Dodge ambulance team assigned to Major Dronne's battalion had been requested to evacuate wounded from the *Richelieu's* contingent at Go Cong. The ambulance crew of two young women had set out with a half-track for security, but en route the half-track had a mechanical breakdown. Knowing how urgent was the need, the women charged ahead alone in their ambulance. They were stopped by a piano key cut in the road and well knew that "the rebels" usually ambushed these positions. They got out of their ambulance and – hearts pounding – ("never mind, it will pass," one thought) looked around. By chance, the position was unoccupied and they began gathering tree limbs and rocks here and there and were able to fill in the trench enough so they could pass. The sailors attending the wounded were stupefied to see an ambulance pull up and two young women alone get out. The Rochambelles themselves, though, thought it was not much.[32]

Leclerc's Style of Leadership

Leclerc was one to take immediate and direct action, little considering his personal safety. One of the first things he had faced upon arrival in Saigon was the problem of Cambodia. After the 9 March coup the Japanese had imposed on the king, Norodom Sihanouk, a prime minister named Thanh who denounced the treaties linking his country to France. He had become very unpopular but was all-powerful, thanks to the support of the Japanese Kempeitai. Thanh plotted against Sihanouk, and those around the king feared a coup and proclamation of a Popular Republic in obedience to the Viet Minh. The king's loyal uncle came to Saigon to see Leclerc and stated categorically that with his help Cambodia would remain in the French Union. On 15 October, accompanied only by two aides, Leclerc had flown to Phnom Penh, the Cambodian capital. He was ushered in to see the premier, spoke a few words and led him outside. The general made a sign for Thanh to get into Leclerc's car. Thanh complied. As Leclerc's auto rolled to the airport, Thanh began asking where they were going. He got into Leclerc's plane without resisting, and an hour later was in the hands of the Sûreté in Saigon. A week later in Phnom Penh, Sihanouk announced that the obstacles which for months had gotten in the way of the traditional friendship between his kingdom and France had ceased to exist. Problem solved.[33]

Leclerc was a sensible, courageous leader, a soldier's general. His men would find him popping up unexpectedly in far-flung operations. On 2 November, after the My Tho operation had been expanded to include other important villages in the Mekong area, he and General Salan were riding in jeeps to see how things were going. The night belonged to the enemy, but basically Leclerc's troops more or less controlled the roads and hamlets during the day. However, returning from their visit to an advance guard unit the jeeps were ambushed during daylight. The generals were unharmed in the exchange of fire but a senior NCO in the jeep behind Leclerc was killed.[34]

On another occasion Lelerc came around a corner in the midst of an engagement in which some of his men had been wounded and killed. He quickly sized up the situation and determined that they needed to get out of the ditches where they had taken cover and maneuver against the enemy. Exposing himself to fire, he went around wrapping the men on their butts with his cane and telling them not to fear, but to get going. They did.[35]

Massu told of an amusing incident which reveals another aspect of the general's personality, and why his men liked him. Leclerc flew in a Catalina flying boat which landed on the Mekong River. Upon the airplane trying to take off again, it got bogged down with floating seaweed and became grounded on a sandbar in the river. Ponchardier, Massu and another officer stripped naked and jumped into the water to try to free the aircraft. Massu said, "The general simply imitated us [by also stripping naked and jumping in to help.]"[36]

Viet Minh Weapons and Munitions

As soon as Opération Moussac was completed, others were launched. Beginning in early November Gracey's forces (Indian, Japanese, French) pushed outward from Saigon. Massu would command an attack on Tay Ninh to the northwest, and again he would have a waterborne force consisting of a mixed bag of legionnaires, colonial infantry from Morocco, and others aboard river craft. They would proceed upriver to Tay Ninh while Massu with his groupement would advance by road.

Massu's ground contingent soon encountered a series of ambushes near Trang Bang, 25 miles northwest of Saigon. The first cost them three dead and six wounded. The enemy would fire from the brush lining the road, then disappear into the forest. A subsequent ambush succeeded in killing a truck driver, which immobilized his truck and blocked the column behind it. The medical officer was seriously wounded while aiding others, and a captain was killed. The head of the Rochambelles was in a nearby ambulance and she drove through the fire to rescue a man who certainly would have died. Then she climbed into the stopped truck and drove it so the column could advance. In the continuing fight, a mounted 75mm gun moved forward to engage the enemy with direct fire, and its commander was killed by a bullet to the head. Then the crew was shot at—with *arrows*. In his book, Massu exclaimed, "A '75 against arrows!! But the brush gave an absolute advantage to the prehistoric weapons!!"[37]

One of the boats in Massu's waterborne force also received arrows twanging off the metal plating. These encounters were not far from the Michelin plantation at Dau Tieng where, as reported in the rubber workers' book, a small resistance band had equipped themselves with bamboo lances and ancient muskets.[38] The Viet Minh would not long have to resort to such means, though, as they were increasingly successful in equipping themselves with captured French weapons, most of them American of WW II, as well as arms they managed to manufacture. The authors of *30-Year War*, an official Communist history, said of Ho's government, "In [Annam], all provinces were allowed to open military plants to repair or fabricate weapons . . . [oganizers collected] iron, steel, copper, and aluminum. Machinery and equipment was taken from industrial plants. The military factories got needed explosives from unexploded bombs and shells used by the Americans and Japanese during the war. . . . These 'military plants' managed to turn out grenades, mines, hand-bombs [satchel charges], pistols, rifles, and bazookas."[39]

In the North, Giap was quite successful in capturing weapons or getting the Japanese to turn caches over to him, but he needed more to support his army, guerrillas, and self defense forces, which toward the end of the year perhaps totaled 5,000. One source was Chinese firearms to be bought from corrupt Chinese officers in the occupying army around Hanoi, or shipped from across the border. But they were expensive. In running the government, Ho found that he needed more funds than were at hand for many purposes—to buy Giap's munitions, to purchase rice and distribute it to the tens of thousands of people who were once again on the brink of starvation due to another drought, to buy trucks, medicines, many things. He appealed to the people of the North and got a warm response. Women sold their jewelry, men sold their chickens and pigs, children sold their toys or pets in what became known as "Gold Week." So it was not just the shouts of acclaim they gave him, but the sacrifice of their hard-earned possessions that demonstrated their support for Uncle Ho.

Situation, End of 1945, Beginning of 1946

America had finally supplied ships for the Expeditionary Corps, and during the last months of 1945, French strength increased notably with the arrival of the 9th and 3rd Colonial Infantry Divisions plus Spitfires acquired from the British, flown now by French pilots. Continuing the focus on Cochinchina first, Leclerc would try to pacify it before any move on the North. The general began sending his units farther out from Saigon.

In mid December French forces pushed into the difficult swampy terrain around Duc Hoa to the west of Saigon without much luck in contacting Viet Minh. By the end of December units to the north in Cochinchina around Ban Me Thuot had turned back south with the objective of eliminating enemy in the rubber plantations to include the second Michelin plantation at Thuan Loi, and in jungle base camps in the double loop of the Song Be River. This feature on the map gave rise to the name we used in 1968 in 11th Cav, "The Testicles," when our cavalry regiment performed the same mission. Leclerc's forces also pushed east and took Nha Trang on the coast of the South China Sea.

Despite these partially successful French moves, the view of Communist historians from Hanoi was positive. "The resistance [in Cochinchina and southern Annam] had lasted over one hundred days. The time and events had caused no few surprises to the famous colonialist generals. . . . Time was on the side of the Vietnamese. The French managed to occupy a number of towns and cities, but vast expanses of rural areas in [Cochinchina] remained under Vietnamese control. Resistance bases were set up in [the Plain of Reeds to the west of Saigon] and in the U Minh Forest [along the west coast of the Ca Mau Peninsula, both places in low wetlands]. In urban areas, including Saigon, resistance bases carried out activities, legally and illegally."[40] In January 1946 Leclerc's units pushed to the southeast to Cap St. Jacques (Vung Tau) on the South China Sea and south to Ca Mau at the very southern tip of Vietnam.

French garrisons now located throughout much of the land south of the 16th Parallel had to be supplied, so the necessity for convoy protection became pressing. The French did just as we did so many years later: they reconnoitered likely ambush sites, cut back the trees and brush from the road, and set up checkpoints. And the Viet Minh did just as the Viet Cong and North Vietnamese Army did those many years later: they found ways to ambush convoys and neutralize checkpoint systems.

Thanks initially to the British and somewhat to the Japanese who, depending on the time and local circumstances were both a hindrance and help to the Allied effort (in some actions, Japanese were actually fighting Japanese), the French had gained nominal control over the South.

The three men in whose hands the fate of Indochina largely rested in late 1945: left to right, British General Douglas Gracey, French Admiral Thierry d'Argenlieu, French General Philippe Leclerc. (NARA)

Nominal is the keyword. Bernard Fall, with several years experience in Vietnam, was close to the mark when he wrote, "Cochinchina was in French hands—to the extent of 100 yards on either side of all major roads."[41] Whereas with difficulty, roads were mostly open to traffic, there were always small-unit guerrilla actions. Although the French Union forces, which contained many more Africans, Vietnamese, and Cambodians than Regular French soldiers, usually could move freely about in the daylight with only moderate concern for security, the nights were another matter, then as in our day. The Viet Minh owned the night. In the darkness, they moved, held meetings, conducted fierce but small-scale operations to kill their enemy, capture weapons, train their cadre and build their strength. They prepared for bigger fights ahead.

Toward the end of 1945, given an improved Cochinchina situation, the French had necessarily begun turning more of their attention to the North. Jean Roger Sainteny had led the French military mission in China and was now both the commissioner for Tonkin and North Annam as well as special envoy of the French government. In Hanoi he and General Salan, military commander in the North, began talks with Ho Chi Minh about bringing French forces back into Tonkin and a Vietnamese nation into a French Union of Allied States. In early November, Ho, ever flexible to accommodate changing circumstances while moving forward his agenda, had found it politic to dissolve the Indochinese Communist Party (ICP). This step, he believed, would attract many Vietnamese to work with the DRV—those who were anti-French and wanted independence but were not Communists. "For the next five years, officially and publicly, there was no Communist party in Vietnam. In fact, however, Party recruitment continued, Party leadership activities went on as usual, and high-level . . . congresses were staged."[42]

To the French, the time seemed right for a new series of moves. Although De Gaulle startled France and much of the world on 20 January 1946 by abruptly resigning as head of the Provisional Government of the Republic of France because of parliamentary discord, the direction of the war in Indochina remained basically unchanged. Through many later shifts in government heads, one thing remained more or less constant: the desire to bring all Indochina states firmly into a French Union. The question was *how*.

CHAPTER 4

Occupation of the North, 1946

* * *

The French Move on Tonkin

Ever since d'Argenlieu had arrived on 31 October 1945 and consulted with Leclerc, the need for doing something about Tonkin had grown into an increasingly pressing problem. For one thing, 3,000 French Union soldiers were still imprisoned in the Citadel fortress in Hanoi and there was great concern for their health and welfare. For another, Ho and his government were getting stronger. And the Nationalist Chinese, 150,000 strong, showed no real intention of withdrawing.

Ho handled what the Communists called "the Chinese problem" in his characteristic fashion: "Our main enemy at present is French colonialism. We need time to consolidate the political power, build up forces and make preparations for a nationwide resistance in case they extend the war to the north. Therefore, we should now take a conciliatory attitude toward Chiang Kai-shek's troops, cleverly avoid a conflict, carry out the motto about 'Chinese-Vietnam friendship' and rely on the support of the entire people to foil the design of Chiang Kai-shek's troops." Ho well knew that "the Vietnamese were full of hatred for them. President Ho always advised local people and officials to avoid clashes with them."[1] The Chinese Nationalists strongly supported two non-Communist Vietnamese independence parties, the VNQDD and the Dai Viet, and "demanded that the Vietnamese reshuffle their government and hand important posts [to them]."[2] Ho did some of this but ultimately would deal with those non-Communists.

Admiral d'Argenlieu, High Commissioner, had been given the mission of "reestablishing French sovereignty in the territories of the Indochinese Union." Leclerc, his subordinate as Supreme Commander, had the mission "to take, under the authority of the High Commissioner, all measures for the reestablishment of that sovereignty."[3] From the beginning the two men had not gotten along. D'Argenlieu was a strange duck. He had no experience in administering a large civilian population or commanding ground troops. A French Naval Academy graduate, he had distinguished himself as a young officer in the First World War. Post-war, he became a monk, took vows as a Carmelite priest, rose rapidly in the order and became Provincial Superior of Paris. Upon outbreak of the Second World War he returned to the navy, was captured by the Germans, escaped and joined de Gaulle. His fierce loyalty to de Gaulle coupled with undeniable talents got him promoted, and he was seriously wounded in an unarmed small boat while on a critical diplomatic mission in North Africa, an attempt to convince the Vichy-loyal governor of Dakar to join de Gaulle. He was appointed commander of French naval forces in Britain and years later paraded with de Gaulle down the Champs-Elysées as they entered liberated Paris. An austere celibate, he expected respect from the Indochinese and ostensibly got it, as shown in a 16 June 1946 film of a parade in which a troop of elephants in a long line approaches the reviewing stand. One by one they face the High Commissioner, kneel under command of the mahout, and then move on. It is a scene one can only imagine played out in a 19th century Eastern emperor's court. One wonders what Leclerc, seated behind d'Argenlieu, must have thought.[4]

The admiral's driving ambition was to be the engineer of France's reclamation of its past role of dominance in Indochina, and he saw force as the way forward. "It was said of d'Argenlieu in France that he possessed one of the most brilliant minds of the twelfth century."[5] Leclerc urged him to adjust to the new conditions and negotiate insertion of French forces in the North. Certainly by February 1946, when the major routes were open in the South during the daytime, and business could largely be conducted in the major cities and villages, Leclerc thought of the enormous sacrifices his men had made and the suffering created on both sides by the war. By the end of that month French Union losses were about twelve hundred killed and thirty-five hundred wounded or missing. Leclerc recognized the even greater costs that would be ahead if the war were to continue mainly as a military contest. However, Leclerc and his staff necessarily began planning for a military move to the North even as they were still trying to consolidate in the South and negotiations between General Salan, Commissioner Sainteny, and Ho were ongoing in Hanoi.

Many factors would be involved in insertion of Expeditionary Corps troops into Tonkin. The two dominant ones were the Chinese occupation and Ho Chi Minh's government. Chiang Kai Shek's Nationalist troops, which had been given the mission of disarming and repatriating the Japanese troops north of the 16th Parallel, had been in Tonkin now for five months. They had proven more adept at rape and pillage than in carrying out their assignment. They were an obstacle to any French attempt to reclaim Vietnam as a member of a French Union. Furthermore, matters of French property and interests within China had to be solved diplomatically before China could be expected to allow French combat units to debark at Haiphong and proceed to Hanoi.[6] Another factor that weighed on Leclerc's mind was that about 17,000 French military and civilian prisoners were still behind bars in Hanoi. He feared that they might be massacred.

Vézinet said of Leclerc: "Very soon convinced that the military action he had to take in the South without prolonged political discourse had no chance of success in the North, he envisaged that a foothold in Tonkin could come about only with political preparation and accompanying diplomacy. He thought that the sole means would be to negotiate with Ho Chi Minh, and to hasten, simultaneously, by negotiations, the departure of the Chinese."[7]

Leclerc's stance made d'Argenlieu furious. At the beginning of January, while de Gaulle was still in office, the admiral had written to the president scornfully about Leclerc and his "capitulators." Then he had said bitterly to General Jean-Etienne Valluy who commanded the 9th Colonial Infantry Division under Leclerc, "I am amazed – yes I am *amazed* that France has in Indochina such a fine Expeditionary Corps and that its leaders prefer to negotiate rather than fight!"[8]

On 6 March 1946 the British mission was completed, with SEAC turning over control to the French. From that point forward, the French were entirely on their own in how they dealt with Indochina. Sainteny had been busy shuttling between Hanoi and Chungking trying to arrange an accord that both Ho Chi Minh and Chiang Kai-shek would accept. Every time the parties seemed close to agreement, something would intervene to prevent it.

The end of March would mark the beginning of the monsoon season in Tonkin when French military operations would become extremely difficult. As days in late February proceeded without an agreement, one after another, relentlessly, Leclerc decided he had to act. He tasked the recently-arrived lead elements of 3rd Colonial Division and the Brigade of the Far East with relieving units in place and continuing pacification efforts in the South, an enormous task for 20,000 men. This released Massu's Groupement and the 9th Colonial Infantry Division to effect the previously planned embarkation for movement north. The tides at Haiphong would be the most favorable on 6 March, and that was selected as the target date for debarkation.

On 26 February 1946 Massu's Groupement embarked in Saigon aboard two LSTs and five other ships. Altogether a flotilla of some thirty ships began forming for Leclerc's move north. Two days later, the French and Chinese negotiators in Chungking arrived at an agreement that the French thought allowed a landing at Haiphong. It soon became apparent that this "agreement" in fact depended upon the French coming to terms with Ho Chi Minh. The news was the same for the flotilla all the way up the coast. Close, but no actual agreement. Finally, on 6 March, the day on which Leclerc said he had to land because he would lose the high tide, which would not return until ten days later, an agreement was announced, the so-called 6th of March Accords.

"France made three major concessions. . . . First, it recognized the Vietnamese Republic as a free state (*etat libre*), with its own government, parliament, army, and finances, although it would be integrated into the Indochinese Federation, which in turn would be a part of the French Union. The term 'free' was a compromise between the Vietnamese demand for 'independence' and the French offer of 'autonomy' or 'self-government,' and the question of full independence was left to the future. The second concession was to promise a referendum among the 'populations' to resolve the question of the unity of the three Vietnamese lands, Tonkin, Annam, and Cochinchina. . . . And the third was to accept . . . that the French military presence north of the 16th Parallel would be limited to 15,000 troops, and to a period of five years."[9]

In his book, *Sept ans avec Leclerc*, Massu describes how the convoy of ships entered the estuary of the river at Haiphong, the cruiser *Triomphant* leading, with General Valluy aboard, followed by Massu's two LSTs. Massu and his men were admiring the scenes on both banks when the ships began receiving fire and taking casualties. His ship's captain first received orders not to return the fire, then after a half hour, to engage the enemy who, it soon became apparent, were Chinese. Naval gunfire raked the Chinese positions, and later Massu learned that those on shore were furious that some of their huge piles of booty waiting to be taken back to China had been set afire by the cannonade and burned up. Massu's unit suffered four dead, 19 wounded. Total losses for Leclerc's force were 37 dead and many wounded. The official Chinese finding was that it was all a miscommunication about the accord that had been signed, but some evidence pointed to a Chinese commander who very well knew of the accord but wanted to give the French a different kind of welcome.

On the 8th, General Giap, accompanied by Sainteny, came to see Leclerc. At that meeting and several following with Vietnamese representatives, Leclerc worked out details of how he and his troops would enter Hanoi. On 18 March, with Sainteny seated beside him, Leclerc drove his jeep into the city at the head of his troops. They made a visit to Ho, with Leclerc saying in greeting: "Well, Mr. President, here we are, now friends."

Leclerc being welcomed to Hanoi by Ho. (Getty)

The discussion soon turned from cordial into confrontational, with Ho stating, "If faced with French unwillingness [to comply with the terms of the agreement], he would not hesitate to kill 'one or two million men' and 'to practice the policy of scorched earth' in order to obtain satisfaction in the matter of union of the three [parts of Vietnam]."[10]

Ho's willingness to come to some kind of agreement with the French is another instance of his flexibility in matters of highest importance – parrying, shifting position, waiting for better opportunity. Paul Mus, a French scholar and author who had been brought up in Vietnam, had fought for the Free French then returned to Vietnam, said that Ho was reported to have remarked, "It is better to sniff the French dung for a while than eat China's all our lives."[11]

Continuing Discussions on the Future of Indochina

In his memoirs, Salan gives fascinating detail of the back and forth between Ho, Giap, and himself. Their meetings in the next few weeks meetings were business-like, always cordial on the surface. On the more social occasions, sometimes Madame Salan was present and received Giap's compliments. Ho was always impressive and polite. At the end of dinner one evening Ho inscribed a photo of himself for Salan, "Best wishes, Ho Chi Minh."

An old Indochina hand, Salan was respectful and cordial, but he was not deceived by the friendly manners of his hosts. Salan said he knew Giap's history, "that he didn't pardon us for the death of his wife in our prison." Salan said, "He is a dangerous debater, very bright, who never remains in one place and attacks without ceasing. He spoke an impeccable French and often reflected on the [French] island prison of Poulo Condore where he had spent numerous years."

Salan was mistaken about Poulo Condore, the most infamous of the French prisons. Giap actually was imprisoned at Lao Bao near the Laotian border. Giap's brother and a 15-year old fervent revolutionary girl, Nguyen Thi Quang Thai, were also held there. Giap fell in love with the girl, later married her, and they had a baby girl. Thai, like so many other famous revolutionary women, left her child in the care of her husband's mother and carried on clandestine activities until she was again imprisoned. Both she and her older sister were to die in 1941, some accounts saying the French tortured her to death. Giap's bitterness over the death of his wife and sister in law, and later his father, at the hands of the French was never to leave him.[12]

During these days of negotiations, High Commissioner d'Argenlieu wrote a letter to the French government saying that Leclerc and Salan were insubordinate, and he requested their relief from Indochina duties and assignment elsewhere. General Alphonse Juin, Army Chief of Staff, was present in Hanoi when an admiral bearing this news in a letter reached Leclerc and Salan. Leclerc told Juin that since his mission was completed, he would return to France. But he was incensed. As for d'Argenlieu's allegations against Salan, Leclerc heatedly stated that Salan had done excellent work and was beyond reproach. Apparently not willing to buck d'Argenlieu, Juin designated Leclerc as Inspector of North Africa, and Salan as president of the military commission for formal peace negotiations. Salan's opinion of d'Argenlieu was that he lacked integrity and was a coward, not daring to tell his subordinates this news face to face.[13]

One day Ho sent Giap to Salan with an invitation to join him as he visited a garrison of French troops, and Salan accepted. Ho took the platform in a gymnasium where Massu and some of his troops were in formation. "'I have been in France,' Ho said, 'in that beautiful country that is yours, and I say to your mothers, your sisters, your fiancées, that all of you have comported yourselves well and that you do honor to your country.'"

"At these words, Colonel Massu faced his troops and cried out, '*Pour le président* Hô Chi Minh: *un triple hourrah*,' and the men responded, '*Hip, Hip, Hip, hourrah!* three times."[14] Massu seems to have been caught up in relief that in the agreement Ho had reached with France, the fighting perhaps was over. Shortly after this he finished his tour of duty and was reassigned to Paris on Leclerc's staff.

An Uncertain Future

As informal discussions were ongoing in the North, and only minor incidents were disturbing the outward calm, the Communists in the South took advantage of the lull. The *30-year War* reported, "Various bases were restored and consolidated. . . . Around Saigon there were a number of small bases linked to the city. Big bases like War Zone D, the Plain of Reeds, the U Minh forest were spread over several provinces. . . . Vietnamese political and military forces markedly developed in rural and urban areas and in the rubber plantation region."[15]

Leclerc had said, "Without doubt, the [6 March] accords are not perfect."[16] This soon became clear with skirmishes in the North between the French and the Viet Minh as well as Chinese, with significant loss of life. Meanwhile, d'Argenlieu had virtually given up on the possibility of a united Vietnam under French auspices. In April he convened a conference in Dalat in the Central Highlands, ostensibly to build on the 6 March Accords. Giap was the primary voice for the North, and although the admiral was supposedly a neutral host, behind the scenes he of course was pulling the strings and the conference ended in failure. In June d'Argenlieu established the Cochinchina Republic, a severe slap in the face for Ho who was insisting on unity of the three parts of Vietnam. The admiral's action also caused deep concern in Paris. Who was ultimately in charge of an Indochina policy, the High Commissioner of Indochina or the government of France?

A conference was planned for Fontainebleau.

With the final departure of the Chinese Nationalists from Tonkin in June 1946, and a deep chasm between Leclerc and the High Commissioner, Leclerc's job was over. He flew off to Paris. Promoted to five-star General of the Army, Leclerc prepared a report on the Indochina situation. While supportive of compromise, he pointed out that "the government in Hanoi was simultaneously negotiating with France and supporting a war against the French in the South."[17]

Meanwhile, developments along the border with China were ominous for the French. The Chinese civil war had been going on for years, and in March 1946, pressured by the Nationalists, the Chinese Communist First Regiment near the border withdrew into the safety of extreme northeastern Vietnam. For a short period, Ho had to deal with the Chinese Nationalists around Hanoi, and the Chinese Communists near the far northeastern frontier. Ho, having received encouragement in his early years from the Chinese Communists, now found himself helping them. He "not only satisfied the Chinese demand for food and other supplies but also provided medicine to treat the Chinese soldiers who were suffering from malaria and dysentery."[18] In turn, Ho saw an opportunity. This regiment was one of Mao Tse-tung's best, and Ho asked this unit which had years of war experience to train his troops and help create an intelligence system. "By July 1947, over 830 officers and soldiers from the Viet Minh army had received training in the camp of the First Regiment. [Additionally, a Chinese-Viet] self-defense force of over 1,000 members had been created, which was later incorporated into the Viet Minh army."[19]

This early circumstance later led to a formal arrangement whereby for the remainder of the wars in Vietnam—French, American, South Vietnamese—Red China would provide fluctuating but significant amounts of military and economic aid to North Vietnam that was crucial for continued conduct of the war. Stalin was also said to have gotten in on the act at this early date. "U. S. intelligence sources had reported in 1946 that the DRV was in direct touch with the Soviet Union, and that Russian and Chinese advisers were training Ho Chi Minh's troops." Qiang Zhai, an author who studied U.S. and Soviet intelligence sources, said that the Chinese in fact sent advisors; however, "It remains highly unlikely that [Stalin] sent any Soviet advisors to the DRV in 1946."[20]

*   *   *

In late 1945 and early 1946, General Leclerc had moved France well ahead in reestablishing French suzerainty in Indochina but was undeceived about winning an all-out war against the Viet Minh, should it eventually come to that. With the 6th of March Accords, Ho had demonstrated consummate skill in diplomacy. Accepting a pittance of French troops to enter Tonkin—only 15,000—and to remain there for just five years—was a small price to pay for what he would gain—time. Finally, from a beginning that was only a seed—Chinese Communist support for his revolution—a ripe harvest was possible.

CHAPTER 5

Fontainebleau and All-Out War, July 1946 -1949

*   *   *

WITH THE 6 MARCH ACCORDS as a basis, a forthcoming conference in France would hold out hope for a more permanent peaceful relationship between Vietnam and France. A new Supreme Commander in Vietnam, though, was to have very different views from Leclerc, and Ho's government would virtually eliminate non-Communist nationalist competition, thus setting the stage for all-out war. Troops and yet more troops would be committed by the French as war was to spread everywhere.

The Fontainebleau Conference, and Purge in Vietnam

Over d'Argenlieu's strong objections, a conference was called in July at Fontainebleau just south of Paris. Although not the designated negotiator, Ho Chi Minh went to France and pressed the issues of independence and unity.

The miffed High Commissioner in Saigon sent a representative to the Fontainebleau conference and in August called another conference of his own at Dalat while the Fontainebleau meeting was in recess. The second Dalat conference, like the first, ended in failure. This was strange business: Two simultaneous conferences—Fontainebleau and Dalat—with the same ostensible goal, furthering the 6 March Accords. Who was in charge, the High Commissioner of Indochina, or the government in France?

Ho welcomed with rendering of honors at Bourget airport on
22 June 1946 by General Paul Legentilhomme, Paris Military
Region Commander (saluting on Ho's right) and Marius Moutet,
Minister of Overseas France (on Ho's left). (NARA)

While Ho was in France, Giap was acting in his place in Vietnam. He issued orders for further repressing the non-Communist Vietnamese nationalists, labeling them as "traitors" to the nation. "He insisted that all parties gather themselves under the . . . Popular National Front. Most refused, knowing that the Viet Minh held all key posts within that front organization."[1] Giap was reported to have closed down *Viet-Nam*, the last opposition newspaper, and to have executed hundreds of members of nationalist organizations, Roman Catholics, and others.

The nationalist Dai Viet party in 1944 and 1945 had developed an anti-French stronghold to the northeast of Hanoi and east of the Communist Viet Bac. Here young men to include Bui Diem had learned martial arts and taken weapons training under direction of their leader Truong Tu Anh. When outright war erupted between the Dai Viet and Viet Minh while Ho was in France, "Giap's methods were blunt. In the Red River provinces his forces launched all-out assaults against nationalist bases. At the same time, Viet Minh urban units tightened their security nets in Hanoi and Haiphong. Nationalist party members went underground or tried to escape to China. . . . Panic struck the parties as Giap's reign of terror swept their ranks with a force that dwarfed previous assassination campaigns."[2] Truong Tu Anh disappeared. There was little question as to his fate. Bui Diem, back in the North at this time after a mission to the imperial court at Hue, was thrust into a long period of avoiding capture by both Viet Minh and the French. He was fortunate in having wealthy or well-off family members and friends to support and hide him as he perilously made his way back south.

Giap had a few things other than war on his mind. During that summer of 1946 he went to see his old professor, mentor, and friend, Dang Thai Mai, and was startled to find that the professor's 4-year old daughter of 1932, Dang Bich Ha, was now a beautiful 17-year old. A widower, he married her, and despite his lack of a settled home life, from 1951 to 1956 they would have four children, two girls and two boys.[3]

During the Fontainebleau conference, the question of unity was highly charged on both sides. D'Argenlieu had already fractured unity with his establishment of a Cochinchina Republic separate from Annam and Tonkin. Ho was adamant. From a short distance outside the conference, he made his voice heard. Ho presented in highly emotive terms the case for unification, integrating Cochinchina into Vietnam: "It is Vietnamese land. It is the flesh of our flesh, the blood of our blood . . . . Even before Corsica became French, Cochinchina was Vietnamese."[4]

The Tiger and the Elephant

David Schoenbrun had been a WWII war correspondent, and post-war was a broadcast journalist. On 11 September Ho told him that he would be leaving France soon to return to Vietnam, and "he would shortly be leading his people in a war against the French." Schoenbrun wrote, "It was the most extraordinary interview I have ever had in my career as a foreign correspondent. It lasted four hours, as he analyzed in great detail all the issues of the conflict, and then, to my astonishment, forecast the future, predicting the early outbreak of the war, describing how it would be fought and how it would end."

Schoenbrun asked Ho to confirm that he "was a Communist and a graduate of the Moscow school of revolution. He laughed at the question: 'I learned about revolution not in Moscow but right here in Paris, capital of Liberty, Equality, and Fraternity.'"

Ho urged him not to be "blinded by the issue of Communism. . . . My people hunger for independence and will have it. . . . Independence is the motivating force, not Communism. The Communists are a small minority in our country. The strongest political element is nationalist. On the issue of independence and unity of the North and South, we are all in agreement, Communists, Catholics, Republicans, peasants, workers."

Ho said that they would fight. Schoenbrun objected that Ho had no modern army, no modern weapons, and that such a war would be hopeless for him. Ho replied, "No, it would not be hopeless. It would be hard, desperate, but we could win. We have a weapon every bit as powerful as the most modern cannon: nationalism. Do not underestimate its power. You Americans above all ought to remember that a ragged band of bare-footed farmers defeated the pride of Europe's best-armed professionals."

The correspondent protested that the weapons of war had progressed markedly since 1776, and that farmers could not fight against them. Ho replied, "The spirit of man is more powerful than his own machines. And we have other weapons that are most effective against machines. We have swamps that are better than antitank guns. We have thick jungles that planes cannot fly through and where the trees are shields against fire bombs. We have mountains and caves where one man can hold off a hundred, and we have millions of straw huts that are ready-made Trojan horses in the rear of any invading army."

"'Then it will be a guerrilla war?' I asked. 'A war of harassment and attrition?'"

Ho possibly was using a common Asiatic anecdote in his response, since Giap is also quoted to have used a similar one. "It will be a war between an elephant and a tiger," Ho replied. "If the tiger ever stands still the elephant will crush him with his mighty tusks. But the tiger does not stand still. He lurks in the jungle by day and emerges by night. He will leap upon the back of the elephant, tearing huge chunks from his hide, and then he will leap back into the dark jungle. And slowly the elephant will bleed to death. That will be the war of Indochina."[5]

And so it was.

* * *

Fontainebleau concluded with no agreement. However, both Ho and Marius Moutet, the Minister of Overseas France, felt that Ho should not go away empty-handed, and after midnight of 15 September, they signed France's proffered *modus vivendi*. It contained eleven articles, one of which was a cease fire to take effect 31 October 1946 in Indochina below the 16th Parallel.

Ho was later to reflect on this period of 1946 as not being a total loss because negotiations had failed to produce an independent Vietnam. As he was in France, negotiating, while military action against the French in Vietnam was at an ebb, Ho said, "Our comrades and compatriots cleverly availed themselves of this opportunity to build up and develop their forces."[6] Indeed, Giap had been busy.

Aftermath of Fontainebleau

On 23 October, back in Hanoi, Ho issued a statement on the *modus vivendi*: "I came to France . . . for the purpose of resolving the problem of Vietnam's independence and of the unity of Central, Southern and Northern Vietnam. . . . . Sooner or later Vietnam will be independent. The Centre, the South, and the North will be reunified."[7]

Ho did not go home with only news of a fragile *modus vivendi*. He had created a legacy which was to pay big dividends. While in France, Uncle had invited Vietnamese students to visit him. When they arrived, he appeared in a frayed, high-collared Chinese jacket, and on his feet were rubber sandals. "Come, my children," he had said and they all sat down on the steps of the house. He wanted them to call him Bac Ho, Uncle Ho. One of the young men recalled, "When Ho realized that among our group there were students from the North, South, and Center of the country, he said gently, but with great intensity, 'Voila! the youth of our great family of Vietnam. Our Vietnam is one, our nation is one. You must remember, though the rivers may run dry and the mountains erode, the nation will always be one.'"

A week later he invited two students from the South to pay him a second visit, this same young man and a young woman. Ho greeted them with, "My children, I'm so pleased you have come to bring me a breath of warmth and comfort from the heroic South. Let's talk a bit and have some tea together." They talked of heroes and duty to defend the Fatherland. The young man wrote, "From that afternoon I was Ho Chi Minh's fervent partisan. His culture and burning patriotism offered me a model that I could follow in my own life." Ho had not spoken to him of Communism, only of patriotism. And thus it was with Ho. Always his role as a revolutionary patriot took precedence over his Communism, and that is why he would do such things as disband the Party in order to broaden the base for recruiting patriots who would fight against the French, and later the Americans.[8]

This young man was Truong Nhu Tang, who would become in 1960 one of the founders of the National Liberation Front of South

Vietnam (NLF). In 1946 his dedication to the cause would cost him his young pregnant wife, who was given to another man when his parents and parents-in-law found he could not give up his work for independence. In 1969 he spent much of his time trying to avoid terrifying B-52 strikes, changing locations often in the jungles not far from me near the Michelin Plantation and Cambodian border during my command of Task Force QuarterCav.

The cease fire arranged at Fontainebleau in mid-1946 soon collapsed. The Southern Viet Minh had taken advantage of the thin spread of French troops ever since Leclerc had taken the bulk of his main force north. Ambushes, acts of terrorism and sabotage had increased dramatically.

Jean Leroy, though, was having great success in the Mekong Delta. His isle of An Hoa with 48,000 inhabitants, ten percent of them Catholic, had become his fiefdom, thanks to his close liaison with high-ranking French officers in Saigon who condoned or supported his moves. His original group of 20 partisans had grown considerably, and he was ruthlessly eliminating the Viet Minh. With the *modus vivendi*, however, his relationship with the French High Command changed. He was summoned to My Tho to see General Georges-Ernest-Émile Duminy, then military commander of Cochinchina. The general received him coldly and demanded that Leroy cease action against the enemy because he was in violation of the accords. The general's reasoning was simple: although Leroy had been duly granted administrative powers he had no authority to make war. Leroy responded, "This *modus vivendi* is an absurdity. If only we respect it while the Viets violate it, then we will all soon be dead and France will be booted out of the country." The general was not amused and ordered Leroy immediately arrested. Leroy says he jumped through a window, ran and escaped. If so, apparently the general had more pressing matters than to hunt down the fugitive because, as Leroy claimed, "A month later I was the master uncontested and uncontestable of my isle. I had extirpated the Viet Minh down to the last one and I lived with my family outside all those governments and all those accords."[9]

An important article of the Fontainebleau accord had been that negotiations would resume in January 1947. This was not to be. The *modus vivendi* solved nothing. Both sides were deeply disappointed, and d'Argenlieu was openly antagonistic. During 1946, despite a supposed cease-fire, armed clashes and Viet Minh attacks in both North and South continued.

The New French Supreme Commander, and Rising Tensions

Upon Leclerc's departure, General Valluy, formerly commander of Leclerc's 9th Colonial Infantry Division, had been promoted and appointed Supreme Commander. As a close adherent to d'Argenlieu's manner of handling things, he was all for a military solution, advocating, relative to the French Indochina Administration, the elimination of the "civil element in favor of a purely military command structure." He told the High Commissioner that, "Instead of contenting ourselves with controlling rebel attacks in the south, we should put serious pressure on the rebels by taking large-scale initiatives in Hanoi and Annam."[10]

On 20 November, tensions between the two sides were at the boiling point. In Haiphong, the French tried to seize a shipment of fuel oil under a ban imposed by them, and a fierce battle broke out. Within three days, buoyed by Valluy's tough stance, the French had bombarded Vietnamese and Chinese quarters in Haiphong with artillery and naval gunfire, and strafed and shelled nearby villages. Viet Minh propaganda claimed 60,000 dead; Valluy said 300, and the generally accepted figure for the "Haiphong Incident," as it came to be called, was 6,000 civilian casualties, dead and wounded.

French military strength at the time was essentially the same as when Leclerc had ridden into Hanoi several months earlier. Valluy wanted ten to fifteen thousand men from France, not North Africa, as reinforcements. In Paris there was discussion of figures as high as 250,000.[11] The pool from which they could come was limited by French law, enacted partly under pressure from strong anti-war groups such as the French Communist Party and Union of French Women. From 1951, by law, conscripts who were French citizens could not be sent to overseas wars unless they volunteered, and the same was true for soldiers from the colonies – all volunteers.

At this time in Paris, Leclerc reflected on the case for negotiations and advised, "Since we did not have the means at our disposal to break the back of Vietnamese nationalism by force of arms, France was obliged to seek every means to bring about the coincidence of French and Vietnamese interests." A new French government listened, and at the meeting of the Indochina Committee, it was determined: "The problem as a whole cannot be settled by the use of force alone. International political opinion would not allow to take such a step, nor would we have the support of the French nation."

Knowing and acknowledging this, it is virtually impossible to comprehend the Committee's next sentence except within a pervasive aura of arrogance and macho intransigence—"But we must make it clear that France does not intend to quit Indochina, and she will defend her presence by every possible means."[12]

Prelude to All-out War

By mid-December 1946 the DRV had made substantial progress in organizing itself, forming military units and civilian defense and intelligence networks. The Communist History says, "At the time, there were 30 Vietnamese regiments in the North and 25 in the South. In addition to rifles and grenades, many units had been equipped with submachine guns and bazookas. Vietnam had nearly one million militiamen, guerrillas and self-defence soldiers."[13] These figures may be exaggerated, but unquestionably in the 15 months since the DRV was proclaimed, the Viet Minh had built up significant forces.

Ho Chi Minh had moved out of Hanoi to a Communist-controlled village 12 kilometers north in the Viet Bac in order safely to continue to plan and direct affairs. Here, at this crucial time, Ho's personal popularity soared. Gone was the animosity toward him in some circles of the Party that had been created when he had allowed French troops into Hanoi in exchange for time to prepare for war. The bush and a thatched hut, not the palace of the Résident Superieur in Hanoi, was just the right place to direct a revolution for a man who came from the people and remained part of them. Giap said that torrential rains had been falling for days, and the streams were all raging. Yet Ho, wearing a shabby cloak, walking toward military headquarters, looked for a place where he might possibly cross and, ignoring the danger, plunged in, successfully making his way to the other side. Encouraged by his example, a small entourage followed him.[14]

Sainteny and Moutet tried to work something out in messages to Ho, to no avail. At headquarters, Ho, Giap, and their staffs made careful preparations: "A detailed plan to encircle Hanoi, besiege the enemy during definite period [sic], and make it possible for the rear area to complete the transfer of all forces to wartime conditions was worked out. Each young man or girl, each citizen found for himself or herself a weapon to fight the enemy. The members of the Women's Union for national salvation were to provide clothes, medicine and other equipment for the army and the self-defence fighters. With the dedicated assistance of city dwellers, the self-defence fighters dug into the walls [of Hanoi dwellings], creating a way to move about secretly and safely during the fight. The major streets around Hanoi were dug up to prevent the passage of enemy motorized vehicles. Large barricades were erected on the roads to the suburbs. Pieces of furniture and big trees were put into the streets, ready to be turned into roadblocks . . . in the areas where French troops were garrisoned. Patrols were secretly increased."[15]

From 15 to 18 December, the French saw that things in Hanoi were going very wrong for a peace settlement. Viet Minh roadblocks appeared on some streets of French residents. Units reported hostile movements around their positions. French Union patrols were fired upon and troops were being killed and wounded. French civilian deaths were mounting.

From the Communists' point of view, the French were the aggressors, with red-capped legionnaires arresting people and firing on Vietnamese tramways.

On the 16th, the "Central Committee sent a message to the [Cochinchina] Party Committee and to all provincial committees in the South: 'In view of the situation in France and the ambitions of the colonialists, the problem of Vietnam's sovereignty can be resolved only by an all out, protracted and hard war.'"[16]

On the other side that day, the French sent an ultimatum to Ho's government that French forces would establish security and order in Hanoi on the morning of 20 December 1946 at the latest.

On the morning of the 18th, Major Jean Julien Fonde, who had been one of Massu's unit commanders, then his executive officer and was now on the general staff in Tonkin, went to Giap's office to protest the Viet Minh's burnt earth policy in which whole villages around Hanoi were being destroyed so the French could not use them or their crops, and the people were being moved to safer areas. After tea and pleasantries, Fonde presented the story, incident by incident. "We must preserve this country," he said.

Giap was no longer smiling, and now lectured the French officer: "That depends on you. Our decision is made. We will yield no longer. The destruction ----- it doesn't matter. Policy takes precedence over economics. The losses ----- a million dead Vietnamese. Of no importance. Some French will die also. We are ready. It will last two years, five years, if necessary. We are ready."

Giap was silent and made a move to rise. Fonde was not ready to go. He reminded Giap that negotiations had gone on for a long time, and that a new French government had been constituted. He said that Giap knew the ideas of the new Prime Minister, Léon Blum, who wanted a negotiated settlement. "The Independence of Vietnam," Fonde continued, "often evoked by General Leclerc, is in the offing. The world is changing apace. What will happen in one year, five years ----- Be patient. Take time. Prevent the irreparable."

Giap answered, "It is up to you." He reeled off a long list of what the Vietnamese took to be French crimes against the people. "*C'est fini*. It's over. We will yield no longer."

Giap rose, extended his hand, and it was over.[17]

Viet Minh Attack in Hanoi

The Central Committee had been meeting with Ho in the village to the north, and the Hanoi representatives had proposed a signal for the start of the war: On the evening of the 19th, the city power plant would be destroyed and electricity cut off.

Although the Committee had given instructions on what was to happen and instructed that people be informed, obviously most Vietnamese had not gotten the word. The morning of 19 December came on bright and clear, and Hanoi life seemed to be returning to normal. After several days of unrest, Vietnamese workers were now back at their jobs, and mixed French/Vietnamese patrols again were making their rounds. Around 1600 hours Fonde was visited by a captain who reported that an agreement had been reached. The Viet Minh had said that, beginning the next day, barricades would be taken down, undisciplined Viet troops would be dealt with, French citizens could return to their normal business unharmed, incendiary and propaganda campaigns would cease, and strict return to order would take place.

That evening a huge explosion ripped through the Hanoi electrical plant, and electricity went off. Two minutes later Fonde heard machine-gun fire and grenade explosions.

The writers of *The 30-Year War* said, "At 2003 hours, all electric lights in the city went out. Explosions resounded from the Lang fortress. Rifles were heard everywhere. The national resistance war had begun."[18]

Fonde's telephone rang. He asked the lieutenant on the other end what was going on.

"The huge clash, I think. *Another 9 March!*" [Referring to the Japanese coup that struck the French throughout Indochina on 9 March 1945.]

Their communication was cut in mid-sentence. The enemy had severed the telephone lines. Sainteny tried to go to the Citadel fortress but his armored vehicle was hit by a command-detonated mine, and he was seriously wounded.

Indeed it was over!

No peace was possible. The war with the French was on, full force, and it would not stop until Dien Bien Phu had fallen and, later, withdrawing French Union troops near Pleiku were decimated in a huge ambush.

The "Start" of the French Indochina War

Many histories, in French and English, date the "start" of the French Indochina War at 19 December 1946 when the power plant was blown up as the signal. Much more correctly, the war built up from 1941 throughout the Vichy French administration in Indochina, to Giap's attacks on the French outposts in 1944, to the "August Revolution" of 1945, and especially the chaos in Saigon which prompted Truong Chinh, later head of the Party, to say of 23 September 1945, *"from that moment, our heroic resistance began."* In October and November 1945, Ponchardier and Massu's men in the Mekong Delta had had no doubt they were at war. Neither did the men with Leclerc who were fired on while attempting to land at Haiphong in March 1946. Nor those who fought at Haiphong in November 1946. In fact, a good case could be made that the French Indochina War actually started in the 1860s with the French takeover of the provinces around Saigon and subsequent Vietnamese armed resistance. That would mean that by 1965 when America entered the war with ground combat units, the Vietnam War had been going on for a hundred years.

Being a combat commander, I had held that the most significant date for the actual outbreak of the Indochina war was 23 September 1945, as Truong Chinh claimed. Finally I found Giap's statement which agreed. He said, "Many people still think that the Indochina war, the longest of the century, broke out on 19 December 1946. In fact it started 15 months earlier, on 23 September 1945 when French troops opened fire in order to recapture Saigon. The war then rapidly spread all over the South and expanded to Northwest Vietnam, Laos, and Cambodia."[19]

Leclerc's Last Try: Make a Deal!

Léon Blum had been Prime Minister for only a week, and the 19 December 1946 crisis was just three days old when he called Leclerc on 22 December and asked him to go to Indochina on an inspection trip and come back with a report and recommendations. Blum had the highest regard for the general, saying that he was the Liberator of Paris and will be Pacifier of Indochina.[20] D'Argenlieu was not pleased, telling Blum by cable that to send Leclerc was unacceptable. The handwriting was on the wall for the admiral. Despite the awe in which those in power still held de Gaulle, and regardless of the admiral's continued strong backing from his mentor, he was on the way out. His ego and the patience of the government were too much at odds.

Leclerc had Massu, now his operations officer, accompany him. They flew in to Tan Son Nhut on 28 December and, without seeing the admiral, on the 31st went on to Hanoi. On 2 January they went to Haiphong to visit Leclerc's son, Henri, who had been gravely wounded. On that day, Ho sent a radio message to Leclerc, praising him as a great general and good friend, and saying, "We still want the independence and unity of Viet-nam." He went on, "Supposing that you wish to fight us for a time, that is problematic, for if you are strong materially, we are morally, with the steadfast willpower to fight for our liberty. . . . We have decided to remain in the French Union, collaborating loyally with France and respecting its economic and cultural interests, but we have also decided to fight for our independence and our national unity."[21] The Viet Minh commander in the South, Nguyen Binh, sent a message to Leclerc saying much the same thing.

Did Nguyen Binh and Ho Chi Minh really want to stay in the French Union? That is a moot question because Ho and his inner circle were always adaptable. They had long proven adept at saying what was acceptable at the

moment but later adjusting or abandoning that position to fit the needs of
the present. They always knew that time was on their side. They could wait.

Viet Minh forces had fought stubbornly for the first few weeks after
19 December but began yielding to French assaults throughout Tonkin.
Giap and his military leaders decided that in some areas they had to go
back to guerrilla warfare long enough to build their main forces stronger.[22] Leclerc considered the situation in Tonkin and believed that reinforcements were urgently needed from France as an interim move to
stabilize the situation, but upon his return to France he again emphasized to Blum that a political solution was what was really required. In
his report, he stated, "In 1947 France will no longer put down by force
a grouping of 24,000,000 inhabitants which is assuming unity and in
which there exists a xenophobic and perhaps a national ideal. . . . The
capital problem from now on is political. It is a question of coming to
terms with an awakening xenophobic nationalism, channeling it in order
to safeguard, at least in part, the rights of France."[23]

Moutet had also been sent to Indochina but returned with a different report: "We can no longer speak of a free agreement between France
and Vietnam. . . . Before any negotiations today, it is necessary to have
a military decision. I am sorry, but one cannot commit such madness as
the Vietnamese have done with impunity."[24]

A military man urges peace, and a civilian urges war.

Ho and Commissioner Sainteny had been on friendly terms, and in
late January 1947 as the recuperating Sainteny and his wife were about
to return to France, Ho sent him a letter with one last appeal: "We
have already had enough death and destruction! What are we to do now,
you and I? France has only to recognize the independence and unity of
Vietnam, and at once hostilities will cease, peace and trust will return,
and we shall be able to get down to work and start rebuilding for the
common good of our two countries."[25]

In Paris, Prime Minister Blum offered Leclerc his old job back,
replacing Valluy as Supreme Commander and then in a short time

taking over from d'Argenlieu also as High Commissioner. Within two weeks Blum was replaced by Paul Ramadier who offered Leclerc immediate succession to d'Argenlieu. The general thought about it, laid out a long list of conditions for the government to consider, and sought the advice of others, most notably de Gaulle who advised him to decline the offer, and instead accept the post of Inspector General of French Forces in Africa. And he did.[26]

In March, Fonde, whom Leclerc knew well as one of his former subordinate commanders, had just returned to France. Admiral d'Argenlieu had been replaced as High Commissioner by a civilian, Èmile Bollaert, and the government was still trying to decide what to do about the modus vivendi signed at Fontainebleau. Leclerc called Fonde into his office, and Fonde passionately began telling the general that the whole thing was a mess, that the old colonial days when the French could dictate to the Vietnamese were long gone. "All of Southeast Asia is moving toward independence. I do not think that France is able or willing to make the effort necessary for a reconquest by force. It almost happened, an agreement at Fontainebleau. Now . . . . "

The general, with a deep frown, interrupted: "Yes, my old friend. It must stop. Your conclusions are correct. I reached that conclusion long ago. The new High Commissioner [Bollaert] seemed convinced when he saw me."

Fonde said that at that moment, the general rose from his chair, took a few steps and clenched his teeth, raised his voice louder, and pointed at his door. Leclerc told Fonde that in that doorway, as Bollaert was leaving, Leclerc once again warned:

"Encore une fois, monsieur Haut-Commissaire – Traitez, traitez, traitez . . . a tout prix."
"Once more, High Commissioner, Make a deal, make a deal, make a deal. At all costs!"[27]

There was no deal.

$*$ $*$ $*$

Leclerc took up his North Africa duties, and in 1947 his aircraft crashed in Algeria, killing everyone on board. He was 45 years old.

1947, Buildup to a Long War

In January 1947, Vincent Auriol was elected President of the new Fourth Republic. In Indochina the hawk, General Valluy, continued as Supreme Commander, with Salan in command in the North and Major General Georges Nyo in the South. The public in France had been shocked by the large-scale uprising of December 1946, and unrest, defiance, and anti-war protests within France were growing. François Billous, the Communist Defence Minister, refused to stand in the National Assembly to pay tribute to the Expeditionary Corps.[28] "French liberals were disheartened and embarrassed by [the colonial war] – particularly as Britain was yielding independence to Gandhi in India and the Dutch were giving up the East Indies."[29]

For several months troops sent by France to Vietnam had been arriving in increasing numbers: armor and armored cavalry units, paratroopers, colonial infantry, artillery, engineers, and support units. The navy and air forces were augmented. The French had recruited Vietnamese and placed them in units under French officers and NCOs. A volunteer Cambodian regiment was a welcome addition, and French Foreign Legion units were being put to immediate work. By 1947 the contribution of Africans and indigenous Indochinese made a big difference: Portions of five Moroccan regiments, four Algerian regiments, and a Tunisian regiment landed. Four battalions of T'ai were formed from hill tribes of the High Region of mountains to the west and northwest of Hanoi.[30]

After the 19 December 1946 conflagration in Hanoi, Salan had moved quickly to take Hanoi, important villages and roads, and control the waterways in a large area of the Delta and beyond. Route Coloniale 4

(RC4), a critical road, was reinforced. It stretched for one hundred fifty miles just south of the border with China, all the way from the Gulf of Tonkin, west and northwest through the important border posts of Lang Son, Dong Dang, That Khe, Dong Khe, and Cao Bang.

Giap conceded, "In January 1947, the French stepped up their military activities in many battlefields. . . . By mid-February, a new phenomenon had occurred: the breakup of [our] war fronts." The French were successful in Hue, and in both the northwest and northeast areas of Tonkin. However, Giap said, "The one-year resistance in [Cochinchina] proved that the French, in spite of their tremendous strength, could never destroy our armed forces if we strictly observed guerrilla tactics." The Viet Minh had built up to battalions and regiments, but were not strong enough for direct confrontations. Therefore, as Giap explained, they resorted to "mobile guerrilla warfare," something in between guerrilla tactics and main force assaults. Once again they had proven capable of adapting well to a situation and patiently doing what they could in attacking the enemy while building their infrastructure and main force strengths. Using the new tactics, "In March there were no more cases of war fronts breaking up." A few months earlier the Viet Minh had developed a crude but effective bazooka. Instead of running up close enough to lob an explosive charge, they could now stand off and destroy armored vehicles.[31] In France, the Communist Party continued to press for negotiations to end the war, but, as Giap acknowledged, even they only wanted Indochina to be a member of the "Indochinese Federation and the French Union," which was not the full independence demanded by Ho.[32]

French forces tried to engage main force Viet Minh units in battle throughout Tonkin, but Giap refused to engage decisively, his units instead inflicting casualties and melting away when faced with too much force, leaving scorched earth behind in an attempt to deny his enemy any sustenance. Constantly building his strength, Giap merged all types of fighters under a unified command, claiming at this time a strength of one million, everything from local small unit militias to main force battalions and regiments.[33] If so, which is questionable, he significantly outnumbered the forces fighting under the French flag although the French armaments and other equipment were far superior. The French had total command of the air, control over the main inland waterways, and less control over coastal waters. The ground was another matter. Where it was not controlled by the Viet Minh it was contested. Giap continued to be patient, biding his time.

In mid-May 1947, with no fanfare, the French tried one more time diplomatically to engage Ho in negotiations. One of the High Commissioner's main assistants, Paul Mus, who had been in Indochina since the 1930s and spoke fluent Vietnamese, was able to arrange a meeting with Ho in the Viet Bac. Their talk was cordial, but fruitless. Before leaving, Mus asked: "'Mr. President, so the war will go on?' Ho replied, 'We desire peace, but not at any price! It must be peace with independence and freedom. . . . ' This was the last contact between Uncle Ho and a representative of the other side during the resistance war."[34]

No More Conferences, Just War

The *30-Year War* history acknowledged that as of May 1947, "After more than four months of massive counterattacks and fierce offensives in [Tonkin and Annam] the French Army managed, at very high cost, to establish its control over a number of towns and cities, strategic communication axes, mining and coastal areas, and border strong points.

"For the Vietnamese side, four months of nationwide resistance had revealed a fact: despite their modern weapons, the enemy was unable to wipe out the Vietnamese main forces and to take by surprise the Vietnamese leadership. Vast areas in the countryside, and even around towns and cities had remained under Vietnamese control."[35]

And there were problems for the French elsewhere. Lao and Cambodian independence resistance forces (Communist-led in most cases) likewise were making themselves felt. In French Madagascar an independence uprising had turned violent, and a brigade on its way to

Indochina had to be diverted to quell the revolt. Algerians too were showing serious signs of unrest.

The fighting in Tonkin, though often fierce, was still mainly on a small unit scale – a company here, a platoon or squad there. Mostly the Viet Minh responded in its characteristic manner, returning fire, then usually melting quickly into the landscape, reappearing only when the times and circumstances were advantageous for inflicting more casualties.

The violence in the North was the topic of the moment, but the South, though quieter in comparison, still had its share of troubles. Speaking about the war in the South at the beginning of 1947, Jean Leroy sarcastically said, "Lucienne Bodard [a French journalist] had called the Cochinchina war, 'the pleasant war,' pleasant for him certainly from his lodgings at the Hotel Continental [in Saigon] but certainly not for others, those who like me fought each day and each night in the mud of rice paddies." Some other French combatants also spoke derisively of Bodard.

On his isle of An Hoa in the Delta, Leroy required all able-bodied males from the age of 17 to be his militia, his Protectors of the Peace, he called them. He organized them in three-man cells, each provided with a short piece of sealed bamboo and a club, which together served as a gong. Their mission was simple, to take positions at night and protect their hamlets by giving coded signals. "Thanks to this method, at the end of 1947 not a single Viet Minh – tax collector, propagandist, or liaison agent—penetrated our isle at night without having been signaled and arrested. . . . One of the Viet leaders . . . named the inhabitants of my district, 'the musicians of gong.'"[36]

Idealism Hardened by Reality

Guy de Chaumont-Guitry was a 23-year old idealistic, religious soldier who had fought with Leclerc's 2nd Armored in Germany. He stayed in the Army, debarked in Saigon in March 1947, and would soon take possession of an armored scout car with three other men in his crew and five Vietnamese infantrymen. He was told that "one cannot leave Saigon except in a convoy. All the countryside is dangerous if you don't go in a group and armed."

His first assignment was at Thu Duc, a short distance to the northeast of Saigon and three miles from my first QuarterCav command post in 1969. On the day of his arrival at Thu Duc he couldn't get over the lush vegetation and brilliant colors of foliage and the clear sky. Maybe they had been wrong in Saigon. "I thought I had found Paradise on Earth." In the area around his headquarters were coconuts, bananas, pineapples – nothing like France. Marvelous. The birds sang while cheerful noises floated from the village where the people went about their business.

"Then came the night." The mosquitoes attacked in hordes, birds let off bizarre shrieks, a lizard or enormous rat would run over his legs, dogs would howl. But most disturbing of all were the tom-toms. They signaled one another in the darkness, an unseen, sinister enemy communicating to one another French positions and movements. Then the sound of distant machine gun fire. Paradise?[37]

A month later a change of mission took Guy down to the Mekong Delta near My Tho. The area was quiet. It too looked like Paradise. Pretty canals, rice paddies. He said he could travel 100 kilometers in a day without seeing a Viet although he could see evidence of their work, such as cuts in the road. Days went by without a single incident in his sector. Then he got a call for help. A convoy had been ambushed. A lieutenant colonel who was the commander of 5th Cuirassiers, his daughter, and two ministers from the Cochinchina government were dead, plus 43 French Union soldiers and a dozen Vietnamese guards. No more Paradise. "The situation in Cochinchina then seemed to get quickly worse. Attacks against convoys multiplied and enemy documents were found which ordered attacks on the railway lines, routes, isolated outposts, etc."

By June this idealistic young man was thoroughly discouraged. He wrote home that "judging by events in our sector, [we are] getting nowhere. We are perpetually on the defensive and nothing more. This is not the way to pacify." Further, he said that, according to letters and newspapers he received, life in France was no paradise. "It is sad to think that people are so much sabotaging our work! . . . . [38] "There are times when we are so discouraged that we want to give it all up. The outposts are always attacked, the roads always cut, convoys which must always be escorted, attacks against isolated positions, bursts of fire in all directions each night, and for encouragement we have the indifference of France and the aid given by some of the French to the enemy, who organizes and equips himself more each day."[39]

Guy observed that the enemy always seemed to know what the French were doing, and the French seemed not to know much about the enemy. Twenty-nine paratroopers were killed and nine wounded in an ambush which resulted from a boy giving information to the Viets. Also, "The Viet Minh are always in one place. . . . If ever [the French command] would leave our units in one place then we could be effective, but with perpetual changing about, it is total mismanagement."[40]

Finally, this highly intelligent, analytical young man concluded, "We fight with a regular army and its European methods against bands which employ guerrilla tactics. . . . We fight the war of Clausewitz and Napoléon."[41]

Operation Lea, The New War of "the Big Battalions"

Ever since the 19 December 1946 outbreak, Ho had been heading his government from hideouts in the mountainous forests north and northeast of Hanoi, the Viet Bac. This was a major problem for the French in terms of trying to control Hanoi itself and the Red River Delta.

The Communists were making headway. They fabricated armaments in numerous small factories hidden in remote areas They continued to eliminate those "traitors" who belonged to other nationalist parties, recruited strongly from a largely sympathetic population, and built their main force and regional units. At the lowest level of the revolutionary forces, but certainly not the most insignificant, were "guerrilla"—or as Giap sometimes called them—"militia" units. He said, "Self-defense militia forces are the broad armed forces of the laboring people who are still engaged in production. They act as an instrument of violence used by the public administrations at the lower levels. In hamlets, villages, industrial enterprises, and city wards, they are organized by combat tasks, conditions, and characteristics. They form a steady, strong force, widespread throughout the country, ready to fight and fight well with all kinds of weapons, from rudimentary to modern ones, with highly efficient combat methods."[42]

Despite having received reinforcements from the metropole, the strength of French Troops in the Far East (the new designation since January, replacing the old title of Expeditionary Corps, though the old term continued to be used) was only about 70,000, with some units in all five territories of Indochina. The South had already been stressed, sending troops north, leaving the South vulnerable to guerrilla operations.

For several months General Salan had been trying to pacify a large portion of the Red River Delta around Hanoi. Now it was time, he thought, for a major strike. This would require concentrating a large part of his forces there, preparing for the strike, thereby making pacification efforts elsewhere in Tonkin and northern Annam all the more difficult. He believed that the potential advantages warranted the risks.

Operation Lea had two main objectives: capture Ho Chi Minh and ensure control of the frontier with China.[43] The plan was to encircle a large area with airborne, ground, and waterborne forces and then destroy the enemy inside the noose.

French intelligence had located Ho's current headquarters in the Viet Bac. No more discussions with him over tea. This time they were out to get him. On 7 October Colonel Sauvagnac's paratroopers, 1,100 strong, suddenly dropped on Bac Kan, 60 miles directly north of Hanoi. And they got Ho! For several minutes radio messages excitedly went back and forth to Salan about the old man with the beard they had captured.

Alas! It was discovered that Ho had narrowly escaped, and the old man turned out to be only a minor official.[44]

Meanwhile, a naval contingent with infantry aboard was making its way up the Claire River from Hanoi as enemy impeded their way with ambushes. The naval element then encountered rapids and had to unload everything and proceed afoot. Before the waterborne engagement played out days later, the navy's casualtires were several boats lost, along with men killed and wounded.

On 8 October, more paratroopers descended to the west of Bac Kan, and on the twelfth, more yet dropped on the critical junction village of Cao Bang on Route 4 near the Chinese border. In subsequent days, additional troops were committed in ground operations and more airborne drops. By the end of the operation on 10 November, the commitment was four parachute battalions, three Legion battalions, a Moroccan infantry battalion, a colonial infantry battalion, an artillery group, a regiment of light armor, and a battalion of soldiers mounted on mules. The direct combat elements were supported by transportation, supply, communications, medical units and a labor contingent of 2,000 "coolies," as they were called. Air force and navy fighter bombers and transport aircraft were busy throughout.[45]

A new stage in the war had been reached: the war of the "big battalions." From now on, operations of battalion, regiment, and larger size on both sides would be frequent in the North.

The official Communist *30-year War* states, "The French strategic offensive of autumn-winter 1947 ended in utter failure," then gives their statistics of French losses, hyped far beyond reason, as was their custom throughout the French and American wars.[46]

The real results of Operation Lea? They had captured Ho's headquarters of Bac Kan, of no importance except psychological. Lea was a modest French success in that while taking casualties, they inflicted many more on the enemy, captured a lot of materiel, and opened routes of communication. During and after the operation they reinforced critical strongpoints along RC4 just south of the Chinese border. Control of this major route was crucial in the effort to stop infiltration of men and materiel from China. As always, however, successes came at a cost. This time it was in heavier guerrilla actions against them throughout Tonkin and, most importantly, a concentration of static French forces along Route 4 that was to have tragic consequences.

At the end of the year Ho and Giap sized up 1947 and declared victory, not final, but a major step on the way. Ho had said, "The enemy forces are like the sunset, arrogant but fading. Our forces become stronger and stronger, like water at its source, like a fire kindled, always going forward and not drawing back." Giap, however, acknowledged that the year had been tough. "Everyone had gotten thinner, had not eaten enough, had spent sleepless nights, and had been constantly on the move. Many suffered from fungus diseases from too many rainy days and constantly damp clothes; their feet became ulcerous and painful."[47] Ho himself was ill but Giap jubilantly attended a large victory celebration.

End of year statistics to date for the French were sobering: 5,345 dead, 9,790 seriously wounded.[48]

1948, A Widening War

The Communist *30-Year War* states, "1948 was to be a year when the war raged everywhere. The French would launch even fiercer mopping up operations in the [Red River] Delta. In [the South] they would . . . bring back Bao Dai to set up a national puppet government. Bao Dai would create an army for that government and set up autonomous regions to divide Vietnam."[49]

Indeed, 1948 started reasonably well for the French with extension of their semi-control of the Delta and adjacent area west of Hanoi. In February General Valluy was recalled to France and Salan became the new Supreme Commander until he in turn would be replaced in April by Lieutenant General Roger Blaizot. In the South, Nyo had been succeeded by Major General Pierre Boyer de Latour.

From the beginning the French had been exercising *tache d'huile* tactics in their efforts to pacify areas with minimum forces. This was an old concept for counter insurgency warfare, a drop of oil to create a stain that slowly spreads farther and farther out from the center. In the South, General de Latour promoted this tactic. A garrison or outpost would be the drop of oil, the center, and the surrounding area represented the enlarging stain to be progressively pacified.

The need for safeguarding routes for convoys and critical locations such as rubber plantations led de Latour to build many outposts along the axes of supply and communication and within the plantations. These garrisons of 30-100 men were spaced about six to twelve miles apart. Standardized outpost designs accommodated both small and medium-sized forts. A triangular construction was chosen consisting of a two-story stone or concrete blockhouse at each of the three corners connected by a stone or concrete wall. The interior would have a redoubt to accommodate an office, supplies, ammunition, and sleeping quarters for the higher ranks. When available, a mortar or small or medium caliber cannon or howitzer would provide extra firepower. Between outposts along a route would be one or more watchtowers constructed of wood, bricks, or stone, a mile and a half or so apart, each about 20-25 feet high, and 16 feet across. The watchtowers were especially scary places, manned by only a corporal or NCO and a handful of men, usually Cambodian or Vietnamese recruits whose loyalty was almost always questionable. My area of responsibility in 1968-69, a large one north of Saigon, contained the ruins of many of these outposts and towers. A stone watchtower at Village 1 in the Michelin plantation at Dau Tieng was still largely intact when I saw it in 2005 and 2010.

The Viet Minh in turn developed a defensive system which served as a base for attacks, first in the South, and then in the North. These were "resistance villages" or "resistance hamlets." "Bamboo hedges, hills, meadows, canals, lakes and ponds around the village as well as communication trenches, tunnels, and dugouts formed a defensive line checking the enemy's advance. . . . fighting pockets, trenches and secret tunnels . . . were linked to one another to ensure mobility in fighting. . . . The people organized their resistance villages in order to stay in their native places and continue production work while fighting the enemy and sabotaging their sweep operations."[50] They also used these villages and hamlets to venture out, day or night, to attack. Their incredible ability to utilize the local population throughout Vietnam to constantly resist and harass the enemy on a small scale, year after year after year, while main force units were preparing for or doing their thing was a major reason for their success.

As Ho's army matured, the need for prescribing ranks to accord with positions had to be met. Meetings of the Central Committee and Government Council resulted in recommendations, and Ho signed a decree. Giap was named general. Nguyen Binh, the commander in the South, was made a major general, and a number of other men were appointed brigadier general and colonel. "Ranks were determined for only key officers, not yet for the whole army."[51]

On 28 May a ceremony was held for Giap. On an altar was a banner with the motto: "The protracted resistance war will be won and unification and independence will be achieved. . . . When news of the event was disseminated on *The Voice of Viet Nam*, a Western correspondent asked Uncle Ho why so many generals and colonels were nominated at the same time, and by what criteria. Uncle Ho gave a simple answer: 'If they could win victory over a colonel they were nominated colonels; if they could prevail over a brigadier general they became brigadier generals. If they were victorious over a general they became generals.'"[52]

French/South Vietnamese politics took a decisive turn on 20 May with formation of a Provisional Central Government under General Nguyen Van Xuan. Bao Dai was preferred by many of the council members and Xuan acknowledged the importance of the emperor by consulting with him. "It was Bao Dai who picked the flag of the central government-----a background of yellow (the imperial color) with three red horizontal stripes across the middle denoting the three areas of Vietnam [a revival of the flag chosen by an emperor in 1890]."[53]

On 6 June in Hanoi a South Vietnamese official announced the establishment of the provisional government. Since the French controlled Hanoi, there was no need yet for placing a government counter to Ho's in Saigon. So now in this crazy war there were two governments of Vietnam, Bao Dai's and Ho's, which for a brief time were headquartered quite close to one another in Tonkin. Ho's had the allegiance of great numbers of Vietnamese in all three areas of Vietnam. "The new . . . government, by contrast, had no territory of its own and little following."[54]

Meanwhile the war went on. In the North, a seventeen year old youth had stood at the Opera House in Hanoi on 17 August 1945 listening to Viet Minh speakers at the start of the "August Revolution." And on 2 September he had heard Ho Chi Minh proclaim Vietnam's independence. Bui Tin became a dedicated devotee of Ho, enlisted in his army and fought the French in Annam. He was to become a North Vietnamese colonel who many years later wrote the book, *Following Ho Chi Minh*. In 1948 his mother had lived in a village outside Hanoi. "During the mid-autumn festival . . . when some French troops were parachuted into the district and made a sweep through the village, an informant pointed out our house as that of the wife of a high-ranking Viet Minh official, meaning my father. Immediately a legionnaire rushed in and shot my mother in the chest with a round of fire from his submachine gun. She died on the kitchen floor. After that it was impossible not to feel vindictive. Whenever I went into battle, behind every opposing gun was the enemy who had killed my mother."[55] Similar events throughout Vietnam continued to recruit many to the Communists' cause.

Northern leaders often held up the guerrilla warfare in the South as an exemplar. Giap said the Southerners had bogged down "nearly half of the French expeditionary corps who had five hundred military posts and carried out sweeps of various scales."[56] Several books by men who were small unit leaders in the French Union forces point to the futility of these sweeps by large garrison units or troops within an outpost. Almost always the enemy knew what would happen and where. Informers within the French units would send the word, or if there were no informers, the local people observing activities could tell when something was up and give warning. In most instances battalion-size sweeps were particularly ridiculous. The troops would go out and thrash around in the jungle or slog through rice paddies for two or three days, and for their trouble either get ambushed or see nothing. The war in the South was fought as if in a spider web. The Viet Minh or local guerrillas, well supported by the local people and extensive spy networks, could tell where in the jiggling web their enemy was and take measures to confront him or disappear.

One bright spot in pacification efforts in the South, or so it seemed to French authorities, was the area commanded by the rabid Catholic, Jean Leroy. His concept of pacification was simple: elimination. By 1948 he had formed "brigades," each directed by an officer, and under him a senior NCO, three sergeants, six corporals, and 49 men. Their armament consisted of three machine guns, three submachine guns, one grenade launcher, one automatic pistol, and 48 rifles. Leroy said this was "the best type of unit to combat the guerrilla," and he was probably right – bigger than a platoon but smaller than a company.[57] General de Latour supported Leroy and in September authorized a large force consisting of thirty "brigades" called Mobile Units for Defense of Christian Communities (UMDC). Their motto: *Pro Deo et Patria*, "For God and Country." Leroy said he "enjoyed the prerogatives and attributions of a corps commander, most particularly in matters of personnel – recruitment, advancement, assignment, transfers, discipline, and instruction." His was, as he said, "a unique Catholic organism."[58] Enjoying support from the commanding general, and promoted to lieutenant colonel, Leroy increased the force he commanded to about 12,000 and was responsible for a large part of the Mekong Delta and area south of Saigon comprising a population of around 600,000. In time, his army would be incorporated into the National Army of Vietnam. Leroy was highly successful in killing Viet Minh (along with many innocents, his enemy claimed, probably with justification).[59] His program of "pacification" allowed de Latour to pull out some French Union units and send them where they were much more needed, Tonkin.

1949: A Momentous Year

In the South, things were not going well for the French. The enemy seemed to be everywhere, constantly inflicting casualties. The young idealist Guy de Chaumont-Guitry was gravely wounded on 6 November and soon died of his wounds. He was buried beside other French soldiers in the cemetery at Vinh Long on the Mekong.

In researching for my earlier book, *One Hell of a Ride*, by a stroke of great good fortune I made contact with a retired French general who in 1949-50 served as a young officer in the Michelin Plantation. The closest French equivalent of the late 1940s and early 1950s to my 1-4 Cav of 1969 was 5th *Cuirassiers*. This armored cavalry unit (battalion size) worked the same terrain we covered and more, stretched thin indeed. Jean Delaunay was a 20-year-old lieutenant, first a platoon leader then commander of 1st *Escadron*, 5th *Cuir* (company size). Ultimately he became a five-star General of the Army and was appointed to the highest post, Chief of Staff, 1980 – 1983. In emails across several years he described his Vietnam experiences, and he sent me articles which he or other French soldiers had written reflecting experiences in the area north of Saigon, accompanied by pictures, maps, and illustrations. He said, "At this time, our enemy was not so strong as yours, using principally mines against us and fighting mostly by ambushes against convoys on roads."[60] By this time in the war, the British and American equipment that had been in reasonably good shape right after WWII was now suffering. "Our equipment," he said, "was very poor with very bad maintenance and lack of spare parts and tires. We used English armored cars 'Coventry' and very light scout cars 'Humber' and some old U.S. scout cars and halftracks.

"My job was to protect the Michelin plantation, the rubber being evacuated by barges on the Saigon river protected by landing crafts of our navy [leftover LCIs and LSTs from the U.S. Navy]. I wonder though if it's really interesting for you to gain information about 'our' war. We had no occasion in South Vietnam at this time to fight (as you did 20 years later) against well equipped enemy units such as were already organized in Tonkin where, four years before Dien Bien Phu, they defeated some of our best battalions in October 1950 on Route Coloniale 4. On the contrary, 'our' war in the South was essentially counter guerrilla, the Viet Minh trying to cut our ways of communications to prevent economic activity in order to take control of the population and prevent the functioning of the young South Vietnamese administration. This general aim, destroying the rubber plantations or preventing them to operate, were their objectives by means of cutting the ways enabling us to import rice, petrol and other goods necessary to the factories and to cut the ways to export the crude dried rubber by river and road. They were killing the French and Vietnamese civilians responsible for the plantation (I saw several of them killed), and threatening Vietnamese workers to force them to join their ranks in the forest. . . .

"The plantation director used the two planes of the Michelin Company. One was an old German Fiesler Storch observation plane which I often used as a reconnaissance plane. I had many occasions to fly in this plane for informal observation missions where I couldn't see anything because the Viet Minh used to take cover when they heard our engine. The pilot was kind enough to evacuate me with this very plane under very bad flying conditions to Saigon Hospital in August 1949 when I lost my right hand to a booby trap. I came back to Dau Tieng some weeks later with a wooden homemade hand.

"We didn't have any organized air support. There was only one air squadron (old Spitfires at the beginning, then King Cobras) for all of South Vietnam, and the air ground liaison was at that time very bad. On the few occasions I had to ask for emergency air support I had no possibility to speak directly to the pilots (as I used to do later in Algeria). In Viet Nam 1949, the planes usually used to fly in circles three or four times around and above the combat area without seeing objectives to fire on. Then they waved their wings to say 'Mission over. I am unable to fire' and they went home. Once or twice, flying aboard the plantation plane for an informal observation mission, I had the opportunity to throw a few hand grenades on Viet Minh hidden in the bushes. I never saw strafing and bombing except in late 1950 napalm dropping tests over supposed Viet Minh columns surrounding Dautieng. At that time, a few 200 liter cans of napalm fuel were pushed out of the aircraft door from an old JU-52, an all-purpose former German transport plane. An incendiary grenade was tied to the can with a piece of string to set it afire.[61] Such at this time was our poor air support. Two years later, things changed, especially in Tonkin due to purchased U.S. equipment such as navy air assault planes and high explosive and incendiary U.S. bombs and radio sets with air-ground possibilities. I don't know if these prehistoric details are interesting for you who fought with armor and air support against a regular Communist army with 20 years of war experience."[62]

I assured General Delaunay that not only I but many others were interested in such details. I knew well the locations of several of the places he described in his many correspondences, places in which my task force had similar experiences some twenty years later.

The New Bao Dai Government

Politically, the French had some reason to hope that their position in Vietnam was improving. President Auriol and Bao Dai had come to an agreement, the Élyssée Accords, which, to Bao Dai, initially seemed to assure the independence of Vietnam, but of course to the French meant something less than that, even though for the first time the word "independence" was part of the accord. Vietnam was to be an Associated State within the French Union. It was to be unified under Vietnamese administration, but France was to remain in control of its armed forces, primarily the Vietnamese National Army (VNA), created in 1949. In July Bao Dai appointed himself as Prime Minister, head of state, relegating General Xuan to the role of Vice Prime Minister.

Proclaiming was one thing, achieving was another. Bao Dai had little following among his countrymen, and he was entertaining the idea of reconciliation with the Communists, even creating positions in his government for them. Bui Diem, the mandarin's son and Dai Viet member who had been hiding out with his family in the North, was to be sent as his party's emissary to meet Bao Dai. He was a non-Communist nationalist whereas his father and older brother were both Communists. Reminiscent of our own Revolutionary and Civil Wars, Bui Diem said, "Regardless of the different political paths we had taken, the war had done nothing to loosen the family bonds between us."[63] Bao Dai had moved to Dalat, the small resort city in the Central Highlands. "From there he sent out invitations to all the politically significant groups and families in Vietnam, asking them to come to Dalat for consultations." Bao Dai cordially greeted Bui Diem and two other important leaders of Dai Viet. He said, "We have a framework for independence. . . . Do you think you can help me put together a government?" Bao Dai did not press for an answer as the Dai Viet and other groups went to work to do just that. Bui Diem noted, "Meanwhile, Bao Dai is in Dalat not doing anything at all. He has his women there and his hunting."[64]

The moment had passed.

As Bao Dai diddled, South Vietnam made an abrupt turn away from a potential compromise government. Ngo Dinh Diem (no relation to Bui Diem), a staunchly Catholic bachelor who had earlier been offered the premiership and declined, set about rallying anti-Communist nationalists. Later he would power his way to the top.

Bui Diem said, "For two and a half decades more I would serve various South Vietnamese leaders, searching always for the many who could meet the nation's needs. Fortunately, I could foresee none of this. And so I did not sense that my search, which was also the quest of Vietnam's nationalists, was touched by doom."[65]

In May 1949 began one of the strangest incidents in the war. The new French Prime Minister, Henri Queuille, sent the Army's chief of staff, General of the Army Georges Revers, to do a thorough investigation of the whole Indochina situation. The year before, Revers had been the French government's representative in drafting the NATO pact. In five weeks of extensive travels in Indochina, the general did a superb job, talking extensively with men from general down to private, and French and Vietnamese civilian government officials from high to low.

As he made the round of visits to sovereigns of Laos and Cambodia and to Bao Dai, he was astonished to discover that a sumptuous Saigon gaming palace, *"Le Grande Monde,"* had been inaugurated in the presence of the High Commissioner and the highest military authorities. It belonged to Bay Vien, the head of the notorious Binh Xuyen, a criminal gang that permeated Saigon and much of the area around it. Bay Vien was paying royalties from prostitution, gambling, and illicit activities to Bao Dai.

In June General Revers returned to Paris with his report. For one thing, even now, after almost four years since the first French forces from France arrived at Tan Son Nhut, he found that the French were not doing well in counter-guerrilla warfare. For another, the government was tainted by the Bao Dai reputation for corruption. One of Revers' recommendations sounded like an early form of the U.S. "Vietnamization" policy. He envisioned that the new Vietnamese army should protect the frontiers and take on the pacification role inside the country. There must be no question of abandonment or evacuation. He thought that the current objectives of the French Forces in Indochina were only hopes and not realistic because they lacked men and materiel. His report was expansive, covering the big picture and many details. All copies were marked "very secret," to be closely held by a select few in the military and government. The copies were carefully logged out and back in. One of the copies went to General of the Army Charles Mast. In August it was suddenly learned that the report had been broadcast by Ho's *The Voice of Vietnam.* Ho, Giap, and all the top leaders of the DRV and its army were now publicizing the thinking of the highest ranking military officer in France, and of his recommendations and the details upon which they were based.

The "Generals' Affair" took many twists and turns, and, astonishingly, evidence pointed to General Mast's having received one million francs as a bribe for his support in naming a certain person the next

High Commissioner for Indochina. The French cabinet fell, and a new Prime Minister, Georges Bidault, took over. Revers himself was caught up in aspects of the scandal, and the result was that both he and General Mast were retired from service as discretely as possible. France's reputation had been sullied during a time when NATO was in its infancy and France was sorely needed in the defensive arrangement against Soviet aggression in Europe.[66]

Yet another new command structure was taking place in Tonkin when on 10 September General Marcel Carpentier replaced General Blaizot as Supreme Commander for Indochina. He had no prior experience in Indochina, but his subordinate, General Alessandri, had been in Indochina since 1940 and had commanded units escaping into northwest Tonkin and China after the Japanese coup on 9 March 1945. Alessandri would be the commander in the North.

Two of Carpentier's friends had been offered and refused to take the post, saying to Carpentier, "You are damned unless you can get 500,000 more men." When he arrived he quickly became aware that General Revers had been wise in counseling the abandonment of the posts on Route 4 along the Chinese border. Allesandri, however, could not bring himself to that view, giving up vast territory that had been purchased with so much blood. Soon after arrival Carpentier learned about the cost of holding it when a large ambush inflicted heavy casualties. Fluctuating in uncertainty, he finally gave the order to evacuate Cao Bang. Alessandri was incensed. Carpentier backed down, making it clear that doing so went against the advice of both Revers and his predecessor, Blaizot. He apparently took comfort in knowing that he would be getting reinforcements, men and materiel: 125,000 Vietnamese from the National Army and 48,000 French, as well as Hellcat dive bombers, C-47 Dakotas, and landing craft from the United States. Tonkin grew calmer, and Annam and Cochinchina were still the same: lots of "minor incidents," but nothing major. Carpentier could breathe a little easier. The stage was set for disaster.[67]

During the Revers investigation, life west of the Iron Curtain had suddenly became much more precarious when on 29 August 1949 the Soviet Union exploded an atomic bomb, launching a nuclear arms race. This, taken with Chinese Communist successes against Chiang Kai-shek's Nationalists, required Washington to consider far more seriously its attitude toward France in Indochina. The French were now perceived to be on the front lines against Communism.

For months the Chinese Nationalists had been suffering huge losses, and Mao's political and military entities were consolidating power. Then, with defeat of most of the Nationalist forces, on 1 October 1949 in Tiananmen Square, Mao proclaimed the People's Republic of China (PRC). Again the western world was electrified. The next day the Soviet Union recognized the new government. By December Chiang Kai-shek had evacuated with significant forces to Taiwan, and Mao's troops were on the northern border of Vietnam.

Giap said, "The year 1949 saw the brilliant triumph of the Chinese Revolution and the birth of the People's Republic of China." Recriminations flew in Washington as to who was responsible for the "loss" of China—with the burden falling on Truman—notwithstanding that China had never been Washington's to "lose." Giap continued, "This great historic event, which altered events in Asia and throughout the world, exerted a considerable influence on the war of liberation of the Vietnamese people. Vietnam was no longer in the grip of enemy encirclement, and was henceforth geographically linked to the socialist bloc."[68]

The war in Indochina changed dramatically with the Chinese Communist victory. The situation was grim for the French. Mao's guide for international revolutionary warfare had prescribed various stages in insurgency, with the creation and employment of conventional armies as the last step. For years Ho and Giap had been progressing in this direction at the same time they were waging guerrilla warfare throughout Vietnam. Without decreasing that kind of local warfare—in fact increasing it—they had been able to build the "big battalions."

CHAPTER 6

Huge Battles and Simultaneous Guerrilla Warfare, 1950 - mid-1953

∗   ∗   ∗

THE EARLY MONTHS OF 1950 were a whirlwind of political activity on both sides of the Iron Curtain. France formally ratified the accords of the Associated States of Indochina. As Ho and Vietnamese Communists vociferously rejected the new federation, the United States, Great Britain, and the Vatican officially recognized it. Britain and Israel, however, recognized Communist China, and the USSR and China recognized Ho Chi Minh's government as the sole legitimate government of Vietnam. The United States did not recognize Red China until three decades had passed.

"[In January 1950], anxious to establish personal contact with the [Chinese Communist] leadership, Ho decided to visit Beijing himself. . . . . [he] walked on foot for seventeen days in Vietnamese jungles before crossing into Guangxi province [China]." He was warmly greeted and taken on to Beijing. After returning to Tonkin, Ho forwarded to the Chinese "a number of aid requests, including the establishment of a Vietnamese military school in China, the dispatch of Chinese military advisers to Vietnam, and the supply of weapons." By April, the Chinese government had established a Vietnamese military school just across the Vietnam border in China and was training Vietnamese in accordance with Mao's military principles.[1]

This beginning of formal Chinese assistance to Ho's government immensely changed the parameters of the war, especially in terms of weapons, uniforms, medicines, and all kinds of other necessary supplies. Many thousands of tons of equipment captured by Mao's forces from the Nationalists (much of it U.S.), as well as newly manufactured modern materiel, would now begin flowing to the Viet Minh. This was an enormous step up from clandestine factories in Vietnamese jungles. At the same time, however, U.S. aid to French forces was far more substantial than Mao's aid to Ho in terms of tonnage, sophistication, and firepower, and it grew from 1951-54. This imbalance continued to be true during the forthcoming war with the Americans. China, the Soviet Union, and the East Bloc countries gave substantial military and economic aid to the North Vietnamese; however, it was dwarfed by the huge American and Allied commitment to South Vietnam.

The Viet Minh Fall Campaign, and War in Korea

The Viet Minh, now officially People's Army of Vietnam (PAVN) but continuing to be called Viet Minh, were planning a 1950 fall campaign which, for the first time in the war, would not only utilize area-wide large attacks by main force units in the North, but also require simultaneous action in the South, a very significant step for the Communists: the first coordinated Vietnam-wide major offensive. The Viet Minh in Delaunay's area of the Michelin Plantation increased their activity in January as preparation for the coming fall offensive, and he was kept busy night and day trying first to protect, and then rebuild, bridges and culverts the Viets had blown.

In Tonkin, emboldened by the Chinese Communist victory, and having built up its main forces, in February the Viet Minh launched an offensive against the Colonial Route 4 garrisons along the border with China. This was Phase 1 of what came to be called Giap's Border Campaign. Despite severe losses, the French units were able to hang onto or recover lost posts, but the fighting drew attention to the deficiencies in the French posture, garrisons and outposts that were far out from Hanoi and difficult to support.

Meanwhile in Washington, the policy of containment of Communism was prompting official action. From *The Pentagon Papers*: "The United States decision to provide military assistance to France and the Associated States of Indochina was reached informally in February/March 1950, funded by the President on May 1, 1950, and was announced on May 8. . . . The rationale of the decision was provided by the U.S. view that the Soviet-controlled expansion of Communism both in Asia and in Europe required, in the interests of U.S. national security, a counter in Indochina. The domino thesis was quite prominent. . . . The importance of the decision was that when the U.S. was faced with an unambiguous choice between a policy of anti-colonialism and a policy of anti-Communism, it chose the latter."[2]

Then catastrophe: On 25 June 1950, North Korean troops poured across the border into South Korea. America was at war. Two days later President Truman stated, "The attack upon Korea makes it plain beyond all doubt that Communism has passed beyond the use of subversion to conquer independent nations and will now use armed invasion and war. . . . Accordingly, I have directed acceleration in the furnishing of military assistance to the forces of France and the Associated States in Indochina and the dispatch of a military mission to provide close working relations with those forces."[3]

This was fulfillment of the 1947 Truman Doctrine: the United States would provide political, military, and economic assistance to all democratic nations under threat from external or internal authoritarian sources. It was a stretch, indeed, to consider South Vietnam as a democratic nation, but from a meager beginning in 1945 when the French Expeditionary Corps entered Vietnam, the United States was now opting to expand, not decrease, U.S. commitment in Vietnam. The U.S. sent Military Assistance Advisory Group (MAAG) there in

September 1950, and with its 35 men America began the long formal relationship between U.S. and South Vietnamese armed forces. Soon, more Hellcat and Bearcat fighters and B-26 bombers arrived from the U.S. The fighters were equipped with bomb racks and machine guns, giving them the capability of being used as fighter-bombers. These aircraft were a great improvement over the earlier Spitfires, King Cobras, and outmoded bombers. Additionally, C-47, DC-4, and C-54 transport aircraft greatly increased French airborne logistics and paradrop capabilities. Two months earlier, before MAAG had even arrived, Ho Chi Minh was already claiming that the Americans, not the French, were the ultimate and most dangerous enemy: "The U.S. imperialists have of late openly interfered in Indochina's affairs. It is with their money and their weapons and their instructions that the French colonialists have been waging war in Viet-Nam, Cambodia, and Laos. However, the U.S. imperialists are intensifying their plot to discard the French colonialists so as to gain complete control over Indochina."[4]

Mao Tse-tung had beaten the U.S. by a few months in July 1950 by formalizing an earlier advisory arrangement as the Chinese Military Advisory Group (CMAG) in North Vietnam. Later, in 1951, China would provide a Chinese Political Advisory Group in keeping with their doctrine of always combining military with political action, and ensuring that within military units there was always a political commissar who not only provided Party doctrine and encouragement but shared in combat decisions. From these beginnings, the Chinese Communist Party (CCP) leadership would develop its position that later played such a dominant role in the Vietnamese war against the Americans: "They would not hesitate to send troops into Vietnam to restore peace and order if the authority of an existing tributary ruler there [Ho Chi Minh] was endangered by either domestic uprisings or foreign invasion."[5] That this threat was real became dramatically apparent when the Chinese stormed across the Manchurian border with North Korea to drive UN forces back south in the Korean war.

The Route 4 Disaster for the French

In Tonkin during the summer of 1950, along Route 4 close to the Chinese border there had been an unusual calm. As a result of the Revers recommendations, smaller posts were evacuated and larger ones were ordered to prepare for evacuation on order. Suddenly on 16 September, the post at Dong Khe radioed to the post at Cau Bang, 18 miles to the northwest on the route, that they were under fierce artillery bombardment. This was the beginning of a nightmare for the French that would not end until a month later. The Viet Minh were now ready to demonstrate that they not only could fight a guerrilla war, but they could field units in a coordinated war of "big battalions."

Colonel Charton at Cao Bang was ordered to evacuate the post. Dong Khe was overrun but then retaken. A force of 3500 men under Colonel Le Page was to move up from Lang Son, 60 miles to the south on Route 4, to Dong Khe. Colonel Charton with about 2,500 troops and 500 or so civilians at Cao Bang had been ordered to destroy his heavy equipment and trucks and move to Dong Khe to join up with Le Page. Charton seems to have disobeyed orders, or was confused by conflicting directions, and took his vehicles with him, hitting ambushes as he progressed. With ten battalions and an artillery regiment, Giap blocked the way to Dong Khe and trapped the French in a gorge where by 8 October they were slaughtered. The losses were appalling: "7,000 men [killed or captured, many of which were wounded], 13 cannons, 120 mortars, 450 vehicles, 3 platoons of armored vehicles, 940 machine guns, 1,200 submachine guns, and 8,500 rifles."[6] Many times in preceding years Ho had publicly stated how well prisoners should be and were treated. About 2,000 of 3,000 French Union prisoners died from neglect and mistreatment during the first months of their captivity in Viet Minh concentration camps.[7]

There was more to come on Route 4. The post of Lang Son had been occupied since the 19th century and was the anchor of the whole Route 4 defensive system. On the night of 17/18 October "it was abandoned intact, with its enormous stocks of supplies, munitions, and materiel, with its hospital and its 150 tons of pharmaceuticals, with its electric plant, its public works shop." That was "enough to equip eight regiments," according to the official Communist history, *30-year War*.[8] A contagious panic set in. Lai Chau and Lao Cai [or Kay], key outposts deep in the High Region to the west, 180 miles from Hanoi, also had to be evacuated. Thus, "Cao Bang, Lang Son, Lao Kay, the three latches [which held the door closed in the French defensive system] along the Chinese frontier, were sprung. Giap could freely arrange the avenues of penetration from China to the Delta. . . . Tomorrow Hanoi?" An important post of the Moïs in the High Region was next to be abandoned under pressure. Other posts were emptied, and Hanoi indeed was in a precarious position.[9]

This Route 4 disaster and succeeding abandonment of posts thoroughly shook France, and it was what had prompted General Delaunay to email me, "We had no occasion in South Vietnam at this time [1949 – 1950] to fight (as you did 20 years later) against well equipped enemy units such as were already organized in Tonkin where, four years before Dien Bien Phu, they defeated some of our best battalions in October 1950 on Route Coloniale 4."

Yet another mission was dispatched to Indochina to assess what went wrong. The French chief of staff, General Alphonse Juin, and the Minister of the Associated States, Jean Letourneau, asked questions and got truthful answers: trying to do too much in far-off difficult terrain against an enemy which had widespread popular support.

At the time French Union forces were taking a beating in Vietnam, in Korea UN forces (primarily U.S. and Republic of Korea) were making a successful amphibious landing at Inchon near Seoul and counterattacking out of their Pusan perimeter. They were fast pushing the North Koreans north toward the Yalu River at the border with Manchuria. Despite General MacArthur's belief that China would not enter the war, on 25 October its troops surged across the Manchurian border. Bitter fighting ensued. France had been one of the UN nations which in August had decided to send troops to Korea even though they were sorely needed in Vietnam. Its "Korea Battalion" was attached to the U.S. 2nd Infantry Division. The accomplishments and heroism of the unit earned the heartfelt praise of General Matthew Ridgway, MacArthur's successor as commander of UN forces.

On 29 November, an elated Ho Chi Minh came to congratulate his victorious three divisions of the Route 4 campaign – now not just guerrilla units, not just companies, battalions, or regiments, but *divisions!!!* – the 304, 308 and 312. "You have left the mountains to descend toward the fertile rice fields of the Red River. . . . In a few weeks we will move into a general offensive of annihilation . . . We will march on Hanoi. I promise you, comrades, by next Tet [6 February 1951] we will enter Hanoi."[10] Following hard on the heels of the disaster on Route 4, Ho's statement was enough to move the French government in Paris to send *le Pasteur*, the largest passenger liner available, to evacuate civilians from Hanoi.[11]

Colonel Bui Tin affirmed, "The situation started to change towards the end of 1950 after we forced the French to abandon their garrisons along the northern border, and the Resistance was able to link up with the People's Republic of China. . . . China was the immense rear area for the Vietnamese Revolution."[12]

The 1950 Fall Offensive was Giap's first operation to bring all forces, North and South, into a synchronized attack with main force units. Simultaneous with the Border Campaign in the North, the so-called Ben Cat Campaign in the South was "an offensive campaign conducted by . . . the 302nd, 303rd, and 304th main force battalions, five independent companies, and guerrilla militia units. . . . The goal of the campaign was to kill enemy troops, intensify our guerrilla warfare operations, cut and eventually liberate Route 13 and most of Inter-Provincial Route 14 and coordinate with and support our operations in Tonkin."[13] The area selected was the crucial road and railway network from the Michelin Plantation south along the Saigon River and east to Ben Cat on Colonial Route 13, and the entire length of RC13 from Loc Ninh south to Ben Cat. "After more than a month of fighting in this campaign, our armed forces had launched a total of 38 attacks against enemy strong-points, mounted two ambushes of road traffic to prevent the arrival of reinforcements, made 43 separate attacks against enemy motorized traffic, conducted two battles against enemy sweep operations, and launched 204 individual harassment attacks."[14] This area in 1969 was the scene of all six of our major QuarterCav battles.

After the disaster of Route 4, not just the French military command and political structures had been shaken to the core by the horrible results of Giap's offensive, but the French people were appalled. They had gotten reports that the war was proceeding quite well, with a lasting political solution possible. Light at the end of the tunnel? And now, crowds rallying for an end to the war included outraged mothers, fathers, brothers, and sisters from across the political spectrum, left to right. They wanted no more of their loved ones to die in that cursed land. Boards of inquiry assessed what went wrong and debated how to fix it. Several senior officers involved in Vietnam War planning and conduct were relieved and the search was on for a savior.

They found their man, they were sure, in the immensely respected General of the Army Jean de Lattre de Tassigny. This time there would be no disagreement between the Supreme Commander and the High Commissioner. In early December de Lattre was appointed to both posts, and hopes rode high that he could get the war and peace process back on track.

America would now be of immense help to the French after more than four years of, first, its condemnation of colonial reconquest, then an ambivalent stance of modest assistance tempered by indifference, then significant help. Congress had reauthorized the Mutual Defense Assistance Program through which arms, equipment, and training might be provided worldwide to other nations for collective defense against Communism, and on 23 December America weighed in heavily when President Truman signed an agreement with France for aid to Indochina.[15]

During these somber days General Salan tallied the enormous loss of men in the French Union forces from 23 September 1945 to

November 1950. Not counting officers from major general down to lieutenant, many of whom were killed, it was 2,900 non-commissioned officers killed, of whom 2,700 were French Union or legionnaires, and 11,500 lower ranks killed, of whom 9,300 were French Union or legionnaires. Adding those missing in action and seriously wounded, evacuated, brought the total to 36,000.[16]

1951, The "Year of de Lattre": a Year of Hope

De Lattre was a "general's general," no-nonsense, no excuses, often wounded in World War I, in World War II enormously experienced at the highest level of French command, and then of post-war European Union affairs. On 17 December 1950 he and his entourage of generals and top civilian officials, to include those of the Associated State of Vietnam, landed at Tan Son Nhut. Following protocol, Special Minister Jean Letourneau descended first from the airliner. Then followed an interminable wait, designed to set the stage appropriately. Finally the general appeared in the door, stepped out and paused, regally. He slowly descended, followed by his deputy Salan and the rest of his officers, hand-picked from veterans of his 1ˢᵗ Army which he had commanded in the previous war. Everyone was in crisp white dress military uniforms or civilian suits. This grand entry was de Lattre's style. Long ago he had been dubbed "*Le Roi Jean*," King Jean, by admirers and detractors alike, each holding to different meanings of the term. He coldly received his predecessors, Messieur Léon Pignon and General Carpentier—two of them for one of him—and upon arrival at his new headquarters began relieving some heads of staff sections, replacing them with men he had brought with him. And he sent the *Pasteur* back with no civilians aboard, only wounded French Union soldiers. The civilians were to stay, he said, and contribute to the war effort. He ordered able-bodied Frenchmen in Vietnam to be put to work as guards.[17] Four days later his airliner flew from Saigon to Dalat, the seat of the new Bao Dai government. But shortly he left, aggravated. He had been unsuccessful in persuading the emperor to accompany him to Hanoi.

General of the Army Jean de Lattre de Tassigny studies
the map of Indochina with his second in command, the old
Indochina hand General Salan, advising him. (ECPAD)

When de Lattre arrived in Hanoi he was taken immediately to a reviewing stand. His new commander in the North, Major General Gonzales
de Linarès, greeted him. De Lattre had given orders for all available battalions to be assembled, some of them coming straight from combat. He
looked at them and exclaimed to General Salan, "They are scruffy!" It
seemed to have been meant in profound admiration, not condemnation.
Only hours earlier they had been fighting. Their combat uniforms were
stained with mud, some with blood, torn. Their faces, needing shaves,
bore traces of dried sweat, but as they passed in review they were in step
with the music. De Lattre felt great pride in being their commander. The
colonel in charge of supplying the disheveled troops did not get away
easily. De Lattre turned to him, seated behind, and said, "Disappear,
colonel!"[18] Then he had the lieutenants and captains assembled, and said,

"I am here. I swear to you that you will now be *commanded*! We will not yield an inch of terrain. I bring you war, but also the pride of this war." Later he sat in front of assembled military and civilian officers, French and Vietnamese, and said, "Our combat is selfless; it is all of civilization that we defend in Tonkin. We do not fight for domination, but for liberation. Never has a war been more noble."[19]

Well-----

One may cringe. Nevertheless, a great many French volunteers in Vietnam believed with him that it was a civil war, and France was helping the non-Communist populace to establish their own country. For many profoundly distressed soldiers and civilians in Hanoi—French and Vietnamese—the general had come just in time, and he was setting exactly the right tone. With an ear to Ho's boast of being in Hanoi for Tet, de Lattre had found the city in a state of near-panic. Civil servants were evacuating their families, and businessmen were selling their factories and stores at fire sale prices. To show that normalcy would return, De Lattre stated he would be joined shortly in Hanoi by his wife. When she landed, the couple set out visiting wounded troops in the hospitals. The general made it clear to staff that those who were enjoying comfortable sinecures while the fighters did without had better begin producing or pack up and get out.

De Lattre was tough on subordinates and would not abide slackers, but he was benevolent among the men who could see the results of his efforts on their behalf. The headquarters for the Supreme Commander and High Commissioner were in Saigon, but de Lattre had always marched to the sound of the guns, and it was near Hanoi that the guns were sounding, so he would spend most of his time in Hanoi close to the fighting. When he had arrived in Hanoi, some of the combat was just 18 miles to the west of the city. The rumble of explosions could be heard. And Ho was not far away. His main headquarters was at Thai Nguyen, only 30 miles north of Hanoi in the Viet Bac. De Lattre was the finest general since Leclerc. For several days he flew in a Morane light observation plane all over Tonkin, maps on his knees, looking down, studying the maps and terrain, getting to know it. Soon he was devising a plan.[20]

Giap, in writing his memoirs, believed that de Lattre had global strategic considerations in mind as he developed that plan. Giap said, "If the Red River Delta, the rice granary of the North, with its 8 million inhabitants, was re-conquered by the Viet Minh, armed by China and the Soviet Union, this would threaten the whole of Southeast Asia. This delta was [the crucial area] in preventing the 'red waves' from flooding down from the north."[21]

In short order de Lattre unveiled a plan with two components. One was a 350-mile defensive line around the Delta featuring redoubts of concrete blockhouses protected by mines, barbed wire, programmed artillery fires, airstrikes, and where possible from the rivers and the Gulf of Tonkin, naval gunfire. It protected Haiphong and Hanoi, the mainstays of the French position in the North. If either fell, the whole French effort in the North would fail, five years of sacrifice of men and money would be for naught, and the ambition to bring all of Indochina into a functioning French Union would end up as a fizzled pipedream.

The defensive line was quickly dubbed "The de Lattre Line." Some existing outposts were eliminated and others strengthened. The line formed a wedge which anchored in the north on the Gulf of Tonkin and border of China at Mong Cai, dropped down to north of Haiphong and included other Haiphong defenses, went west past Mao Khe and Vinh Yen to Viet Tri, then curved southeast, enclosing Hanoi, and south to Nam Dinh, continuing south to anchor once again on the Gulf at Sam Son.

This sounded like the Maginot Line which in 1940 failed so spectacularly to keep the blitzkrieg out of France. However, it was no static barrier. As the second component in his plan, the general also ordered a mobile defense: every available unit which could be equipped for mobile warfare was to be positioned in critical locations within this perimeter. These regimental-size strike forces were the best, most combat-tested troops he had. The line was intended to hold any Viet Minh main force advance in place long enough for the strike forces to react. Upon order the mobile units were to rush to the location and counterattack, assisted by all available ground, air, and naval support, and crush the enemy.

General de Latour had moved from command in the South to command in the North. He evacuated a post, which angered de Lattre. "Not an inch, general!" De Lattre relieved him and told his deputy, Salan, to take command.

De Lattre was making a strong push with the Vietnamese national government to raise and strengthen Vietnamese forces to take over the war. He told them that France would help them, but ultimately it was up to them to defend their country against the Communists. Also, the general went around to the various military schools where, with largely French officers as the leaders and teachers, young Vietnamese were learning to become soldiers and officers. At these schools, in government assemblies, and in youth groups he called upon Vietnamese young people to defend their freedom, telling them that the fate of their country was in their hands. On one occasion in a Saigon lycee he urged them to make a commitment: "'Be men! If you are Communists, then join the Viet Minh—there are some good people there, fighting well for a bad cause. But if you are patriots, then fight for your country, because this is *your* war. . . France can only fight it for you if you fight with her.' His uneasy audience responded with only polite applause."[22]

For many young Vietnamese, there was not much sense of "country" for them to defend. With France still so obviously the leader in the fight against Ho's DRV and the Viet Minh, it was difficult for that idea to take hold. De Lattre early on found that Ho was giving the Vietnamese something to die for—independence—whereas it was difficult for France to motivate Vietnamese into something to live for—an Associated State within the French Union.

Mindful of Ho's promise to enter Hanoi by 6 February in time for Tet celebrations, Giap's first objective was to overrun fortified Vinh Yen, which would crack the de Lattre Line. He had his forward command post installed in the nearby remains of bombed out cellars of mountain summer houses formerly used by Bao Dai and the French governor general. On the night of 12/13 January 1951, Giap's main forces attacked. French accounts vary as to the size of enemy forces, with some saying that four enemy divisions were used, either at Vinh Yen itself or to the north and south in secondary attacks. Giap said he used five of his regiments, the equivalent of almost two divisions, at Vinh Yen.[23] Whatever the size, Giap's attack was fierce, using regular, battle-tested troops. They penetrated the village and set a fuel depot afire, and the defenders were in deep trouble.

De Lattre was in Saigon when he was notified. He ordered mobile units to counterattack and directed that reserves in the South, the best units he could get quickly, be assembled at Tan Son Nhut to be sent north by continuous airlift. He got some aircraft by requisitioning civilian airplanes as they landed at Tan Son Nhut, unaware they were going to be shortly on their way north, loaded with soldiers.[24] De Lattre was flown to Hanoi, then climbed into his light observation plane to fly to Vinh Yen to take charge personally. With tracers from antiaircraft fire whizzing by his plane, and told that the position below him was about to be overrun, nonplused, he landed and was taken to the fort. It was a pathetic scene of dead and wounded. Seeing that the situation was critical, he ordered another mobile unit into battle and told the air force to use everything they had. This included a new weapon, used in this battle extensively for the first time by the French – the napalm canister. It inflicted horrible casualties. A Viet Minh leader later wrote, "It was hell in front of me, fire which fell from the sky. . . . 'What is it'? one of my terrified men asked, 'an atomic bomb?'"[25]

Mobile Groupement 2 commanded by Colonel Christian de Castries reinforced the defenders, but without its commander. At the head of the convoy, in the dark de Castries' vehicle had hit a mine and he was seriously wounded. Giap's Division 308, the one that had done so much damage on RC4, attacked, but in desperate hand-to-hand fighting it was stopped. By the night of 16/17 January, Giap's troops were in retreat, having lost many dead, wounded, and captured. De Lattre's men had also suffered severe casualties, but they had stopped Giap. Lacking reserves of ground troops and air forces, de Lattre was unable to mount an effective pursuit to exploit his victory.

But French Hanoi was ecstatic. International television, radio, and newspaper journalists clamored for stories. Ho's boast that he would make it into Hanoi for Tet was fodder for jokes. De Lattre was riding high. "At his arrival everything bad. . . . A month later everything had changed. . . . Confidence, resolution, audacity animated the same men. . . . The expeditionary corps reached its apogee. . . . The French had feared a new disaster; suddenly they believed in victory. It was a resurrection."[26]

Ho had not made it into Hanoi by Tet in February, but he was busy with an important political development. In order to attract a broader spectrum of people to his cause, since November 1946 Vietnam had not had an official Communist Party. But in February 1951 in the far northwestern reaches of the Viet Bac, just south of the Chinese border, Ho convened what came to be called The Resistance Congress, attended by 211 Vietnamese delegates as well as observers from the Chinese and Siamese [Thailand] Communist parties. "The Dang Lao Dong Vietnam, or Vietnamese Workers Party, was inaugurated with Ho as chairman. . . . It made respectable, at least legal, that which had been secret and, in a sense, illegitimate. . . . It helped internationalize the Party and integrate it into the worldwide Communist movement as an orthodox element. Joining the international mainstream was given as the reason for dropping the name *Indochina* in favor *of Vietnam*, as well as the use of *worker* instead of *Communist*, asserted to be ideologically fashionable."[27]

De Lattre flew back to France to try to pry 15,000 more men and supporting materiel out of the government. While he was there, on 24 March the second blow of Giap's campaign fell. Three divisions attacked, this time with the intention of opening up the way from the north to Haiphong. Giap quickly overran some small posts. General Gonzalez De Linares, the new commander in the North, wanted to counterattack immediately but de Lattre telegraphed him to wait. De Lattre rushed back to Hanoi and, believing that the village of Mao Khe, 20 miles north of the city, was the key to stopping the assault he ordered the small posts there to be reinforced, and other mobile units made ready to move on order. He and de Linares had visited the posts a month earlier so he knew the terrain. The navy ordered a powerful Dinassaut unit up a river estuary to support.[28]

Division 312 struck hard at the Mao Khe posts with mortars, artillery, and ground assault. French naval gunfire responded from a cruiser, two gunboats, and LSTs, along with Hellcats firing rockets, and dropping bombs and napalm canisters. An intrepid forward observer in his tiny Morane plane coordinated the fires. The Vietnamese partisan unit defending the posts had their wives and children to protect, and they fought like demons to hold on. Paratroopers, legionnaires, and marines reinforced the partisans, and despite continued vicious attacks they punished the enemy with their strong stand and heavy supporting fires. Giap's two-division attack at nearby Dong Trieu likewise failed. After 12 days of bitter fighting, night and day, Giap withdrew.

For the next two months de Lattre was busy trying to get the South Vietnamese government to do as much as possible to defeat the Communists by enlisting soldiers. Meanwhile, French Union units were conducting sweeps in the Red River Delta to try to consolidate their victories in turning back the two major assaults, on Vinh Yen and Mao Khe. The Viet Minh divisions, as was their custom, had pulled back to reorganize, reequip, and retrain for the next main thrust. Meanwhile, guerrilla activity went on unabated, always pressuring the French and gaining recruits.

De Lattre was now in a position to attempt pacification of the Delta, and he ordered several relatively small operations. One of them was "Medusa" southwest of Haiphong, and his son Bernard distinguished himself at the head of a company of Vietnamese infantrymen during two weeks of tough fighting. Some days after the operation ended on 2 May, a very proud father pinned the Croix de Guerre on his son. Bernard de Lattre, 23 years old, gaunt from the rigors of combat, shows a hint of a smile, standing a head taller than his renowned father.

General de Lattre, proud father, decorates his
cherished son Bernard, May 1951. (ECPAD)

It was about at this time that de Lattre discovered he had liver cancer, but he kept working. Giap's third attack was to test de Lattre as
never before. Ninh Binh was the most advanced position in the de
Lattre line. It lay on the Day River 60 miles south of Hanoi, good
rice country at the edge of Moïs mountainous terrain to the west.
Two of Giap's divisions struck on the night of 28/29 May. Bernard's
unit was one of the first to respond, assaulting and gaining a rocky
point during the night. One of the enemy's first mortar rounds
killed him.

Bernard had been an extraordinary young soldier. At age 14 he had
helped his father escape from a German prison in France, and then he
made his way to North Africa where at age 16 he rejoined his father
and, because he was underage, had to get permission to enlist in the
Free French forces. Later he fought in southern France, was wounded,

and upon recovery fought in Germany, receiving two of France's highest decorations for valor.

The general got the terrible news. He was struck to the core of his being. His only son, the young man he so deeply loved, the young fellow who was well on his way to carrying on the proud de Lattre tradition, was dead. In a dreadful telegram to his wife, now in Paris, he asked forgiveness for not being able to save their son. "The next day he confided to some intimates in a sob, 'Bernard, he did not die for France. They can write that on his cross, but it is not true. Bernard, at Ninh Binh, he died for Viet Nam.'"[29]

In the Battle of Day, de Lattre had again stopped Giap. After that terrible summer of 1951 for the Viets, they never again would pose a serious threat to Hanoi and the fertile delta area. Viet Minh desertions were at an alarming rate, and Giap would have to review his strategy of attacks by main force divisions. Ho even called a meeting of the Central Military Committee and he proposed relieving Giap of his position of commander in chief of the army. Ho seemed to have done this pro forma because the motion was defeated mainly because Ho opposed own proposal. It may have been put on the agenda just to clear the air or perhaps, as Bernard Fall pointed out, "Giap was retained because the erroneous decision to launch the offensive had been made collectively by the whole senior Party hierarchy."[30] This event shows how important military, as well as political, decisions were made, soliciting the advice of the entire Central Military Committee, a practice which carried over into the war against the Americans and South Vietnamese government.

For de Lattre, grieving, quite surely there was no feeling of personal accomplishment. He had fallen in love with Vietnam. He thought the people were courageous, industrious, proud. He had faith in their future, and he had gone a long way toward "Vietnamization," more politically than militarily. Later in Paris at the funeral of Bertrand and two of Bertrand's men who had been killed beside him, struggling with deep sorrow and suppressed passion, the general told the mourners, "For many years the best blood of France was being spilled in Indochina and the people of

France did not acknowledge it. With Lieutenant Bernard de Lattre and his companions, the anonymous dead of the rice paddies have the right to the tears of France."[31]

The general and his wife returned to Hanoi, and he continued with his duties, devastated, ill, but resolute. Giap's Vinh Yen setback, followed by failures up to the Day River debacle, convinced the Chinese advisors that "it was premature for the Viet Minh to achieve a decisive victory through big offensives in a region where the colonial army, close to its base [Hanoi and the Delta] could utilize its superior firepower."[32]

General Westmoreland, 14 years later, before ordering search and destroy in jungles, might well have reviewed de Lattre's tactics of mobile defense of critical areas with significant populations of civilians to protect. But he apparently did not.

Ho and Giap acknowledged that their forces had been insufficiently prepared, and there were to be no more division-size attacks by the Viet Minh for months. They had been severely hurt and needed time to recover. Instead of big unit battles, while they were recuperating and preparing once again for major combat, they shifted for a time to assassinations and guerrilla warfare throughout Vietnam and in northern Laos.

De Lattre showed his appreciation for faithful service to the French Union by decorating men from diverse nationalities for their heroism – Moroccan, Vietnamese, Moung. And his efforts at urging the Vietnamese to take charge of their own future took a step forward on 14 July when the Bao Dai government announced the official birth of the Vietnamese National Amy and decreed general mobilization. In execution the draft had its weaknesses, with many, but not all, sons of powerful and rich men finding ways to avoid service, but it was an important step forward.

In the fall, Giap's 312th Division was attacking villages and outposts around Nghia Lo in the High Region 100 miles northwest of Hanoi, and Salan responded with parachute assaults. In November de Lattre parachuted units into Hoa Binh on the Black River 40 miles southwest of Hanoi in an effort to interdict enemy north-south communication at the point which became one of the most important funnels for personnel and materiel on the later-named Ho Chi Minh Trail. Mobile units now operated outside the de Lattre Line. On 19 November the general came to congratulate the men who had retaken the area. The next day, gravely ill with cancer, he sorrowfully bade goodbye to his staff, and he and his wife lifted off for Paris. Somewhat like the regal MacArthur ten years earlier, he left, promising that he would return. Unlike MacArthur, that was not to be.

*   *   *

In 1951, the obvious strength of the Viet Minh and recognition of this internationally, and the rising success of Red China in gaining influence among global Communist powers had led to official reestablishment of the Communist Party in Vietnam (now Lao Dong) in hopes it could take a greater part on the world stage. Ho was named Chairman and Truong Chinh was selected Secretary General in what was perhaps the beginning of Ho's somewhat diminishing influence, serving more as elder statesman, diplomat and advisor while Truong Chinh and others took on Central Committee duties of establishing policy and seeing that it was carried out.

Continued Guerrilla Warfare in the South

A rising star in the South was Le Duan. Born in north Annam in 1907 to a poor family, as a young man he moved to Tonkin, worked as a railroad clerk and became caught up in anticolonial activities during which he recruited railway workers. He appeared later as a Viet Minh commander in the Mekong Delta. Le Duan was a very different kind of leader from Ho and Giap, both of whom had been well educated in the Mandarin or French traditions. Slight in stature, speaking like the country people he came from, he was basically self-educated and had good common sense and a keen mind. His documents reveal a prodigious intellect, impressive analytic skills, and mastery of language. An early 1930s Party member, he was imprisoned twice for five years each time, first in 1931-1936 like his friend and later right-hand man Le Duc Tho, and again in 1940-1945. Le Duan rose to prominence in the Party due to his courage, patriotic fervor, competence, overall administrative skills, and burning desire to be the top man. His guerrilla strategy made life miserable for the French in parts of the South. By 1951 he was directing political and military operations throughout the South.

Le Duan. (Corbis)

French Foreign Legion

One type of French unit opposing le Duan's guerillas was the legionnaires. In addition to General Delaunay, another Indochina combatant responded to my request for information which I had addressed to the

French Defence Department. General Paul Simonin corresponded with me and sent me his book, *Les Bérets blanc de la légion en Indochine*. He was a lieutenant in 1951 commanding a company of the 13th Demi-brigade of the Foreign Legion. As a career officer, he said, "I did not choose to do only wars that I thought were just. I was only doing my duty to obey. . . . Who were the soldiers who came to fight for a cause of which for the most part they were ignorant? Career military, enlistees from France, North African or Senegalese tirailleurs."[33]

Years earlier, Simonin had been a leader in the Resistance, then served in the Free French forces. To go to Indochina he had to leave behind his wife and three young children. He now had Vietnamese volunteers to command, many of whom were of Khmer (basically Cambodian) origin. They were not authorized to wear the *kepi blanc* – white hat—distinctive of Foreign Legionnaires, but after their training, those who had survived the rigors proudly wore white berets. This privilege marked them as quasi-members of the Legion, not the Vietnamese National Army. Simonin's company was part of a battalion of "juani," yellows, composed of two companies of Vietnamese and two of Khmers. When Legion NCOs and corporals were killed, wounded, or missing and could not be replaced by other legionnaires, the best of the indigenous *berets blanc* could attain these ranks.

Simonin said that de Lattre had stated, "The war in Indochina is not a colonial war; it is a war against Red colonization. We fight for the peace and liberty of the Vietnamese people."[34] With that in mind, Simonin and his men set out to do what they could to defeat the enemy.

This lieutenant's first experiences were in the Mekong Delta, but some months later his whole company with their families and minimal goods was packed onto a barge and after three miserable days off-loaded in Saigon. His mission was to secure the rubber shipments coming south from the Michelin. He established his headquarters at Di An, where I had my first command post in QuarterCav eighteen years later. He was ordered to construct and garrison two new outposts on the east bank of the Saigon and take charge of the area. Like Lieutenant

Delaunay before him, he was to protect both convoys coming south down the road, and river shipments of latex from the Michelin. The 5th Cuir, to which Delaunay had belonged the year before, was still headquartered at nearby Thu Dau Mot, and would provide the mobile reaction force in case of trouble.

The war, now five years old, showed its hand in that the villages along the road that paralleled the Saigon River were gone, "abandoned and burned, as well as the villas of the [French rubber] planters and houses and huts of the Vietnamese, pagodas included."[35] Simonin learned that all posts on Route 13 from Ben Cat north would be rebuilt by the ironically named "Joyeux" battalion—Joyous – young Frenchmen who had been sentenced to prison and were now doing their time in military service in Indochina. Simonin said they didn't inspire him with confidence. Also his confidence was not improved by the fact that his posts would border the forest of Anson which was known to be a vast complex of enemy tunnels. In my time, we called this area the Iron Triangle, still laced with tunnels but denuded of trees by huge Rome plows intended to expose the enemy, probably the sons and daughters of the ones who occupied the tunnels in Simonin's day. When Simonin set about his work in 1951 there was nothing in his area to show for five years of sacrifices on both sides of the war except scars on the landscape and hatred in the people.

A Legionnaire in the Michelin Plantation

Legionnaire lore included the story of General François de Negrier who in 1893 had addressed legionnaires on their way to Tonkin to fight Chinese, and many of them took to heart his famous saying: "You, you Legionnaires are soldiers in order to die, and I am sending you where one dies." In 1951 a Brit who had been in the Royal Navy enlisted in the French Foreign Legion and served for two years of a four year enlistment. He had been well indoctrinated. He said in his excellent 1955 book, *In Order to Die*, "It was part of the Legion's job to get killed."[36]

By strict custom, in telling of adventures, no legionnaire must ever divulge the true names of himself, his comrades, or dates, times, or places of events which could result in retribution on the participants – in many cases, severe, even deadly. To write his compelling book this young man used the pseudonym Henry Ainley. His tales are of particular interest to me because, as was the case with Simonin, the actions were in places I came to know well some 18 years later.

Soon after arrival at regimental headquarters in the Cu Chi-Ben Suc-Hoc Mon area northwest of Saigon, Ainley heard gory tales of legionnaires who had been captured and hideously tortured during slow, agonizing deaths. Soon he learned that this happened on both sides. He said, "The next two years were to confirm what I sensed the first day. Torture and brutality were routine matters in the questioning of suspects, and frequently I was obliged to be an unwilling and disgusted witness, powerless to intervene. Unfortunately, brutality and bestiality were not exclusively reserved for official suspects. Rape, beating, burning, torturing of entirely harmless peasants and villagers were of common occurrence in the course of punitive patrols and operations by French troops, throughout the length and breadth of Indochina."[37]

Although assigned as secretary to a battalion commander because he could read, write, and speak French, which few men in the Legion could do proficiently, he also was posted to guard duty and patrols. On one of the latter which an Armenian sergeant led, the sergeant methodically robbed some peasant women and children of whatever "little money and odd bits of jewelry they had. The last . . . was a girl of about sixteen, who had been trying to hide in a corner. . . [He] stretched out his hand and with a violent downward wrench ripped open her jacket and tore down her trousers . . . . Without thinking, I grabbed him by the shoulder, pulled him off the girl and told him he couldn't do that. . . . I realized that I had laid my hands on a superior and the consequence could be terrible. [The sergeant] was so amazed that he finally burst out laughing and in the friendliest way told me that I would soon get used to a little friendly rape."[38] Soon the sergeant and others were busy burning down the hamlet and stealing chickens and pigs.

Ainley took no comfort in such behavior, but when his unit moved on and came upon a horrible massacre at one of the French Union posts. "The NCO and the two Légionnaires, who had been in command of the native auxiliaries, were dead and had been beheaded by machetes, a dozen of the auxiliaries dead and a score wounded. . . . Several of the auxiliaries womenfolk had been scalped or ripped open or both, and three were dead, as well as two small children. . . . One of the women who had been ripped open was pregnant; she was not dead, and in her arms she held a small child half of whose scalp was missing."[39]

The war in the North was having a serious effect on Ainley's battalion. "We still hadn't received the reinforcements we had hoped for. . . . The new troops arriving from Africa were all vitally needed for the Regiment's two battalions in Tonkin, and to supplement four other regiments of Foreign Legion infantry and parachutists who had been suffering heavy and consistent losses [there]. The rare driblets effected to our battalion were those too old or too untried to be of any use for the heavy fighting up North. . . ."[40]

After two years, Ainley was hospitalized with physical and mental fatigue, and eventually evacuated back to France. He reflected on why he had joined the Legion: "I had fondly imagined that the Indochinese war was an all-out effort to protect an innocent people against the unwelcome attentions of the communists. . . . Not even in my wildest dreams had I realised that I was to become part of a mercenary army deliberately trained to devastate. The men of the Foreign Legion were first-class soldiers, but they had nothing whatsoever to do with a mission of pacification and political re-education. The Foreign Legion was brilliant at two things—killing and dying well, both of which the Légionnaires did frequently and with *éclat*. But that had little to do with protecting the quiet little yellow men who surrounded us, hated us cordially and occasionally got around to murdering us when they saw the chance."[41]

*   *   *

Another person to tell his story involving terrain I flew over many times was General Guy Simon who served as a lieutenant and captain from 1951-56 in the fertile rubber plantation and rice cultivation area between Bien Hoa and Xuan Loc. He was an officer with a battalion of Moïs tribesmen recruited from the jungles of War Zone D. Their conduct was another example of why the war could not be won by the French. His book tells of his tirailleurs (infantrymen) going on a foraging mission. "The crime of the [local cultivators of rice] was habitual to a region not controlled by us and which furnished rice to armed roving bands [of Viet Minh]; for punishment we had burned their villages, flooded their rice (because it was difficult to burn), broken their jars, confiscated their chickens and ducks, killed their pigs, and driven the people on leashes to the village of Trang Bom which offered them some thatched roof huts [as part of the 'pacification' program]. Needless to say that the Moïs tirailleurs, who hated [Vietnamese], do not pray to 'convert' the Viet Minh cultivators of the region."[42]

In 1951, helicopters played an increasing role. Drawing on American and their own seminal experiences in Korea, the French in Indochina found air medevac much in demand. Captain Valérie André, a member of the French Resistance, was not only a neurosurgeon but parachutist and helicopter pilot, the first woman to fly a helicopter in combat. She flew some of her first missions out of Tan Son Nhut and also Bien Hoa Airbase where in 1968 I was the senior staff officer of 11th Armored Cavalry Regiment. Her flights took her into War Zone D which I often flew over in my helicopter and in which I several times landed to assist in the actions below me. To have such high level skills as hers available on the spot where a soldier had been seriously wounded was very special to the troops. After many hazardous missions around Tan Uyen, northeast of Bien Hoa in War Zone D, she traveled to the Central Highlands far to the north. One of her missions there took her to the northern Laotian boondocks where at a tiny post a man was gravely ill and could not be moved by road. If she had had a helicopter available, she could have flown in, but there was none, so she got a ride out on a cargo plane and parachuted down alone, landing in the small drop zone only a few meters from a sergeant. A lieutenant trotted up and scolded the sergeant, "'What are you waiting for to help the doctor?'

"Bewilderment paralyzed the sergeant.

"'But lieutenant,' he stammered, 'I expected a different kind.'"[43]

Serving two tours in Indochina, Captain André was acclaimed for her courageous rescues under fire and surgical skills in several parts of Vietnam, Laos, and Cambodia and went on to become modern France's first female general.

* * *

In December 1951, as the end of the year approached, Giap attacked the Hoa Binh area southwest of Hanoi with two divisions in an attempt to open up a major route to the South. Salan, now both interim High Commissioner and Supreme Commander, reinforced his defending units by dropping paratroopers. Among them was the 1st Vietnamese Parachute Battalion which got its baptism under fire fighting other Vietnamese. So the year ended in Tonkin much as it had begun, with Salan conducting sweeps inside the de Lattre line, Giap attacking with main forces while guerrilla war was ongoing everywhere, and the French defending and consolidating their positions through "pacification."

1952: U.S. Raises Its Ante

The new year in France opened in the National Assembly on 3 January with addresses by Prime Minister Plevin and Minister of the Associated States, Jean Letourneau. The U.S. embassy in Paris reported to Department of State: "These statements . . . set forth French government policy toward Indochina. They show the present preoccupation . . . with [negotiations to end the Korean War and] a conjectured Chinese Communist invasion of Indochina.... They indicate that the French Government has no present intention of abandoning Indochina and that it considers that Indochina must stay in the French Union. They reject, although not categorically so, any idea of negotiation with Ho Chi-Minh. . . . It was important that France's allies realize that the French effort in other areas must depend upon the French effort made in Indochina. . . . The only sentiment for negotiation came from the Communist side."[44]

The statement about France's allies reflected a continuing U.S. concern for the level and strength of the French commitment to defense of Europe within the NATO alliance. This fostered an increase in U.S. financial and military aid for Indochina.

On 12 January France's Defence Minister shocked a country which had been ill-prepared to receive the news. De Lattre was dead. "General de Lattre de Tassigny has given everything to his country—his victories, his son, and his life."[45] On that same day the National Assembly posthumously elevated him to the rank of Marshal of France. Dignitaries from around the world would attend his grand state funeral, with pallbearers to include Field Marshal Bernard L. Montgomery and General of the Army Dwight D. Eisenhower. And on the day de Lattre died, the Viet Minh cut the supply lines to the French forces in Hoa Binh despite the French command's earlier insistence they could hold that position indefinitely.

The question of Communist China invading Indochina continued to play a large role in U.S. thinking. On 30 January U.S. Ambassador Donald R. Heath in Saigon cabled that he had said to Bao Dai, "At present time only Fr[ench] Union forces kept Vietnam from becoming Chi[nese] Colony."[46]

A top secret State Department policy study report of 11 February 1952 said that U.S. objectives were "to prevent Indochina (as well as Southeast Asia as a whole) from passing into the Communist orbit, to assist the Indochinese people to develop the will and ability to resist Communism from within and without and thereby to contribute to the strengthening of the free world. . . . General Juin [French Army Chief of Staff] informed General Bradley [U.S. Army Chairman of Joint Chiefs of Staff]. . . that the forces of the French Union and the Associated States could liquidate the Viet Minh in about eighteen months provided that:

a. Chinese assistance to the Viet Minh was not increased significantly beyond its present level;
b. U.S. assistance to French Union forces arrived on schedule; and
c. no massive Chinese intervention materializes."[47]

In 1952, troops of the Vietnamese National Army were doing reasonably well. Ambassador to France David K. E. Bruce cabled on 12 February that a fact-finding mission from the French government to Indochina "was particularly impressed with progress made in formation Vietnamese National Army, excellent results obtained by this army in pacification work and satisfactory manner in which Vietnamese units have performed against Viet Minh in Tonkin. Chief problems said to be cadres but mission considered Vietnam Army gave hopes for future."[48]

French evacuation of their untenable position at Hoa Binh on 22 February was a strong indication that 1952 was not going to be *"l'année du Salan"* as the previous year had been "The Year of de Lattre." In France, the new government of Prime Minister Edgar Faure fell in less than two months, succeeded in March by that of Antoine Pinay. The U.S. National Intelligence Estimate of 3 March was also not much comfort: "There has been little significant change in the political situation within Vietnam, the most important of the Associated States, . . . and the factors discussed [in the preceding estimate] which limit the development of a strong Vietnamese government still apply. The death of General de Lattre has had an adverse effect upon Vietnamese morale as have the suspicions of the Vietnamese that the French may be weakening in their determination and ability to defend Indochina. We believe that the spirits of the Viet Minh leaders have been raised by the recent death of General de Lattre, the expanded scale of Chinese Communist assistance, the debilitating effect which the sustained Viet Minh offensive has had upon the French, the reoccupation of Hoa Binh by the Viet Minh and their discernment of a weakening Franco-Vietnamese will to resist. The consolidation of Communist control within the Viet Minh area continues and has effectively countered internal opposition. The food shortage is being alleviated by rice gained from within the French perimeter. There is no evidence of serious friction between the Viet Minh and the Chinese Communists."[49]

The intelligence estimate proved to be optimistic. The National Government of Vietnam was now changing prime ministers almost as quickly as was France itself. In June its fifth head in four years took the uncertain reins of state. Despite some decent performances by units of its army, the government could not excite the admiration or support of the people to any degree approaching that of Ho's DRV. In France, anti-war sentiment continued. But counter-arguments pointed to unrest in other colonial areas—Madagascar, Syria, Lebanon, Tunisia, Algeria, Morocco, and others. If France gave the impression it was being driven out of Indochina, would that not give hope to revolutionary movements elsewhere? Besides, the United States categorically rejected negotiation from a position of weakness in Indochina.

The Nature of the Soldier and Citizen, North and South

A view of ARVN General Tran Van Don may be appropriate at this point, given that a Vietnamese national government of sorts and a Vietnamese national army had been in existence for a few years, both of which had been receiving increasing U.S. aid. General Don held high military and government posts in South Vietnam beginning in 1963, to include finally being commander of ARVN and Minister of Defense. He had grown up in Saigon and the Mekong Delta where the year-around favorable climate made production of food easy. Virtually no one went hungry. On his first trip to the North as a boy with his father in 1935 he saw how different were the conditions. "Instead of the gentle monsoon, which gives a warm 'tropical paradise' feeling to life for southern rich and poor alike, the northern wind produces cold and highly disagreeable weather. I have seen peasant girls standing up to their bare knees in rice paddies in January planting rice, bravely suffering the effects of both low temperature and chilling winds. Their more frugal existence and more difficult life make the northern people 'harder.' Used to the perversity of nature and frequent privation of insufficient food, the North Vietnamese have a quite different attitude toward life than we do in the South. They work harder, endure more, and know less of creature comfort. It is no wonder that they were able to fight so courageously and continuously over so many years while living an austere and cheerless existence."[50]

Self-criticism and the Three-man Cell

Colonel Bui Tin explained a development in the Viet Minh that, despite aspects which many of its practitioners quietly despised, nevertheless seemed to enhance their fighting capabilities: "From the beginning of 1952, every unit had to set up three-man cells. Each evening after they had eaten, these cells had to examine together their actions during the day. Every member . . . had to reveal his fears of hunger, hardship and death as well as his thoughts of envy, lust or enjoyment. This system was said to be necessary to maintain discipline, but it weighed heavily on human dignity and the personality of the individual who was always forced into repentance."[51]

"Criticism and self-criticism was just something we had to cope with. There was no sincerity involved. You criticize me so I criticize you as strongly; you forgive me so I do the same."[52] This technique of self-criticism was the last point in the ten-point pledge that Giap's first 34 fighters took in 1944: "To use self-criticism for personal improvement."[53]

The three-man cell was the lowest unit in the Viet Minh's tripartite arrangement for its combat units – three regiments to a division, three battalions to a regiment, and so on down the chain. At the lowest level the closeness of three men, forced or not, paid off in combat. One took care of another both during heavy fighting and in periods of rest and recuperation. This is well documented in prisoner of war accounts: "From induction, each soldier was taught that his three-man collective team was more important than his individual rights or desires. . . . the three-man cell forced a bonding akin to brotherhood, which was essential for coping with fear in battle and boredom in camp." An NVA private first class said, " The three-man cell was very helpful to me. For example, during the infiltration south, the other men in the cell gave me a lot of assistance such as carrying my gun and ammunition and other items for me when I was tired or sick. The attitude of the other men in the cell was so encouraging that I was even more determined to endure the hardships in order to arrive in the South." A three-year veteran said, "When I was wounded the first time on an operation, the other two men helped me to get out from the battlefield."[54]

This system endured to the end of the American war. I first heard of it in 1968 from prisoners, and at the time I read several accounts of it in our prisoner of war reports.

Late 1952, Early 1953, A New Front in the High Region

Ho and Giap changed strategy, and this was to have profound effect on the course of the war. Despite what seemed like insurmountable hardships, Ho's government had strengthened its support among the populace from north to south. It also had been able to improve the training and equipping of all aspects of the military – main force, regional and local units, and guerrillas. Now was the time, Ho and Giap believed, to open a new front. It would be in the High Region of Tonkin, the Tay Bac, that rugged mountainous area that stretched from southwest of Hanoi north to the Chinese border and west to Laos. Giap had seen some of this country in 1939 on his way to China, right after he left his first wife, Thai, to participate fully in Communist activities, never to see her again. He and Pham Van Dong, the future prime minister in Ho's government, surreptitiously had taken a train from Hanoi all the way up the Red River Valley to Lao Cai near the Chinese border. There they abruptly left the train to avoid the police and walked the rest of the way into China where they met Ho.

In 1944 French special forces detachments had parachuted into the High Region to recruit indigenous Montagnard tribes to fight the Japanese, and they had landed at the rudimentary Dien Bien Phu airstrip. After the Japanese surrender, these detachments continued to make headway in recruiting Montagnards, mainly T'ai, and forming them into meagerly armed units. Many of the hill people in this vicinity blamed Vietnamese for racial discrimination that forced them out of the fertile valleys into the hills. In 1953, while Viet Minh guerrilla and main force actions were making headlines elsewhere, many small French posts, supplied almost entirely by air, remained operating in the High Region despite Viet Minh harassment. Dien Bien Phu was not one of them. Salan had withdrawn the French outpost, and the village was soon occupied by his enemy.

Not all High Region indigenous people supported the French. In September 1952 while Ho had attended a meeting at military headquarters in the Viet Bac, he met with his commanders and staff as they prepared for the campaign which would take them through Montagnard tribal country to the west. Historically, the Viet Minh had been highly successful in recruiting tribal groups in the Viet Bac; now they had to turn their attention westward. He spoke to the group of the critical nature of behavior among the minority people: "The Government has issued policies concerning the national minorities; you and the troops must implement them correctly. This is a measure to win over the people, frustrating the enemy's scheme of 'using Vietnamese to harm Vietnamese.' We must so do that each fighter becomes a propagandist. You must behave in such a way that the people welcome you on your arrival and give you willing aid during your stay and miss you on your departure."[55] Generally this dictum guided the behavior of main force units throughout the long wars, whether among minority or Vietnamese populations, and was a factor in their successes. Ho's guidance had worked reasonably well in the Viet Bac; a significant number of the minority people supported the Viet Minh against the French.

Several signs were good for Giap. In France, the financial and human toll after more than seven years of war, and strong anti-war sentiments, resulted in the government's decision in May to decrease the effective strength of its Indochina force by 15,000 men.[56] Then too his forces had been able to feed, clothe, and equip themselves on the periphery of the de Lattre Line in the Delta even though the French controlled the richest rice land. Could they not do the same if a large part of its main forces were to move west?

Such a move would have three main advantages. First, it would "liberate" the region and threaten Laos, which hopefully would lead to a much easier route for supplying the South, down along the Mekong through rich Laotian rice lands instead of south through the rugged central mountains of Annam while trying to evade French blocking forces.

Second, it could require the French to commit large mobile forces far from their bases near Hanoi and Haiphong. The French would have to move them into mountainous terrain which highly favored the Viet Minh. If that happened, those French units would have to be supplied from a great distance by air, and could be isolated and destroyed.

Third, by sucking out French strength from the Delta, the local Viet Minh there would be able to build strength internally and supply more clandestine rice to main force units and the people whose support was so necessary..

A major Viet Minh move to the High Region, though, would be daunting. Giap said, "The way of overcoming this difficulty was to repair the roads in order to use motorized vehicles. And we had to mobilize a large number of *dan cong* (the people who voluntarily took part in the supply to the front). But if the number of *dan cong* increased, the need for food also increased."[57]

That the Viet Minh were able to accomplish their moves is one of the greatest achievements of the war. They repaired roads, especially the one from the China border south to Lai Chau, just north of Dien Bien Phu. It became capable of supporting heavily-laden Chinese trucks. Also, they replaced the earlier backpacks of coolies with sturdy pack-bicycles that could be pushed, each carrying up to ten times as much as a backpack.

Giap's bicycle supply line. (Getty)

In addition, a strategic deception plan worked well. Suddenly on 20 September main force divisions started using different call signs, their old ones still operating in the same places with dummy staff. This deception would enable regiments of the 308th and 312th Divisions to begin a move west and position themselves for battle, with elements of the 316th and 351st Divisions soon to follow. Separately, for a period, Giap's 149th Independent Regiment garrisoned Dien Bien Phu.

Salan and the base aéroterrestre

The French were not entirely fooled by Giap's moves, especially after cracking the new radio code, and in October 1952 having their base at Nghia Lo, deep in the hills east of Dien Bien Phu, fall to the 312th Division. "To counter the threat . . . Salan initiated the concept of the *base aéroterrestre*, a distant air-ground base with a usable landing strip that could be improved and was placed in a strategic location out of which his forces could reconnoiter and attack enemy units, diminishing the threat of a move on Laos. The base would be a logistics center, resupplied by air, to support attacks from it against the enemy's lines of communication. [In November 1952] he put the first such base at Na San in a small valley opening, some 150 air miles west of Hanoi."[58] Salan also reinforced the position at Lai Chau, 20 miles north of Dien Bien Phu.

There was no French general who knew Indochina and the Viet Minh better than Salan. In 1924 he was in Tonkin as a lieutenant, traveling from Lang Son to Cao Bang, then 15 kilometers west to a company headquarters at Nguyen Binh where he was assigned as administrative officer under the captain commanding. His district was large and diverse, encompassing two different Montagnard tribes and Vietnamese and Chinese people. He set about learning at least the rudiments of all their languages. Before his arrival he had studied the writings of the French governors and military officers who preceded him, especially of Joseph Gallieni who had commanded in Tonkin as a colonel in the late 19th century. This was the officer who with his "oil spot" technique has influenced counterinsurgency thinking to this day. Within weeks Salan had been asked if he would volunteer for a post in northwest Laos, and his eager response was "*oui!*"[59] For the next 13 years Salan was in colonial administration.

Additionally, Salan had medium and high level command experience in World War II. Near the end of the war he had commanded a Senegalese infantry regiment and then the 9th Colonial Infantry Division (9th DIC). Salan had been back in Indochina almost continuously since October 1945 when Leclerc sent him north to command French Forces in Tonkin and southern China. Later, de Lattre had put him in command of the counterattack at Vinh Yen using two mobile groups and the air force, and Salan had stopped Giap's advance. So by 1952 this general was well experienced in high level command, and he had had many face to face meetings with Giap, and some with Ho. He well knew the terrain and the ways of the Indochinese. When he came up with the concept of the *base aéroterrestre* he had reason to believe that Giap would emerge from the jungle with an attack by a division or two, and thus put his forces in a position to be severely mauled by French artillery, air strikes, and counterattack.

Salan sent several battalions of infantry, some engineers, and artillery units to Na San under a gritty commander, Colonel Jean Gilles. They dug in and erected formidable defenses, inviting a set-piece battle in which the French could bring enormous firepower and counterattack to bear on an exposed enemy. The base, though, turned out to be not much of a threat to Giap's forces. With some difficulty the Viet divisions could bypass it on their way to Laos. Also, the French had a tough time reconnoitering around it in the mountainous terrain, and they suffered casualties from main forces outside that invested the distant fortress.

Although there were never enough troops to conduct pacification operations in the Delta and attack decisively elsewhere, Salan thought he could create a large mobile reserve for use in the High Region by drawing down his sweep forces in the Delta. But Na San, Lai Chau, and the small outposts of the High Region were a long way from Hanoi, and his air resources were strained to supply them. Fortunately for him, aircraft furnished by the U.S. had arrived in increasing numbers. C-119 *Flying Boxcars* and C-47 *Dakotas* for supply and paradrop missions, and B-26 *Invaders* for bombing were replacing the aged JU-52s. F6 *Hellcats* and F8 *Bearcats* for dive-bombing and strafing were welcome improvements.

It seemed Salan had been right about this concept of attracting large enemy formations to attack, then annihilating them. The French at Na San, using heavy air support, beginning at the end of November repelled a two-division Viet Minh attack after four days of bitter fighting and heavy Viet Minh casualties while incurring only moderate losses themselves.

The French GCMA, *Groupement* de *Commandos Mixtes Aéroportés*, had been active in recruiting minority tribesmen in the High Region, and had been highly useful in the Na San defense. A Communist history testified to the effectiveness of the GCMA, organized similar to later U.S. Special Forces in Vietnam. The GCMA operated in extremely hazardous circumstances among the various hill tribes. The history said, "This new force was viewed as the 'backbone' of the effort to collect information and to sabotage resistance facilities and organizations in order to support the final steps of military adventurism that the French would take in the war. . . . In December 1952 the enemy sent [a three-person young female] spy team out to infiltrate into . . . the gateway to our Northwest Region and to our resistance base area. . . . All three of these spies were Catholics. . . . The team's missions were to collect information on resistance headquarters organizations, military units, supply caches, etc., in order to provide targeting information for air strikes. The team was also ordered to obtain information about the defensive deployment of our armed units to support plans by [our] Occupation Headquarters to launch an offensive campaign to capture and occupy Na San and to build a military strong-point at Dien Bien Phu."[60]

✳   ✳   ✳

After being repulsed at Na San, Giap replenished his units and began to move on Laos with three divisions. The French position at Sam Neua in Laos near the northeastern border with Tonkin was garrisoned with 1,700 men. A division was now threatening it, and in mid April 1953 the post commander received orders to destroy what he could and evacuate to the south. The column was ambushed and its Laotian partisans deserted and fled in panic. The French commander had to give the remnants the order to disperse, essentially "every man for himself." Salan countered by applying pressure in the Delta, and Giap, considering his rear and how far he was moving from his support base, halted further advance into Laos. But northeastern Laos was now largely in the hands of the Viet Minh and their Pathet Lao allies.

CHAPTER 7

Dien Bien Phu and the End, mid-1953 - 1954

* * *

LECLERC, DE LATTRE, SALAN—THEY WERE France's best generals. Given their meager resources to commit to such a war, and the terrible conditions in which they had to fight it, they did what they could, and generally did it well. After eight dreadful years, the French government, the French people wanted it to end. No one could know in early 1953 that the end was approaching.

But not as the French hoped.

Geneviève

On 5 May 1953 a young woman, Geneviève de Galard, arrived in Hanoi during her first tour of duty in Indochina. She was born in 1925 into a family that traced its roots back to Clovis in the sixth century. One of her ancestors had ridden in the Crusades and another had fought with Jeanne d'Arc. After the terrible period of German occupation in World War II she could have had an easy life. Instead, she wanted to find some meaningful way to serve others. She said, "I was proud and at the same time eager to prove myself worthy of these famous [ancestors] who had proved their loyalty to their Christian faith, to their native soil, to a spirit of service and honor."[1] She became a nurse and joined *les Convoyeuses de l'air*, the French military flight nurses service.

She had experienced a few days of heat and humidity in Saigon, then flown north. She said, "The climate of Hanoi felt delicious. But I was mostly happy to be sent to Tonkin so soon, where the heaviest fighting was taking place." Her first mission was to Luang Prabang in northern Laos. "We were to evacuate a number of soldiers who had tramped through the brush on an exhausting march of sixty kilometers. They were the survivors of battles at Sam Neua and of the entire region around Luang Prabang."[2] Some of her missions took her to Lai Chau, capital of the T'ai tribes of the area north of Dien Bien Phu deep in the High Region. On her flights to care for the wounded, she was awed by the beauty of the country. "I never ceased admiring the view when the aircraft flew, hedge-hopping, over the Claveau Pass before making a 45-degree right turn to start down the valley toward the airfield at its other end. Along the road that skirted the field, T'ai women walked in single file at their graceful pace, so elegant in their traditional costume, a white top held close by silver hooks, a long skirt of dark fabric, a wide, flat straw hat."[3]

Geneviève also made several trips into Na San evacuating casualties, and one night after a serious battle stayed to help treat the wounded. "That night I had a foretaste of what I would experience, though far more dramatically, ten months later in Dien Bien Phu."[4] She had no idea that her service would require such extreme courage, skill, and devotion.

The Penultimate General

Two days after Geneviève first landed in Hanoi, Prime Minister Mayer announced the appointment of the new Supreme Commander to replace Salan, General Henri Navarre. "Mayer's charge to Navarre seems to have been vague, essentially to go [to Indochina] and create conditions of strength from which France could negotiate an end to this endless war. And by the way, don't expect any reinforcements or increase in budget."[5] Just before the next prime minister, Pierre Mendes-France, took over three weeks later, Mayer publicly stated that the only possible outcome would be by negotiation—a faint echo of General Leclerc's point some seven years earlier?

Navarre had been a cavalryman in World War I, an intelligence officer and regimental commander in World War II, and after the war chief of staff to General Juin, supreme commander of NATO. He had no Indochina experience. Arriving in Vietnam, he soon proclaimed that he saw "light at the end of the tunnel."

General Henri Navarre confers with Chief of
State of Vietnam, Bao Dai, May 1953. (Corbis)

Navarre selected for his commander in the North an artilleryman, General René Cogny, a huge man who had been captured by the Germans at the Maginot Line. Cogny escaped, joined the Resistance, was recaptured and tortured by the Gestapo and sent to Buchenwald from which he barely emerged, virtually a skeleton, and with a severe limp that required him to use a cane for the rest of his life. He was one of de Lattre's men and had commanded a division in Tonkin. In a bitter exchange of recriminations after Dien Bien Phu, the volatile "Cogny would . . . refer to [Navarre] as a freezing, 'air conditioned general' and as a disconcerting 'electronic computer.' [Navarre] was accused of approaching military operations as an intellectual exercise, and of calculating acceptable levels of casualties with cold logic. This quality is certainly unattractive; but it has been shared by many of history's most successful generals, including Napoleon."[6] One might certainly add, and Giap.

Salan had left behind a plan for a *base aéroterrestre* at Dien Bien Phu, and in July Navarre ordered that it be executed. For his base commander Navarre chose another cavalryman, Colonel Christian de Castries, who had a previous tour of duty in 1946 and then in 1951 had led a mobile group under de Lattre in the fighting at Vinh Yen and been wounded. "The combination of Cogny and de Castries seemed ideal – firepower of artillery, mobility of cavalry. Dien Bien Phu, about eleven miles long and five miles wide, was one of the very few valleys – indeed the largest one – in northwest Tonkin that was open enough to accommodate a large force. An added benefit was that it produced much of the rice that supported the Viet Minh troops in the High Region. Additionally, its opium bought Chinese weapons. On the map it appeared that its seizure could seriously handicap Giap's operations there and in Laos."[7] The village was a strategic intersection of three roads, one north 50 miles to China, another west 30 miles to Laos, and the third east 220 miles to Hanoi. All were in poor condition almost all the way, but passable with difficulty.

Navarre's plan for establishing a base at Dien Bien Phu provoked strong objections among some of his staff and commanders. Colonel Dominique Bastiani, a tough paratrooper, warned that "In this country you cannot bar [the enemy from taking a direction]. The Viet goes where he likes – he's proved that well enough in the Delta."[8] The air force pointed out its limited capacity to support an operation 180 air miles from Hanoi. It would need to expend enormous air strike, paratroop drop, and supply lift resources in weather that was often terrible. Cogny, after the French war, adamantly insisted that he had counseled Navarre against such a move, but there is scant evidence of this assertion.

In answering his post-battle detractors, Navarre pointed to Na San's successful defense. The losses of the defenders had been relatively small weighed against the hundreds of enemy bodies found on the barbed wire encircling the position. But the brash Colonel Gilles, who had commanded at Na Son during the battle, stated he had been lucky. Good French soldiering, he said, was only part of the reason for the good results. The rest was due to the bad mistakes made by his enemy. The upshot was, "when in August 1953 Na San was successfully evacuated under pressure in order to concentrate the reserves, this seemed to the Navarre air-conditioned headquarters in far away Saigon assurance that [Dien Bien Phu] would succeed in putting a huge dent in Giap's plans."[9] After all, Navarre would have his air force overhead and his artillery inside Dien Bien Phu. And he was planning for some light tanks to be air-lifted, and aircraft to be based at the airstrip. He would have an excellent mobile strike force capability. The enemy would be punished even more than at Na San. And, if necessary, Dien Bien Phu could be evacuated, like Na San.

Navarre did not envision that "Giap could move five divisions into position around the DBP defenders, little damaged by the many airstrikes directed against them; or that they could be supported by masses of laborers building roads and trails for artillery and supplies; or that when French battalions moved out of DBP on reconnaissance in force missions they would encounter inordinately tough going in the difficult terrain and incur heavy casualties; or that antiaircraft fire from hidden positions would prove deadly against planes trying to land or drop men and supplies; or that the Viet artillery could be dug into the forward slopes of the hills surrounding DBP to provide heavy direct fire onto the airfield; or, incredibly, that this enemy artillery could survive massive counter battery fire and air strikes and itself become dominant."[10]

The Street Without Joy

While preparing for occupation of Dien Bien Phu, Navarre had struck out in several directions: in the Delta and in the South. In July 1953 he claimed a victory in central Annam. The stretch of Route 1 from Hue to Quang Tri consisted of 18 miles of heavily fortified enemy villages, trenches, and tunnels that housed large supply depots and a hospital. For good reason it had earned the moniker, "The Street Without Joy." French convoys and units entering the area had been trapped in a kill zone and took heavy casualties.

For this operation, though, Navarre's attacking ground force initially consisted of six infantry battalions, three companies of amphibians, two artillery groups, and three marine companies. Two paratroop battalions were dropped. The air force furnished 32 C-47s and two groups of B-26 bombers. The navy had a dozen ships offshore for bombardment, and three LSTs, three LCTs and one LCM were used in amphibious assault. All in all this was a huge force against a single Viet Minh regiment. But it was the 95th Regiment, well dug in, one of the very toughest fighting forces in the Viet Minh army.

The attackers faced formidable obstacles. Many sand dunes on the sea side were 60 feet high and extremely difficult to surmount. On the inland side an almost impassable marsh backed up to the road. In the amphibious assault, Legionnaires, Muongs, and Senegalese soldiers became dreadfully seasick and upon landing required time to become usable. In some sectors there was no contact. In others, cuts in the road, pits with poisoned bamboo points, and booby traps, mines, machinegun fire, bazookas, and mortar fire greeted the assault. Ten percent of one parachute battalion was wounded or killed by machine gun fire raking them as they neared the ground. Success was imperative because Route 1 with the parallel railroad was the single easiest means of communication, supply, and troop movement between North and South Vietnam. Most of the fighting was over by dark of the first day, but several more bloody days were required to clean out what could be found of defenders, their weapons and caches of munitions.

A French victory as Navarre claimed? Within a few months the 95th Regiment and its local militia were back at it, mining and cutting the railroad and road and ambushing trains and convoys. Once again, a temporary French success had been gained at the cost of an enormous expenditure of resources and significant losses in killed and wounded.

Evacuation of Na San

Na San had never effectively fulfilled its purpose of cutting Viet Minh communications in the far northwest. Garrisoned with 12,000 men, it ultimately just sat there far from Hanoi, taking casualties from daily forays outside the wire. Cogny needed those men as part of his reserve, and evacuation was fixed for 7 August. The memory of the Route 4 disaster was still painful, so movement by road would be impossible. But to evacuate that many men and their equipment and supplies by airlift would be a huge and risky undertaking. Sixty-five sorties of C-47s daily for four days would be required.

To execute the evacuation, first, a strong force from the garrison attacked the Viet Minh surrounding the base and drove them away. Next, a company of colonial parachutists was flown in to give the impression of reinforcing the garrison, not abandoning it. Then, 700 men of the recruited hill tribes moved in to provide ground security outside the perimeter. The planes began landing empty, one after another, and taking off loaded. For once the enemy seemed not to have gotten advance intelligence and could not react effectively in time. Unfortunately, many of those tribesmen who had assisted the evacuation with their attacks outside the fort would be killed three months later in fighting Viet Minh, and their French leaders slowly tortured to death.

The End: Dien Bien Phu

This part of the French Indochina War basically from the French point of view has been treated in depth by historians in French, English,

Vietnamese and other languages. An excellent place to start is Martin Windrow's book, *The Last Valley: Dien Bien Phu and the French Defeat in Vietnam*. Windrow says his book is a "synthesis of secondary sources." Most of those sources, though, are in French and, as he says, "may therefore not be familiar to Anglo Saxons."[11]

Only an outline of major actions, incorporating testimony of some combatants, should be necessary here. Books by the DBP combatants are powerful testimony to incredible courage, endurance, and concern and care for one's comrades on both sides during mostly miserable, cold, wet weather. No human being should ever have had to face such conditions, but tens of thousands did – the defenders in mud and icy water-filled dugouts on the inner lines of defenses, the attackers in equally horrible artillery dugouts and assault trenches.

American concern over the consequences of a Communist victory were reflected in the September 1953 presidential approval of additional aid for France, and President Eisenhower was somewhat optimistic that the Navarre Plan might work. "Admiral Radford, chairman of the Joint Chiefs of Staff . . . [said] 'this was the first time that the [French] political climate had improved to a point where military success could actually be achieved.'"[12]

Major Marcel Bigeard commanded 6th Colonial Parachute Battalion (6th BPC). He had been in the High Region earlier, leading the 3rd T'ai Battalion, and had parachuted into "The Street Without Joy," as well as several other such exotic places. He was renowned as a tough fighter in World War II, coming up the ranks from private to major, and everyone knew him by his WWII radio call sign, "Bruno." On the evening of 19 November 1953, as he recalled in his memoirs, "Officers, NCOs, men were proud and happy. A fine new mission. For me to see again that picturesque village so calm and welcoming where I had landed in a Dakota seven years earlier. What would we find for our reception committee?" Major Bigeard was thinking of the Viet Minh who had taken over when the French closed down that small outpost some time earlier.

"The intelligence was fuzzy," he said. "The 148th Viet Minh Regiment lay some fifty kilometers to the northwest."[13]

At daylight on 20 November 1953 a command and control C-47 Dakota bearing three generals – two army, one air force – circled over the village of Muong Thanh, the T'ai name for Dien Bien Phu. They were concerned about the *crachin*, the persistent ground fog of the High Region that on the best of days did not begin to burn off until about an hour after dawn, often much later or not at all on some days. In Hanoi, 65 Dakotas had sat for almost two hours, loaded with paratroopers, burdened with the backpack of their main chute and the reserve pack on their chest, below which was strapped a knapsack to which was attached their personal weapon, ready pockets of ammunition, some changes of clothes and personal items. At 8:15 AM the command aircraft over Dien Bien Phu radioed the go-ahead, and the planes began trundling down the runway, one after another. In the air they took assault formation. As they flew over the High Region, Bigeard looked down. "Viewed from on high, it was beautiful with all those mountains so green. If we could remain up here, us, we paratroopers, life would be much simpler." They had been flying for almost two hours, much of it in the windy conditions that prevailed over the mountains. Bigeard said, "Crammed into the Dakotas, flying three by three, the wingtips some 30 meters from one another, some men were pale, others vomiting."[14] Those of us who were paratroopers well know this experience as the plane bounces through rough winds. You just want to get out and get the firm earth under your feet again no matter who might be down there to greet you.

Finally the commands: *Stand up—Hook up—Check your equipment—Shuffle to the door* ----- *(LOUD BUZZER)—GO!*

Suddenly dozens, then several dozens, then hundreds of parachutes descended. As they neared the ground Bigeard's troopers began receiving fire. He heard rounds zipping by him. His battalion medical officer was shot dead in his harness before he landed.

Paratroopers descending to establish Dien
Bien Phu, 20 November 1953. (NARA)

Bréche, as he was called—Major Bréchignac—with his 2nd Battalion, 1st Parachute Light Infantry Regiment (2/1 RCP), was close behind Bigeard dropping on another nearby landing zone, encountering no enemy resistance. When the empty Dakotas returned to Hanoi they loaded up with Major Jean Souquet's 1st Colonial Parachute Battalion (1st BPC) and dropped them at about 1600 hours into a secure landing zone. By nightfall about 2,700 men, French and their Vietnamese comrades, were on the ground, and the initial objectives were secure.

The units that had jumped that day were the headquarters of 1st Airborne Group (GAP 1), its three parachute battalions, a company of engineers, and two batteries of artillery. Casualties on the French side were 15 killed, 34 wounded, 13 jump injuries. The enemy had lost 115 uniformed dead and four prisoners.[15] When the first paratroopers were jumping to reestablish Dien Bien Phu, this time as a major French fortified position, a poll in France was showing that only 15 percent of the people favored prosecuting the war toward military victory.[16]

On the second and third day, three more paratroop battalions dropped, along with their headquarters (GAP 2), and other units. Sufficient repairs had been made to the landing strip so that General Cogny could land for an inspection visit. About 4,650 troops were now present, and reconnaissance in force units began thrusting out into the surrounding hills. On the next day, the 1st T'ai Partisan Mobil Group (GMPT 1), marched into the garrison, and the first bulldozer arrived by parachute. On the sixth day the first DC-47 Dakota landed and the airbase became operational with a control headquarters. On that same day, two Viet Minh divisions were identified moving toward DBP. It appeared that the *base aéroterrestre* concept had proven successful in attracting enemy main forces into a classic open pitched battle which would give the French a decided advantage.

The base was now beginning to take the shape it would finally reach. The central position was in the village itself on the western bank of a small river, the Nam Youm, and on that side and across the river, atop small hills were strongpoints. To the south by three and a half miles was Isabelle, a second smaller, virtually independent position with its own airstrip. In a few weeks, joining the infantry and artillery in that position, would be a company of ten tanks which were flown in disassembled, then reassembled.

On 29 November, Navarre and Cogny landed along with U.S. Major General Thomas Trapnell, the third commander of Military Assistance Advisory Group (MAAG) which had been in existence since 1950. All of them liked what they saw, an increasingly impregnable position. High level government and military visits would continue for the next four months.

While DBP continued to build, Giap kept the French occupied elsewhere. Viet Minh units pressed the French in both the Delta and in central Annam with regional units and guerrilla forces. Pressure in Cochinchina by guerrilla actions continued. Elements of two Viet Minh divisions struck west from Annam into Laos and by 26 December had captured Tha Ket on the Mekong. Navarre had to withdraw Bigeard's and Bréchignac's parachute battalions from DBP plus three parachute battalions from the Delta and commit them to Laos. Tha Ket was retaken in January but French casualties were high, and significant French Union forces were tied down far from either DBP or the Delta.

On 5 January 1954, Giap arrived at a forest headquarters nine miles north of Dien Bien Phu to take personal command. His cave bunker would be expanded until it comprised a large complex of underground tunnels with several feet of overhead rock cover. About at this time, two ominous developments were reported by French intelligence. One was that 37mm antiaircraft guns were arriving around DBP, and they would put airstrip use and parachute drops in considerable jeopardy. The other was the phenomenal success in the face of enormous obstacles that the enemy engineers (Vietnamese and Chinese) were having in improving roads for use by Chinese-supplied trucks.

Of the U.S. visitors and short-term advisors to the French at DBP, to include Lieutenant General John W. O'Daniel, the new head of MAAG, none is recorded to have expressed strong pessimism as to whether DBP could be successfully defended.

On 20 January Navarre launched a major operation in Annam, Operation Atlante, a planned six-month drive to trap large Viet Minh forces. Although the major troops to be used were those of the National Vietnamese Army (VNA), this operation, long in planning, took air and airborne assets away from DBP. It was in several respects a test for that army. They failed. "On 26 March [Navarre] admitted in a letter to General Paul Ely, Chief of Defence Staff: 'It is now clear that, however skeptical I was when Monsieur Pleven asked my opinion on the possibility of the Vietnamese relieving us in the short term, I was still too optimistic. They are incapable of doing anything serious for several years yet.'"[17] These nationalist Vietnamese units were no match for the Viet Minh who had long since proven to be a formidable foe.

A diplomatic development would have major impact on the coming battle. On 25 January, the Big Four (U.S., Britain, France, Soviet Union) met in Berlin to discuss Korea and Indochina. They agreed to meet again in April to begin a wider conference at Geneva. This dramatically raised the DBP stakes. A military victory before Geneva, after nine exhausting years of war, would give the winning side enormous bargaining power. This meant that Giap would have to attack so fiercely he would overrun the position whereas Navarre would have to defend so successfully that the five Viet Minh divisions would be *hors de combat* and the Communists might be inclined to settle on terms more favorable to France. Thus the Navarre Plan would have succeeded.

By late February, although adjustments would be made as the battle progressed, Dien Bien Phu had taken essentially its final shape with strongpoints on the small hills surrounding the central position and airstrip, and a heavily fortified Isabelle position to the south. Before the battle was over, the main position in the north and Isabelle together would be defended by seven parachute battalions, ten infantry battalions, an armored cavalry company, all or elements of seven mortar/artillery battalions, all or elements of two engineer battalions, three commando groups, several medical teams, and three communication companies from the army. From the air force there was an airbase control detachment, fighter group, two artillery observation groups, and a signal company. Supporting units included maintenance, supply, transportation, traffic and provost, and postal personnel. Bernard Fall put the total French Union strength as of 13 March at 10,814, and subsequent airborne reinforcements at 4,291 to total 15,105 plus 2,440 Viet Minh prisoners, men who had been kept for long periods for menial and medical duties. Many of them performed faithfully and heroically for their French captors. Other sources put the total at somewhat over 16,000.

Farther out from the French positions, overlooking the valley, were numerous larger hills, and dug into their forward slopes with camouflaged openings were Viet Minh artillery positions. Many of these had direct line of sight to the two airfields. The gunners could look through the cannon bores and see the airstrips beyond. They had put out aiming stakes and plotted data for their targets, from which they would make adjustments after the command to fire. Near the French positions were four enemy divisions and one independent regiment, dug in and camouflaged as they were digging trenches, meter by meter, for their advance closer to the French positions. Giap confirmed that these trenches came within 10-15 meters of the French defenses. Combatants from both sides could and did lob grenades at one another. In support was Giap's reinforced 351st Heavy Division consisting of an engineer regiment, a heavy weapons regiment, two artillery regiments, an antiaircraft regiment, and a field rocket unit. The planning and effort it took to emplace and support all this, so far from populated centers, across such poor roads and trails, across rivers and streams through such difficult mountain terrain, is one of the greatest feats of modern warfare. Each of Giap's divisions had about five to six thousand men at full strength, supported by impressed or volunteer civilian labor in strength from 100,000 to 300,000 according to times of use and various sources.[18]

Giap Attacks

On 13 March 1954 at 5 PM, ringing the hills and looking down, were at least 30,000 combatants, probably more. Looking up toward them were about half that number – not bad odds for the dug-in French, considering their powerful artillery and air.

Or so it seemed.

Upon command, FIRE, the Viet lanyards were pulled and some seconds later the ground around the French erupted in a hellish din. A fight to the finish had begun.

That night and for several more days and nights the fighting was vicious. Bigeard's men, supported by tanks, were able to open the road to Isabelle in heavy fighting. A Vietnamese parachute battalion was dropped to bolster the defenses. Artillery replacements parachuted into Isabelle. De Castries busied himself keeping in contact with Hanoi, calling for support while Lieutenant Colonel Pierre Langlais took de facto control of operations. With French positions being overrun, Bigeard was given command of several units and counterattacked. The T'ai battalion at strongpoint Anne-Marie deserted. Early on, the air force had succeeded in landing some C-47s for supply and evacuation of wounded, but the antiaircraft fire was getting more vicious.

Geneviève de Galard's medevac Dakota flew in at night, wounded were quickly loaded, and she was off again. That night and on succeeding days and nights, several aircraft were shot out of the sky. Geneviève came in on another night mission and due to miscommunication, the ambulances were not at the airfield. The enemy shelling became so intense the pilot had to take off without the wounded, and Geneviève was crushed, knowing the despair those men must have felt. Back in Hanoi she wrote to her mother, hoping that the letter "would help her understand that if I didn't return, I did not die for nothing."[19]

On 28 March at 4:15 AM she was off again to Dien Bien Phu. In terrible visibility the pilot made two approaches but had to pull up both times since the airstrip was not under him. He was able to land on the third attempt, but the plane skidded off the landing strip and into some barbed wire. The wounded were hurriedly loaded, and just as they were to take off, the mechanic reported that the oil reservoir had been punctured and the tank was empty. No oil pressure. "There was no way we were going to be leaving," Geneviève said. Nothing to do but unload the wounded.

The crachin cleared around 10:00 AM and the Viet artillery zeroed in, hitting the plane on the fourth round. Hanoi said she could fly out on the next aircraft. In the meantime she visited wounded, cheered them up, and took their letters to be posted when she got back to Hanoi. At the command post she met de Castries, who greeted her amicably. She helped out at the underground hospital where desperately wounded men turned to her in their last gasps of breath. Then days went by and no plane landed. More strongpoints fell, and the flow of wounded and dying at times overwhelmed her and the medical staff. The fighting was fierce and virtually continuous. Finally it became apparent that the airspace and landing strip were so dangerous no more planes would be able to land.

Geneviève was trapped.

*　　*　　*

In June of 2009 I received an email from General Delaunay asking if I would help Geneviève de Galard get her book published in English in America. It had been published in French on the 50th anniversary of the fall of Dien Bien Phu and been awarded the *Grand Prix de l'Académie des sciences morales et politiques*. For decades she had resisted many efforts to get her to tell her story, but finally "her boys," the veterans of Dien Bien Phu, had prevailed upon her.

I knew about Geneviève de Galard. While I was a second year cadet at West Point I had read about her in accounts of the battle. In 1954 the whole world had known about her. Teletype, radio, and television carried the news daily to those who were fixed on Dien Bien Phu.[20] Everyone wanted to know more about the incredibly heroic little nurse, the only French woman in the battle.[21] Offers poured into the command post for rights to her story.[22] Geneviéve, trying to save the men who could be saved, and giving the kind of comfort only a woman could give to the dying, ignored these distractions and kept working, sometimes going out with a helmet clapped on her head to positions at strongpoints under fire to do what she could.

Geneviève de Galard atop a berm at Dien
Bien Phu. (Courtesy Geneviève de Heaulme)

Last Throes

From 1 April, Dien Bien Phu continued to receive reinforcing paratroopers, with some landing behind the enemy who killed or captured them. Week after week went by with desperate fighting, the Viet Minh capturing the airfield and slowly progressing toward the central position. A strongpoint would fall, and Bigeard would counterattack. Then another, and he would do it again. Airborne reinforcements continued to trickle in through the antiaircraft fire and shelling. The losses on both sides were appalling. Viet Minh morale had plummeted, and desertion now became a serious problem. The French, with no evacuation possible, could do nothing about their situation other than continue to defend fiercely and keep as many wounded alive as possible. But Giap could. He had freedom to slow the pace of attacks, give some rest to units, and come up with something to buck up spirits. In typical Giap fashion, when things were not going well, there was always "the right" to blame. "*A rightist and negative tendency* appeared among our officers and men, in various forms: fear of casualties, losses, fatigue, difficulties and hardships, underestimation of the enemy, subjectivism and self-conceit." The Political Bureau of the Party Central Committee came up with an immediate psychological program, and Giap was the target of severe criticism and maneuvering to replace him. He narrowly managed to hang on to his position, and "after this conference, a campaign of ideological education and struggle was launched from the Party committee to the cells, from officers and soldiers and in all combat units." As a result, "all the Party members, officers and men had more confidence in the final victory and an unshakeable will to destroy the enemy completely."[23]

That episode, coming in the midst of this horrendous battle, reflects how well the Communist manifesto of independence and freedom was able to appeal to the most basic instincts of an enormous number of Vietnamese, not just the men on the line in the worst days of DBP, but throughout the country. Victory was so near it must not be allowed to slip out of their hands through lack of understanding of the goal and resolve to reach it. With renewed energy, the Viet Minh divisions at DBP pressed home their attack.

On the day the Geneva Conference opened, 26 April, fifty aircraft were struck and three shot down. Still, a small number of Foreign Legion paratroopers were successfully dropped on Isabelle. Cold monsoon rains left mud in the trenches and dugouts up to three feet deep. By 4 May it was patently obvious what would be the fate of the defenders, yet paratroopers were still trying to reinforce. De Castries reported the circumstances to Hanoi, closing with: "The situation of the wounded is particularly tragic. They are piled on top of each other in holes that are completely filled with mud and devoid of any hygiene."[24] On 5 May a few qualified paratroopers dropped, and on 6 May some more of 1st Colonial Parachute Battalion, half of whom were Vietnamese. Between 1,800 and 2,600 (depending on the source cited) paratroopers had dropped in the last days, all volunteers. "Of these, about 700 unqualified volunteers would actually be dropped during April and early May, the great majority making their first jump over Dien Bien Phu."[25] All most certainly knew what fate awaited them, but they jumped anyhow.

The CIA, successor to the OSS, had covertly set up a supposedly civilian company to fly C-119 Flying Boxcars for the French. On 6 May, James B. McGovern, a WWII American ace fighter pilot called "Earthquake McGoon" because of his huge size and brash personality, was flying his 45th mission over the valley, and his plane was badly hit. A radio transmission from him seemed to say, "Looks like this is it, son," before he crashed, killing all aboard.[26] At noon, Katyusha rockets with their characteristic howl came crashing in, the first use in Vietnam of these weapons which would become so familiar to us in the American war.

End of Dien Bien Phu

Finally on 7 May there was no hope. Hanoi notified de Castries that he should cease firing at 5:00 PM and surrender but not raise a white flag. This set about a great exhausting scramble to burn money and documents, disable the few remaining howitzers and the one workable tank, and explode the paltry remaining stock of ammunition.

In the last few minutes, Captain Yves Hervouët was in his bunker. He had commanded his ten tanks with both arms in a cast from his wounds, right down to his last two battle-scarred tanks. One of his men "raised high a bottle spotted with dirt. '*Mon capitaine*, there is no way that the Viets are going to celebrate their victory with our champagne.' Hervouët agreed.... [He said], 'Let us drink to the freedom we are about to lose, to the satisfaction of having done the best we could to avoid getting where we are. You have no reason to blame yourselves. I will do my utmost to see that justice is done to you one day. Good luck!'"[27]

Geneviève tells of her final minutes until the surrender. "We were all close to tears, Langlais and Bigeard hugged me .... Back at the unit I informed my patients that the combat would stop at five. They were greatly relieved. I distributed the last cigarettes. Calm and a strange silence settled over the valley, and we waited."[28]

In his memoirs, Bigeard, "Bruno," tells of his last radio messages to and from his remaining commanders:

> "Brèche to Bruno: They are coming en masse. I'm smashing my radio. Goodbye, Bruno.
>
> "Botella to Bruno: This time we're fucked. Goodbye, Bruno.
>
> "Bruno to Botella: Goodbye . . . I'm wiping tears running down my face. No, it is not possible."
>
> Then---------
>
> Bigeard noted, "A great calm, a silence of death hovered over the citadel, crowned by a clear blue sky. It was indeed the end. Is it possible?"
>
> He reflected, "Ah, if we had been victors. But we are vanquished, humiliated, diminished, and I am just one poor guy like all the others."

Foreign legionnaires and paratroopers were especially hated by the Viet Minh. Bigeard defiantly propped his red paratroop beret on his head moments before the enemy entered the command post. He was a prisoner "of these little Vietnamese who, in our French army we once felt that they were only good for being medics or drivers. These high-spirited men began at zero in 1945 with an ideal, a mishmash of arms, a purpose: drive out the French. In nine years Giap beat – no question about it – our Expeditionary Corps."[29]

I asked Geneviève if she were not terrified, thinking of what the enemy would do to a woman. She said she had been too busy and exhausted to think, and her men still needed her, so she just kept on doing what she could, checking their bandages, passing out the last cigarettes, comforting them.

At 5 pm, 7 May 1954, the Viet Minh arrived at de Castries' command bunker, marking the beginning of the end for the French Colonial Empire.

Capture of command bunker, 7 May 1954. (Getty)

The Aftermath

For days Geneviève's captors kept after her to write a letter to Uncle Ho for clemency and to congratulate him on his 64th birthday on 19 May. After struggling with the idea she finally decided to do it, "afraid that a refusal might compromise [my patients'] freedom. . . . As I saw it, the letter had no political import; it was a letter from a nurse whose only concern was to help her patients, for whom evacuation was becoming more critical with each day."[30]

Giap said, "All the enemy troops stationed at Dien Bien Phu . . . . were taken prisoner and were kindly treated."[31] Kindly? Windrow, who carefully studied all available sources, French and Vietnamese, cited what he considered the most authoritative. It concluded that somewhat over 9,000 prisoners, about a third of them wounded or sick, were marched away, and "perhaps half of them would die or disappear."[32] When Giap had set out on his quest with his 34 fighters in 1944, he had heard Ho state that prisoners must be treated well. In his first action Giap had killed them, and in the following days and weeks had killed not only more French Union prisoners but those "rightists" from Vietnamese nationalist non-Communist groups who could not be made to see the light. Ho set the policies. He saw the results. To suggest that Uncle Ho, who had such a remarkable sense for being attuned to people, knew nothing of this in nine years of war goes against considerable evidence to the contrary, inferences from his own statements, and common sense.

After the battle and Geneviève's release from captivity and return to France, she was showered with honors. President Eisenhower invited her to the United States, where the American press was calling her "The Angel of Dien Bien Phu." She was welcomed with a tickertape parade up Broadway, then taken to Congress and received a standing ovation. At the White House the president decorated her with the highest medal awarded to other than U.S. military, the Medal of Freedom. Geneviève was sent off on a tour of major U.S. cities, where she was received with honors and enthusiastic large crowds.

President Eisenhower decorates Geneviève de Galard, the "Angel of Dien Bien Phu," with the Medal of Freedom as French Ambassador to the United States Henri Bonnet and U.S. Congresswoman Frances P. Bolton look on, 27 July 1954. (Courtesy Geneviève de Heaulme)

I had told General Delaunay I would be delighted to do what I could to get her book published in America. For a year and a half Geneviève and I worked to enlarge her short French text. I suggested additions, translated them, added a chapter of pre-DBP history, did the annexes and maps, and edited the book, *The Angel of Dien Bien Phu*. It was a marvelous experience working with this extraordinary woman and her husband who were so warm and personable with Sandra and me. Later, being with them in Washington and Paris, they became our close friends.

At least two things were made abundantly clear by the French-Vietnamese war. First, if any person had doubted Giap when he told

Fonde, just before the 19 December 1946 breakout of total war, that it was of no importance if one million Vietnamese would have to die, his side would triumph in the end, the outcome proved Giap correct. It is unclear as to how many Vietnamese had died by the end, but given the violence combined with famine and other disasters aggravated by the war, the one million number is quite certainly too low.

Second, from its early beginnings in 1944, the leadership of the North demonstrated a remarkable cohesiveness in making the big decisions that guided the war on their side. Yes, Ho Chi Minh was the leader, but more as a first among equals than dictator. In fact, often with no input from Ho, many others in the early decades had done the spade work which made the creation of the Democratic Republic of Vietnam possible. The building of the Viet Bac as a sanctuary for the Viet Minh movement is a prime example, having been established by slow, careful work just north of Hanoi by Ho's predecessors in the Communist movement within Vietnam while Ho was out of the country. The Party, and not just one man, usually made the decisions after long discussions, and with input from many subordinate leaders. This resulted in a cohesiveness representing a broad base leading to major actions. When the decisions turned out to be wrong, the causes were debated and corrective measures directed. Political and military action were inextricably linked, and this cohesiveness in leadership and results did the French in and would bode ill for the Americans and South Vietnamese government in the renewed war to come.

During the eleven years from 1945 to 1956 when France finally withdrew, the North had one president and one general in charge—Ho Chi Minh and Vo Nguyen Giap (although Le Duan had become increasingly powerful). The political and military leadership on the French side, though, was like a revolving door. During that period, France had five presidents, fifteen prime ministers, eight High Commissioners of Indochina, and six Supreme Commanders of French Union forces. Also, the various Vietnamese governments of the South, starting with the Republic of Cochinchina and ending with the Republic of Vietnam, changed eight times. One side was obsessed with independence and unity, the other was bedeviled by an outmoded colonialism that no other country in the world supported and the French themselves vacillated over dumping, but could not quite bring themselves to do it.

Bernard Fall was the most insightful of war correspondents and historians to cover both the French and American wars in Vietnam before being killed in 1967 by a mine in "The Street Without Joy," the place about which he had written the book by that name. He thought that de Lattre, if he had lived, like Leclerc, would have strongly pushed the French government to negotiate when he saw that the war "had become hopeless." Whether or not he was correct, in fact General Navarre in his 1956 memoirs, *Agonie de l'Indochine*, "stated that the war simply could not be won in the military sense" and that "all that could be hoped for was a draw."[33]

Part Two: The American War - Many More Bullets

*   *   *

General Creighton W. Abrams:
"In the whole picture of the war, the <u>battles</u> don't mean much."
Saigon, 29 August 1969

*   *   *

CHAPTER 8

America in Support, Advisory Mission, 1954-1964

* * *

THE FALL OF DIEN BIEN Phu had dramatically shaken France. The people's earlier knowledge that things had not been going well did little to soften the impact. An objective military analysis would reveal that about four percent of the French Union and Associated States forces had been lost, and there was no reason in terms of battlefield power, main force against main force, that the war was lost. But the resultant psychological shock surging throughout France swamped that kind of reasoning.

Nevertheless, with the fall of DBP the war was not over, and the immediate problem for Navarre was to protect Hanoi and the Delta where the great bulk of the French civilians and military were located, along with Vietnamese who had for years resisted Communism. Mounting up in Chinese trucks and moving at night, much of Giap's army was leaving the High Region headed toward the Viet Bac and perhaps Hanoi itself. The French withdrew exposed French posts outside Dien Bien Phu and elsewhere to reinforce the Delta's mobile forces and reserve.

Of course the disaster resulted in another military and political shakeup of the French command structure. On 3 June General Paul Ely was appointed both Commissioner General and Supreme Commander, succeeding Maurice Dejean and General Navarre. And France itself got yet one more prime minister, this time Pierre Mendès-France whose goal was to get a Geneva settlement under the best terms possible.

The Question of Independence for South Vietnam

The disaster of Dien Bien Phu profoundly affected South Vietnam. Non-Communist nationalists in Bai Dai's government had long been pressing for France's recognition of independence for the South's State of Vietnam, just as Ho had done for the North's Democratic Republic of Vietnam.

South Vietnamese General Lam Quang Thi wrote that as a young officer after the fall of Dien Bien Phu he had observed the hopes of the Vietnamese for independence to soar, not just in the North, but also in the South. "I knew that the fall of Dien Bien Phu was the beginning of the end of the French presence in Indochina. . . . I hoped that the Americans would step in to stop Communist expansion in Asia in accordance with the U.S. policy of 'containment.' . . . Further, the French departure would mean true independence for our country. With the help of the Americans, we would have a good cause to fight for."[1] France before DBP had been reluctant to grant it, still caught in its colonial past, but now on 4 June France signed treaties of full independence and association with the southern State of Vietnam.

By "independence for our country" General Thi was not thinking of unification of Vietnam, probably conceding that the DRV had gone too far in the war, as had the South, to allow that. He said, "Looking back on the Indochina War, I think the main causes of the failure of French policy in Indochina were the opposition of the French government to progressive and orderly development of South Vietnam toward independence under a genuine nationalist government, and more importantly, not allowing the creation of a strong Vietnamese Army."[2]

Indeed, if the French had been willing and able to "Vietnamese" the Vietnamese National Army sufficiently, they would have given it a much better chance of fighting independently. Similarly, the Americans would later fail to emphasize "Vietnamization" soon enough and forcefully enough.

America's Increased Role, and the Triumph of Ngo Dinh Diem

As France was in the throes of impending loss of empire, not just in Indochina but in North Africa and elsewhere, America had begun taking upon itself a more direct role in a global drama. This, as General Thi said, was no less than containment of the advance of Communism in Southeast Asia. Eisenhower, in a press conference a month before the collapse of Dien Bien Phu, used the term "falling domino principle." He did not invent the domino theory—that a collapse in Vietnam would lead to Communist takeover of the rest of Indochina, Thailand, Malaysia, Burma, and extend potentially to Indonesia and even Australia, New Zealand, and India—but it now was on the front burner. The president and his advisers felt that whether or not the Soviet Union in fact was guiding a worldwide Communism, the Indochina situation was a threat that had to be met before all of Southeast Asia succumbed.

Ho Chi Minh and some in the inner circle of the Central Committee were fully aware that the Dien Bien Phu victory, crucially important as it was, did not spell the end of the struggle. Only one day after DBP fell, Ho wrote to the army, its logistical support members, and the people to congratulate them, saying: "This victory is big, but it is only the beginning. We must not be self-complacent and subjective and underestimate the enemy. We are determined to fight for independence, national unity, democracy, and peace. A struggle, whether military or diplomatic, must be long and hard before complete victory can be achieved."[3]

The United States had well enough shown that it was now the main enemy of Vietnamese Communism. Strong voices within the Party had been urging a continuation of the war before the Americans could act to prevent a takeover of the South. But they were being counseled by both the USSR and China to go slowly so as not to provoke the Americans into establishing bases in South Vietnam, Laos, and Cambodia, taking the place of the French.

On 1 June 1954 Colonel Edward G. Lansdale landed in Saigon to set up the Saigon Military Mission. He had been a key figure in the successful neutralization of insurgency in the Philippines and now was tasked with doing everything possible to support the Southern government and weaken the Northern. It was hoped that this new American initiative, added to the already ongoing MAAG efforts, would stiffen the Bao Dai government.

Before DBP, Bao Dai had continued for some time to be recognized by France and the U.S. as head of state, even as he was enjoying the pleasures of women and gambling in Europe. But after DBP, in what was to have momentous consequences, the nominal emperor could do little more to shore up the State of Vietnam's shaky government than on 16 June to appoint Ngo Dinh Diem, a long-time thorn in his side, as prime minister.

Diem, a strict Roman Catholic with a bishop for a brother, had a strong constituency among Vietnams' Catholics, many of whom resided in the North in the Red River Delta. He had been maneuvering for power for years, and with this appointment, a whole new era opened. Despite warnings from the French and doubts within the U.S. administration itself, Diem was accepted in Washington as America's best hope for providing a bulwark against a perceived Red Tide from the north.

Geneva, Independence and Unification

There had been no cease fire after DBP, and sporadic small-scale fighting took place throughout most of Vietnam. Late in June, in central Annam a major battle was fought, the last of the French Indochina war. French Groupement Mobile 100 of about regimental size was ordered to abandon its positions at An Khe in the Central Highlands and withdraw to Pleiku. Suffering from poor leadership decisions, it was ambushed multiple times and lost hundreds of dead and most of its vehicles and equipment. The nucleus of GM 100 had been the proud French "Korea Battalion." Having earned the praise of General Matthew Ridgway, commander of UN Forces in Korea, it was now virtually wiped out. Weeks later, between 27 July and 11 August, allowing for time to disseminate orders in various parts of Vietnam and Laos, the cease fire agreement reached at Geneva went into effect.

Pham Van Dong, the DVR's lead representative at Geneva, drew up a draft declaration that was deemed unacceptable. "Although Viet Minh representatives had met with their Chinese and Soviet counterparts before the conference to formulate a common negotiating strategy, it had become clear that neither Moscow nor Beijing was eager to back the Viet Minh in a continuation of the war, nor were they willing to give blanket support for [North] Vietnamese demands. [They] favored a compromise based on the division of Vietnam into two separate regroupment zones, one occupied by the Viet Minh and the other by the Bao Dai government and its supporters."[4]

As negotiations progressed, the French and DRV negotiators came to a final sticking point: at which parallel should the two countries be temporarily divided until elections to unify them? The French proposed the seventeenth parallel. This would give the South considerably more territory than would be the case if the former dividing line, the sixteenth parallel, were chosen."When Pham Van Dong appeared reluctant to accept the compromise, [Chinese delegate Zhou Enlai] argued that giving French Prime Minister Pierre Mendez-France a means of saving face was a small price to pay for obtaining the final departure of French troops." Zhou is said to have promised, "With the final withdrawal of the French, all of Vietnam will be yours."[5]

The United States deliberately kept a low profile at the conference, not sending its highest level negotiators, unlike the other countries. By now, the Eisenhower administration realized that it was the ultimate, and probably sole, power that could in one way or another continue containment of Communism in Southeast Asia, and both the Soviet Union and China had moved toward a position of detente.

The Geneva Conference closed on 21 July 1954 with an agreement signed by France and the DRV. The South Vietnamese government believed it had been sold out by both France and the United States and it refused to sign. The U.S. was wary of some of the provisions and likewise did not sign. The agreement stipulated that Vietnam would be divided at the seventeenth parallel, somewhat north of Quang Tri, with Democratic Republic of Vietnam in temporary charge in the North, and State of Vietnam in the South. The only mention in the Accord itself of elections to unify Vietnam was a phrase in Article 14: "Pending the general elections which will bring about the unification of Viet-Nam."

A "Conference Final Declaration," issued by the British chairman of the conference, provided though that "general elections shall be held in July 1956, under the supervision of an international commission composed of representatives of the Member States of the International Supervisory Commission, referred to in the Agreement on the cessation of hostilities. . . . [The International Commission] shall be composed of representatives of the following States: Canada, India and Poland."

The South Vietnamese and United States governments did not approve this declaration of a specific date, believing, with good cause, that given two more years for the Communists to use their methods of coercion on the populace, the election would be rigged and the South would be certain to lose.

Instead, the U.S. produced a unilateral declaration, issued by Walter Bedell Smith on 21 July 1954: "In connection with the statement concerning free elections in Vietnam, my Government wishes to make clear its position, which it has expressed in a declaration made in Washington on June 29, 1954 as follows: 'In the case of nations now divided against their will, we shall continue to seek to achieve unity through free elections, supervised by the UN, to ensure that they are conducted fairly.'"[6]

Vietnam had nominally been united as one nation since 1802, the beginning of the Nguyen Dynasty with Emperor Gia Long on the throne in Hue. In the minds of Ho Chi Minh and the Communists, from the time of the August Revolution in 1945 the country could remain a unified nation if only the great majority of the people would support the revolution and throw out the French. Although warfare had split the nation, not until 6 June 1948 with the announcement of Bao Dai's provisional government were there technically two governments of one nation, the DRV under Ho and the State of Vietnam national government under Bao Dai, the latter claiming administrative authority over all of Vietnam.

Regroupment

The reality then and in particular in 1954, of course, was far different. When Bao Dai appointed Diem as prime minister of the State of Vietnam, the split into North and South was formalized. In the so-called "regroupment" provided for in the Accords, almost a million Vietnamese would be transported from the North to the South, with perhaps 80,000 – 100,000 going the other way. In the latter group would be many who would be militarily and politically trained by the North to be later infiltrated back into the South to support the war against the South Vietnamese and Americans.

In some ways the North got the better of the regroupment deal. The U.S. had heavily proselytized the approximately 600,000 Vietnamese Catholics in the North to go south, reminding them that Communists historically had persecuted Catholics. Beginning in the fall of 1954, hundreds of thousands of North Vietnamese Catholics used the regroupment provision of the Geneva Accords to come to the South, many of them enduring grave hardships to do so, voting against Communism with their feet. This movement on the one hand strengthened the South, since the Catholics tended to support its government, but it also removed a large thorn in the side of the North, largely denuding the Delta area of people who could have been a real problem for the North, perhaps even the nucleus of espionage and insurgency.

In an action resembling American decrees which had allowed settlers to rush westward into Indian territory, thus causing much discontent among the Indians, Diem settled perhaps two hundred thousand Catholics on lands the Montagnards in the Central Highlands thought of as their own, thereby embittering the hill people who had enjoyed a large degree of autonomy under the French. Finally, in 1964 the Montagnards rebelled in the Ban Me Thuot area, and although the outbreak was quelled, the hard feelings which remained were to have significant consequences when in 1975 the North Vietnamese chose this area to make their initial massive attack and were tacitly or directly supported by many Montagnards.

The two-edged sword of the regroupment situation for Diem became especially apparent when he so much heavily favored these and others of his fellow Catholics that he caused widespread resentment among the majority non-Catholic population of the South.

The DRV's Politburo Differences over Unification

"The goal of unification, one Vietnam under the Party's banner, became an objective as soon as it became a problem at the 1954 Geneva Conference. . . . At some point, or perhaps from the very start, unification passed from mere Party policy to holy crusade, from goal to obsession. Consider this typical passionate assertion from Ho Chi Minh: 'Each day the Fatherland remains disunited, each day you (of the South) suffer, food is without taste, sleep brings no rest. I solemnly promise you, through your determination, the determination of all our people, the Southern land will return to the bosom of the Fatherland.'"[7]

Reunification of Vietnam had long been Ho's goal, and he had spoke often of it. However, the North had suffered greatly in the long war with France—economically, culturally, militarily. After 1954, for some time in the North there were two divergent views of how to proceed with unification. The "North-firsters"—prominently Ho Chi Minh, Pham Van Dong (Finance Minister), Vo Nguyen Giap (Defense Minister), and Truong Chinh (First Secretary of the Party) wanted to focus resources and energy on building up the North, confident that the South would eventually be united to the North basically by growth of socialism in the South and widespread dissatisfaction with ineffectual Southern government—if not by that, then later by revolutionary violence led by the North.

A very different view was held by other powerful members of the Politburo. Several of them had long grumbled among themselves about what they considered three huge failures of Ho. First, in order to disguise Communist intentions and broaden the base for independence-minded adherents, in 1945 he had officially dissolved the Indochinese Communist Party. Then in 1946 he agreed to let French troops into Tonkin for a period of five years while he was strengthening his DRV government and negotiating to accept a place in the French Union in return for a French pledge of full independence. Then during the 1954 Geneva negotiations, the dissenters thought he had succumbed to Chinese and Soviet pressure to accept a "temporary" division of Vietnam at the seventeenth parallel to be followed in 1956 by elections for a permanent government of a unified Vietnam, elections which hardly anyone believed would indeed be held. The "South-firsters" wanted to continue the war immediately in the South and win it before the imperialist Americans could become so strongly entrenched that they might have to be forced out.

During this period, the South-firsters gained strength when the land reform program in the North led by First Secretary Truong Chinh was an enormous failure, resulting in widespread executions, displacement of small landowners, and other privations. The resentment was so great that in 1956 the military had to be called in to put down uprisings, causing more deaths and destruction. A full division was required to suppress the revolt in, of all places, Nghe An Province, Ho Chi Minh's birthplace. Truong Chinh was ousted (for awhile) and in 1959 Le Duan took his place, thus inaugurating an era in which Ho—still revered, but no longer the center of actual political power—was basically relegated to diplomatic issues, and Giap was initially sidelined by Le Duan's enmity toward him. If we are to believe Colonel Bui Tin, several years after the end of the Vietnam War Le Duan compared himself to Ho: "I remember extremely clearly how he talked about his own exploits compared with those of Ho Chi Minh. In very elated fashion, Le Duan said, 'As for me, well, I am better than Uncle Ho. He opened his mouth and talked along the lines of the Confucian code of morality, like human dignity, loyalty, good manners, wisdom and trustworthiness. What is that? It is outmoded feudalism. As for me, I am for collective mastery by the workers.'"[8] What is certain is that Ho was revered by many and Le Duan was feared by all.

U.S. Assistance to South Vietnam

By agreement with the French, on 9 October 1954, Viet Minh troops had marched into Hanoi. The DRV was now secure in the knowledge it had really won the war and could claim Hanoi as its capital. Certainly among French officers and men who were present when the tricolor was lowered for the last time in the North were some who wondered what had happened. What in hell happened? We did our best. We won battles. They wore sandals and backpacks. We were strong, a modern army with a navy and air force. But we lost.

The war had inevitably shifted from under them. Not only had they lost, but America was now in de facto charge. On 24 October 1954, President Eisenhower made a strong commitment to South Vietnam when he wrote to President Diem:

"We have been exploring ways and means to permit our aid to Viet-Nam to be more effective and to make a greater contribution to the welfare and stability of the Government of Viet-Nam. I am, accordingly, instructing the American Ambassador to Viet-Nam to examine with you in your capacity as Chief of Government, how an intelligent program of American aid given directly to your Government can serve to assist Viet-Nam in its present hour of trial, provided that your Government is prepared to give assurances as to the standards of performance it would be able to maintain in the event such aid were supplied.

"The purpose of this offer is to assist the Government of Viet-Nam in developing and maintaining a strong, viable state, capable of resisting attempted subversion or aggression through military means. The Government of the United States expects that this aid will be met by performance on the part of the Government of Viet-Nam in undertaking needed reforms. It hopes that such aid, combined with your own continuing efforts, will contribute effectively toward an independent Viet-Nam [South Vietnam] endowed with a strong government. Such a government would, I hope, be so responsive to the nationalist aspirations of its people, so enlightened in purpose and effective in performance that it will be respected both at home and abroad and discourage any who might wish to impose a foreign ideology on your free people."[9]

Diem had started late. Ho had been at his business of building an independent Vietnam [all of Vietnam] much longer, and had constructed a formidable political and military infrastructure tested by years of war against the French. The bulk of the people—virtually all in the North, and many in the South)—admired Ho and shared his yearning for independence. Diem had none of the charisma and little of the profound commitment to his people at the lowest levels that so consumed Ho. Diem's government of nine years, 1954-1963, in length about equal to the French Indochina war itself, would never be "so enlightened in purpose and effective in performance that it will be respected both at home and abroad." Instead, it caused deep scars and skepticism among the South Vietnamese people that would be a poor base upon which his successors would need to build.

Before the end of 1954, Eisenhower would get bad news from his special emissary, head of Mission to Saigon, General J. Lawton Collins, a much respected soldier/diplomat. Collins doubted Diem's "capacity to stabilize the government or rally support for his regime. He recommended Bao Dai's return be considered [from France where he had gone after DBP], but if this were unacceptable, recommended the U.S. withdraw from Vietnam."[10]

That the White House and State Department were pulling the Vietnam strings – or thought they were—is abundantly clear in many executive branch records such as the 19 December 1954 transcript of meeting: "[Secretary of State John Foster] Dulles was sure Diem could succeed with proper direction." Proper direction! Dulles was more sure that no other viable candidate existed.[11]

By contrast, several men around Ho had shown the capability to lead the North if anything were to happen to him. Almost all of them had paid their dues by being held in prison by the French, or in Ho's case the Chinese, suffering great physical and mental abuse. From the very beginning of America's close involvement with South Vietnamese affairs, there never was a pool of strong candidates at the top of the Southern government who could step in if the current head of government were to die or be incapacitated. By contrast, the Politburo, despite differing opinions, acted collectively. In the South, with the exception of the trust Diem placed in his family, there never was trust that someone was not plotting against the head of state. The North experienced plenty of internal maneuvering for favor and power, but none that was a danger to effective leadership.

Diem's Rise to Power

Not that Diem lacked courage. He had plenty of it. He was well known as an anti-Communist. In 1945, arrested by Viet Minh near Hue on his way to see Bao Dai, he had been imprisoned in the North and fell desperately ill. Ho was interested in getting Diem's help in converting Catholics to the Viet Minh cause, and in 1946 directed that he be medically treated. Later in a face to face meeting, Ho offered him a high position in the Communist government. Diem angrily rejected Ho's overture, asking him if he should forget that in the previous year Ho had had his brother and his brother's son buried alive. When Ho said that he had nothing to do with it and that mistakes had been made in the early days of the revolution, Diem asked him if he was free to go. Ho said he was but warned that it might be dangerous for him to try to do so. Diem said he would take his chances and angrily stormed out. Ho subsequently had him condemned to death in absentia but presumably became too busy with events in the North to follow up.[12]

Very early in America's involvement in Vietnam, nationalist Diem knew it would be good policy to get strong American support. He had sailed for New York in late 1950, stopping in Rome for an audience with Pope Pius XII. In America he began making the rounds of low level Washington personages, hoping to work his way up to the Secretary of State. This was not to be, but Cardinal Spellman of New York became highly interested in him, and Diem accepted the cardinal's invitation to stay in a seminary in New Jersey and another in New York where he remained for more than three years. Lecturing to interested groups of Americans, Diem maintained that an independent Vietnam under his leadership would "satisfy the Vietnamese population that they have something to fight for."[13]

That is what, precisely, Diem was never able to do – inspire the bulk of the population to fight the Communists. It was about in 1955-56 that in the South, Diem's government was beginning to refer to the Viet Minh contemptuously as Viet Cong, Vietnamese Communists, an abbreviation of Viet Nam Cong San. The VC would carry on the fight.

Diem was to prove a much tougher nut to crack than Collins thought, and Collins kept up a constant drumbeat with Dulles to get Diem replaced. The first clue to Diem's intransigence might have been when in November 1954 Diem forced Bao Dai's appointee, General Nguyen Van Hinh, commander of Vietnam National Army (VNA), to leave the country and turn over the post to General Nguyen Van Vy. At this time, with virtually no backing, Diem seems to have accomplished this by means known only to himself. Then, as of 1 January 1955, American money started going directly to VNA instead of through French channels. So now Diem definitely controlled VNA. When a crisis soon erupted, the VNA was fiercely loyal to Diem.

One of Diem's greatest problems was the criminal gang of thousands of members with its own army, the Binh Xuyen. From a compound in Saigon with rooms of pythons, leopards and tigers, and a moat filled with alligators, General Le Van Vien [aka Bay Vien], the leader, ran a huge gambling, prostitution, and opium ring in the city and its environs.

Bao Dai received a handsome cut, and it was this situation that had so enraged General Revers when he made his visit in 1949.

In a neat arrangement with Bao Dai, Bay Vien had been the person who appointed the Saigon police chief. But now Diem, as prime minister, was the real power, not Bao Dai. Bay Vien was a major threat to Diem's authority. Diem ordered the Vietnamese National Army to seize the Saigon police headquarters, and they maneuvered to attack. General Ely, the French commissioner general, got wind of the move and told Diem he should call it off. Collins was enraged that Diem had taken such a drastic step after Collins had urged him to negotiate. Collins told Diem that "if he continued his present course we [the American government] would be under heavy pressure to support a change in [his] government." Collins told him "to consult with Ely and me before taking any additional critical steps whatever." Diem replied that he would think it over.[14]

Diem in Charge

Diem didn't think long. On 27 April 1955 fighting erupted between the VNA and Binh Xuyen, engulfing the Cholon/Saigon complex in artillery and mortar fire and causing by some estimates hundreds of civilian deaths and thousands of people to be homeless. A week later, Bay Vien's compound was in ruins, the menagerie of exotic animals that had been in it was dead, and Bay Vien himself was fleeing to Paris. The U.S. Congress and American newspapers applauded Diem, the little man who had taken on such a huge task and won.

Diem had plenty of family help. His brother Ngo Dinh Nhu in effect was vice premier, a man so powerful it often was thought that he and not his brother in reality ran the show. Nhu had founded a political party that infiltrated or controlled much of South Vietnamese politics and life. It espoused an abstruse position between Communism and capitalism which promoted the wellbeing of the group instead of the individual. And there was no group so deserving as the Ngo Dinh Diem family.

Because the celibate Catholic Diem was a bachelor, Nhu's gorgeous wife, Madame Nhu, or "the Dragon Lady," served as "First Lady." Diem's other brothers were an archbishop, a warlord, and an ambassador to the UK. In-laws and other relatives also did well. "U.S. embassy official John Mecklin recalled, 'There probably had never before in American foreign affairs been a phenomenon comparable to our relations with the Ngo family. It was like dealing with a whole platoon of de Gaulles.'"[15]

Diem followed up his victory over the Binh Xuyen by going after the anti-Communist leader of the Hoa Hao religious sect, having him guillotined. The Cao Dai—another religious sect with an army, a temple in Tay Ninh, and revered holy people, almost saints, to include Jesus, Buddha, Shakespeare, and Victor Hugo—was also cowed into submission. Then there was the matter of elections. Diem, with Communists so strong in the South, certainly was not going to allow a country-wide election by July 1956 in accordance with the British-authored "Conference Final Declaration" which Diem and the U.S. had not accepted. Eisenhower said that if the elections were held, possibly 80 percent of the votes would go to Ho instead of Bao Dai. So Diem's next major step was to hold a general election in South Vietnam, ostensibly for the people to choose between him and Bao Dai as head of a new Southern government. Not surprisingly Diem won with a vote of 98.2 percent. He now was president of the First Republic of Vietnam (RVN), with a constitution which he virtually wrote, giving him ultimate power over the executive, legislative, and judicial branches. He also now remodeled his army as the Army of the Republic of Vietnam (ARVN) which discarded French rank and salutes, adopted their own rank insignia, and now used the U.S. Army's style of saluting and system of organization at about half the U.S. strength.

After Dien Bien Phu the American government had pressed the French to keep their troops in Vietnam as long as possible to give the South Vietnamese time to stabilize and to deter any Communist violation of the cease fire agreement. Diem went along at first but later wanted the French army out, and by mid-1955 the Americans were now ready to see them go. In January 1956 Diem turned down a French request to build and man an aero-navale base at Cap St. Jacques (Vung Tau), telling them, "The presence of French troops, no matter how friendly they may be, was incompatible with Viet-Nam's concept of full independence."[16]

In 1956 the last French combat units left Vietnam, leaving behind them French plantations and other businesses which often had to deal with both the governments in Hanoi and in Saigon. Diem's statement is a reminder that many Vietnamese in both North and South had long wanted full independence and did not trust words on paper when a French military force was still on the ground. Ho and the Politburo wanted independence for all of Vietnam after they had gained mastery over the South. Diem and his National Assembly wanted independence for South Vietnam. Neither the DRV nor the RVN wanted foreign troop presence other than as trainers and advisors, but both sides had it—the South, of course, with the later huge American force much more so than the North. When the French departed and the Americans were then the only foreign power on the scene, Ho and his circle claimed that America had now gotten what it wanted all along, an unimpeded chance to fulfill its imperialistic ambitions.

General Thi said, "I believed at that time that Diem was the man of the hour. He had rescued South Vietnam from bankruptcy after the 1954 Geneva Accords. He had created a unified national army by defeating the armed religious sects and assimilating various semi-independent paramilitary forces left by the French. He had successfully resettled one million refugees from the north. From the ashes of the 1945-1954 war, he had created a strong, prosperous, and internationally recognized Republic."[17]

Despite some doubters in the Eisenhower administration, Diem seemed to be the man of the hour also in the United States. The lobby group American Friends of Vietnam arranged an impressive U.S. tour for Diem for May 1957. President Eisenhower and Secretary of State John Foster Dulles welcomed him to Washington, DC. Diem addressed a full session of Congress, then was welcomed to New York with a tickertape parade up Broadway, visited the seminary where he had been a resident some years earlier, then toured cities on the West Coast. Eisenhower, Dulles and major U.S. newspapers heaped praise on him as the Iron Man of Vietnam, a courageous savior of his country.

President Eisenhower and Secretary of State Dulles greet Ngo Dinh Diem, President of Republic of Vietnam, at National Airport, 8 May 1957. (NARA)

Return to Revolutionary War in the South

Everywhere in the South, it seemed, the Communists were a threat, usually not so much militarily as politically and socially. During the French war they had built up a strong Viet Minh presence with significant public support. Then during the period 1954-1959, under direction from Hanoi the Communist cadre in the South worked diligently at gaining more adherents and supporters, especially among the rural population. In sparsely populated areas they instituted small but effective civic action programs to show the people they were on their side. They subordinated Communist ideology, which could be a hard sell, to nationalism which was easily accepted, and spread their influence across many areas of South Vietnam.

After Dien Bien Phu, the North began working intensively on consolidating its power and developing its economy in anticipation of further efforts to unify the country. While his prestige remained high among the population as the victor, Giap had used this time to rebuild his army through training, enhancements in weaponry, and most of all, logistics and administration to support a modernized force. With his eye on the South, he believed he needed time, that precious commodity that had served so well in the eventual victory over the French. But by 1959 Diem's campaign to eradicate Communists had caused severe setbacks, and Giap had lost considerable personal power in the often vicious inner politics of the Communist Party. Although he voiced objections, wanting to keep time on his side, in January 1959 the Central Committee came to the conclusion that they had to end the four-year period of relative quiet before progress in the South was further hindered. By adopting Resolution 15, they proclaimed a return to "revolutionary violence," the Marxist-Leninist term often used by the Vietnamese Communist leaders to describe the war. In a neat bit of double-talk, Le Duan said, "We won't use war to unify the country, but if the United States and its puppets use war, then we have to use war, and the war that the enemy has initiated will be an opportunity for us to unify the country."[18]

For centuries a basic network of trails had existed from north to south, cutting through rugged terrain in Laos and western South Vietnam. Major work was now started to develop this primitive patchwork into a highly effective system which could be used to transport troops, munitions, and supplies to the South, the so-called Ho Chi Minh Trail. Simultaneously, the ability to move men and materiel by water through the South China Sea was improved. The stage was being set for expanded war in the South.

Revolutionary Nguyen Thi Dinh

Diem embarked on a series of measures to rout out Communists, nearly all of which had enormous negative effects among the populace. Part of his anti-Communist strategy was the government's Agroville Program, a resettlement effort based on earlier French attempts. Its results are a central part of the story of Mrs. Nguyen Thi Dinh in her book, *No Other Road to Take*. Dinh was born in 1920 in the province of Ben Tre, the most populated and richest one in the Mekong Delta. This is where Massu struck in 1945, and where Colonel Jean Leroy was commanding that area. It was Leroy who was trying to eradicate Communists like Mrs. Dinh, employing "brutal and indiscriminate killings," as acknowledged by the South Vietnamese government during the American war.[19] (It was also the province of the 1968 much-quoted statement of an American officer: "We had to destroy the village in order to save it.")

In 1930, when Dinh, daughter of a peasant family, was ten years old her brother was a local Communist who held secret meetings in her father's house and surreptitiously planted a red flag with yellow hammer and sickle at a busy river crossing point. She heard people talking when they saw the flag, saying, "The Communists in Ben Tre Province will soon rise up like those in Phu Rieng." The reference was to the Michelin Plantation uprising to the northwest of Saigon earlier in that year, the one which Tran Tu Binh had described as a hell on Earth. (*The Red Earth*)

Dinh became an ardent revolutionary in her teens, later married another cadre and had a child. When her husband was arrested by the French and sent to Poulo Condore prison, she vowed to fight for independence. She was soon arrested, sentenced to prison, and had to hand her seven-month old baby over to her mother to raise.[20] After three years she developed heart trouble and was sent back from prison to Ben Tre under house arrest where she hoped to meet her husband but learned he had died at Poulo Condore. For months afterward, in despair she finally concluded, "I must live to bring up my son and to avenge my husband and comrades." She worked at menial jobs to support herself and her son. "It was only in 1944 when the Viet Minh movement became strong that I succeeded in establishing contact with the organization."[21] Her dedication led in 1946 to her being chosen to go north to meet Ho. She asked him for arms to fight, and after numerous close calls was able to return by sea with a large shipment of them and was able to deliver them personally to Tran Van Tra, a leader of guerrilla units in the South who went on to become a famous general. "After [this] I continued to operate in Ben Tre province. . . . In the years 1950, 1951, and 1952, the French colonialists poured out all their energies to expand their oil spot to cover all of South Vietnam."[22] Hunted by Colonel Leroy, once more she had to leave her son with her mother in order to continue her work, and she remarried, again a Communist cadre. Leroy himself, though, ceased to be a problem. He had tangled with Colonel Christian de Castries and the State of Vietnam government, and as a result in 1953 was kicked upstairs and out of the Mekong Delta.

Dinh said that at the end of 1953 and in early 1954, "in coordination with the Dien Bien Phu battlefield, guerrilla warfare in the South erupted violently. . . . In each area that [we] liberated . . . the peasants were simultaneously given the land and allowed to keep all their crops. Many villagers told me with tears in their eyes: Only the Party and Old Mr. Ho have taken care of us like this."[23] After the Geneva Accords, her teenage son regrouped to the North, and her ill husband wanted her to go too, but she stayed to continue the fight. Now it was against the Diem regime which was struggling to convince a multitude of farmers, who had gotten their land from the Communists and no longer had to give back most of their harvest to landlords, that they would be better off with the Southern government than with the Communists.

Diem's 1959 Agroville Program promised the people better services and marketing for their products, and most importantly, security against what were by now being called the Viet Cong. Under the program, villages were destroyed and the inhabitants were either moved back into a rebuilt fortified village on that site or out of the area into a new village. Dinh described how it impacted life in Thanh Thoi village, Mo Cay district, Ben Tre province: "The villagers were angry . . . because they had been ordered by Diem and the Americans to tear down their houses and move within a month. An entire area of fertile rice fields, luxuriant fruit trees, and densely populated settlements—. . . over ten kilometers in length – had to be completely evacuated for the establishment of an agroville. . . . The villagers told us, 'If we're going to die, we're going to die right here, we're not going anywhere.' . . . A month passed without any villagers obeying the order to dismantle their houses. . . . Two companies were brought in to blanket all neighboring villages. Every day they set fire to houses, cut down trees, and crushed lush rice fields with tractors. . . . After the Dien Bien Phu victory the [Communist] revolution [had given a widow] three cong of land to farm and support her five young children.[24] She painstakingly built an embankment to grow tangerines, clod of earth by clod of earth. The tangerines were beginning to ripen when the soldiers came to cut them down. Watching them destroy what she had constructed with sweat and tears, she shouted in anger, 'What kind of government is this that can be so cruel?' . . .

"A couple of old people came forward and protested, 'The government said it was concerned about the life of the people but hasn't done anything to prove it. Now it is forcing us to tear down our houses, destroy and burn our properties, dig up the graves of our ancestors, and perform exhausting [uncompensated] labor tasks. How are the people going to survive?"[25] (During the subsequent Strategic Hamlet Program, in 1968-69 I witnessed reactions of villagers affected by this program, then carried out by the Thieu government. At the time I did not see how it could possibly succeed in anything other than embittering generations of people.)

Dinh said, "Also in this period Diem concocted [a law] under which anyone who entertained thoughts of opposition—even if he did not take any concrete action to oppose the regime – would be labeled Viet Cong and guillotined. The mobile guillotine was taken everywhere and prisons mushroomed."[26]

This description could be taken as propaganda, a concoction of a dedicated Communist who had been harshly treated by the French and was now being hunted by the Diem regime, were it not for plenty of evidence that this happened in the life of the Agroville program, 1959-61.

Diem in fact revived the use of the guillotine which, in the hands of the earlier French colonials, had lopped off heads that were then stuck on stakes as a warning.

The entry for Dinh in *Military Encyclopedia of Vietnam*, Hanoi, 1996, states: "In late 1959-1960 [Dinh] was the person who started and was the key leader of the Ben Tre Simultaneous Uprising Movement (17 January-20 April 1960). On 17 January 1960 she personally directed the victorious insurrections in three villages . . . of Mo Cay district, which began the high tide of insurrection throughout the entire province and the lowlands regions of the Mekong Delta and Eastern Cochin China." She went on to become a high ranking Party member and a Deputy Commander of the South Vietnamese Liberation Army.[27]

In Diem's time, as during the French war, the Communists remained fully as capable of bestiality as was the other side in this *guerre sale*, "dirty war." Dinh says that during the 1960 insurrection in Ben Tre province, "The villagers felt very satisfied, especially when the policemen, tyrants, officials, and landlords with blood debts were led out to be executed in front of the people. However, in accordance with the lenient policy of the revolution, only the gang leaders – the most cruel and treacherous of them all—were executed. The others, those who had blood debts but confessed their crimes and acknowledged their guilt, were only given a suspended death sentence. They were ordered to move to the . . . towns to live in repentance, and if any of them committed new crimes they would be executed."[28]

After the war a South Vietnamese general, Tran Dinh Tho, wrote, "Under President Diem's secret directives, province chiefs were allowed to 'dispose of' [Viet Cong infrastructure (VCI)] members in whatever way they deemed appropriate, including murder, without legal justification." In discussing the later Phoenix program under President Thieu, he pointed out that even measures far short of murder, such as the initial step of detention, could have deleterious effects. "To the innocent people detained . . . because of suspicion, detention was apt to alienate them from the GVN cause and, under Communist proselytizing influence, could well turn them into sympathizers and eventually members of the VCI."[29]

Diem's attempt at land reform to gain popular support met with mixed results. Some people who got land they could not otherwise have possessed naturally liked the policy. But previously well-off land owners were embittered at having to give up their land, and peasants were dismayed in many cases to find they now had to pay for land the Viet Minh had given them free. And many were adversely affected by Diem's rounding up of suspected Communists. Friends and family members sometimes just disappeared.

But no matter how well Diem was able to forge a quasi-police state, partly because of American presence and pressure he and his brother Nhu could never match Le Duan and Le Duc Tho in the North in gaining strict control of their state.

The War Changes: National Liberation Front (NLF)

In December 1960, the National Front for the Liberation of South Vietnam was formed, widely known as the National Liberation Front, NLF. The Front was a concerted, armed military and political effort to sink the entire Southern regime. Truong Nhu Tang, who as a student had met Ho in France and become an instant disciple, was one of its founders. These men and women wanted the organization to represent a broad spectrum of people with nationalist and neutralist views, not just those of Communists. Tang spoke to his friend, Albert (Pham Ngoc) Thao, about the NLF. He found that Albert had no need to become an NLF member because he was already performing invaluable service as a spy in the highest levels of Diem's government, a man who "had the implicit trust of the president and his brother." This was an excellent arrangement, to get inside information yet keep Diem in power since the NLF was not anxious to get rid of him and Nhu because they were causing such widespread hatred of their regime.[30] Tang was later arrested and while in prison found that

Albert had been exposed. It was rumored Albert was tortured before being executed.

The NLF was no makeshift insurrection such as the Ben Tre affair which had started with sharpened sticks for weapons. The People's Liberation Army of South Vietnam (PLAF – Quân Giải Phóng Miền Nam Việt Nam) was formed as the armed branch of the NLF and it became the official name for Viet Cong. PLAF was a name not much used by the Americans. I still have the captured NLF/Viet Cong flag which Major Chau gave me in 1969. A horizontal band of red represents Communist North Vietnam. Under it is a blue horizontal band (South Vietnam). The gold star in the center is taken from the North's PAVN flag, solid red with a gold star in the center. The red and blue "signified the two halves of the nation, united under the star—in a single purpose [Liberate the South]."[31]

For a long time the Communists had established "shadow" governments at the lower levels—hamlet, village, district, province—and the creation of the NLF in 1960 was a major step toward a shadow Communist government at the national and international levels in South Vietnam (to be achieved nine years later when the Provisional Revolutionary Government, PRG, was formed).

Many fine French men and women such as Jean and Geneviève de Heaulme truly believed that they had fought to support anti-Communist patriots in a civil war against Communists, and that their efforts were part of a global battle to contain Communism. And now in 1960, if not before, Vietnam indeed seemed to have a civil war on its hands, Northern government and military against Southern government and military. It was further complicated in the South by the government rooting out and punishing not just Communists, but also many non-Communist individuals and groups with differing positions on civil rights and governance, the reverse of what had happened in the North.

Nhu Tang was arrested and imprisoned. He said of his "trial": "I received only two years [and was instead immediately released], the result of a $5,000 bribe my wife paid to the tribunal president, a man who was to become special adviser for security under Thieu."[32] This tribunal head was said by others in the government to be the most corrupt man in South Vietnam—yet Thieu kept him in this position of rooting out Communists, apparently a lucrative position indeed.

The sixty delegates, including Tang, who promulgated the NLF represented many groups, not just Communists, but others of varying beliefs: intellectuals, university students, professional people, Montagnards, Khmer, Chinese, Cao Dai, Hoa Hao, Catholics, and others. The NLF's broad platform stressed patriotism and was highly successful in taking this route, particularly since it also included such ostensibly neutral and popular proposals as land reform and civil liberties. Many neutralists—professors, lawyers, doctors, businessmen and women—would soon join the NLF. Unfortunately for them, as it turned out, the Politburo had its own ideas as to who would control the war in the South, and it definitely was not Southerners, not the NLF.

The DRV, Increasingly a Police State

Le Duan recognized that the DRV had to control tightly what went on not only in the South, but within the North itself. He determined that reinforced discipline was necessary to enable a full national commitment to defeating the Americans who were increasing the size and scope of their advisory mission. Ho Chi Minh's manner of conducting affairs, cruel in effect as it often had been during the French war, was not tough enough.

Lien-Hang T. Nguyen was the first scholar to gain access to the Archives of the Vietnam Ministry of Foreign Affairs, and as she says, "accumulated a wealth of high-level documents never before seen."[33] Her findings confirm that during 1960-63, Le Duan and his deputy, Le Duc Tho, had created "a formidable police state."[34]

CIA analyst Merle Pribbenow agreed. He sent me documents he translated relating to *Plan 69*, 14 December 1960, entitled "Preparations of all types to deal with the U.S.-Diem plan to start a war":

"After studying documents collected during the course of our battle against enemy spy networks and reactionary organizations, we learned of the plans and intentions of the Americans and the puppets to expand the war ".... The Plan of the Ministry of Public Security stated that "Public Security was the core force and that all other forces, staff agencies, and localities must absolutely carry out the requests of Public Security agencies and Party chapters and committees at all levels .... Counter-reactionary forces at all levels carried out a number of tasks: they ... established political files from the village level up; intensified intelligence and surveillance operations; and developed plans to deal with suspect individuals and reactionary organizations and networks."

This plan to tighten security in the North gave impetus to a country-wide hunt for "traitors," spies, and any others believed to be opposed to the DRV government. Catholics in particular were specified as "counter-revolutionary elements." Security forces "increased their efforts to mobilize the people to turn every cadre, every Party member, every citizen into the eyes and ears of Public Security and to persuade them to work together with us.... From 1961 until 1965, we sent a total of 11,365 individuals considered dangerous to our security and social order to collective re-education [prison].... our new policy also focused on carrying out the tactic of "surrounding an area and detaining the reactionaries.... In this way in a short period of time the majority of elements considered dangerous to security were either punished or neutralized, and clean areas were created."[35]

Giap himself was not spared from the hunt for 'revisionists.' Colonel Bui Tin discovered that some of those arrested were asked, "What about Giap? When and where did you meet him? .... Did Giap have anything to say about Le Duan and Le Duc Tho?" Three high-ranking members of Giap's staff were arrested. Bui Tin later asked Giap why he did not intervene. The reply was that Public Security was too powerful, and he was powerless and had to be careful in order that his colleagues not be detained longer.[36]

In the email to which Pribbenow attached the documents relating to *Plan 69*, he said, "North Vietnam was definitely a police state. They knew how to conceal their steel fist inside a velvet glove (Ho Chi Minh was especially adept at this), but it was a police state by any definition of the word. Individuals were suspected, detained, placed under house arrest, etc. without judicial process, sometimes based simply on who their relatives were or who their friends were. Everyone was constantly monitored by Public Security officers and their massive network of informers, and anyone who expressed dissatisfaction was instantly the target of suspicion. . . . What really kept the country together and inspired the troops to fight was the almost universal Vietnamese tradition of fighting against 'foreign aggression' and the desire to reunite Vietnam into a single country. The North Vietnamese troops, like Russian troops in World War II under Stalin, fought for the cause of 'defending the Fatherland,' not for the dictatorial police state that governed them."

The Kennedy Administration: Increased Commitment

The Eisenhower administration had cooled considerably in its enthusiasm for Diem, but in January 1961 John F. Kennedy came into office with solid credentials as a Diem supporter, offering expanded U.S. aid. Kennedy had other problems, though, that demanded more immediate attention than Vietnam. The Soviet Union and North Vietnam were supporting the Communist Pathet Lao, NVA units, and neutralist allies in Laos against a pro-American government, and were gaining the upper hand. Kennedy had said, "Bear any burden, fight any foe." The CIA set out to do this in Laos. The action controlled by them was called the "Secret War" in that details were kept from the American public. The CIA recruited Hmong tribesman to fight an unconventional war, many of them children age fourteen or less,[37] and the U.S. Air Force bombed targets in Laos designated by the CIA.

Then in April 1961 came the deeply embarrassing Bay of Pigs fiasco. On its heels, Kennedy could not afford to show a perceived weakness in Southeast Asia, and in May, Vice President Johnson barnstormed Vietnam. He praised Diem to the world press as "the Winston Churchill of Southeast Asia." Privately, Johnson knew better and confided his reservations in reports to Kennedy. So the question was how much support, and of what kind, should the U.S. continue to give Diem.

Vice President Lyndon Johnson and President of the Republic of Vietnam Ngo Dinh Diem confer in Independence Palace, 12 May 1961. (NARA)

The growth of U.S. military commitment in Vietnam is reflected in casualties. The first American soldier to die in Vietnam after World War II ended had been OSS Lieutenant Colonel A. Peter Dewey, killed by gunfire in September 1945 while driving to Tan Son Nhut for a flight back to the United States. Dewey had protested French conduct toward the Vietnamese to General Gracey who had previously told him to stop meddling, and then ordered him out of the area. The assumption was that Dewey was killed by Viet Minh who stopped his jeep, but no one is sure, and his body was never found. Air Force Technical Sergeant

Richard B. Fitzgibbon, Jr. was killed in Vietnam by another airman on 8 June 1956. Then on 21 October 1957 Special Forces Captain Harry G. Cramer, Jr. was killed by Viet Cong while training South Vietnamese in ambush tactics. The next KIAs in MAAG were in 1959 when the numbers of dead from enemy action began to mount as advisers were allowed to accompany their units in action.[38] In the fall of 1961, the VC were becoming increasingly bold against their countrymen and overran Phuoc Vinh, a village where I had some responsibilities several years later. They decapitated the province chief and stuck his head in a toilet.

The American military commitment ratcheted up in December 1961 when two army helicopter companies arrived in Vietnam, the first complete U.S. units which would support ARVN soldiers. Then in February 1962, Military Assistance Command Vietnam (MACV) was created as an expansion of MAAG and commanded by a four-star general, Paul D. Harkins. By February of the following year, Department of Defense acknowledged that U.S. pilots were flying Vietnamese operational missions and were authorized to make air strikes.

Harkins was a sharply-pressed-uniform, swagger-stick-carrying general who lived in a plush villa near the Cercle Sportif, the former French tennis, swimming, and social club. Called "General Blimp" by some of the press for the hot air he exuded about nonexistent South Vietnamese successes, he had little credibility among those who were close to the war and knew what was really going on.

During the early Kennedy presidency of 1961, U.S. civic aid had also increased. Funds for Diem's "rural development-civic action program" were programmed. By now, Diem had abandoned the failed Agroville Program and instituted his brother Nhu's Strategic Hamlet Program, a similar effort that tried to correct some of the Agroville problems and was instituted on a nationwide basis. "Designed to transform villages and hamlets into antiguerrilla bastions, the basic idea was to oppose the Communists with a ubiquitous resistance and defense system whose 'main and long front line' was the villages and hamlets themselves. With each village and hamlet fortified and armed, the enemy would find it very difficult to select a weak point to attack. He would find strong resistance everywhere. . . . The army would be kept at a reasonable size and improved in combat effectiveness; it would concentrate primarily on enemy base areas and main-force units. The people would become the primary force in the fight against enemy guerrillas. Toward that end, they would organize the defense of villages and hamlets by themselves and fight the enemy by employing 'people's guerrilla tactics.' . . . By the end of 1962 statistics showed that, out of a total of 11,864 hamlets [designated to become Strategic Hamlets], 3,235 had been completed and about 34 percent of the total population was considered as living under the GVN protection."[39]

The concept sounded great, the statistics impressive. The problem was that those statistics nowhere near matched reality. Instead of "ubiquitous resistance" to Communists, there appeared to be ubiquitous Communists resisting the government, many within the fortified hamlets themselves.

Upset at the Joint Chiefs of Staff for what he considered bad advice during the Cuba venture, Kennedy recalled General Maxwell D. Taylor from retirement to serve as a presidential advisor, and soon Taylor virtually supplanted the JCS. In trips to Vietnam Taylor assessed the situation and felt that Diem must be supported, and that up to 8,000 additional U.S. troops might be required in a training mission. He believed that despite Diem's deficiencies he could hold the country together. General Taylor and Secretary of Defense McNamara might reasonably be credited with the original American "light at the end of the tunnel" view.

Southeast Asia matters were soon shoved aside by the developing Cuban missile crisis of August-October 1962, in which the Soviet Union and the United States came close to a nuclear confrontation. After it was resolved, attention swung back to Vietnam, and Taylor became a prominent player in the process of trying to get something done about the deteriorating situation. Assassinations of district and village chiefs were up, and South Vietnamese government and military performance seemed stagnated.

1963: A Terrible Year for ARVN and the South Vietnamese Government

The year was to begin badly and end worse. On 3 January 1963, South Vietnamese forces of 7th Division attacked a Viet Cong battalion at Ap Bac, a hamlet in the Mekong Delta 35 miles southwest of Saigon and 12 miles northwest of My Tho. They quickly found themselves in a hornets' nest with well dug-in VC raking them with automatic weapons fire, and then inflicting heavy casualties on reinforcements brought in by both armored personnel carriers and helicopters. "Viet Cong losses had been 36 captured, an unknown number wounded, and perhaps 50 or more killed. Saigon's casualties were 66 dead, including 3 Americans, and 115 wounded, of whom 6 were American. By those terms the battle had been a draw, another of a long series of clashes. . . . [The Viet Cong] could take smug comfort in the severe damage they had inflicted on U.S. helicopters and in the undeniable fact they had held off so powerful a force. . . . [The whole purpose of the South Vietnamese] once the situation became clear was to disengage, to terminate the battle. . . . For the rest of the war, Ap Bac remained a landmark of Viet Cong progress. . . . Ap Bac was a decided victory for the Viet Cong and an ignoble drubbing for the 7th Division and its American advisers."[40] This battle was followed by others which the North claimed as victories more than two years before U.S. ground troops arrived: "After the Ap Bac victory. . . our People's War against the Americans to save the nation expanded rapidly."[41]

The summer of 1963 was even worse than Ap Bac and other setbacks for the government of Vietnam (GVN—the term most often used by Americans instead of RVN for Republic of Vietnam). Televised scenes of Buddhist monks immolating themselves in the streets of Saigon and Hue electrified the world. The monks were protesting discriminatory treatment and violence against Buddhists by the largely Roman Catholic Diem regime. The Buddhist "crimes" were to support a neutralist position in the war and to hold large, raucous rallies which degenerated into violence when the authorities confronted them. Madam Nhu called these immolations "barbecues," offering to give fuel and matches to the Buddhists. The American public, Congress, and the White House were horrified.

General Cao Van Vien, the highest ranking general in South Vietnam, respected by the Americans, was Diem's chief of staff and a great admirer of Diem. He believed that Diem had indeed saved South Vietnam from succumbing to Communist-directed revolution. When the United States applied pressure on Diem to exile the Nhus, Vien said that Diem could no more do that than cut off his own head. "Mr. Nhu was not only the president's brains, he was his most loyal and trusted advisor and supporter." Then some units of Vietnamese Special Forces attacked pagodas, quite certainly under Nhu's orders, beating monks and nuns. Schools and universities were ordered closed because professors and students supported the monks. General Vien said, "This heavy-handed repression . . . . ended support for the Diem regime at home and abroad."[42]

More bad news for South Vietnam during mid-summer was Giap's greatly enhanced weaponry. The RPG-2 and 57mm and 75mm recoilless rifles came into the inventory, deadly weapons against both infantry and armor. Even more noteworthy, he replaced the early mishmash of rifles with Kalashnikov AK-47s supplied by the Soviet Union, and later with knock-offs by China and East Bloc countries. South Vietnamese units were armed with ineffective light U.S. carbines, submachine guns, or left-over WWII M-1 Garands and other heavy rifles. Due to the shooter's small stature, the latter were brutes to handle, and the soldiers found themselves greatly outclassed in firepower by the AKs which came to be history's most successful, most used, still-used individual weapon.

But the worst was yet to come. In late summer 1963, President Kennedy was becoming more frustrated with Diem and his government. Kennedy wrote a long letter to Diem about the necessity to win over his people, and if he did not take strong measures to accomplish this, America could not continue to back him. Kennedy told a television interviewer, "Diem could regain the support of the people and win the war only 'with changes in policy and perhaps with personnel. . . . I don't think the war can be won unless the people support the effort and, in my opinion, in the last two months the government has gotten out of touch with the people. . . .In the first analysis, it is their war. They are the ones who have to win it or lose it. We can help them, we can give them equipment, we can send our men out there as advisors, but they have to win it, the people of Vietnam.'"[43]

Diem had survived assassination attempts, one at close range in 1957 when shots missed him. He shrugged it off and delivered an address minutes later as if nothing had happened. Then in February 1962 two of his Air Force officers bombed the presidential palace and he escaped without a scratch, although because of the damage he had to move to Gia Long Palace, which had been Leclerc's headquarters. But at the end of October 1963 a serious coup against him by some of his high-ranking military officers was in progress. On 1 November 1963 five paratroop battalions seized key locations in Saigon and surrounded the palace. Their demand was that Diem could stay in office if he would institute reforms. Diem would not capitulate; rather, he stalled while word went out to other ARVN units who might support him, and soon there were battles, ARVN soldier against ARVN soldier. Diem and his brother Nhu escaped from the palace in the dark, but on 2 November they were picked up in a Cholon church by an armored personnel carrier. Ostensibly they were to be taken to a meeting with coup plotters to work out concessions which would allow Diem to continue in office. On the way they were murdered.

Diem's assassination was to result in a year and a half of political chaos in South Vietnam. At first General Duong Van Minh ("Big Minh") put together a loose, fractious junta of generals which had no cohesiveness or direction. Then, three weeks after Diem died, Kennedy was assassinated. Within a day, President Johnson announced that U.S. support for South Vietnam would continue. A day or two later Johnson "said failure was not an option against the Viet Cong. Lyndon Johnson is not going to go down as the president who lost Vietnam."[44]

Diem's assassination threatened to collapse the whole South Vietnamese war effort. The military juntas would last for a few days, weeks or months. Then a civilian was chosen to head the government, an arrangement that lasted only half a year before the generals again took charge in an uneasy coalition.

1964, a Year of Even Greater Crisis Requires a New General: Westmoreland

With Kennedy dead and Lyndon Johnson now the president, the Vietnam situation demanded rethinking and new major players. Late in December 1963, General Earle G. Wheeler, Army Chief of Staff, had told Lieutenant General William C. Westmoreland he would be going to Vietnam as Deputy Commanding General, MACV, and that he would likely take over the top spot in mid-1964 from General Harkins.

Why was Westmoreland chosen for this critical position? There were other generals to consider.

Westmoreland was the right age, a West Pointer, and an airborne commander with an impeccable record. Most importantly, he had high-level sponsorship. The army of the late 50s and early 60s was greatly influenced – some say dominated—by West Pointers who were World War II airborne generals. Matthew B. Ridgway, USMA 1917, commanded the 82nd Airborne Division in combat in Sicily 1943, helped plan Operation Overlord, and jumped with his division into Normandy. In 1944 at the head of XVIII Airborne Corps, he was in on ill-fated Operation Market Garden (*A Bridge Too Far*), and the Battle of the Bulge. In 1950 Ridgway commanded 8th Army in the Korean War, and when President Truman dismissed MacArthur, Ridgway became the UN Forces Commander. This was followed by being named Supreme Allied Commander, Europe and finally in 1953, Chief of Staff, United States Army.

If Westmoreland programmed his own rise, which to a large degree his record and other evidence indicates he did, he could not have done better than to be a protégé of Maxwell D. Taylor, USMA 1922. Taylor had been one of Ridgway's men. He had commanded the 82nd Airborne early in World War II, then the 101st Airborne, jumping with his troops into Normandy on D-Day. Taylor was with his men during Market Garden as one of Ridgway's division commanders. When Ridgway retired in 1955, Taylor replaced him as Chief of Staff. Soon growing at odds with the Eisenhower Administration, Taylor believed that its emphasis on nuclear weapons at the expense of training and maintaining battle-ready ground combat forces was dangerous. He naturally caught the eye of Senator John F. Kennedy and Robert Kennedy, and when JFK became President, Taylor was recalled from retirement to become his military advisor. In this role he ruffled the feathers of the Joint Chiefs of Staff by effectively taking their place, and in 1962 Kennedy appointed him Chairman of the Joint Chiefs .

Taylor had been followed as Army Chief of Staff in 1957 by another general who had commanded the 11th Airborne Division post-war. General Lyman L. Lemnitzer, USMA 1920, went on to become Chairman of the Joint Chiefs in 1960, the man JFK got so exasperated at during the Bay of Pigs fiasco that he turned in disgust to Taylor to determine what went wrong. So, during the early 60s when airborne commander Westmoreland was rising to lieutenant general, he was highly indebted to that happy concurrence of senior airborne generals from West Point.

William C. Westmoreland was born 26 March 1914 to a wealthy Southern family. A decent student, popular among his classmates, he was an Eagle Scout. In 1932 he entered the Military Academy. He achieved the highest cadet rank, First Captain, in his last year just as Robert E. Lee, John J. Pershing, and Douglas MacArthur had done before him. Commissioned in artillery, during World War II he commanded a field artillery battalion of the 9th Infantry Division in North Africa, then as a colonel was with the division in Normandy, Battle of the Bulge, and the Remagen Bridgehead. Lieutenant General Philip B. Davidson, who was Westmoreland's J-2 (Intelligence) on the MACV staff, said that in

World War II Westmoreland "impressed some powerful senior officers, people who would further his later career. The most prominent of these were the three 'greats' of the army's airborne arm – Generals Matthew Ridgway, Maxwell Taylor, and 'Jumping Jim' Gavin. Their friendship and support would be invaluable in Westmoreland's climb to the top."[45]

In the post-war army, Westmoreland knew how and where to steer his career. He transferred from artillery to infantry branch, qualified as parachutist—Airborne all the way!—and served as regimental commander and then chief of staff in the elite 82nd Airborne Division. According to Davidson, General Eisenhower, then Army Chief of Staff, had the most senior officers in the army give him names of rising stars, and Westmoreland was on the final list of the ten best, along with Creighton Abrams and John Michaelis.[46]

Late in the Korean War Westmoreland commanded a paratroop regiment that saw little action, and he was never to be wounded or receive any battlefield awards for valor, unlike Ridgway, Taylor, Gavin, Abrams, Michaelis, and others who became senior generals. He continued to land choice assignments: Secretary of the General Staff in the Pentagon, Commander of 82nd Airborne Division, and Superintendent of West Point, in which role he was again following the illustrious footsteps of Robert E. Lee, Douglas MacArthur, and especially the man who would become his patron, Maxwell Taylor. Just before Westmoreland's Vietnam tour, he was commander of XVIII Airborne Corps.[47]

Other Possible Choices for the Position of COMUSMACV

Lewis Sorley in his fine book on a great man, General Harold K. Johnson, USMA 1933, Chief of Staff of the Army 1964-68, recorded in a footnote, "In a White House meeting with Generals Wheeler and Abrams, Lyndon Johnson said: 'I like Westmoreland. He was one of four recommended to me. The other three were: General Abrams, General [Bruce B.] Palmer, and General Johnson. Westmoreland has played on the team to help me.'"[48] This presumably referred to Westmoreland's recent appointment as deputy to General Harkins.

There may have been others who did not make the list of the final four but who should be considered in determining whether any general other than Westmoreland could have "won" the war:

General Ridgway, USMA 1917? He was much too senior, had fought two wars and been Chief of Staff. In 1963 when Westmoreland was chosen, Ridgway had been eight years retired and was 68 years old. General Taylor? Similar professional reasons—too senior and 62 years old. General Lemnitzer? Similar and 64. General Wheeler? No one could expect him to give up his current post as Chairman, Joint Chiefs of Staff to go to Vietnam. The same applies to Wheeler's successor, General Harold K. Johnson, who though only 51 had been a Bataan Death March survivor and Japanese prisoner during all of WWII. His courage, character, and subsequent professional accomplishments made him an attractive candidate. Perhaps, though, the horrible physical depredations of the prison camps and ships weighed heavily in the presidential decision to make him instead the next Army Chief of Staff. Another candidate might have been General Williston B. Palmer, USMA1919, former Army Vice Chief of Staff, age 64, but he was outspoken and had made some unpopular decisions.

Of younger men, lieutenant generals in 1963, Hamilton H. Howze would seem to have been an attractive candidate. He was a West Point graduate of 1930, former commander of 82nd Airborne and head of the group which developed the airmobile theory, organization, and tactics that played such a major role in the Vietnam War. He went on to command XVIII Airborne Corps and, as a four-star general, the United Nations Command in Korea.

An interesting possibility for the post in Vietnam could have been James M. "Jumpin' Jim" Gavin. Probably an illegitimate child, he was adopted out of an orphanage, worked hard as a boy and was able to enter West Point and graduate in 1929. Gavin was an early innovator of airborne tactics in the U.S. Army, having learned from studying the

Soviets and Germans. In WWII he commanded an airborne regiment of the 82nd during the Sicily invasion and was awarded the nation's second highest military award for valor, the Distinguished Service Cross. On 6 June 1944, now a brigadier general, he led the parachute assault of the 82nd into Normandy, and three months later led the division in Market Garden. He fell out of favor with the Eisenhower administration because of his outspoken views on how to conduct modern warfare, which required rebuilding of conventional forces. In 1958 he retired as a lieutenant general from his post as Chief of Research and Development. Shortly thereafter in his 1958 book, *War and Peace in the Space Age*, he stated that limited war was to be our bane. "It was exasperating. Wouldn't the Communists ever provide us with the right kind of war?" Well said, but contributing to his demise at the highest levels of the army had been such views as: "We could have settled Korea and Dien Bien Phu quickly in our favor. Tactical nuclear missiles, sky cavalry and increased assault airlift can contribute decisively to that kind of operation."[49]

Would Gavin have been enticed back into service, as had been the case with Taylor, and would he have accepted the MACV command if offered? A moot point. There was zero chance that any soldier favoring tactical nuclear warfare in an insurgency environment would have been asked.

Two other men who like Westmoreland ultimately became four-star generals were lieutenant generals in late 1963: John H. Michaelis, and Creighton W. Abrams, Jr. Interestingly, both were Westmoreland's USMA 1936 classmates. Another classmate was Bruce Palmer, Jr., a senior major general at that time, soon to be promoted, who was said to be one of the four generals considered by the president.

Michaelis became famous during his command of the "Wolfhound" regiment in the Korean War. Called "Iron Mike" by his men for his tough standards and extraordinary heroism, he earned the Distinguished Service Cross. During my first two years at West Point, Brigadier General Michaelis was our much-respected Commandant of Cadets. He later contracted throat cancer (in 1960) and could barely talk, which probably would have disqualified him for the Vietnam post.[50]

Bruce Palmer graduated 5th in the class, somewhat over 100 seats ahead of Westmoreland, and was commissioned in Cavalry. While chief of staff of 6th Infantry Division in the South Pacific he was awarded the Silver Star. Shortly after the Westmoreland appointment, Palmer was promoted and moved into the prestigious slot of Deputy Chief of Staff for Operations (DCSOPS). Later, for five months in 1967 he was commanding general of the corps-size II Field Force Vietnam (IIFFV). Then Westmoreland made him Deputy Commander of U.S. Army, Vietnam (USARV), the subordinate MACV headquarters responsible for all support operations which, in essence, Palmer commanded. After Vietnam, Palmer ended his career as Vice Chief of Staff, then acting Chief of Staff of the Army.

Creighton Abrams would become Westmoreland's successor.

Westmoreland Arrives

Attractive as that small stable of well-qualified candidates was, it was Westmoreland and not one of the others who landed in Saigon in late January 1964. The situation that he found would have been ludicrous had it not been so deadly serious. He said, "Life in Saigon in those days was curiously lethargic. . . . The South Vietnamese simply called off the war—or ignored it—on weekends and holidays and took long siestas at lunch time."[51] The statement reveals the Americans' impatience in fighting a new war that was old for the South Vietnamese—going back 19 years—and was just about to really get going for a gung ho new U.S. advisory group commander. Since the enemy had been fighting even somewhat longer than the South Vietnamese, it also highlights the difference between their lackadaisical attitude and the Viet Cong's go-go-go offensive spirit. As Westmoreland looked around he found that "The temporary gaiety that had followed Diem's downfall had disappeared. The atmosphere fairly smelled of discontent—workers on strike, students demonstrating, the local press pursuing a persistent campaign of criticism of the new government."[52]

In February, the Viet Cong dramatically drew attention to their goals to kill Americans. Only a few days after Westmoreland arrived, enemy attacks in the Mekong Delta, a bomb in Saigon killing five U.S. personnel and wounding four dozen, attacks in Tay Ninh Province in III Corps zone, and an attack on the U.S. advisory compound in Kontum in II Corps served notice that the enemy was serious about the war. While the enemy was busy making gains, General Nguyen Khanh and the generals in his junta seemed to be spending more time plotting how to stay in power and in fighting for the top spot than in fighting the enemy. In succeeding months, attacks which continued all over the country brought McNamara and Taylor, then chairman of the Joint Chiefs of Staff, to Vietnam to assess the situation for the president. McNamara told the president bluntly, "The situation unquestionably has been growing worse. . . In terms of government control of the countryside, about 40 percent of the territory is under Viet Cong control or predominant influence. In twenty-two of the forty-three provinces the Viet Cong control 50 percent or more of the land area. . . . in the last ninety days the weakening of the government's position has been particularly noticeable."[53]

During 1964, the enemy's first complete division had been raised in the South, the 9th Division, and its units were particularly effective in December. Late in that month, Maxwell Taylor, now the U.S. ambassador and furious over a serious instance of yet more infighting, insisted on a meeting with Khanh. The GVN general, his hackles raised, instead sent his principal assistants, four generals including Nguyen Van Thieu and Nguyen Cao Ky. Ambassador Taylor began the meeting, "Do you understand English?" he thundered. Then he dressed them down for the abysmal failure to form any kind of stable government. Taylor wrote, "Devoted as we were to the cause of Vietnam, I assured them that we were not prepared to take any more of this suicidal nonsense. . . . After reporting back to Khanh, and, I suspect, instigated by him, they let it be known publicly that I had insulted them and the armed forces by treating them like American puppets."[54] No doubt this incident, in the

North's view, more than justified their long denunciations of the South as a "puppet regime."

The North Sends Units South

Since 1959 when Le Duan became First Secretary, the most powerful man in the Politburo, eclipsing both Ho and Giap, he had urged continuation of the war in the South, and he was taking steps to consolidate control over the fighting of it. Colonel Bui Tin said, "The decision to step up the struggle in the South was taken at the 15th Party Plenum held in 1959. . . . During 1959 and early 1960 we did not send whole units to the south, but instead secretly selected individuals from among those Southerners who had regrouped to the North in 1954."[55] By 1962 Central Office South Vietnam (COSVN) had been created to control the struggle in the South.

In December 1963, the 9th Plenum of the Party Central Committee in Hanoi adopted a resolution which was to have immense consequences in the American war: *"Efforts to Move Forward to Gain A Great Victory in South Vietnam.* [It] . . . laid out . . . directions for . . . . sending main force troops to the South [in 1964], and intensifying massed combat in South Vietnam in order to, shoulder to shoulder with the entire population, defeat the 'special war' being conducted by the American imperialists. Besides those cadre and soldiers being sent off to battle in South Vietnam as individual reinforcements and as 'framework units,' in 1964 our army began to send to the battlefield complete units at their full authorized strength of personnel and equipment. . . . The 101st, 95th, and 18th Regiments of the 325th Division were the first mobile main force regiments to march south into battle as complete regiments."[56]

I asked Merle Pribbenow by email: "Did any main force units of battalion size or larger get sent south earlier [than late 1964]?"

Pribbenow's answer: "There were certainly battalion-sized and regimental-sized 'framework' units of Southerners that were sent from North Vietnam to the South prior to late 1964, but I have also found reference to at least three regular NVA battalions, two from the 312th Division and one from the 308th Division, being sent to fight in South Vietnam prior to the fall of 1964. The 312th Division sent a battalion south to fight in the spring of 1963; the 308th Division sent a battalion south in the fall of 1963; and the 312th Division sent another battalion south to fight in the spring of 1964."

Pribbenow provided excerpts from North Vietnam division histories which he had translated, including: *The Victory Division: A Report*: "In the spring of 1963, the first battalion of the division [312] to be sent South, 600 cadre and enlisted men, crossed the Ben Hai River [the Demilitarized Zone] into the Tri-Thien battlefield."[57]

By the time of the 9th Plenum, the powerful, militant Le Duan was particularly annoyed with Giap who had long counseled patience in sending units south, very concerned that the time was not yet ripe for such aggressive actions. Giap had seen patience pay off in spectacular fashion at Dien Bien Phu. Originally, under Politburo orders, his massive attack was scheduled for 25 January 1954. The DBP defenders, though, had noted the buildup, and braced to receive the onslaught. On one of Hal Moore's trips back to Vietnam, Giap told him, "I disobeyed my orders. . . . At the time I wasn't sure if this would cost me my life."[58] Just hours before the assault was to begin, Giap ordered all units to withdraw to their previous positions. Giap sensed that his force would not be strong enough, particularly artillery, and if he attacked he would take casualties he could not replace. He needed more time to tunnel in from the reverse slopes of the hills to emplace howitzers at concealed entrances on the forward slopes where they would be virtually immune to counter battery fire and air attacks. Upon receiving the order to withdraw, Giap's hyped up troops were greatly demoralized, and some deserted. Giap came under intense criticism from other generals and some Politburo members, and they demanded his dismissal. He was saved only by Ho, who had not lost faith in him. And Giap was proven right. His patience had paid off. The attack, launched finally on 13 March, inflicted huge losses on the

French forces and began the slow, grinding progress toward the fall of the bastion on 7 May.

During 1963 Giap had been advising caution, taking more time for training and equipping PAVN. Duan allowed him to remain Minister of Defense but secured the appointment of General Nguyen Chi Thanh as commander in the South, working out of COSVN headquarters. Thanh was an early revolutionary. "When [Nguyen Chi Thanh] was arrested for 'illegal, anti-French activities' in the 1930s, the judge at his hearing asked him why he chose to be a Communist. . . . [He] responded, 'I fight for the people, for democracy, for our livelihood, so what is the sin? I haven't yet understood Communism, so how can I be a Communist? But Communists are patriots and fight for the masses so what is wrong with that?'"[59]

Thanh had earlier been promoted to full general, equal in rank to Giap. Similar to Le Duan, Thanh was a Southerner from a lowly background, a peasant. He was very different from Giap who had been raised as an intellectual. Giap's fall from grace was temporary. His devotion to training troops and ensuring their logistics, an enormous task, ensured him a position of formidable power as the war was to take another major turn.

With the assassinations of Diem and Kennedy, and the resolution of the 9th Plenum to send complete main force regiments, and later, divisions, to the South, America had been thrust into a new era of the Vietnam War. Whereas COSVN always conducted guerrilla war, and in time, so-called "VC" divisions[60] were to launch coordinated attacks in the South, PAVN main force units up to division size would be pitted against South Vietnamese regular forces with their American advisers and support. As a measure of how much the war in the South was not just influenced by the North, but in fact taken over by it, Merle Pribbenow wrote to me, "Every one of the division commanders, including the commanders of the so-called 'VC' 2nd, 3rd, 5th, and 9th Divisions, was a native of North Vietnam."

With the North fully committed, war on a huge scale was soon to follow.

CHAPTER 9

General Westmoreland, Attrition, Search and Destroy, 1964-1967

*   *   *

WESTMORELAND MAY HAVE BEEN PROMOTED beyond the range of his competence, as Lewis Sorley contends in his book, *Westmoreland: The General Who Lost Vietnam*. Westmoreland had done well indeed at lower levels of command, but now, despite impressing others as being comfortably in control, now having received his fourth star and being appointed as COMUSMACV, he indeed may have been in over his head. The chaotic situation he inherited, which might be summarized as foreign troop support in a country which abhorred foreign presence and was on the verge of collapse, speaks for itself. But dire situations have sometimes been converted into victory. Much more to the point, consideration of the organization, equipment, and training of the United States Army of that time, coupled with its command culture, handicapped him, just as it would the two generals who succeeded him as COMUSMACV.

Westmoreland, as Shaped by Advice and the Command Culture of the U.S. Army

The American army of 1964 had been organized and trained to fight a conventional war in the manner of World War II and Korea, with front lines protecting extensive logistical rear areas. The so-called triangular division was the norm for infantry and armor – three regiments, generally of three battalions with three companies, and so on down the line in threes. This kind of division, at about half the strength, is what the French, North Vietnamese, South Vietnamese National Army, then ARVN used in Vietnam.

All the senior American generals who shaped policy for the army in the 1950s and 60s had commanded in World War II, and some of them also in Korea. Post-war, most of them had influenced in one way or another the way the current army was organized, trained, and equipped. Naturally they were part of a command culture, learning from and influencing one another. In his memoir, Westmoreland recounts a 1962 visit to the Academy by the aged General MacArthur when Westmoreland was superintendent. "We entered my office, the office he had occupied as superintendent, following World War I. Sitting in his old chair, he leaned back and lost himself in thought." Following a parade, "at lunch in the cadet mess . . . . Speaking without notes . . . he hypnotized his audience. . . . General MacArthur spoke with emotion of his years in uniform, his love of West Point, his respect for the Academy's motto. To the cadets he charged: 'Your mission remains fixed, determined, inviolable – it is to win our wars.'"[1]

A year later, when Westmoreland had received his Vietnam assignment, he visited General MacArthur in his suite in the Waldorf-Astoria in New York. The old general began talking about Southeast Asia and continued for an hour and a half, nearly nonstop. He said, "Your assignment there will be ripe with opportunity but fraught with danger."[2] Finally, "he turned to the war itself." MacArthur, thinking in terms of the armed forces he had commanded in World War II, urged Westmoreland to make sure he always had plenty of artillery because the Oriental greatly fears artillery.[3]

Westmoreland also recounted a visit which President Kennedy made to West Point in June 1962 to deliver the commencement address. "'Yours are not strictly military responsibilities,' he said [to the audience of graduating cadets]. 'Therefore they will require a versatility and adaptability never before required in either war or peace.' He spoke of 'another type of war, new in its intensity, ancient in its origin – war by guerrillas, subversives, insurgents, assassins, war by ambush instead of war by combat, by infiltration instead of aggression, seeking victory by eroding and exhausting the enemy instead of engaging him.

"'Where there is a visible enemy to fight in open combat,' he went on, 'the answer is not so difficult. . . . But when there is a long, slow struggle, with no immediately visible foe, your choice will seem hard indeed.'"[4]

Here were two sets of advice for the man who was to conduct America's war in Vietnam—one from the old general who had led America's fight across the Pacific to defeat Japan: "Make sure you have plenty of artillery."

The other, from the young naval hero of that war in the South Pacific: "Yours are not strictly military responsibilities—They will require versatility and adaptability." This would be "another type of war."

Westmoreland chose the old course, analogous to using plenty of artillery, almost certainly because that is what he, all of his contemporary generals, and those of us who had been captains, majors, and lieutenant colonels during the Vietnam War had been brought up on: *firepower.* As cadets at West Point, 1952-56, my class had no instruction in insurgency warfare. Shortly after graduation, as a lieutenant in the armor basic course I learned a great deal about tanks and low-level armor tactics but nothing about using tanks in the jungle. Then in Europe during the Cold War our training and field exercises were designed to fight the World War II kind of war, holding off superior Soviet forces arrayed against us just across the West German border. As a captain in the armor advanced course in 1961-62, there was nothing about the Vietnam-type war beyond a few brief paragraphs in our training brochures. The Army's senior generals, as more junior officers, had commanded in World War II, and America had won that war. So what could be wrong with the choice of making sure you applied massive firepower at the right place and time—that you had "plenty of artillery"?

That kind of thinking was not unique to the Army. The Air Force, Navy, and Marines likewise thought in terms of superior firepower. All armed services during the Cold War were focused on first defending against the Soviet Union, then winning a war against them, utilizing the concepts, training and, except for nuclear weapons, much the same type equipment that had brought victory in World War II. We had a command culture fixed on past victories, and it was not well suited to the war we would fight.

MACV, Mission and Resources

In July 1964, just after Westmoreland assumed full command of MACV, President Johnson had named Maxwell Taylor as ambassador to Vietnam, with the following charge: "[To] have and exercise full responsibility for the effort of the United States Government in South Vietnam. . . . I wish it clearly understood that this overall responsibility includes the whole military effort in South Vietnam and authorizes the degree of command and control that you consider appropriate."[5]

Not only was Taylor a respected military man but he had been a patron of Westmoreland, so the Taylor/Westmoreland relationship would seem to bode well for a unified approach to the military conduct of the war. However, as Westmoreland pointed out, "MACV was but one component, albeit the largest, of what was known as the 'United States Mission' or 'Country Team.' Under terms of the Mutual Defense Assistance Act of 1949, the U.S. ambassador headed the Mission. Aside from MACV and the Department of State, other organizations involved were the Central Intelligence Agency, the Agency for International Development. . . the Joint United States Public Affairs Office . . . and the Mission Economic Counselor. It was a complex, awkward arrangement."[6]

Each of these other agencies had a role in what went on militarily in Vietnam, especially after American combat units arrived, but none was in Westmoreland's chain of command. Perhaps more problematic was his link to the president as Commander in Chief. As Westmoreland said, "MACV functioned not directly under the Joint Chiefs of Staff in Washington but through CINCPAC [Commander in Chief, Pacific Area Command]. . . . What many failed to realize was that not I but [Admiral U. S. Grant Sharp, CINCPAC] was the theater commander in the sense that General Eisenhower . . . was a theater commander in World War II. My responsibilities and prerogatives were basically confined within the borders of South Vietnam. Admiral Sharp commanded the Seventh Fleet, over which I had no control . . . . When the bombing of North Vietnam began in February 1965, Admiral Sharp controlled that too. . . . The big B-52 bombers that were later employed in South Vietnam were under the Commander in Chief, Strategic Air Command, but I was responsible for selecting targets for final approval by authorities in Washington. . . . My task would have been eased had I headed a 'Southeast Asia Command.'"[7] In short, Westmoreland was not the supreme commander of military operations over and in North Vietnam or Cambodia or Laos,[8] and within South Vietnam were several agencies of the U.S. government functioning in a quasi-military manner over which he had no direct command responsibility and therefore no control except through coordination and persuasion.

Cold War Major Threats

Even had Westmoreland been given a unified combined command with operational authority over all components of the U.S. military in Southeast Asia as well as Allied forces in Vietnam (called Free World forces)—principally those of South Vietnam, Thailand, Philippines, Australia, New Zealand, Republic of China, and Republic of Korea—he and any other commanding general would have been subject to the political and military restrictions confining U.S. military action. As enunciated in turn from Truman to Nixon, the biggest threat to America in the Cold War was not North Vietnam but the USSR. Our primary military consideration in terms of both nuclear battlefield and conventional war necessarily was Europe. The concept of mutually assured destruction constrained both sides to ensure that it never occurred. That left non-nuclear warfare as the sole military means of containment of Communism. When Westmoreland arrived in Vietnam in 1964, the Soviet Union seemed to be moving into a policy of wary, non-violent coexistence.

Chinese intervention in Vietnam, though, was still a possibility. Truman had been roundly trashed for "losing" China in 1949, although one could not lose what was never possessed. Eisenhower had China in mind, perhaps even World War III, when he turned down massive bombing or nuclear weapons as an attempt to save the French at Dien Bien Phu. With America deeply into its advisory role in 1964, presidential campaign bluster of Goldwater and LeMay was hardly the kind of rhetoric for guiding responsible military action.

HOP TAC

We must take Westmoreland's pronouncements in his book, *A Soldier Reports*, with more than a grain of salt. Nevertheless, they reveal major beliefs and events that shaped the war, and thus are valuable in assessing his role and the war as a whole. One of his first actions, surprising in terms of what happened later, was to stress pacification. He takes credit for designing a pacification plan which, he says, "I code-named HOP TAC . . . cooperation. . . . It was designed to expand security and government control and services – pacification – gradually outward from Saigon into six provinces that form a kind of horse collar about the city. . . . When I presented this at the Honolulu conference[9] in June 1964, I received authority to conduct HOP TAC, and thus in effect obtained for MACV the role of executive agent for pacification around Saigon, the role that I believed the military should have for the entire country."[10] Thus Americans, not Vietnamese, were the center for planning and conducting pacification, and this was to have profound consequences.

In later evaluating the program, Westmoreland said, "HOP TAC's problems can be summed up in two words: political instability. With everybody at South Vietnamese top levels concerned about the next *coup d'etat*, few gave more than minimum commitment to the program."

Westmoreland added, "[HOP TAC] was in effect, a 'spreading oil spot' concept. If successful around Saigon, similar programs might be conducted in the environs of such other cities as Danang, Qui Nhon, and Can Tho, until eventually all might merge."[11] In other words, all of South Vietnam could become pacified. This was at a time when U.S. advisory strength was approaching 23,000, US ground combat units were only a matter of discussion, and the South Vietnamese were fighting losing battles in all arenas, political and military.

The *Pentagon Papers* researchers said, "So unsuccessful was [HOP TAC] that during its life span the VC were able to organize a regiment . . . in the Gia Dinh area surrounding Saigon.[12]

"Even during the dark days of 1964-1965, most Americans involved in the war paid lip service, particularly in official, on the record statements, to the ultimate importance of pacification. But their public clichés about 'winning the hearts and minds of the people' were not related to any programs or priorities then in existence in Vietnam."[13]

Commit Ground Combat Units?

In his excellent book, *Choosing War*, Fredrik Logevall uncovers in great detail steps leading to the fateful decision by President Johnson to commit ground combat units. The three most influential voices in the president's coterie were Secretary of State Dean Rusk, Secretary of Defense Robert McNamara, and National Security Advisor McGeorge Bundy. Walt W. Rostow of the State Department could be considered a fourth. Johnson inherited them from Kennedy and kept them on, intensively grilling them on why the war was necessary. All, in the beginning, were inveterate hawks. McNamara, though, relatively soon saw that the war would not only be difficult in the extreme, but probably unwinnable, yet he spoke publicly about winning it and forged ahead with fighting it.

McNamara includes a chapter in his memoirs, *In Retrospect*: "The Decision to Escalate":

"The most critical phase of America's thirty-year involvement in Indochina, the six months between January 28 and July 28, 1965, saw the United States embark on a course of massive military intervention in Vietnam, an intervention which ultimately destroyed Lyndon Johnson's presidency and polarized America like nothing since the Civil War. How did it happen? Why did we fail to foresee the implications of our actions? What hopes, fears, perceptions and judgments—accurate and inaccurate—shaped our thinking and actions?"[14]

Johnson agonized over the war he hated, the war that interfered with his Great Society program. He tried to rationalize a way out, yet he and his advisers kept coming back to the bedrock of prestige: the *prestige* of the United States was on the line, and it was essential in this Cold War to uphold it. Their personal prestige, too, was inextricably wrapped up in the mess, and they could not, or would not, loose themselves from it. Johnson was caught, like Macbeth:

"I am in blood
Stepp'd in so far, that, should I wade no more,
Returning were as tedious as go o'er."

III.iv.136-38

The President's Decision

Telford Taylor, U.S. Chief Counsel at Nuremburg, bluntly summarized the choices: "If the objective of our Vietnam policy be stated over-simply as 'to stop Communism at the 17th Parallel,' there were at most two ways to do that. The first, which has been our stated policy, is to gain and hold the political allegiance of the South Vietnamese to a non-Communist government, while giving them defensive assistance against any military means used by the North. The second was to ignore the South Vietnamese people, treat South Vietnam as a battlefield, and kill all the North Vietnamese or Viet Cong found on or moving toward the battlefield. The sad story of America's venture in Vietnam is that the military means rapidly submerged the political ends, and the first method soon gave way to the second."[15]

By 1964 it was abundantly clear that our immense American aid program—military, economic, and societal—had failed. South Vietnam was in crisis. In essence, President Johnson had two basic choices: support the South by any and all means necessary, or withdraw. He could make a further enormous military commitment to include inserting ground combat troops in the South, bombing North Vietnam, and blockading its harbors. He could even invade the North, which would require a very large ground force and bombing so intense it would approach the carpet bombing destruction of World War II. Then, in order to ensure the safety of the South, an occupation of the North would be required. For how long? Five years? A decade? A century? Congress, the American people, and allies rightly would never support such a course.

The president's other choice was to withdraw—an enormously difficult task politically—while trying to get the best deal possible for the South Vietnamese. "Unlike the situation in 1954, when the Secretary of Defense and all the Joint Chiefs except Admiral Radford had opposed [US] intervention [at Dien Bien Phu], in late 1964 there was near unanimity among the civilian and military leaders of the Defense Department in favor of doing what was necessary to save the situation."[16]

Johnson heard and could not ignore contrary advice. Being advised both ways, and absorbing the stress the country was now exhibiting, Johnson continued to struggle with the problem. His real mark in history could be made, he knew, by the success of his Great Society Program. And this damned Vietnam War was torpedoing it. He was a Texan. How could a *Texan* lose a war to little yellow men in sandals in "that damn little pissant country"? How could *he*, Lyndon Baines Johnson, go down in history as the first American president to *lose* a war?

At the end of 1964 when President Johnson was tussling with the enormous Vietnam problem – Should America cast down the gauntlet and commit ground troops to war in South Vietnam?—American military deaths in Vietnam and adjacent countries as a result of the Vietnam War from 1955-1964 stood at 416.[17]

It would have taken enormous courage for President Johnson to have acted other than as he did. The true test of presidential character in weighing a war decision should be ultimately a personal, not political one: *Would I subject my son or my daughter to the dangers and sacrifices I will order other people's sons and daughters to face?*

>*My son!*
>*My daughter!*
>*Luci Baines Johnson?*
>*Lynda Bird Johnson?*

If America's core interests unmistakably require the president to answer—*Yes I would, I have to send my son, my daughter*—then fight, and fight fiercely and intelligently America must. If *No, I will not send my son or my daughter*, then an alternative must be found.

But President Johnson did not have that kind of character. Under the circumstances he inherited, would *any* American president have had it?

When the last American death was recorded in the Vietnam War, the number was more than 58,200. Wounded were over 153,300.

1965: America Goes All In

Two events in particular shaped America's Vietnam decisions in late 1964 and early 1965. The first was the so-called Gulf of Tonkin incident when in August 1964 North Vietnamese patrol boats in the Tonkin Gulf were reported to have attacked a destroyer, the *USS Maddox*.[18] That incident led to the Congressional resolution: "The Congress approves and supports the determination of the President, as Commander in Chief, to take all necessary measures to repel any armed attack against the forces of the United States and to prevent further aggression." The president ordered retaliatory air strikes on North Vietnam. Then on 7 February 1965 sappers struck the American advisers compound at Pleiku, killing eight U.S. soldiers and wounding another 126.

That did it.

The president ordered increased air strikes against North Vietnam that led to Rolling Thunder and other bombing campaigns against the North which, with some halts, were to continue almost to the end of the American war. Marines landed on 8 March 1965. One report stated, "First ashore was the Battalion Landing Team 3/9, which arrived on the beach at 8:15 a.m. Wearing full battle gear and carrying M-14s, the Marines were met by sightseers, South Vietnamese officers, Vietnamese girls with leis, and four American soldiers with a large sign stating: 'Welcome, Gallant Marines.' Gen. William Westmoreland . . . was reportedly 'appalled' at the spectacle because he had hoped that the Marines could land without any fanfare. Within two hours, Battalion Landing Team 1/3 began landing at Da Nang air base."[19] These two battalions were intended for a limited mission, security of the American base at Da Nang. But combat boots on the ground were sure to prompt more requests, and within two weeks, MACV asked for and got two more battalions; furthermore, the president authorized them to engage in "active combat." A request followed from the Joint Chiefs of Staff for a Marine division to go to the northern provinces and an Army division to the Central Highlands.[20] For the time being, the president held off on approving these requests, but the die was cast. Marines ashore, along with a soon-approved troop level of 175,000, clearly signaled that the war had changed from one of denying the enemy a victory by defending to—in Westmoreland's words—"taking the war to the enemy." The buildup to over 543,000 troops had started.

By early April 1965, 17 non-aligned nations were calling for negotiations, and, whereas President Johnson welcomed this idea, he also said, "We will not be defeated. We will not grow tired. We will not withdraw, either openly or under the cloak of a meaningless agreement."[21] The president had concisely proclaimed the exact opposite of what would happen.

With American ground combat troops ashore, a major question was how the Americans and South Vietnamese would interact at the highest levels. What missions would the Americans have? Republic of Vietnam Armed Forces (RVNAF)? The South Vietnamese ambassador to the U.S., Bui Diem, wrote: "At the top levels of the [U.S.] administration there is no evidence to suggest that anyone considered the South Vietnamese as partners in the venture to save South Vietnam. In a mood that seemed mixed of idealism and naïveté, impatience and overconfidence, the Americans simply came in and took over. It was an attitude that would endure throughout the remainder of the conflict. The message seemed to be that this was an American war, and the best thing the South Vietnamese could do was to keep from rocking the boat and let the Americans get on with their business.[22]

Remembering all too well that Chinese forces had poured across the border into North Korea when the Americans had gotten too close, Washington had speculated on a possible Chinese reaction to U.S. troops ashore in Vietnam. The Chinese Central Committee had made plain to the North Vietnamese leadership its intent: "You may wage the boldest struggle against U.S. imperialism. You need not be afraid of the expansion of the war, its expansion into China. If the war expands to China, we will fight shoulder to shoulder with you."[23]

In April 1965, very soon after the first American combat units landed, patriotism in the North reached a fever pitch. "The Party's Three Readiness Campaign . . . called for 'readiness to join the army, to partake in battle, to go wherever the fatherland deems necessary. . . . Mobilization drives more than doubled the ranks of the PAVN in the first few months of [the new] war."[24]

Victory in Vietnam records: "On 25 July 1965 Chairman Ho Chi Minh appealed to the citizens and soldiers of the entire nation: 'No matter if we have to fight for five years, ten years, twenty years, or even longer, we are resolved to fight on until we achieve complete victory."[25]

Search and Destroy

While planning HOP TAC back in 1964, Westmoreland had his staff come up with terminology to describe the initial military actions intended to push government control outward from Saigon. "Search and destroy" was the unfortunate choice. This, he said, "was nothing more than the infantry's traditional attack mission."

Attack mission? That is an astonishing statement in recapping a pacification mission. Westmoreland went on, "Many people, to my surprise, came to associate it with aimless searches in the jungle and random destroying of villages and other property."[26]

Perhaps because that so often happened, and the term seemed appropriate?

Soon after he had launched HOP TAC, Westmoreland was to have something more to concern him than a failing pacification operation in the Saigon area. Earlier, North Vietnamese reinforcements had been infiltrated individually and in small groups into the South, most of them originally Southerners who had regrouped to the North after the Geneva Accords. But by the fall of 1964, entire regiments were being sent south. As if the very term "search and destroy" had triggered something in Westmoreland in 1964, shortly after he got combat forces ashore in 1965 he would send them on missions to search for enemy main forces and destroy them. This, on the surface, may seem reasonable enough, given the U.S. military's organization and command culture.

What was behind search and destroy? Westmoreland and every American army officer since the end of World War I studied the "Principles of War," the tenets that were intended to guide modern military combat. After World War I, British military strategist B. H. Liddell Hart analyzed the essence of wars and stated what he considered the time-tested principles for conduct of war. Following Hart's lead, the various armies of the world then expressed their principles of war in manners unique to their circumstances. All of them, though, in one way or another gave great weight to the two cardinal principles as later stated in *Department of the Army Field Manual 3-0*, 1965:

"Objective – Direct every military operation toward a clearly defined, decisive, and attainable objective. The ultimate military purpose of war is the destruction of the enemy's ability to fight and will to fight.

"Offensive – Seize, retain, and exploit the initiative. Offensive action is the most effective and decisive way to attain a clearly defined common objective. Offensive operations are the means by which a military force seizes and holds the initiative while maintaining freedom of action and achieving decisive results. This is fundamentally true across all levels of war."

As for *objective*, critics have long pointed out that the U.S. government had trouble devising a statement of objective for Vietnam that satisfied the public and the Congress. What we were doing or trying to do in Vietnam seemed murky and led at first to confusion and distrust, and later to civil disobedience, riots, and demands for withdrawal.

Patton said there are only three principles of war: Audacity, Audacity, *Audacity!* No American military manual or military school taught that wars were won by being on defense. It was indeed important to learn the ingredients of a good defense, and to practice them when necessary. But defense was taught as a temporary means of regaining the offense. Westmoreland's first combat units ashore initially would be used defensively, to secure critical installations such as airfields and coastal facilities, but as quickly as possible, they would go on the offense.

So where did Westmoreland go wrong? Or did he go wrong?

Command Culture and Its Consequences

U.S. soldiers had learned in past wars they must *attack*. By the time of the Vietnam War, commanders well knew they must hit the enemy in the middle, or hit them on the flank, or go around them. Go, go GO! The best defense is a good offense. And that was absolutely true, proven time after time in the wars prior to Vietnam. No commander wants to be known as hesitant or weak. As a cadet, then lieutenant, then captain in the 1950s and early 60s, I immersed myself in the history of World

War II. I watched the many movies of WWII combat, read the books, listened to the veterans, and attended the service schools. We Americans have a *can do* attitude. The offense was how WWII had been won: *Attack!*

In General Bruce Palmer's book, *The 25-Year War*, he revealed how command culture had tragic consequences for America and South Vietnam: "The JCS [Joint Chiefs of Staff] seemed to be unable to articulate an effective military strategy that they could persuade the commander-in-chief and secretary of defense to adopt. In the end . . . . General Westmoreland . . . made successive requests for larger and larger force levels without the benefit of an overall concept and plan. . . . Not once during the war did the JCS advise the commander-in-chief or the secretary of defense that the strategy being pursued most probably would fail and that the United States would be unable to achieve its objectives. The only explanation of this failure is that the chiefs were imbued with the 'can do' spirit and could not bring themselves to make such a negative statement or to appear to be disloyal."[27]

Attrition, Search and Destroy, Body Count, Kill Ratio

In *The Pentagon Papers* and other official reports, the terms "attrition," and "search and destroy" as "strategies" are seen over and over—in MACV communications, discussions in Washington circles, and orders conveyed to Westmoreland in Vietnam. More correctly, attrition was the strategy Westmoreland chose, and search and destroy his tactic for achieving it. Body count and kill ratio evolved naturally out of those concepts.

McNamara said, "Between 1965 and 1967 Westy intensified his pursuit of an attrition strategy aimed at inflicting more casualties on the Viet Cong and North Vietnamese than they could replace. . . . The body count was a measurement of the adversary's manpower losses; we undertook it because one of Westy's objectives was to reach a so-called crossover point, at which Viet Cong and North Vietnamese casualties would be greater than they could sustain."[28]

In other words we would reach a point at which we would be killing Viet Cong and NVA faster than the enemy could replace them, thus ultimately ensuring our dominance over them. As command policy this concept, coupled with the kill ratio – the ratio of enemy to friendly killed – ia appalling. Soldier-scholar Dave R. Palmer wrote, "Attrition is not a strategy. It is, in fact, irrefutable proof of the *absence* of any strategy [Palmer's emphasis]. . . . [The commander] uses blood in lieu of brains."[29]

When it was certain that American combat units would be sent to Vietnam, Westmoreland seems to have shifted gears from thinking of himself as top American military advisor to the South Vietnamese government—which he was—to that of battlefield commander—which he also was. While minimizing efforts to get pacification moving and building ARVN into a capable army through Vietnamization, he focused instead on those NVA main force units, and he would attack. As soon as U.S. troops came ashore in 1965 and secured base installations, Westmoreland sent them on search and destroy missions, The first major one was by the 173rd Airborne Brigade under Brigadier General Ellis Williamson. They went into War Zone D, the immense jungle to the northeast of Saigon,[30] and found not much of anything. But a search and destroy later in 1965 far to the north was to have much different results.

The Battles of the Ia Drang

The 1st Cavalry Division (Airmobile) began arriving at An Khe in the Central Highlands in early August 1965 under command of Major General Harry W. O. Kinnard. The 1st Cav was the culmination of General Howze's earlier work on army aviation and air cavalry, and was a superb fighting unit. The division had 435 helicopters, enabling it to do wide-range patrolling, intelligence-gathering, and fighting. Hal Moore said, "The helicopter, Gavin believed, held the possibility of making the battlefield truly a three-dimensional nightmare for an enemy commander."[31] As it turned out, it also made the battlefield a nightmare for Moore when he was ordered to air assault into deep jungle.

The division had trained hard in the months before shipping out, but personnel problems over which it had no control resulted in some of its units or individuals in them not getting the full period of training, in fact only a small part of it, and they would have to learn on the job.

Hal Moore's 1st Battalion, 7th Cavalry arrived at An Khe in mid-September 1965, flying over the site where French Mobile Group 100 met disaster eleven years earlier. His initial mission was to build a base camp. "We stepped off the choppers into a tangle of trees, weeds, and brush, in the middle of what would become our airfield. . . . The men of the division and some two thousand Vietnamese laborers cleared the site by hand, with machetes and axes. . . . They also built a heavily fortified twelve-mile-long and hundred-yard-wide defense perimeter . . . around the base."[32] Moore learned right away that bases ate up combat manpower, not just initially in building them, but also later with guard duty and a multitude of other tasks to perform in maintaining and defending them. Then a particularly virulent form of malaria, against which the yellow pill of the time was insufficient defense, resulted in 56 troopers from his battalion being evacuated. Expiring enlistments took a further toll, and from an authorized strength of 767 he was down to 679.

Moore's companies conducted some relatively minor operations out of Plei Me fort, an old French position, "patrolling south and east, finding nothing and growing more frustrated by the hour." The Corps commander paid a visit and said "our primary mission was: Find the enemy and go after him."

Find 'em, fix 'em, fight 'em. That's one of the main things an airmobile battalion was designed to do. On the afternoon of 13 November, UPI reporter Joe Galloway said he had heard that Moore's battalion would launch into the jungle the next morning. Shortly, Colonel Thomas W. (Tim) Brown, 3rd Brigade Commander, gave Moore his orders: "Here is your area of operations – north of Chu Pong in the Ia Drang Valley. Your mission is the same one you have now: Find and kill the enemy."

Search and destroy.

Brown would provide 16 UH-1D Huey helicopters to move the troops, and would position two 105 millimeter howitzer batteries within range to support them. Major Bruce Crandall would be in charge of the helicopters. Moore said, "We had not yet been in any battalion-size fight in Vietnam, and Bruce Crandall's helicopter pilots were likewise unblooded."

Moore would be going after North Vietnamese units operating in rugged jungle close to the Cambodian border. On the map, he searched for "possible landing zones in that rough scrub-and-jungle region."[33] His main concern was that once he selected a landing zone (LZ) he could insert less than 80 men before the Hueys would have to return 15 miles to pick up another load, and then continue the shuttle until he could get the 450 men of his three rifle companies, his combat support company, and a slim headquarters command element on the ground. The region had long been a Viet Minh, then Viet Cong sanctuary.

In 1965 Chu Huy Man was a general in command of a large area in Central Vietnam, and Moore was to meet him many years after the war. He told Moore, "I was confident the Americans will use their helicopters to land in our rear, land in the Ia Drang area. It was our intention to draw the Americans out of An Khe. We did not have any plans to liberate the land; only destroy troops." Moore recounts that General Man's three regiments attacked Plei Me and then regrouped in the Ia Drang-Chu Pong base area. "Under the jungle canopy were excellent training areas and wide trails on which troops could move, even during the day, without being detected from the air. Best of all, the Ia Drang Valley was convenient to the inviolable sanctuary across the Cambodian border. . . . General Man could also call on the local veterans of the H-15 Main Force Viet Cong Battalion, six hundred strong, for duty as porters, guides, and fighters."[34]

Moore would have preferred not to have to make an aerial recon to select a landing zone since the enemy knew there could be a good reason for aircraft over a particular area. But he had no viable alternative, never having seen the terrain. Early on the morning of 14 November he flew high to minimize the chances of alerting the enemy, rejected two possible landing zones as too small, and decided on the third, Landing Zone X-Ray. "It was flat; the trees weren't all that tall; and it looked as though it could take up to eight helicopters at one time."[35]

Moore flew back to Plei Me and "issued orders to the assembled company commanders, liaison officers, pilots, and staff: 'Assault into LZ X-Ray to search for and destroy the enemy.'" Division artillery would fire a twenty minute preparation, blasting the landing zone. This would be followed immediately by 30 seconds of helicopters firing rockets, then 30 seconds of their machine gun fire, with the lift ships carrying the infantry hard on the gunships' tails. Moore and his small command group loaded with the first flight and they were off. Moore said that on 14 November 1965 at 10:48, "as the chopper skids touched the ground I yelled, 'Let's go!' and jumped out, running for the trees on the western side of the clearing, firing my rifle."[36] The LZ, a semi-clearing no more than a football field in size, was cold. But it was soon to get hot.

On one of his trips to Vietnam after the war, Moore also met Lieutenant General Nguyen Huu An, who as a lieutenant colonel commanded the NVA troops in the battle. Together, Moore and An went to LZ X-Ray and studied the battlefield. General An said, "When you landed here, you landed right in the middle of three of our battalions of the 66th Regiment, our reserve force. It was the strongest we had. [At] full strength the battalions each had about four hundred fifty men. [To include the headquarters units] the regiment's total strength was about sixteen hundred men."[37]

For Moore's men, it was the beginning of three days and two nights of horrific battle at LZ X-Ray. Moore's battalion, soon reinforced by elements of other infantry battalions, were heavily supported by artillery, cav gunships, Air Force flare ships, and fighter bombers. The enemy had been operating in this area for some time and knew it well, helped by the local guides. In most places the jungle was dense, and in the semi-clearings along stream beds and in occasional openings of double and triple canopy trees, heavy growths of elephant grass reached to five feet. With mountain streams to provide water, jungle foliage for concealment, and a Cambodian sanctuary close by to the west, the NVA were in an ideal position for the actions they were good at: concentrating quickly, hitting hard, and then if necessary withdrawing back into the jungle.

Even with all of its mobility and firepower, the 1st Cav was at a great disadvantage, so much so that one has to question seriously why Moore's unit was given such a mission in such terrain. Across broad swaths of formidable jungle the cav could not land its helicopters except in some small clearings that were known to the enemy, and then often only one or two ships at a time. Moore said, "This clearing [X-Ray, about a hundred yards long] was the only decent helicopter landing zone between the slopes of Chu Pong and the Ia Drang [River] and for two miles east or west." That in itself spelled danger.

The ability to move so that the commander can exercise initiative is key to success or failure. In terrain which allows flexibility of movement, airmobile units can be deadly. In the jungle that all but engulfed LZ X-Ray, though, Moore's unit was quickly pinned into position, and once the firing started, even to get his own men into the LZ, to say nothing of reinforcements, required immense courage, skill, and determination.

General An said, "When you dropped troops into X-Ray, I was on Chu Pong mountain. We had a very strong position, and a strong, mobile command group. We were ready, had prepared for you and expected you to come. The only question was when. The trees and brush limited our view of the helicopters landing but we had an observation post on the top of the mountain and they reported to us when you dropped troops and when you moved them."[38]

At the time of the assault, back at 3rd Brigade headquarters the assistant division commander was briefing the division commander: "When General Kinnard arrived I showed him a situation map. He took one look and said, 'What the hell are you doing in that area?' I replied, 'Well, General, the object of the exercise is to find the enemy and we sure as hell have.'"[39]

The battle, night and day, was close in and vicious. After having reinforced piecemeal by air, on the third day, after X-Ray had fallen quiet, Colonel Brown finally landed for a brief visit. Moore had gotten no sleep since he had caught a few hours the night before the assault. He said, "I could still think clearly but I had to tell myself what I intended to say before I opened my mouth. It was like speaking a foreign language before you are completely fluent in it. I was translating English into English." Only soldiers who have gone through battle for two or three days and nights with little or no sleep can truly know that feeling.

For three days the enemy dead had been rotting in the heat. "Now came the body count," Moore said. "Hating it, I asked my company commanders for their best estimates of enemy killed." The men pushed outward from their final line to be greeted by ghastly scenes of carnage. Moore finally gave 634 as body count plus an estimated 1215 killed and wounded by supporting fires, and six prisoners. "We had lost 79 Americans killed in action, 121 wounded, and none missing."

On the morning of 17 November, the fourth day, when the sounds of war no longer buffeted X-Ray, Lieutenant Rick Rescorla said, "We were flown away, but the stench of the dead would stay with me for years after the battle."[40] The townspeople of Gettysburg knew and were haunted by this stench. My troops and I well knew the smell of a battlefield in tropical heat, and we will never entirely rid ourselves of it.

LZ Albany

The withdrawal by air of what remained of Moore's battalion was not to be the end of the horror. The LZ X-Ray battle was followed immediately by an even deadlier day and night for 1st Cav sister units in the jungle, in and near close-by LZ Albany. The two reinforcing battalions which remained at X-Ray after Moore's men departed were ordered to march to landing zones, one of them two miles distant, and the other four miles away by the route they took.

March!

This, despite the fact that part of one of those reinforcing battalions had gone through heavy fighting on their second and third days at X-Ray. Although the third night had been relatively quiet, both battalions had been on one hundred percent alert all night long, meaning that no one had slept.

Why did the brigade commander, Colonel Brown, order a march through the jungle under such conditions? The 1st Cav had 435 helicopters.

March?

A B-52 strike had been scheduled for the lower slopes of Chu Pong mountain. For safety, the troops had to be at least two miles from X-Ray by the time it hit. Why wasn't the strike moved farther up the mountain or diverted to an alternate target so the men who had remained at X-Ray could have been extracted by helicopter? Whatever the answer, sending dead-tired men miles through jungle in proven proximity to a tough enemy invited tragedy.

In *We Were Soldiers . . . .* Moore described what happened, but he was not there at Albany. Larry Gwin was. On that day Gwin was a lieutenant, executive officer of Alpha Troop, 2nd Battalion of the 7th Cavalry. In his book, *Baptism: A Vietnam Memoir,* he describes how his battalion in column formation, without sleep for 48 hours, each man carrying a minimum load of 60 pounds in stifling heat, struck out for LZ Albany.

Gwin said they had no air support during the march, and other reports confirm his statement. It is incomprehensible that in a division with so many helicopters there was not even one overhead to guide them, and no gunships to provide instant support if they needed it. After marching a long time they came upon "a ragged row of [abandoned] Montagnard huts. . . . Battalion ordered us to burn the huts." *Burn huts?* Probably not the smartest thing to do—send up a smoke signal in country that contained NVA main force regiments, to say nothing of "winning hearts and minds." Gwin said that after another hour or so of difficult going, they were then less than five hundred meters, they thought, from LZ Albany where they would be picked up. No problem.

They crossed a stream and "the terrain changed dramatically, and the jungle seemed to engulf us. Tall, triple-canopied trees, festooned with hanging vines and mosses, towered overhead, shutting out the sun. The undergrowth changed from the tall dry grass and scrub brush of the valley, to the in-your-face heavy, broad-leafed vegetation of a tropical rain forest. It enshrouded us like the night, and all was obscured in a dim, eerie light. The men in front of me virtually disappeared as if they'd been swallowed by the earth."[41] The progress slowed to a crawl. But ahead was a clearing, the first one they had seen in two hours. LZ Albany. Hopefully.

With the bulk of the battalion column strung out in the jungle behind him, disaster loomed. Gwin made his way forward to a clump of trees ahead of him where he saw the battalion commander's small group. Suddenly a burst of fire was followed by another and then a deafening crescendo, the onset of chaos. Cav soldiers desperately returned fire as rounds from AK-47s whacked into elephant grass and underbrush so tall they could not see the man standing next to them, or the enemy firing at them. Screams of anguish and "cease fire, cease fire, we're shooting into our own men" at first went unheard in the din of battle as men pulled triggers, tried to kill the enemy, and struggled to survive. To Gwin's rear the strung-out battalion column was overrun, and the slaughter was horrendous. Later, with fighter bomber and artillery support and reinforcement by helicopter, the battle ebbed, but after dark, "pop, pop, pop" was heard as the NVA went among gravely wounded Americans and executed them. By the next morning, "the battalion, roughly four hundred strong when it left X-Ray, had suffered more than seventy percent casualties – 155 dead, 124 wounded. Charlie Company was the hardest hit, losing all but 9 of its 110 men." The survivors and reinforcements spent the day policing up the battlefield, evacuating dead and wounded. The stench of American and Vietnamese bodies, Gwin said, was much worse even than at X-Ray. "At Albany it filled your nostrils and permeated your soul."[42]

Westmoreland on Battle Results

A few days after the survivors had returned from Ia Drang to their base camp they looked forward to Thanksgiving dinner. General Westmoreland showed up and wanted to address the troops. Gwin relates that his battalion had been on its way to a hot turkey dinner when they were lined up around the general standing on a stump. "It was a nice speech, full of praise for the great job we had done, and the great victory we had won." After the talk, Westmoreland departed with his entourage of colonels and other officers, and Gwin and his buddies found themselves at the end of the chow line, looking around for "a place to sit and eat their cold and lumpy dinners."[43]

Westmoreland's connection with the Ia Drang, an important test of his search and destroy tactic which he proclaimed a resounding victory, is oddly tenuous. He said in his memoir, relative to enemy actions against Plei Me and in that vicinity, "I directed the commander of 1st Cavalry Division [Kinnard] to find the enemy and seize the initiative from him." Then he erroneously referred to Moore's brigade commander during the battle as a Colonel Clark whom he had known, instead of Colonel Brown. He went on mistakenly to refer to the battle as lasting six days, commanded by Moore, when in fact Moore commanded for two days and part of a third. And the general does not mention in his memoirs the horrific battle of LZ Albany, taking place on the fourth day and the night leading into the fifth day and then a sixth day – the last two days spent policing the battlefield after having taken enormous casualties. Moore and the surviving men of his battalion had been back at Pleiku during the entire battle of LZ Albany and its aftermath.[44]

In his book Westmoreland also takes no note of the cold Thanksgiving dinner for the remnants of the battalion that was so mauled at LZ Albany, probably because no one had told him who they were. However, another incident occurred to indicate Westmoreland's distance from the men at times when it really mattered. Gwin said that after the general left the unit at Thanksgiving, "I wondered if he had any idea of what the battalion had just been through. It turned out that General Westmoreland had no idea of what had happened to us at Albany. While Colonel Moore had been able to brief him about the fight at LZ X-Ray, no one had told him about the debacle we had suffered at Albany. The 1ˢᵗ Cav brass were too embarrassed or ashamed to tell him the truth – the truth being that we'd suffered roughly seventy percent casualties in that fight. . . . They covered it up."[45]

Lewis Sorley, in his book on Westmoreland, sheds further light on this important matter. "Westmoreland contacted Lieutenant General Stanley Larsen, commanding general of I Field Force, Vietnam, and asked for an explanation. Larsen personally investigated the matter and was told by the division commander, assistant division commander, and brigade commander of the forces involved that they said nothing to Westmoreland about what happened at LZ Albany because they had not known about it at the time. . . . Larsen stated, 'They were lying and I left and flew back to my headquarters and called Westy and told him so, and told him I was prepared to bring court-martial charges against each of them. There was a long silence on the phone, and then Westy told me, 'No, Swede. let it slide.'"[46] Was he protecting them or, having so widely expressed his satisfaction with the "victory" of the Ia Drang, protecting his career?

Confirmation of Attrition as a Strategy

Moore wrote of the aftermath of the 1ˢᵗ Cav Division's Ia Drang campaign: "In Saigon, General William C. Westmoreland, and his principal deputy, General William DePuy, looked at the statistics of the [entire] thirty-four days of the Iadrang campaign—3,561 North Vietnamese estimated killed versus 305 American dead—and saw a kill ratio of twelve North Vietnamese to one American. What that said to the two officers who had learned their trade in the meat-grinder campaigns in World War II was that they could bleed the enemy to death over the long haul, with a strategy of attrition."[47] Never mind that body count was always suspect, and never mind that the loss of a single soldier ought to cause a commander to strive for ways of conducting war that would minimize those losses, attrition it was.

When Westmoreland told [a senator from South Carolina], "We're killing those people at a ratio of 10 to1" to that [the senator] responded, "Westy, the American people don't care about the ten. They care about the one."[48]

General Bruce Palmer stated that he had examined "approximately 250 national intelligence documents, most of which were produced by the CIA, covering the 1965-75 period."[49] As a result he found that "in assessing North Vietnam's capabilities to fight a prolonged, grinding war of attrition, the CIA during the period 1964-72 consistently concluded that the North Vietnamese manpower base was adequate. (In 1967-68, North Vietnam's population exceeded eighteen million, while South Vietnam counted only about twelve million people.) The CIA pointed out that North Vietnam's own industry contributed only marginally to the war effort, practically all material support coming from the Soviet Union or China; that the diversion of substantial manpower to a very large air defense effort and to the large work force required to repair damage from U.S. air attacks was manageable; that North Vietnamese force levels had been readily expanded to keep pace with the allied troop buildup in the South; and that Hanoi's available manpower resources were clearly adequate to sustain the war indefinitely."[50]

Evolution of the Search and Destroy Concept

Westmoreland's first step in progression to his search and destroy tactic had been a rejection of the so-called enclave concept which Ambassador Taylor had advanced early in 1964 when discussions about committing U.S. combat troops became more serious. The Taylor concept would have put arriving U.S. troops in critical coastal spots which they would defend as logistics bases for supporting the South Vietnamese, and out of which they could conduct some limited combat actions around those bases. Westmoreland had increasingly failed to see eye to eye with his patron, and said, "I disagreed with the enclave strategy."[51]

In May 1965 Westmoreland was using the term "enclave" differently: "I forwarded to Washington my concept of how operations were to develop. In Stage One the units were to secure enclaves, which I preferred to call base areas. . . . In Stage Two the units were to engage in offensive operations and deep patrolling in cooperation with the ARVN. In Stage Three they were to provide a reserve when ARVN units needed help and also conduct long-range offensive operations."[52] This went well beyond Taylor's concept, but Washington bought Westmoreland's plan.

The 1st Air Cav's experiences partially fulfilled Stages One and Two as they built their base, patrolled and conducted limited operations. Then they leapt into the Ia Drang—without ARVN, contrary to plan. U.S. forces would be the whole show.

Westmoreland's Stages Two and Three prescribed aggressively going after the enemy's main forces. He said, *"Although a commander must observe caution, he wins no battles by sitting back and waiting for the enemy to come to him."*[53] This was a natural statement for a soldier brought up in the command culture of the offensive, and it is so important in an exploration of why no American or South Vietnamese general could win in Vietnam that we will come back to it.

Any American general of the time could make that statement with no argument from his peers. In fact, the two Army generals in the JCS strongly supported it. But it was contrary to what Westmoreland had earlier espoused, his belief in his role as being twofold – one: to support Vietnamese pacification efforts, two: simultaneously, to train and support ARVN forces to fight their own war, "Vietnamization." If, with more U.S. combat forces arriving, Westmoreland were to employ them primarily in that manner – pacification and training ARVN—it would take time and patience, a lot of it.

Dave Palmer's analysis of time and patience is instructive: "To Americans, raised in a free, competitive, capitalistic society, time is a precious commodity. It is the one thing that cannot be bought or built. We can't bear wasting it. A moment lost is never regained. . . . To Asians, steeped in Confucian concepts, time is an endless stream flowing from an infinitely regenerating source. It is precious enough, a commodity to be valued, but because it is of unlimited abundance one can hardly use too much of it. Thus, that which we husband the most carefully they expend the most liberally. . . . A quick victory is strictly a western concept. In war our attitudes and expectations lead us to seek the lightning stroke of victory."[54]

Instead of taking the slow approach of pacification and improvement of ARVN so that hopefully they could fight their own war, Westmoreland had decided to use his forces in another fashion. Speaking specifically of the airmobile division, he said he would "gain the initiative, penetrate, and whenever possible eliminate the enemy's base camps and sanctuaries." Then referring to his forces generally, "Invading the sanctuaries also might bring the elusive enemy to battle, affording an opportunity to destroy his main forces. . . . Furthermore, since the enemy's large units would be met most often in his base areas, the greater mobility of American units would provide them with an advantage."[55]

In his base areas? Greater mobility? An advantage?

Did Westmoreland have Europe in mind with armies maneuvering rapidly against one another? Or, as Jaubert had cautioned Leclerc, the Sahara with its hard-baked sands and vast, open maneuver areas?

Where were those base areas to which Westmoreland referred? Most were in deep jungle, carefully selected to provide natural cover, concealment, and terrain barriers.

As for "the greater mobility of American units?" In the air, surely— but the enemy's main force units were not in the air. The jungle, like the night, was the enemy's friend. So Westmoreland's strategy was to pit U.S. ground forces against the enemy's main forces where the enemy had the advantage—in the jungle. I had more than a little experience fighting in the enemy's jungle base areas with my armored cavalry, mechanized infantry, infantry, and air cavalry. We were ordered to go there, to seek out and destroy the enemy. We went and tried to do that. We can attest that the advantage was with the enemy, not with us.

Westmoreland went on to state, "Two additional tasks were to be pursued throughout all three phases [of his three-staged plan]: pacification and strengthening the ARVN."[56] His phrasing clearly indicates his priorities – these were "additional tasks" which came after the primary one, U.S. troops attacking enemy main forces in their jungle bases. In any event, these additional tasks turned out to be hardly more than lip service at first. Later, when he had committed U.S. forces so much to enemy main force destruction, backtracking and reinventing priorities would have been difficult indeed.

So, search and destroy it was, and would continue to be.

The Marines – A Different Concept

Brigadier General Frederick J. Karch, a Marine who had fought in the South Pacific was assistant division commander of 3rd Marine Division. He had made several visits to Vietnam in the year before he became commander of the 9th Marine Expeditionary Brigade. On those visits, "He did not like what he saw. In his opinion the ARVN were so weak that if Marines were to land in Vietnam he felt they should make it North, not South V Vietnam. "If we go into Da Nang we'll disappear into the countryside and never be heard from again.'"[57] He sounded like George Ball speaking to President Kennedy some four years earlier: "Within five years we'll have three hundred thousand men in the paddies and jungles and never find them again." Karch was the general in charge when his Marines were so warmly greeted on the beach.

Marine Lieutenant General Victor H. Krulak served for two years in the Pentagon, 1962-64, as special assistant for counterinsurgency to the Joint Chiefs of Staff. Then in 1964 he became commander of Fleet Marine Force Pacific with responsibility for all Marines in the Pacific area to include Vietnam. He was certain that Kennedy had been correct in placing great emphasis on counterinsurgency rather than big unit warfare. Krulak said, "I went to Vietnam eight times between 1962 and

1964. In those early years I learned something of the complex nature of the conflict there. The problem of seeking out and destroying guerrillas was easy enough to comprehend, but winning the loyalty of the people, why it was so important and how to do it, took longer to understand." Krulak had several meetings with Sir Robert Thompson, acclaimed for his methods of countering insurgency in Malaya, and Krulak was mindful of Thompson's principles: "The people's trust is primary. It will come hard because they are fearful and suspicious. Protection is the most important thing you can bring them."

Krulak said, "The 'spreading ink blot formula' [pacification]. . . should have been at the heart of the battle for freedom in Indochina. Many people applauded the idea, among them Army generals Maxwell Taylor and James Gavin. General Westmoreland told me, however, that while the ink blot seemed to be effective, we just didn't have time to do it that way. I suggested to him that we didn't have time to do it any other way; if we left the people to the enemy, glorious victories in the hinterland would be little more than blows in the air --- and we would end up losing the war. But Defense Secretary Robert S. McNamara expressed the same view as Westmoreland to me in the winter of 1965---'a good idea' he said about the ink blot formula, 'but too slow.' I had told him in a letter dated 11 November 1965, 'In the highly populous areas the battleground is in the peoples' minds.'"[58]

This difference in concepts – search and destroy versus pacification with its primary emphasis on security for the people – was to strain Third Marine Amphibious Force relations with MACV throughout the war. By 1968 Krulak had gone to Vietnam 54 times, in periods ranging from five to twenty days, and he saw the country from the DMZ in the north to Ca Mau Peninsula in the south. He met a lot of people, went on operations with the Vietnamese Marines and ARVN, and observed how large enemy forces could melt into the landscape. "Everything I saw kept bringing me back to the basic proposition that the war could only be won when the people were protected. If the people were for you, you would triumph in the end. If they were against you, the war would bleed you dry and you would be defeated."[59]

An official Marine history said that General Krulak "sought to persuade [Admiral Sharp, Commander in Chief, Pacific, who had command authority over Westmoreland], that there was no virtue at all in seeking out the NVA in the mountains and jungle; that so long as they stayed there they were a threat to nobody, that our efforts should be addressed to the rich, populous lowlands. . . . It is our conviction that if we can destroy the guerrilla fabric among the people, we will automatically deny the larger units the food and the intelligence and the taxes, and the other support they need. At the same time if the big units want to sortie out of the mountains and come down where they can be cut up by our supporting arms, the Marines are glad to take them on, but the real war is among the people and not among these mountains."

However, "General Westmoreland's staff reinforced his doubts about the Marine Corps concentration on the small-unit counterguerrilla campaign south of Da Nang. . . . Brigadier General William E. DePuy, the MACV J-3 [Operations], reported to General Westmoreland . . . .that the Marines 'were stalled a short distance south of Da Nang' because the Vietnamese were 'unable to fill in behind Marines in their expanding enclaves.' Although impressed with the Marine professionalism and concern for the 'security of the people and the pacification process,' . . . .Depuy believed that [the Marines] should use part of its force 'as a mobile element throughout the Corps.' He recommended to General Westmoreland that the Marines 'be directed' to launch large-unit offensive operations against VC base areas with two to three battalion forces during at least two weeks out of every month.'"[60]

And so Westmoreland directed.

A Marine Platoon Leader in Search and Destroy

Second Lieutenant Philip Caputo had landed at Da Nang Airbase on 8 March 1965, the first day ashore for U.S. combat units. He was a rifle platoon leader in Karch's brigade. Caputo was soon caught up in Westmoreland's directive to the Marines to conduct search and destroy operations. "General Westmoreland's strategy of attrition . . . had an effect on our behavior. Our mission was not to win terrain or seize positions, but simply to kill: to kill Communists and to kill as many of them as possible. Stack 'em like cordwood. Victory was a high body-count, defeat a low kill-ratio, war a matter of arithmetic. The pressure on unit commanders to produce enemy corpses was intense, and they in turn communicated it to their troops. This led to such practices as counting civilians as Viet Cong. 'If it's dead and Vietnamese, it's VC' was a rule of thumb in the bush."

In his memoir, *A Rumor of War*, Caputo says, "The conflict in Vietnam combined the two most bitter forms of warfare, civil war and revolution, to which was added the ferocity of jungle war. . . . Communists and government forces alike considered ruthlessness a necessity if not a virtue. . . . A sergeant in my platoon, ordinarily a pleasant young man, told me once, 'Lieutenant, I've got a wife and two kids at home and I'm going to see 'em again and don't care who I've got to kill or how many of 'em to do it.'"

Caputo entered the war with the idealism of youth, wanting to serve his country and do a good job. But "by autumn what had begun as an adventurous expedition had turned into an exhausting, indecisive war of attrition in which we fought for no cause other than our own survival. . . . Out there, lacking restraints, sanctioned to kill, confronted by a hostile country and relentless enemy, we sank into a brutish state."[61]

Calley of My Lai should never have had leadership responsibility at any level. By contrast, Caputo was a highly intelligent, thoughtful, concerned leader, yet as he and his platoon fought he fell into a mood in which at times he thought he might be going mad, and he wanted to kill. It was horrible for him – the losses in his platoon, the ghastly sights of his men dead, the grotesque enemy bodies mutilated by platoon fires including his own, the ferocity and insanity of killing enemy who were trying to surrender, the burning of small hamlets while shooting anyone thought to be VC, the recovery of Marine bodies after the VC had gotten through with their tortures and executions. Caputo struggled and became more Calley-like with each incident. Then as bad luck would have it, he was assigned to regimental headquarters in a position that would further stress him. For five months he was Officer in Charge of the Dead, as he called it.

Caputo's duties were to do all the paperwork on casualties, and to confirm them – which often meant to view them as they were brought in for processing. Some had been out in the sun for a long time and they stunk of death. Others were in pieces or mangled. He had to confirm that the wounds appeared to be of such or such cause so the reports would be accurate. One of the bodies was of his classmate from officer's candidate school, a lieutenant who had led a 28-man patrol. Only two survived an ambush and execution of the surviving wounded. They had crawled under the bodies of the dead and feigned death. Caputo said, "We paid the enemy back, sometimes with interest. Some line companies did not bother even taking prisoners; they simply killed every VC they saw, and a number of Vietnamese who were only suspects. . . . 'If he's dead and Vietnamese, he's VC.'"[62]

To escape this horrifying duty he asked for reassignment to a line company. Incessant monsoon rains added to the misery as he led his new platoon. Except for the daily rain and the painful jungle rot it caused on his legs, nothing had changed. He was back with the killing and burning, especially of one village. "It was as though the burning of Ha Na had arisen out of some emotional necessity. It had been a catharsis, a purging of months of fear, frustration, and tension. We had relieved our own pain by inflicting it on others. . . . I could analyze myself all I wanted, but the fact was we had needlessly destroyed the homes of perhaps two hundred people." Caputo went over the reasons, some of which at the time he thought good, and concluded, "None of that conventional wisdom relieved my guilt or answered the question. . . Why?"[63]

The final step for Caputo was to be charged with murder. Some of his platoon had said they knew where confirmed VC were in a nearby hamlet, and Caputo knew he wanted them dead – not saying so, exactly— but his men could read the unspoken language with which he gave them their mission, and he and they went off to accomplish it. Two Vietnamese villagers were killed, one a mere boy. If they were VC there was no proof.

Caputo, waiting for a verdict, was told that the enlisted man who actually pulled the trigger was acquitted and the general was considering dropping the murder charges against all the rest. He said, "I paced nervously for fifteen or twenty minutes. It looked as if my instincts had been right: the higher-ups wanted this case off their backs as much as I wanted it off mine. . . . I would atone in some way to the families of Le Du and Le Dung. When the war was over, I would go back . . . and . . . and what? I didn't know."[64]

Search and destroy was over for Caputo. He would get a letter of reprimand. The charges against him and the others had resulted from the village chief going to the district chief to report the murders. One can imagine what the villagers thought when they heard the verdicts—letters of reprimand—and how their subsequent attitudes and actions may have contributed to the outcome of the war.

Civil War, Almost

Lewis W. Walt was "a Marine's Marine." He had fought in WWII, Korea, and now Vietnam. Twice wounded, he had received numerous awards for valor to include The Navy Cross, equivalent of the Army's Distinguished Service Cross, our nation's second highest military medal. In Vietnam he was promoted to Lieutenant General and appointed Commanding General, III Marine Amphibious Force, and Senior Advisor, I Corps. By 1966 General Walt had established a close working relationship with General Nguyen Chanh Thi, the Vietnamese I Corps commander. General Thi appreciated Walt and he reciprocated, being highly supportive of Walt's Marines and the program they called the Combined Action Unit. In his book, *Strange War, Strange Strategy*, Walt said, "We had found the key to our main problem – how to fight the war. The struggle was in the rice paddies, in and among the people, not passing through, but living among them, night and day, sharing their victories and defeats . . . . Then suddenly, came a terrible blow – not on the military but on the political front. . . . Swiftly and unexpectedly, our hopes were collapsed. Not by the Viet Cong, but even more tragically by our friends and allies, the South Vietnamese themselves."[65]

Concerned with General Thi's popularity and power in I Corps, and fearing a coup, when Ky was prime minister and Thieu a figurehead, Ky summarily relieved Thi. Thi's units, as well as the predominant Buddhist leadership around Da Nang, supported Thi against Ky, and fighting and riots broke out. Caputo said, "South Vietnamese soldiers were fighting street battles with other South Vietnamese soldiers as the two mandarin warlords contended for power. And while the South Vietnamese fought their intramural feud, we were left to fight the Viet Cong."[66]

In a manner reminiscent of Diem's Buddhist troubles, the city of Hue joined in the struggle, and a spreading strike disrupted airfields, ports, and supply installations. The loyalty of several military South Vietnamese leaders to their government was increasingly questionable. Buddhists, loyal to Thi, demonstrated, and anti-Ky/Thieu government sentiments became widespread. In Da Nang, ARVN personnel took part in the demonstrations. At Hue, RVNAF personnel joined civil servants and students in protests.

Then, in crisis mode two Vietnamese Marine Corps battalions, loyal to the government, landed at Da Nang, and Ky's Vietnamese air forces patrolled the skies. Ky's Saigon troops were seizing critical locations in Da Nang while Thi's opposing troops, including an armored force, were moving on the city. For several days and weeks the situation went back and forth, with General Walt trying to placate the contending parties and dampen a civil war. Exchanges of gunfire killed and wounded some military on both sides, South Vietnamese against South Vietnamese. When Ky's planes fired rockets that fell into the U.S. Marine compound and wounded several men, though, a fed-up Walt launched his own jets with orders to shoot down the Vietnamese aircraft if there was any further attack. Now it was U.S. against South Vietnamese.

While awaiting final decision on his case, Caputo was at his division's command post on a hill "which gave us a ringside seat. Looking to the west we could see [U.S.] Marines fighting the VC; to the east, the South Vietnamese Army fighting itself. . . . I knew then that we could never win. With a government and an army like that in South Vietnam, we could never hope to win the war."

The insurrection ended on 25 May. Caputo said, "General Walt sent a message to all Marine units in I Corps: . . . the 'rebellion' had been crushed and that we could 'look forward to an era of good relations with our South Vietnamese comrades-in arms.' The message shocked me. Even Lew Walt, my old hero, was blind to the truth. The war was to go on, senselessly on."[67]

Ultimately, high-level meetings of Vietnamese and American officials had led to a meeting between Ky and Thi, with Ky prevailing and Thi being exiled to the United States. During the weeks of chaos, a new corps commander, a division commander, and other high-ranking officers had supported the dissidents. There had been serious concern that ARVN units would go over to the Communist side. The disaffected generals were tried, dismissed from service—and three of them became senators![68] All sides went back to the war against the VC and NVA, but the problems of civil unrest and military favoritism, corruption, and political appointments of generals, province and district chiefs rather than appointments based on merit, continued to plague the South Vietnamese conduct of the war.

The Marines' Combined Action Program (CAP)

The Marines, trained to attack straight up the middle when they thought they had to, were also a highly innovative lot. They had much the same civil affairs kinds of programs the Army had, providing medical, nutritional, minor construction services, and the like in the hamlets and villages. But they took it one step further with what they called the Combined Action Program (CAP). General Walt, a tough man with high standards, saw the futility of search and destroy. In his chapter titled "Rice Roots Support," he said, "Of all our innovations in Vietnam none was as successful, as lasting in effect, or as useful for the future as the Combined Action Program. Like many good ideas, the system was basically simple: Help the local defense forces at the hamlet level with training, equipment, support, and the actual presence of American fighting men. . . . The local Popular Force soldier—the hamlet and village guard—was the poorest equipped, least trained, and most inadequately supported of all the government forces in the Republic of Vietnam, yet none was more important to the security of the people. . . . He was defending his own home, family, and neighbors. The popular force soldier knew every person in his community by face and name; he knew each paddyfield, trail, bush, or bamboo clump . . . . He knew in most cases the local Viet Cong guerrilla band, and it was not uncommon for him to be related to one or more of them by blood or other family ties."[69]

General Walt pointed out to Westmoreland that the huge proportion of inhabitants in the large I Corps area lived in hamlets and villages basically along the coast and on streams that reached back toward the mountains to the west. Walt was not in favor of chasing the enemy in its own lair, that difficult jungle terrain to the west; rather, through his pacification program he would cut them off from the support they found and very much needed in the populated areas. He was not successful in dissuading Westmoreland, who thought the Marines were dragging their feet on search and destroy, but nevertheless Walt was able to devote significant resources to pacification while, following MACV orders, he committed the rest to search and destroy. He recognized that it made little sense to sweep through a village, taking and inflicting casualties, then go on to some other place and have to come back and do it all over again. He wanted his teams to have a continuing presence in the hamlets and villages. The schizophrenic contrasts between Marine search and destroy missions and Marine CAP missions reveal much of why the war could not be won. Lieutenant Caputo and his men during search and destroy showed the terrible dark side of military operations which may exist at one level simultaneous with CAP at another level within a single command.

A CAP Team

Barry L. Goodson explained what it was like, being a CAP team member. "Generally, each unit consisted of six to eight men including one radioman and one corpsman (medic)."[70] CAPs worked with Popular Force soldiers integrated into the units. Sometimes they were lucky and had an interpreter, sometimes not and had to get along with whatever Vietnamese language they could learn themselves. The Marines both taught and helped the PFs and villagers, and in turn learned from them. During the day the CAPs might be in the hamlet, with some of them sleeping after a night on ambush in the adjacent jungle or in some surrounding terrain that provided concealment. As night approached, part of Goodson's unit would then go back into the jungle or surrounding terrain to ambush. On some days, a Marine Civil Affairs unit would hold a MEDCAP (Medical Civil Action Program) in the village, examining the inhabitants, inoculating them, and providing whatever medical and dental assistance they could, sometimes evacuating patients to a U.S. or GVN facility for further treatment.

Life as a CAP was tough and dangerous, and some Marines undoubtedly were not a credit to their service in their conduct with the local people, but overall the results seemed to make a favorable impression on the Vietnamese. The Marine CAPs saw and experienced many gruesome things, sometimes including the PFs torturing prisoners, or seeing the bodies of mutilated PFs which the VC had spirited away from their homes, or wounded or dead villagers caught in crossfire.

Before his tour as a CAP, Goodson was with a platoon on search and destroy missions. He said, "Yes, I was part of the action that destroyed villages, rampaged throughout rice paddies, burned huts and performed hundreds of other wantonly destructive deeds. I wasn't proud of it either, but in the Marines. . . yours is not to reason why. The next few days, as well as the remainder of my stretch in 'Nam, would reinforce my realization of how terribly I had wronged the Vietnamese people in my previous service."[71]

The Marines' Combined Action Program came reasonably close to being effective, at least for awhile. With the minimal resources which Westmoreland's directed search and destroy operations left them, General Walt and his Marines down to squad level did as much as could be done to make their pacification concept a reality. In some areas, for some periods, they succeeded in establishing relatively secure hamlets and villages and gaining the loyalty of the people—loyalty, it unfortunately turned out, more to the Marines than to the government of South Vietnam.

This is demonstrated in the case of another CAP squad. Captain Bing West and a squad of twelve Marines left their fire support base (FSB) on 10 June 1966 to live in the Vietnamese village of Binh Nghia on the South China Sea near Chu Lai. Their story was one of fear, courage, commitment, discouragement, and heart-rending loss of men in the squad and of PFs who worked with them during many months of trying to turn the village away from VC to GVN control, basically by training and working with the village PFs. Sometimes it was a story of success – the VC were virtually forced out of the village, though one could never be sure, and the people were supportive of the Marines, though one could never be sure. West came back to the area in December 1967, wanting to go to the village and talk with Captain Phil Volentine who now had responsibilities there. "Volentine didn't like the way things were going. In the three months since I had last been there, he said, both the [U.S.] Army and Koreans had moved in more forces. . . . He said most Army troops were far out in the hills and the Koreans were behind a massive defensive barrier. . . . He considered the [South Vietnamese] Revolutionary Development (RD) teams a liability since, by Saigon order, they required a high degree of PF protection and had done nothing he could judge to be of lasting value. . . . Although several hamlets had been labeled 'Ap Doi Mois' (pacified New Life hamlets) [the successor term to Strategic Hamlets], he said he had never seen one where the people were actually organized or where they expressed in any way a spirit of hostility toward the VC." Volentine was told by a civil affairs colonel that "large rake-offs were a normal part of aid distribution and that he should not buck the system. . . . The colonel told Volentine to cheer up, that we were winning the war and that the Americal Division had the NVA regiments out in the hills completely on the run.[72]

West's trip back to Binh Ngia was delayed that day by an invitation to dinner with some generals. While they were eating, Captain Volentine was dying. He had raced to a command bunker to direct the defense against an enemy attack and was killed by a satchel charge. The extraordinary courage of a few Marines and PFs and their commitment to the people in Binh Ngia was not enough to ensure security and progress.

The Allure of the Big Unit War

That employment of arriving U.S. forces might turn the tide by their simultaneous use in pacification and building a capable ARVN (Vietnamization), Westmoreland had no doubt. He expressed this in his memoir in various ways, including: "As colonial masters, the French could never command the broad support of the people, but for all South Vietnam's political difficulties, it was possible for the government to attract support. That same condition made it possible to create an ARVN far more effective than the weak national army that had fought with the French, and a combination of the ARVN and American and Allied units constituted a military force far larger and more effective than the French Expeditionary Corps that at peak had had but 180,000 men."[73] He might have added that the French Union forces at their peak were only one-third as large as U.S. forces at their peak and were spread throughout all of Vietnam and parts of Laos, not just South Vietnam.

Westmoreland seemed to discount the kind of war the enemy had been conducting. South Vietnamese General Tran Dinh Tho wrote,

"American military policy sought to train and equip the Vietnamese military as a conventional force to face an eventual conventional invasion. However, this invasion first materialized under the unconventional form of subversion, sustained by guerrilla warfare. The RVNAF, tailored to the U.S. Army image, were hard-pressed to fight this kind of war, for which they were ill-prepared. Increased U.S. military aid and the availability of U.S. combat support assets failed to solve the basic problem of the long-term conflict."[74]

Subversion sustained by guerrilla warfare had produced the people who dug the piano key ditches that stopped Massu's column back in 1945, the people who followed Nguyen Thi Dinh in her insurrection in 1960, and the people who did not warn the South Vietnamese forces they were entering a trap at Ap Bac in 1963.

Big unit battles, not subversion and guerrilla warfare, were Westmoreland's priority. During his four years in command, 1964-1968, and especially after ground combat units arrived in 1965, he could have devised ways to use his U.S. units around selected villages and cities to provide security and other assistance for pacification efforts that might have reduced subversion and guerrilla attacks. Simultaneously he might have strengthened ARVN, Regional Forces (RFs), and local Popular Forces (PFs) through Vietnamization. Instead, Westmoreland rejected the Marines' clear and hold tactics which fought subversion and local guerrillas. His mantra was search and destroy. He would fight the big-unit war, going after the enemy where they had the advantage and were most likely to hurt his troops.

Sweeps and Their Results
Search and destroy operations were not directed exclusively at deep jungle base camps. There was plenty of tough but more open terrain along the coast from the DMZ south, around Saigon, and even some in the Mekong Delta which presented other types of challenges.

Such was the case with 1ˢᵗ Squadron, 1ˢᵗ Cavalry, 1ˢᵗ Armored Division (1-1 Cav) which had reasonably open terrain in which to operate. The squadron was manned and equipped exactly as was my 1ˢᵗ Squadron, 4ᵗʰ Cavalry, 1ˢᵗ Infantry Division (1-4 Cav), my battalion-size unit which formed the core of the Big Red One's armored cavalry task force. But with TO&E – Table of Organization and Equipment—the similarities ended between my unit and 1-1 Cav. Our modes of operation were very different.

1-1 Cav, not to be confused with 1ˢᵗ Cavalry Division or one of that division's units, was alerted early in 1967 that it would be detached from 1ˢᵗ Armored Division and sent to Vietnam as a separate unit. Lieutenant Colonel Richard H. Herrington's experiences were completely foreign to my personnel situation in 1969. He was deluged with well-qualified men. In order to get the units down to what was still over-strength at the platoon levels, during the months of preparation Herrington had his staff sort through them as they trained and demonstrated their skills. In the book, *Search and Destroy: The Story of an Armored Cavalry Squadron in Vietnam*, Keith W. Nolan takes the story of 1-1 Cav from Fort Hood, Texas, to provinces of I Corps south of Da Nang in the northernmost region of South Vietnam where the Marines were working.

Nolan, a military historian, was the son of a Marine but he himself had no military service. He coauthored another excellent book, *A Hundred Miles of Bad Road: An Armored Cavalryman in Vietnam 1967-68*, the story of a trooper in 3ʳᵈ Squadron, 4th Cavalry, 25ᵗʰ Infantry Division. Except for *The Red Badge of Courage*, I have never read books by non-military men which so accurately depict troops and actions down to the smallest details which could not have been known except through total immersion in the subject, and uncanny understanding of combat circumstances.

Nolan wrote *Search and Destroy* as a revelation of the brutal truths of 1-1 Cav's combat—courageous and commendable, and cowardly and despicable, with the emphasis on the former. He depicts the squadron commander as distant from what was happening on the ground, a man who never rode his ACAV in battle, who with his sergeant major lolled around base camp, who was awarded a Silver Star for who knows what. Contrary to this performance Nolan describes how dedicated and courageous many of the men were under circumstances which brought out the best and worst in them.

The 1-1 Cav's battlefields were not the jungle, rubber plantations, and roads through jungle that for months were my domain. And the divisional command situation was entirely different. The 1-1 Cav was placed under operational control of a brigade of division-size Task Force Oregon. This huge task force was created in Vietnam of disparate brigades that had not worked together within a division. It was soon renamed the American Division. My 1-4 Cav, by contrast, was part of the continuous history since WW I of the famed Big Red One, and its units in Vietnam were often cross reinforced so that commanders worked together and usually knew one another. Under my operational control I had straight leg infantry companies, mechanized infantry companies, tank companies, armored cavalry troops, air cavalry units, and some engineers. In most cases I knew the battalion commanders of the division. We had an ingrown cohesion that was lacking in American, the division of the My Lai massacre. Nolan's book, not focused on My Lai, nevertheless provides insights as to how such a horrible situation could develop.

An early sign of trouble in 1-1 Cav appeared just before the squadron went ashore, "Final briefings were held in the crowded troop compartments [of the ship taking the squadron to Vietnam]. Noting that the enemy wore black pajamas like the locals, and sometimes even disguised themselves as government soldiers, one senior noncom warned: 'If they aren't wearing a uniform like yours, they're the enemy.' 'How 'bout the Marines?' a joker called from the crowd. . . . The squadron had been instructed to only fire when fired upon and to refrain from reconning-by-fire, a standard tactic to flush the enemy out of hiding. [Platoon Sergeant] Boyd disagreed. 'I'm not going to lose any people over this kind of bullshit,' he growled. 'If we see something we'll shoot first and get in trouble later.'"

The squadron's first operations were near the coast in generally open, rice paddy terrain near Chu Lai. A platoon of A Troop got mortared, losing two killed, ten wounded, and it killed no enemy in return. "Platoon Sergeant Boyd, vexed by their losses, had an uncomplicated message for that night's ambush patrol: 'Bring me back some fuckin' meat.'"[75]

Casualties mounted from mines. Charlie Troop was going to exact retribution."We blew the road where the platoon leader's track got blown up, and we also drove our tracks through their rice fields, tearing them all to hell,' wrote [Max]Pryor. . . . You should have seen the people asking us not to ruin their rice crop. But it didn't do them any good. They all knew where the mine was and now must pay for it. However, I realy [sic] don't think we did enough to them. I realy [sic] wish we'd burn their homes.'"[76]

In addition to deliberate damage there was the expected kind of destruction to dikes and paddies when tanks and ACAVs got stuck or just moved across them. Then there were the many villages, some fortified by the enemy with bunkers, some not. "Incident by incident, the hearts of the dragoons [77] hardened. Max Pryor's scout section came under fire while securing a bridge late that month. Pryor returned the fire, either killing the sniper or putting him to flight. 'I also shot hell out of a little village about 1000 yards from where the shots came from,' he wrote. 'I figured they probely [sic] knew who it was that shot at us. I don't know if I hit anyone their [sic] or not. . . . I'll tell you one thing that village I shot at last night ain't the same today. I put 100 rounds of 50 Cal in it.'"[78]

In another incident a 1-1 Cav platoon was working with the Marines when eight military age males were rounded up in a fishing village. One of them bolted and ran into the surf. A Marine amtrac [amphibian] chased him, was swamped and three men on it drowned. "According to the squadron log, the detainee who bolted into the sea was shot . . . . The log also indicates that two other detainees attempted to escape and were killed as well. 'Not exactly, says David Eady. Instead, Staff Sgt. Beverly Martin – a hot-headed ex-Marine to be twice wounded and twice decorated for valor in the months ahead – forced the remaining detainees to their knees, then walked down the line with his .45, and popped 'em in the head: *bam, bam, bam.*' John Guzic recalls Eady, and others, describing the executions upon returning to Hill 29. Eady was dismayed by the incident, thinking those shot were simple fishermen – they seemed too old to be regular guerrillas."[79]

Then there was a joint operation with ARVN in what was known as the Pineapple Forest. An ARVN officer pointed to Lieutenant George E. Norton's map and said, "'All V C. Go kill all.' The dragoons had no intention of acting so wantonly, but what was planned was rough enough: the hamlets were to be razed and the forest itself stripped to bare earth with bulldozers. The inhabitants . . . were to be moved to the resettlement villages along Highway 1. . . .'Man, if anyone thought the Americans were bad, ' muses Norton, 'they should have seen the ARVN go through the area: looting, burning, taking the chickens, taking the pigs, taking everything.'"[80]

Nolan relates other acts of callousness, cruelty, criminality, and murder by the dragoons, but also of kindness in helping villagers, and of incredible courage in protecting and caring for one's buddies, and sometimes also the people. Unfortunately, generous and courageous acts were quite certainly not as apparent to the people as those in which they were mistreated and killed. In their search and destroy operations, not many hearts and minds were likely won in 1-1 Cav's area.

Search and Destroy in 1st Infantry Division's Area of Operations

Many U.S. unit search and destroy sweeps were taking place throughout South Vietnam. They grew in size and intensity as the war progressed from 1966 into 1967 until division and multi-division-size operations took over the headlines. The war in the area of operations of 1st Infantry Division north of Saigon is instructive. I became familiar with most of that area and some of the adjacent 25th Infantry Division's area during my service with 11th Armored Cavalry Regiment and 1st Infantry Division.

The first major battle of the Big Red One after it began arriving in July 1965 was on Highway 13 five miles north of Lai Khe. Operation Bushmaster I in November was a two-brigade search and destroy which was finding not much of anything. Then on 12 November, two days before Hal Moore would assault at LZ X-Ray far to the north, a mechanized infantry company, artillery battery, and Troop A, 1-4 Cavalry in a night defensive position (NDP) at Ap Bau Bang were attacked at dawn by a regiment of the PAVN 9th Division. A vicious daylight three-hour fight in open terrain, heavily supported by artillery, helicopter gunships, and fighter bombers resulted in 146 enemy dead and 20 Americans killed, seven of them from A Troop, and about five dozen Americans wounded. Three and a half years later, this same spot was to be one of my 1-4 Cav temporary command posts where our ACAVs and tanks – some of them probably the same battle-scarred vehicles that had gone through the earlier fight—in moving into and out of position churned up skeletons of the enemy dead who had been buried in shallow graves scraped out by bulldozers.

This fight was to demonstrate several things that became a continuing experience. The enemy picked the time and place – in this case, not a good one for him because for some reason he seems to have been delayed by several hours in launching his attack during the darkness of early morning hours. He learned a lesson, and this mistake of attacking Americans in fixed positions during daylight was not often repeated. When he determined it was time to withdraw back into the nearby jungle where he would be largely immune from further harm he did so. Although his casualties were high, he soon replaced them and was back in business without seeming to miss a beat.

On the U.S. side, several things became apparent. First, a relatively large number of men in a fairly small perimeter made an excellent target. Our organization for conventional war, and our tactics of pushing out fire bases farther and farther into the boonies to support search and destroy operations virtually ensured that night attacks would be launched and we would take casualties. Second, an artillery battery always had to be protected, and this defensive role fell to a minimum of one rifle company, often more. This ate up combat resources which could have been used in other ways. Third, if an enemy chose to expose himself in open terrain, day or night, he was surely going to get hurt by our superior firepower and ability to maneuver. At Ap Bau Bang, after the initial shock of the defenders and repulse of the enemy from the perimeter, the cav troop's ACAVs burst out of it and into the attackers, disrupting the ground assault.

But Bushmaster and Ap Bau Bang were small potatoes compared to what was to come in 1st Division. In 1966 sweeps by U.S. units grew larger – Operations Mastiff, Abilene, Birmingham, El Paso II and III. The infantry walked, rode APCs, ACAVs, and tanks, and air assaulted while armor and armored cavalry crashed through jungle into War Zone C to the northwest of Saigon and War Zone D to the northeast. In 1966 this was tough, tough going in mostly jungle terrain, and remained just as tough three years later when I was doing the same thing with my task force.

CHAPTER 10

The Big, Big Unit War, 1967 - Mid 1968

∗   ∗   ∗

IN 1967 CAME THE MOTHER of all search and destroy operations. Actually, Mother One and Mother Two. General Westmoreland was particularly proud of these, especially the second operation. After returning from Vietnam in mid-1968, from then until 1972 Westmoreland served as U.S. Army Chief of Staff. One of his projects was to task senior army officers with producing a series of monographs, *Vietnam Studies*. He chose Lieutenant General Bernard W. Rogers for the Department of the Army study, *Cedar Falls-Junction City: A Turning Point*, written in 1971 and published in 1973 as a book. Rogers as a brigadier general had been assistant division commander of 1ˢᵗ Infantry Division during these two operations.

In May 1966 General Westmoreland had directed the IIFFV commander, Lieutenant General Jonathan O. Seaman, to plan an operation in War Zone C, northern Tay Ninh Province, to start at the beginning of 1967. The planning associated with this operation was strange. Normally, enemy circumstances cause planners first to select an objective to deal with those circumstances. Next comes consideration of the forces required to attain the objective, and the detailed planning begins. Not so in this case. Westmoreland was envisioning an operation over seven months away, an extraordinary circumstance when division-size operations were usually conceived one day and executed within the next few days. Rogers wrote, "[Westmoreland] further indicated that it should be a 'big operation.' Over the next several months the operation, to be known as Junction City, was planned. As approved by General Westmoreland it was to start on 8 January 1967, was to be multidivisional, and was to include a parachute assault."[1]

This has to be one of the weirdest sequences of events in conducting a large-scale operation in any war, getting the cart before the horse. It cries out that a major desire of the MACV commander—who had been an airborne division and airborne corps commander—was to get his U.S. Army parachute forces, two brigades, doing what they were designed to do, and what had not been done since the Korean War – make a combat jump. And this had to be in conjunction with a multi-division operation. In short, the size of operations to date would not do. However, fate played the general a bad hand. Intelligence events intervened, and Junction City was delayed until Cedar Falls could be launched into a somewhat more southern area, the Iron Triangle north of Saigon.

Rogers said, "Operations Cedar Falls and Junction City took place during the first five months of 1967 and were the first multidivisional operations to be conducted according to a preconceived plan. They were to result in a turning point in the war."

Turning point? When the book was written in mid-1971, the U.S. was well on its way out of the war. That these operations of four years earlier could be considered at any time "a turning point" is astounding. Rogers continued, "They confirmed that such operations do have a place in counterinsurgency warfare today; they brought an end to the enemy's thinking that his third phase of the war – large-scale operations throughout the country – would be successful; they caused the enemy to reevaluate his tactics and revert to smaller-scale guerrilla operations; they destroyed his camps, pillaged his supplies, and killed hundreds of his best troops; they proved to the enemy that his old sanctuaries were no longer inviolable, thus causing him to depend primarily upon those located over the border in Cambodia; they helped convince the enemy that the maintenance of large bases and main force units near urban areas was risky business; and they enhanced immeasurably the confidence of the Allied forces in South Vietnam, a confidence which had been growing since the dark days of the first half of 1965."[2]

It is profoundly disappointing that this assertion stands as official history of the United States Army.

*   *   *

The objective area for Cedar Falls was the Iron Triangle, that triangular piece of scrub jungle between the confluence of the Saigon River on the west, the Thi Tinh River on the east, and an imaginary line running from Ben Cat on Route 13 on the east to the Saigon River on the west. (See Map 4, p. xx) The concept was classic conventional warfare: an anvil (blocking force) would be positioned so that a hammer (assaulting force) could drive the enemy against the anvil, and swing down and smash it. Rogers said, "The destruction of the enemy's Military Region IV headquarters was the principle objective of the operation." In addition to the region headquarters, units thought to be in the area were the equivalent of six battalions which at full strength could be 250 or more men each, but at the time were probably somewhat less. Three other battalions were also possibly in the area. All told, the planners believed, there conceivably could have been up to 3,000 enemy to be eliminated. "The triangle itself was to be scoured for enemy installations, cleared of all civilians, stripped of concealment by huge Rome plow dozers, and declared a specified strike zone." This type of zone was more commonly called a free fire zone, meaning that henceforth no authorization by South Vietnamese officials was necessary for harassing and interdictory (H & I) artillery fire, or engagement of any target by any means, artillery or air, or target practice, or unloading of unexpended bombs or rockets. When friendly units entered these zones they needed to be careful to keep U.S. and Vietnamese authorities aware of their positions to avoid being hit.[3]

The task organization for Cedar Falls was huge: major elements of two U.S. infantry divisions (1st, 25th), plus one ARVN division (5th), two squadrons of the 11th Armored Cavalry Regiment, the 173rd Airborne Brigade, and the 196th Light Infantry Brigade. Supporting U.S. forces were elements of the 7th Air Force, 1st Logistical Command, 3rd Tactical Fighter Wing, IIFFV artillery, 12th Combat Aviation Group, and 79th Engineer Group. Supporting RVNAF forces included 3rd Riverine Company (Navy), 30th River Assault Group (Navy), and three Regional Forces boat companies. "Cedar Falls was to be the largest and most significant operation to this point in the war."[4]

A major objective for the operation was the total elimination of the village of Ben Suc which lay just outside the northwestern corner of the Triangle in a big loop of the Saigon River. It was a rich rice paddy area and also produced a variety of other crops and farm animals. Since 1955 the government had maintained an ARVN outpost in the village which lasted nine years to 1963 when the outpost finally was eliminated by the Viet Cong, along with most of an ARVN battalion. That the outpost had been allowed to exist for so long is a bit of a mystery except that the NLF always played to its advantage. Probably the outpost was an excellent source of intelligence as a contact point for agents, or it provided black market goods, or weapons which some ARVN officers sold to the Viet Cong for a tidy profit, among them some from General Thuan's 5th Division, headquartered at Ben Cat, as was acknowledged by an NLF official. The politics of Ben Suc and three other nearby communities – Rach Kien, Bung Cong, and Rach Bap – all on the bank of the Saigon in the Triangle, and all also excellent producers of agricultural products, were no mystery. During at least those nine years and probably many more before that the people of those villages had been solid revolution supporters. At first the Viet Minh, then Viet Cong gained sympathizers by propagandizing and helping the villagers, but when it became necessary for selective terror, they did that too. They kidnapped and later executed the Ben Suc village chief and set up their own government. Presumably they finally did away with the handy ARVN outpost when for some reason it no longer was an asset.

The search and destroy operation was a masterpiece of timing and coordination. "The II Field Force, Vietnam, tactical command post for Operation Cedar Falls opened at 0700 on D-Day at Long Binh. Under its direction the twenty battalions allocated to the five brigades of the 1st and 25th Divisions were ready for Phase II of Cedar Falls – the destruction of the enemy force." Ready were 30,000 U.S. ground troops, about 10,000 ARVN, and enormous engineer and air resources. The estimated 1,500-3,000 enemy were outnumbered at least fifteen to one.

Ben Suc was the first objective. The 1st Division paper, *The American Traveler*, 28 January 1967 issue, carried the story: "In the early morning hours, January 8, people in Ben Suc Village went calmly about their tasks. At exactly 8 a.m., total confusion erupted. The once clear sky filled with 60 helicopters. The choppers swooped in, allowing the division soldiers to unload and begin a seal of the village. Minutes later the sky was filled again as the aircraft vanished as quickly as they had appeared."

The Hueys had landed in an open area within Ben Suc itself because mines and booby traps were known to be thick around the periphery. As soon as the Hueys lifted off, a psychological warfare helicopter came in low, broadcasting over its loudspeakers the message in Vietnamese: "Attention people of Ben Suc. You are surrounded by Republic of Vietnam and Allied forces. Do not run away or you will be shot as VC. Stay in your homes and await further instructions."

Lieutenant Colonel Alexander M. Haig was commanding 1-26 Infantry, 1st Infantry Division, the battalion that landed in Ben Suc. He was later to become White House Chief of Staff under President Nixon, Supreme Commander of U.S. Army Europe and NATO commander, and Secretary of State under President Reagan. "By 1030, 8 January, Ben Suc was securely in the hands of the friendly forces and the 2nd Brigade command post had been established in the village."[5]

As that operation was underway, 50 Rome plows with their huge blades were at work, first clearing back the trees in a swath of 50 yards along both sides of the very poor and heavily mined roads in the Iron Triangle. The plan was to scrape the entire Triangle flat, but that proved to be far beyond the capabilities of the engineers during the 19-day operation. "Only 7 or 8 percent of the sixty-three square miles of jungle area could be cleared in that time. Therefore, only strategic areas such as those along roads and landing zones would be cleared, plus spaced swaths to permit rapid deployment by mechanized and airmobile units in future operations."[6] They were also able to knock down everything above ground in Ben Suc plus the three other villages on the bank of the Saigon. Four villages ceased to exist. Later that year, the Rome plows came back and finished scraping away the remainder of the scrub jungle.

"A total of 5,987 persons was evacuated (582 men, 1651 women, and 3,754 children.) Also moved to the relocation site [Phu Loi] were 247 water buffalo, 225 head of cattle, 158 oxcarts, and 60 tons of rice.)" Rogers' report makes no mention of the chickens, ducks, pigs, and dogs which were always numerous in Vietnamese villages. A reporter who accompanied the operation said that the ARVN battalion killed and roasted many chickens, some of which were shared with American troops.

Regarding the ARVN battalion that was landed on the first day to provide the search inside the village, "It was no coincidence that the South Vietnamese battalion selected was the same one that had been driven out of Ben Suc in 1964." In fact it was a reconstituted battalion because the original one had been overrun and virtually destroyed. One can imagine that there were some scores to settle. Within the village the ARVN found "a number of bunker and tunnel complexes," and "engaged the enemy sporadically for three days and nights."[7] Before the operation terminated, two more ARVN battalions landed to relieve the Americans sealing the village on its perimeter, and two to relieve 1-4 Cav in its blocking role.

Rogers said that about half of the villagers from the four villages destroyed were transported to the resettlement camp at Phu Loi, at first by Vietnamese Navy and helicopters, along with household items, farm animals, and some rice. The other half went by truck convoy over the terrible roads that by now had been mineswept. "It would be weeks before the [South Vietnamese military and civilian agencies] could restore a sense of normality to the evacuees. Eventually they would have their own village with its school, raise their own crops with access to the Saigon markets, and have much-needed medical assistance available."[8]

Such happy people? The displaced villagers did not much appreciate the government's largess, and were sullen.

The assault at Ben Suc and throughout the triangle had been met with only light resistance. Identification of VC was more than dubious since almost all farmers wore black pajama-like clothes, the same as many VC who carried rifles. And not all VC wore those clothes. In one case a tank crew opened up with 90 millimeter canister on a raft on the Saigon River and "destroyed the raft and killed all occupants."[9]

In a chapter titled, "The Results," Rogers said, "Cedar Falls compiled some impressive statistics. U.S. and South Vietnamese forces accounted for nearly 750 confirmed dead and 280 prisoners. In addition there were 540 Viet Cong *Chieu Hoi* ralliers, 512 suspects detained, and 5,987 refugees evacuated."[10]

In 1968 and 1969 I planned and participated in many village seal and search operations. Through my excellent interpreters I talked with villagers, with Hoi Chanhs [returnees in the Chieu Hoi Program] and their families. What were supposedly Hoi Chanhs in many cases, upon closer look, were just villagers who found it advantageous to claim that status for the time being. And the identification of VC was tenuous indeed when dealing with rural people with little access to the government to obtain identification papers.

In the four chapters on tactical operations, Rogers described the actions of each of the components of the 24 battalion-size American and Vietnamese mobile forces. In a 2nd Brigade action he says that 60 VC were killed and "friendly casualties were light. The enemy withdrew under cover of darkness. . . . According to the 2nd Brigade's report, 'this was the only incident during the entire operation in which the Viet Cong elected to fight.'" Other encounters throughout the 19 days produced fewer reported enemy killed. . . . Two battalions of 1st Infantry

Division attacked and had "only light and occasional contact . . . with the enemy." Such reports of light action continued. A company of 196th Light Infantry Brigade reported that it had "engaged 14 bushes floating upstream [on the Saigon River] resulting in 10 KIA (Possible)."[11] If the company had watched a bit longer it no doubt would have seen many bushes floating upstream, a perfectly natural occurrence and not proof that VC were under the bushes and maneuvering upstream. When the tide comes in, ever-present living, floating clots of vegetation, some as much as 50 yards across, float upstream. I have watched this phenomenon of the Saigon River even at the Cu Chi tunnels about 60 miles upriver from the South China Sea.

I was in many small contacts with enemy from two or three individuals to platoon size, and in large, violent battles against battalions and a reinforced regiment. I do not see how it is possible for General Rogers to have claimed 750 confirmed dead at the same time he was reporting mostly light contacts. The two just do not go together. He said, "The 1st, 7th and 8th Viet Main Force Battalions of Military Region IV did not conduct an organized defense of their areas, apparently having been directed to disperse and avoid contact." In other words, of the six enemy battalions that were supposed to be in the Triangle, plus three others that might be, only three are mentioned as actually being there, and they put up a weak defense. Twenty U.S. battalions had thrown a supposedly tight noose around the Triangle, over which there was continuous daylight observation from the air. Where were the enemy? If in fact they were there at 0800 on 8 January when Cedar Falls began, most of them either slipped wholesale through the noose, or, more logically, they had been tipped off and slipped out beforehand, this despite the secrecy in which the operation had been planned. That this was quite certainly the case is confirmed by events during the subsequent Junction City operation. In such conditions, it is difficult to conceive of 750 confirmed dead.

General Rogers asserted, "From every aspect, the enemy had suffered a great defeat. General DePuy [Commanding General, 1st

Division], in his analysis of Operation Cedar Falls stated: 'Although I do not expect the war to end quickly, I believe this has been a decisive *turning point* [italics by Rogers] in the III Corps area; a tremendous boost to the morale of the Vietnamese Government and Army; and a blow from which the VC in this area may never recover.'"

If in fact there had been such a blow, the enemy quickly recovered. General Rogers, apparently not realizing he was contradicting himself, said, "Only two days after the termination of Cedar Falls, I was checking out the Iron Triangle by helicopter and saw many persons who appeared to be Viet Cong riding bicycles or wandering around on foot." Did he subscribe to the theory that anyone wearing black pajama-like clothing was VC? The general continued, saying how some other "VC" had been engaged, and the air cav troop of 1-4 Cav had descended and rounded up 31 men "who were suspect." Worse, he reported, "During the cease-fire for Tet, 8-12 February, the Iron Triangle was again literally crawling with what appeared to be Viet Cong. They could be seen riding into, out of, and within the triangle. . . . Periodic reconnaissance of the triangle confirmed Viet Cong activity within it." Despite all this, Rogers proclaimed, "In nineteen days, II Field Force, Vietnam, had converted the Iron Triangle from a haven to a sealed battleground, and then to a military no-man's land. . . . A strategic enemy base had been decisively engaged and destroyed. "[12]

Preposterous!

Junction City

Cedar Falls was big. Junction City was to be bigger, in fact the largest planned operation of the Vietnam War. Committed were major elements of two U.S. infantry divisions plus four South Vietnamese battalions and fourteen artillery battalions. (Westmoreland had not forgotten MacArthur's advice to make sure he always had plenty of artillery, for the Oriental greatly fears artillery.) Junction City would also include the first major U.S. combat parachute assault since the Korean War.

The primary stated mission would be "search and destroy to eradicate the Central Office of South Vietnam (COSVN) and Viet Cong and North Vietnamese Army installations." The enemy's base was in what was called the Duong Minh Chau area in Tay Ninh Province. It had been heavily used by the Viet Minh during the French war, and this gave the current occupants plenty of experience operating within it.

Westmoreland had envisioned "a parachute assault by both the 1st Brigade, 101st Airborne Division, and the 173d Airborne Brigade." However, by D-Day, 22 February 1967, Westmoreland had had to use the 101st men in conventional ground operations far to the north. That left the 173rd to drop 845 paratroopers of 2nd Battalion, 503rd Airborne Infantry Regiment; A Battery, 319th Artillery Battalion; and headquarters elements of the 173rd.[13]

Junction City and Espionage

Two aspects of the enemy's Junction City resistance in early 1967 are especially instructive. The first, espionage, is one of the factors that greatly contributed to making this war unwinnable for American and South Vietnamese generals. General Bruce Palmer said, "At times the government had been penetrated all the way from the [Independence] palace down to small units in the field. When I first visited the 25th ARVN Division headquarters in Duc Hoa, the division commander would discuss only trivial matters in his office; he took me outside well away from any building, with only the two of us present. Here he explained that he strongly suspected that his own division G-2 (intelligence officer) was a Viet Cong agent; thus he did not dare discuss operational matters in his own command post."[14]

That the opposing side had a highly developed intelligence and espionage net is well known. Merle Pribbenow sent me an annotated list of some of the most prominent agents who penetrated the highest French and South Vietnamese government and military offices, to include those of the Chairman of the South Vietnamese Joint General

Staff and the President of the Republic of Vietnam. What is not so well known are the details of their operations. Merle included translations of some of their mind-boggling activities. According to two Vietnamese journalists (Hoang Hai Van and Tan Tu) writing in 2004, "There were many among them who had led lives filled with danger and excitement, but they all lived quiet lives – they lived to serve. This moral character strongly attracted us, but it also caused us [as journalists] more than a few difficulties, because they do not want to talk about themselves."[15]

One who did tell enough of her story that it was published in a book was Colonel Dinh Thi Van, a spy who was awarded the title of "Hero of the People's Armed Forces," a very high award. Her story reflects deeds similar to those of many other Northern spies. Near the end of the book is her account of espionage affecting Junction City.

Van was born in the North and was active in espionage against the French. Immediately after the fall of Dien Bien Phu she was sent to Hanoi to gather intelligence. The French still had most of their forces available and could present a renewed threat, and the United States in the last stages of the war was supplying 80% of the equipment and funds to fight it. There was concern that the United States might actually enter the war to pick up where the French left off. Her superior told her, "You ought to know the enemy's strategic schemes, what is new about their military assistance and their equipment, and how U.S. forces can become involved in Vietnam. The value of this information can equal the strength of a division."[16]

Like so many dedicated Communists, Van was prepared to sacrifice her family life and her life itself for Uncle Ho. She had a husband and a mother she loved very much, but she urged her husband to find another wife so she could continue her espionage, and her mother told her she indeed had a higher duty to perform. After the Geneva Accords, unable to say goodbye to her mother, brothers, and sisters, and taking advantage of the resettlement agreement, with a fake ID card she left the North on a French boat and landed in South Vietnam at Vung Tau. There she and the other evacuees got a rude reception from

Southerners who didn't like or trust Northerners, and didn't want them as immigrants.[17]

For five years she worked carefully in the South to establish a growing network of agents who started off in minor civil and military positions and then worked their way up. She traveled from Saigon north to the DMZ and back, ostensibly as a vendor of various goods while recruiting agents and helping to set up the network necessary for communication with first Hanoi, then COSVN. Through her contacts in Central Vietnam she visited several high officials: the province chief of Quang Tri, the commanding general of South Vietnam's 1st Division, an official in the Public Security Ministry, and even President Diem's sister and his brother, Ngo Dinh Can, the powerful warlord.[18]

Then one of her agents was captured and he, to save himself, informed on her. She was tortured for weeks while maintaining she was only a vendor. Through every horror she said, "I remembered Uncle Ho's words, 'never surrender to violence,' and I mumbled: 'My Uncle, I will hold on to the end, I may die, but I will never surrender to the enemy. I will live up to the honor of being a member of your Party.'"[19] Across many months then years of imprisonment her interrogators inflicted multiple tortures that left her unconscious and in pain, and they tried every conceivable psychological ploy to get her to reveal her contacts. They brought some of those contacts before her, those who had been discovered and given the choice to help reform other cadre or die. Still she refused to admit to anything other than being a vendor.

Finally, never having revealed anything, in 1964 she was released in terrible health. She discovered that in the five years of her imprisonment, one of her agents had worked his way up to become Nguyen Khanh's bodyguard. Khanh was the general who overthrew Duong Van Minh, the general who succeeded to power when Diem was assassinated.[20] This agent had bribed Khanh's interrogators of a captured high-ranking intelligence cadre, giving them "a huge sum of money" to secure his release.[21] Two other agents recruited by her were officers in the Ministry of Defense.

Another agent, Ha Dang, whom she loved and had informally adopted as her son several years earlier, became a company commander in the ARVN 5th Division headquartered on Route 13 at Ben Cat. He gave her information on the defense system along that main highway which, in 1969, I was tasked to secure. One day she and another agent visited Ha Dang at his camp on the highway. He said that he and two U.S. officers regularly used a U.S. Army L19 observation plane to reconnoiter the whole route system up to Bu Dop, and he gave her that information plus operational plans of the 5th Division which led to a "victory" over GVN forces in a battle. She said, "As a lieutenant and a skillful scout, Dang had won the liking of senior colonel Pham Quoc Thuan, Commander of the division. [Dang] told us that in the office, he was allowed to . . . hear all the reports. In many of Thuan's visits to examine the units, Ha Dang was chosen to be the liaison officer. It was time to assign him a specific duty . . . their defense system plans. . . . [and] the enemy's military activities in the tactical zone . . . . : 'Keep track of the station of U.S. units, particularly the 'Red big brother' 1st division.'" [sic]

I operated in that area in 1968-69 and I was with now-General Thuan a few times. On one occasion I attended a ceremony at 5th Division followed by a reception by Thuan who, with a luscious young woman on each side of him, conveniently saw to it that Colonel Patton and I each also had one beside us. It was abundantly clear that if we had wanted to avail ourselves of his generosity, they were ours. We thanked him, declined, and left. Thuan was a joweled, paunchy political man who had a terrible reputation among the American advisors and unit commanders. Not only did they view him as a lousy combat leader, but suspected him of selling weapons and other items to the enemy. However, he was a close supporter and confidante of President Thieu.

Dinh Thi Van was receiving so much information from a source in Thieu's General Staff, and spending so many hours copying it that she solved the problem by getting the agent a camera with which to photograph the documents. Two of Van's agents in departments of the General Staff were given transportation by the Staff, one a car, one a jeep, which greatly facilitated their conveyance of documents they brought home to copy after duty hours.

Another of Van's agents, Phiet, as a junior officer had established a close friendship with a lieutenant colonel in the G-3 office of the General Staff. This office was responsible for South Vietnamese military plans and operations throughout South Vietnam and thus was a gold mine of information. The lieutenant colonel was not a Communist or sympathizer, just incredibly trusting and careless. Phiet became virtually a part of his family, taking the colonel's wife and children on outings, driving the colonel's young son around in the family auto, telling him the story of "'White Snow and the seven dwarfs.' . . . Therefore, through their intimate conversations, Phiet grasped all stages of the U.S.-puppet's 'three [-stage] search and destroy spearheads' campaign [Junction City]." When the lieutenant colonel was promoted, Phiet gave him a Japanese crystal lamp. The colonel "shared with Phiet crucial and secret information concerning the enemy's operation plans and the deliberations between [the colonel] and General Westmoreland and Cao Van Vien, Chairman of the South Vietnamese Joint General Staff."

Generals Cao Van Vien and Westmoreland. (Corbis)

One evening in the colonel's home, two officers came in and the colonel told Phiet to rest in the bedroom while he received the officers. With the door closed, Phiet found a bound 20-page English language manuscript entitled, "The Session with the General Staff's Advisor and General Cao Van Vien – for submission to the president." He was reading fast and trying to remember details when he got to page twelve and heard footsteps, so he quickly put the document back in its place. The manuscript was about launching a huge campaign aimed at destroying COSVN and would require 40,000 soldiers: Operation Junction City.

"One month and two days later, the Janson-City [sic] campaign was launched. Our Command had known about a number of the campaign's battle plans and had been well prepared to strike back."[22] Sometime after the operation ended, Dinh Thi Van got news that the Party had awarded a medal to Phiet for his great work in uncovering the American plans for Junction City.

COSVN's System of Defense for Junction City

The second aspect of Junction City that is instructive on why the war was unwinnable militarily flows naturally from the espionage, and that is the system of defense devised by COSVN. Parts of two enemy histories sent to me by Pribbenow treat the 9th Division's defense and COSVN headquarters' role in Operation Junction City.[23]

As a colonel, General Hoang Cam was the commander of the regiment that had attacked the 1st Infantry Division's NDP at Ap Bau Bang in 1965. At the time of Junction City he was the senior colonel commanding 9th Infantry Division of about 9,000 men. Having been well briefed on what espionage had uncovered, he said that COSVN stated: "This will be the largest operation that the Americans and the puppets have ever conducted, and the primary direction for the enemy's first attack prong will be to destroy our base area and to find and destroy the headquarters and leadership agencies of COSVN and the 9th Division in order to win a military victory of decisive importance . . . and create a turning point that will transform the war and give the Americans the advantage at the negotiating table."

Westmoreland had a three-part plan for conduct of the war: destruction of main forces, pacification, and Vietnamization. Cam said, "Defeating this operation will be of tremendous significance, because the failure of the enemy's first attack prong [destruction of main forces] in Eastern Cochin China will have a significant effect on the enemy's 'pacification' prong, the second prong of his attack."

Cam explained that COSVN had only two choices, defend the base area or retreat into Cambodia to "try to create an opportunity to attack them [later]." Believing they could inflict serious damage on the Americans in this jungle arena, they chose the first, defend. In order to unify command and use all troops to the maximum, to include COSVN headquarters, the base area was divided into "districts" and further into "villages," each with its own commander. Additional weapons were issued, and headquarters troops trained as infantry squads, platoons, and companies and rehearsed various scenarios. (They had plenty of time to do this, given Westmoreland's seven-month planning stage.)

Cam asked if he would get help from other main force divisions and was told no, they were needed elsewhere. "The 9th Division's main force troops, who had been issued additional heavy weapons, and especially B-40 anti-tank rockets [RPGs], were stationed at locations from which they could easily move in any direction." After studying COSVN's directives and plans, and "most directly, those of Tran Van Tra, the [COSVN] military commander," Cam briefed his staff and commanders. His concept was "to force the enemy to fight the kind of battle we wanted to fight."[24]

"The kind of battle we wanted to fight"—always the ideal goal which our enemy trained carefully to accomplish.

Junction City was planned for three phases. Phase I established a "horseshoe" with the open end in the south and the northernmost extension within a few miles of the Cambodian border. On D-Day, to form the horseshoe, eight infantry battalions assaulted by helicopter, and one parachuted into a drop zone. Only one battalion received sporadic small arms fire. The other insertions were unopposed. Rogers said, "Throughout the day enemy contact and casualties remained light with four Americans killed and twenty-three wounded; enemy losses were unknown." The next day two squadrons of 11th Armored Cavalry Regiment and 2nd Brigade of 25th Division "thrust northward through the open end of the horseshoe." They found significant caches of supplies and equipment. "Only four minor contacts, however, were made during the day's search." Around the horseshoe itself, "contact remained light." On the third day of the operation, "resistance was light and scattered throughout the day and into the night. . . . By the end of the third day. . . all was still going according to plan. Forty-two of the enemy had been killed and 1 prisoner and 4 ralliers taken; U.S. losses were 14 killed and 93 wounded."

Phase I lasted for 18 more days. "During this 21-day period the action was marked mainly by contacts with small forces (one to ten men) and the continual discovery of more and more base camps."

To have 40,000 U.S. and Vietnamese troops engaged in search and destroy within a confined area and not have some sharp engagements would have been unusual since a full enemy division plus COSVN headquarters units were thought to have been there. Only scattered contacts with small forces for the first several days of an operation in a major base camp area, especially since it was headquarters for COSVN which controlled all resistance in the South, needed explanation. In a 1969 day-long battle, my task force of battalion size had to fight through a bunkered base camp that enemy units fiercely defended in order to protect only a regimental headquarters, not the Junction City grand prize of COSVN itself. The logical explanation for light contact during Junction City is that Cam did not yet see conditions right for fighting the kind of battle he wanted to fight. Additionally, because the key agencies of COSVN headquarters had by this time certainly left the horseshoe area, 9th Division did not have to worry about defending them.

Rogers gives details on two of what he calls "major battles" during Phase I and says of one of these battles, "Eleven enemy were killed with U.S. losses 5 killed and 19 wounded." In another, "The enemy lost 39 killed and the U.S. 20 killed and 28 wounded." In that battle a U.S. company was making extremely slow headway "through the thick and tangled jungle, " and "then came to fallen trees and brush – deadfall" when they were hit by an enemy battalion.[25] In another battle, part of a U.S. mechanized battalion was protecting an artillery battalion and engineers in a circular position around an air strip when they were struck at night by two battalions. Rogers said, "By now in Junction City two of the [9th] division's [four] regiments had attacked and been badly defeated. The remaining regiments would make their appearance in Phase II and be bloodied as well." (Badly defeated, bloodied? Rogers' own account gives no such evidence.)[26] Rogers then said: "During the twenty-nine days of Phase II operations in which intensive searching and destruction were performed, there were only three major battles, all initiated by the enemy."[27] One of these battles, indeed a major battle, under then-lieutenant colonel Haig is treated later.

Phase III continued for another twenty days, "but the organized enemy units became almost impossible to find. Most of the contacts made were with relatively small Viet Cong groups."[28] The operation concluded on 14 May. Rogers said, "The statistical results of Junction City are impressive. All the regiments of the Viet Cong 9th Division had been trounced. The final total carried 2,728 enemy killed and 34 prisoners taken. . . [and] 139 Chieu Hoi ralliers. . . . American personnel losses were 282 killed and 1,576 wounded."[29]

Aside from highly suspect counts of enemy bodies, I fail to see how an enemy who chose to bide his time, then attack, then withdraw at will without being impeded can be considered "trounced," especially when he left so many dead and wounded Americans behind him. Westmoreland had chosen once again to go after the enemy in his jungle lair, employing his enormous force against perhaps 9,000 enemy combatants. And COSVN, the primary objective, escaped.

The Admiral Sharp/General Westmoreland official *Report On the War in Vietnam* stated, "Junction City convinced the enemy command that continuing to base main force units in close proximity to the key population areas would be increasingly foolhardy. From that time on the enemy made increasing use of the Cambodian sanctuaries for his bases, hospitals, training centers, and supply depots."[30]

That statement, made to bring the official report up to date as of 30 June 1968, only five months after the Tet '68 offensive began, makes one wonder: Had Westmoreland forgotten that the enemy was able soon after Junction City ended to base his divisions again in War Zone C – the location of Junction City – and in War Zone D – where several subsequent search and destroy operations had failed to find much of anything? Had he forgotten that from those two war zones during Tet '68 enemy divisions had emerged to attack Saigon and the outlying populated areas? It has been claimed many times that we never lost a battle, that when the firing ended we were always the owner of the battlefield. Almost always true, if we speak of battalion level and above. Our firepower and ability to reinforce assured it. And true if we speak of the hours during and immediately following the battle. But where was the enemy the next day, the next week, the next month, the next year? If he wished, he was back in those same locations, up to strength again, usually performing as before, or better.

The official enemy history of the war, *Victory in Vietnam*, made the usual preposterous claims as to their great victories over the American aggressors in their operations of Cedar Falls and Junction City – thousands of Americans killed, brigades eliminated, hundreds of aircraft and armored vehicles destroyed. But when one cuts that nonsense out, some painful truths are left, summarized by the history as follows: "The Duong Minh Chau base area lay in a large, sparsely populated jungle mountain area in Tay Ninh Province. First formed during the resistance war against the French and further built up during the resistance war against the Americans [we prepared the battlefield]. . . . All staff organizations and military units were issued a three-month supply of food and ammunition. Combat fortifications were consolidated and extended. A command communications network was extended out to each individual area. Soldiers and self-defense forces of staff agencies trained and conducted field exercises in accordance with the combat plan."[31]

The enemy had gotten early warning by espionage and were well prepared. Despite being on the defensive, according to Rogers' report they gained the initiative by attacking where they chose, when they chose. The enemy relinquished the battlefield only for awhile, raising the question: Which is better, to be the force standing on the battleground after the battle, or be the force that returns and retains it until the war is over?

Frustrations of Search and Destroy for Westmoreland

Westmoreland said, "Our strength was too limited to maintain enough troops in War Zone C to prevent the enemy from reentering it later."[32] Westmoreland was speaking from afar, but Rogers directly witnessed the problem. He said, "One of the discouraging features of both Cedar Falls and Junction City was the fact that we had insufficient forces, either U.S. or South Vietnamese, to permit us to continue to operate in the Iron Triangle and War Zone C and thereby prevent the Viet Cong from returning." Rogers had confirmed for Cedar Falls that the Iron Triangle was again "literally crawling" with enemy. The problem was the same with Junction City. Rogers reported, "Reconnaissance flights over War Zone C following Junction City revealed that the enemy was returning." In 1969 my task force captured prisoners and documents which made clear that the enemy knew the safest place to be was in the area where American troops had just completed an operation. American troops did not hang around. They were ordered to go on other search and destroy missions.

Despite having an enormous number of troops, many times more than the enemy's main forces, it is true that Westmoreland did not have enough to enable him to stay in these areas even though in the case of Junction City he had wished to do so. But why should he wish to stay in jungle? In almost all cases, it was a mistake to go there in the first place, and would have been a bigger mistake to stay. Search and destroy itself was a mistake. The enemy conducted war across the full range of his capabilities – guerrilla, regional, main force – and did so at all times with at least guerrilla forces across much of South Vietnam. A search and destroy fixation required meeting those challenges, so Westmoreland hopped his divisions and brigades around to meet the trial of the moment, Whack-a-Mole fashion.

The aftermath of the two biggest operations of the Vietnam War was frustrating for General Rogers. He spoke of how even before those operations "our engineers had changed the face of Vietnam. . . . The success of the jungle-destruction operation using Rome Plows, bulldozers, and tank dozers was particularly impressive. However, the discouraging aspect of such operations is that it takes but a short time for the jungle to grow again."

The jungle did not cooperate. The enemy was no better. Rogers said, "It was a sheer impossibility to keep him from slipping away if he were in terrain with which he was familiar – generally the case. The jungle is usually just too thick and too widespread to hope ever to keep him from getting away; thus the option to fight was usually his."[33]

Did those generals – Westmoreland and Rogers – have any clue that what they said about their search and destroy operations was so damning to them? They had invested enormous resources in those operations in areas where in most cases the enemy had the distinct advantage, where he could do pretty much what he wanted when he wanted. The generals, fighting with conventional war tactics, claimed victories when hundreds of their soldiers were killed and thousands wounded in areas which the enemy quickly regained. And they kept on doing more of the same.

Covert War by MACV's "Studies and Observation Group" (SOG)

The North Vietnamese and NLF/Viet Cong were highly success-ful in carrying out covert war against the South. How did the South Vietnamese government and Americans fare in covert war against them?

Developments in the war in Laos were to have impact in Vietnam. In 1966 Theodore Shackley, CIA station chief, "'had been dispatched to Vientiane to run the war. . . . He came into meetings, embassy officer Mark Pratt recalled, 'and spoke as if he were the Lord Almighty with nothing but the highest truth, and everyone else was badly informed until he spoke.' It was all can-do. 'I wondered if he ever reflected at any time on why he was doing all this.'" One of Shackley's superiors said, "It was great fun. You sit in the Ambassador's office, deal with leaders of the Lao government, arrange for Thai artillery strikes, map out strategy . . . send orders to field commanders. It had everything."[34]

Shackley loved to quantify things in the Robert McNamara fashion, and he immediately began sending far more reports to Langley than had been the case earlier. His efforts, though, to include attempts to inter-dict the Ho Chi Minh Trail, at best were only marginally effective, and some resulted in large losses of the tribesmen he used.

Later, Shackley was promoted to station chief in Vietnam. "In the sessions with his senior field officers Shackley inevitably turned to a chart that listed every province and district in the country. . . . He pressed his subordinates to recruit assets [espionage agents], run operations, and churn out reports, lots of reports. . . . He demanded high-level penetra-tions, spies in the upper regions of the Viet Cong. . . . But the chart did not lie. Shackley read down the list of the provinces and districts and noted the number of penetrations . . . : zero, zero, zero, zero. . . ."[35] Although the Americans and South Vietnamese were able to place some spies of their own in enemy units in South Vietnam, the results were nowhere near as beneficial to them as was espionage to the North and NLF.

President Kennedy had been enthusiastic about not just special forces operations generally, but conducting covert warfare specifically.

At first he relied on the CIA, but by 1962, after the 1961 Bay of Pigs failure, Secretary of Defense McNamara was shepherding a transition of responsibility for covert operations to the Department of Defense, and by July1962, planning was underway for what in January 1964 became the highly secret MACVSOG—MACV's euphemistically labeled "Studies and Observation Group" (SOG). Their four covert missions were agent networks and deception programs, maritime raids, psychological warfare, and cross-border operations against the Ho Chi Minh Trail.[36]

The CIA had been virtually unsuccessful in conducting any kind of covert war against North Vietnam. This was hardly surprising in view of that country's reputation as the most difficult to penetrate of what in intelligence circles was called "denied areas"—the other areas being the Soviet Union, countries in the Soviet Bloc, Communist China, and North Korea.[37]

The DRV had highly efficient internal security involving several of its agencies, as well as population control. Ultimately SOG was little more successful than the CIA. SOG's composition was: U.S. personnel from all military branches, CIA, South Vietnamese military and security members, minority personnel within Vietnam, and some Lao, Cambodian, and Thai personnel, ultimately over 10,000 strong. Virtually all became highly trained, and teams that were inserted were superbly courageous. However, with the exceptions of operations against the Ho Chi Minh Trail which provided useful intelligence, and some clandestine radio relay stations, in the long run the rest was almost fruitless. The North quickly caught on to insertion teams and captured, killed or turned virtually all of them into working for the North. In 1968, the CIA and Defense Intelligence Agency "evaluated every team's message traffic, intelligence reports, and movements, all case officer reports, and related materials. . . . The conclusions were devastating. Nothing had worked. All the teams that [SOG's Airborne Operations Group] thought were legitimate were actually under enemy control and being run back against MACVSOG. It was a complete double-cross, a seven-year spoof that had seen nearly 500 agents inserted into [North Vietnam] but none brought back out, or exfiltrated, in SOG jargon."[38] The fate of many is unknown, but it is believed that not one agent inserted into the DRV ever returned during the war. Some were released after the war, beginning in the late 1970's, having suffered years of torture and cruel imprisonment.[39]

*   *   *

The South Vietnamese election of mid-1967, which critics claimed with more than a little justification were rigged, saw Thieu now elected as president with full powers of a presidency. The bitter Ky was vice president, an arrangement not likely to bode well for strengthening the South but which more or less worked until Ky later dropped out of formal politics and reverted to his air force role. With Thieu's gain of power, the arrangement provided a measure of stability over the highly volatile politics of the past.

Major General Frederick C. Weyand, commanding general of 25th Infantry Division 1964-67, believed that pacification, providing security for hamlets and villages was the way to success, not Westmoreland's search and destroy. His New York Times obituary on February 13, 2010 stated, "At a cocktail party in Saigon in 1967, General Weyand, speaking of Westmoreland, had told Murray Fromson, a CBS news correspondent: 'Westy just doesn't get it. The war is unwinnable. We've reached a stalemate, and we should find a dignified way out.' . . . Mr. Fromson said: 'He was very candid, and a very decent guy. A lot of the generals felt that way, but he was willing to sit down and talk about it.' General Weyand later expanded on his views in an off-the-record conversation with Mr. Fromson and R. W. Apple Jr. of The New York Times [reported in the Times, August 6, 1967]. Swearing both reporters to secrecy, he painted a grim picture of American prospects. 'I've destroyed a single division three times,' General Weyand said. 'I've chased main-force units all over the country, and the impact was zilch. It meant nothing to the people. Unless a more positive and more stirring theme than simple anti-Communism can be found, the war appears likely to go on until someone gets tired and quits, which could take generations.'"

President Nguyen Van Thieu (on President Lyndon Johnson's
right) and (then) Premier Nguyen Cao Ky (on left), with
Defense Secretary McNamara behind Ky during honors at
the Honolulu Conference, 6 February 1966. (NARA)

Westmoreland reportedly was furious at this leak. Looking at the
overall Vietnam scene he saw much progress. When he went back to
the U.S. in November 1967 to meet with President Johnson and address
Congress, he used the phrase, "light at the end of the tunnel."

President Johnson and General Westmoreland at
the White House, 16 November 1967. (NARA)

1968, the Tet Offensive, a Refutation of Search and Destroy

And then two months later—Tet!

So much has been written about the Tet Offensive which erupted on 30 January 1968 that there is no need to detail it here. What is not well known is that planning for it had its genesis in Le Duan's 1959 rise to power. Reluctantly he had shelved for the time being his desire to move aggressively on the South, uneasy and inwardly resentful at Ho's and Giap's warnings that the North was not ready to push for a general offensive/general uprising in which main force units would attack and overrun the major cities of the South, and the Southern people would simultaneously respond in a massive uprising. Le Duan got his chance in mid 1967 when Senior General Van Tien Dung (the same rank as Giap) maneuvered to remove himself as Giap's deputy and get chosen by Le Duan to plan, together, the 1968 offensive. In mid 1967 Le Duan's internal security forces began purging moderates in the Party who would oppose such a move in what came to be called "The Revisionist Anti-Party Affair." By October some of the highest ranking members had been placed under house arrest, including generals on Giap's staff.[40] Giap saw the handwriting on the wall and "left for Eastern Europe and did not return until well into 1968. The defeated Ho Chi Minh followed suit and left for Beijing [ostensibly] to convalesce [from his illness of 1967]."[41]

The relationship of Le Duan with both Ho and Giap during and shortly after Tet in terms of power seems to have been one of accommodation. What is clear is that Ho returned, still very much revered for his past leadership. Giap returned and resumed his duties as head of the Central Military Committee and as Defense Minister, his talents still much needed in the aftermath of disastrous Tet casualties.

Although Westmoreland was never to acknowledge it, the Tet '68 Offensive starkly revealed the failure of his attrition strategy and its trappings: search and destroy, body count, kill ratio. For the enemy, Tet '68 was a military defeat but a huge psychological and political victory. For the Americans, Tet '68 virtually extinguished the light at the end of the tunnel and soon kicked Westmoreland upstairs, out of Vietnam to become Army Chief of Staff in the Pentagon.

General Giap sharing a moment of camaraderie, 1968. (Getty)

An Alternative Strategy?

The enemy's strategy was the offensive, always the offensive. Giap said, "Our military art is permeated with the idea of active attack on the enemy. It is mainly the art of attack. Imbued with the strategic idea of offensive in the revolutionary war, let us in our armed struggle actively attack the enemy in a resolute, continuous and thorough manner with all forces and weapons, in all forms, on all scales, everywhere and at all times."[42] And so it was: In all forms—from sniping to major assault; on all scales—from the single guerrilla to a full division and more; everywhere and at all times. For 30 years throughout the country from north to south, in daylight and darkness the French colonialists, American "imperialists," and their "puppets" were subjected to resolute attack.

Tet '68 reveals how an alternative U.S. strategy could have yielded far better results from 1965 to mid-1968 during Westmoreland's tenure in Vietnam. He had said he would not sit back and wait for the enemy to come to him. He did not sit back, but in Tet '68 the enemy came to him – in spades. Main and regional forces left their jungle base camps and exposed themselves in fiercely attacking cities and villages, aided by local units and guerrillas who also necessarily revealed themselves in order to accomplish their missions of guiding the main units, and sabotaging and attacking critical installations. The attackers at all levels were hurt badly by a combination of rigorous defense and punishing counterattacks, quickly improvised by American, South Vietnamese, and other Free World military forces.

Early on, Westmoreland had recognized that in the long run the South Vietnamese would have to carry out their own pacification and fight their own battles against enemy main forces. He had expected the Vietnamese to carry the brunt of the pacification efforts while the Americans and some ARVN units would keep the enemy's main forces from interfering. But he did not follow through. Instead he used the bulk of his U.S. main force strength in search and destroy missions in mostly jungle terrain.

When American combat units arrived in 1965, a defensive-offensive strategy throughout South Vietnam coupled with pacification and true Vietnamization might have been an excellent choice if planned well and executed intelligently and aggressively. When Westmoreland and other generals were junior and mid-level officers they had studied fundamentals of the defense along with other forms of warfare. Army field manuals such as FM 100-5, *Operations* (1965) discuss how valuable a mobile defense can be: "Mobile defense orients on the destruction of the enemy force by employing a combination of fire and maneuver, offense, defense, and delay to defeat the attack. . . . Defenders place minimum forces forward, forming powerful forces with which to strike the enemy at his most vulnerable time and place." Westmoreland's airmobile infantry, mechanized infantry, armor, armored cavalry, and air cavalry could move, shoot, and communicate better than any other forces in the world. As to fixed defensive positions which could blunt or channel an enemy attack so that mobile units could engage them, Westmoreland's straight-leg infantry and ARVN could have well handled that.

Major General William E. DePuy, Commanding General of 1st Infantry Division 1966-67, was widely recognized for his innovative ideas on defense. Working within Westmoreland's search and destroy concept, DePuy needed to protect permanent fire support bases and fixed installations, and he wanted passionately to ensure the safety as much as possible of his grunts in the boonies when they finished the day's sweep missions and moved before dusk into night defensive positions (NDPs) or temporary fire support bases (FSBs). In a detailed division directive he prescribed and diagrammed how these positions should be constructed, and he insisted on their use.

DePuy's concept for construction of bunkers, fire support bases, and installation defenses continued to be used by subsequent division commanders and many other U.S., Allied, and South Vietnamese forces throughout the war. For example, Alexander Haig tells how his battalion came under fierce attack at night during Junction City. Before dark Haig had ensured that his men dug in at their night defensive position, using the DePuy plan which, by then, was second nature to the infantry. "As soon as darkness fell, I visited every bunker, ordering that they be improved if they were not properly dug and sandbagged, that the firing ports be correctly aligned, that the claymore mines in front of each position, at least one for each American, be properly emplaced. I told each man to be alert and ready, because I was sure we were in for a big fight."[43]

After a mortar barrage the enemy launched a vicious ground attack, and the big fight erupted, joined quickly by artillery and air strikes around the perimeter. Haig said that the next morning 491 dead enemy were found, 34 of them within the perimeter. Fierce, courageous defensive-offensive action, incorporating well-planned and dug-in fighting positions along with enormous artillery and air support kept his losses to nine killed and 32 wounded.[44]

In most cases, in order for the enemy's combat forces to strike populated areas they would have to leave their jungle base areas and expose
themselves in open or relatively open terrain. They did this in Tet
'68. And they paid a horrible price. The aggressive defensive-offensive
actions by American, South Vietnamese, and Allied forces during Tet
'68 exacted a terrible toll on them.

Instead of search and destroy – from which the enemy was always
able to recover and reoccupy the ground temporarily lost—American
and Allied forces could have worked closely with Vietnamese in pacification and simultaneously equipped and trained them (Vietnamization) if
that had been Westmoreland's intention. He spoke of it, planned it, even
tried it, but the reality was that under him the plan did not work well
because search and destroy was his priority. Westmoreland's units could
have been integrated into defensive-offensive configurations around
selected cities and villages. They could have patrolled extensively out
from them, ambushed, and used special forces in a manner which suited
them well: longer range reconnaissance patrols to locate the enemy. One
can think of other ways in which, from 1965 when our first ground combat units arrived, they could have been employed other than to pit them
against enemy main and regional forces in terrain where the enemy
always would have the advantage.

A problem with allowing enemy forces to remove from his bases
to attack populated areas was that if he could secretly move and strike,
as he did in Tet '68, then civilians and their property would be badly
hurt in trying to eject him, and they would lose further faith in the
South Vietnamese government. This was a conundrum which persisted
throughout the war. It might not have come to this so dramatically as in
Tet '68 if, instead of conducting search and destroy operations in deep
jungle, troops had patrolled and ambushed aggressively out from the
fringes of pacification zones in order to detect and identify enemy units,
and as these units tried to move on populated areas, struck them in a
mobile defense before they could do so much damage. That is what the
Marines wanted to do early on in I Corps, but Westmoreland wanted

them out on search and destroy. General Bruce Palmer, briefly commander of IIFFV, later deputy to Westmoreland as essentially the commander of USARV, said, "Our greatest battle successes occurred when the enemy chose to attack a U.S. unit well dug in and prepared to defend its position. As enemy forces learned about the devastating impact of greatly superior U.S. firepower, both ground and air-delivered, they became less inclined to attack."[45]

In discussing Tet '68, Westmoreland said, "In the prior months of fighting, I had learned conclusively that it was when the enemy came out of hiding to make some major attack that American firepower could be brought to bear with tremendous effect. Even though we might incur some temporary setbacks if he came out of hiding to make a 'maximum effort', it would be the beginning . . . 'of a great defeat for the enemy.'"[46]

Yes!

Yes, Yes, YES!!

That is exactly what happened during Tet'68 in February, and in much weaker follow-up attacks we called "mini-Tet" in April and May. The enemy was hurt so badly, as admitted in their histories, that the Viet Cong infrastructure took months, in some places years, to rebuild. Although the NVA main forces were able to rebuild and retrain more quickly, and there was plenty of fighting against NVA main forces later in 1968 and 1969, as my soldiers and I can attest, the enemy was hurt so badly that it was spring of 1972 before they could again muster the kind of main force strength they had had at Tet '68. Since enemy histories loudly proclaim great victories, preposterously inflating the losses they inflicted on their enemy, when they acknowledge weakness, this is noteworthy. Their comprehensive official history, *Victory in Vietnam*, admitted this, relative to Tet '68: "Our soldiers' morale had been very high when they set off for battle, but because we had made only one-sided preparations, only looking at the possibilities of victory and failing to prepare for adversity, when the battle did not progress favorably for our side and when we suffered casualties, rightist thoughts, pessimism, and hesitancy appeared among our forces."[47] Translated into the actual circumstances of the battles of Tet '68, those words are an admission that the counterattacks on their exposed forces of all types – guerrilla, local and regional units, and main force units – were devastating. Some of the division histories are much more honest than the official history, and describe how difficult were their circumstances and how terrible their losses.

If Westmoreland knew, as he said, that when the enemy exposed himself he was hurt badly, why then from mid-1965 to the end of his command in April 1968 – nearly three years – did he persist in sending American troops into the jungle after base camps where we suffered so many casualties? He might have been able with a strong pacification and Vietnamization campaign, using U.S. combat troops in the defensive-offensive manner sketched above, or some such other concept, to have strengthened South Vietnam's chances for survival.

That a defensive-offensive concept had merit at the highest U.S. military level was acknowledged in post-Tet comments made during a Weekly Intelligence Estimate Update (WIEU) briefing by General Abrams, the commander who succeeded Westmoreland. In attendance was General George S. Brown, Deputy COMUSMACV for Air Operations, and Commander, Seventh Air Force (1968-70). Brown replied, "It's clear that we kill more troops, we kill troops best, when they mass and they're attacking. That's when you can really mow them down. Now if you then adopt an attitude of chase them around in the bush, and keeping them off balance all the time so they never can get massed, and on the other hand you can't <u>find</u> them, you're not killing troops as rapidly as if you did something else for a while, let him mass, and <u>then</u> bashed him."[48]

Khe Sanh, A Different Kind of Battle

Khe Sanh, like Dien Bien Phu, began as a place nobody in the outside world had ever heard of. McNamara's planners of his 1966-67 defensive barrier line—"McNamara's Wall, or Fence, or Jungle Maginot Line"— incorporated this small outpost on Route Coloniale 9 as one of many along the line which lay just south of the demilitarized zone separating North and South Vietnam. Route 9 had been important as a colonial east-west trade route from Savannakhet on the Mekong River that was the eastern boundary of Laos, all the way across Laos and then across Vietnam to Quang Tri on the Gulf of Tonkin. As an indigenous outpost with a U.S. Special Forces detachment and a small airstrip, Khe Sanh was intended to interfere with any enemy movement out of Laos toward Quang Tri, a vital city in I Corps in the populous lowlands along the coast. Westmoreland and General Walt, the Marine commander, became concerned about a reported two-division buildup of enemy forces just across the Laotian border. They flew in to Khe Sanh to inspect. Walt would have preferred to use his Marines in CAP situations in populated areas in the lowlands, but Westmoreland was looking to provide a base of operations for SOG to interdict the Ho Chi Minh Trail. Westmoreland's strong belief in the value of Khe Sanh led to improvement of the airstrip, movement of the main fortification a bit farther west, garrisoning it with Marines and strong artillery support, and outposting the surrounding hills with Marines.

Except for patrolling and jostling back and forth for positioning, for a year not much on a large scale happened. Then during the night of 20/21 January 1968 shells rained down on the camp and the enemy attacked fiercely behind a massive artillery barrage. Soon two divisions had virtually encircled the position and thus began a 77-day battle and siege, the longest, costliest, most discussed battle in a single location of the American war. It has been so much documented that there is no need to detail it.

As the size and ferocity of the battle at this distant, forsaken spot quickly mounted, President Johnson showed his concern. A large terrain model was erected in the Situation Room where he received continuing updates. Apocryphally he extracted assurances from Westmoreland and all of the Pentagon's top generals that Khe Sanh would hold, guaranteed by their metaphorical "signatures in blood," and supposedly a pledge from Westmoreland that "he would not pull a Dien Bien Phu on him."

That nonsense aside, it is a fact that he got assurances from his military men to include Westmoreland that the enemy would not take Khe Sanh. Enormous airpower and ground reinforcement capability ensured it. The media and armchair generals around the world were so fascinated with what they saw as parallels to Dien Bien Phu that Americans were glued to the battle in front of their television screens. That is—until the Tet Offensive erupted on 30 January, a week after the initial Khe Sanh attack. Then the viewers had two critical situations confronting them.

*   *   *

At the time of Tet I was at Command and General Staff College, Fort Leavenworth, with orders to Vietnam upon completion. My dearest friend, Major John Martin, was an engineer in a unit near Hue. On 7 February 1968 I went to teach an evening class for University of Kansas at a branch campus in Leavenworth. When I returned home, an ashen-faced Sandra met me at the door.

"What's wrong?"

She put her hands on my shoulders and said, "John Martin is missing."

Before John had left, Kaki had insisted that the SOB not get killed on her. They had five wonderful children, a marvelous, rambunctious family. All Sandra knew was that an aircraft had been shot down near Hue with John in it and he was missing. We had two weeks of waiting, not knowing. Then on 21 February we got word. All aboard had been killed. The cost of the war came down hard.

*   *   *

As the fighting at Khe Sanh dragged on, with the garrison, the nearby Lang Vei strongpoint, and the outposts in the hills absorbing ferocious attacks, and with artillery, tactical air strikes and B-52s pounding the enemy positions, it became apparent that the final casualty figures would be huge, and they were. The accounting was confusing, but for certain the friendly KIAs were in the several hundreds, and enemy dead in the several thousands. In the war there was not another battle on such a scale in which essentially the Americans defended a fortified position while pounding enemy outside it with massive artillery and air strikes. Westmoreland viewed it as a victory: "Khe Sanh had evolved as one of the most damaging, one-sided defeats among many that the North Vietnamese incurred, and the myth of General Giap's military genius was discredited."[49] Giap also viewed it as a victory, having successfully drawn significant forces away from cities which were attacked during Tet. Perhaps Khe Sanh can best be described as a bloody draw. In late June, a week after Westmoreland left Vietnam for good, the new MACV commander, General Abrams, ordered the base closed. The NVA had lost interest and, after U.S. forces left, committed only a company to reoccupying it and raising their flag over the razed ground as a psychological statement.

$$*\quad*\quad*$$

The nature of the war had changed dramatically in 1967, but no one outside the most secret inner councils of the Politburo would know it until 1968. The highest levels of political and military leadership in North Vietnam had decided in meetings from June-August 1967 that guerrilla and small unit warfare would continue, as always, but from Tet '68 forward, the war would essentially turn on the success or failure of "big battalions," "big battles." Americans and South Vietnamese in Tet '68 had opportunity to employ enormous firepower on massed enemy. They would have it again in 1972, and the South Vietnamese would finally have it in 1974-75.

CHAPTER 11
General Abrams, "One War," Mid-1968 to Early 1969

*   *   *

General Creighton W. Abrams. (NARA)

IN THE AFTERMATH OF THE Tet Offensive, President Johnson's address to the nation on 31 March 1968 dramatically launched a new era in the war, one in which the United States offered to stop the bombing of North Vietnam and withdraw troops in exchange for the other side withdrawing forces to the north and entering peace talks. He electrified the world by stating, "I shall not seek, and I will not accept, the nomination of my party for another term as your President." On 13 May, representatives of the United States and the Democratic Republic of Vietnam met in Paris to explore talks.

After Westmoreland left Vietnam to become Chief of Staff, in early June 1968 General Creighton Abrams officially took command of MACV. Lewis Sorley cites Abrams' role in commanding "MACV Forward" in the northern part of South Vietnam during Tet '68, and in the May Mini-Tet fighting which followed it, saying "The message traffic makes it clear that he was in de facto command much earlier."[1]

"One War"

General Palmer, as IIFFV commander, had an initial discussion with Abrams when Abrams visited Vietnam in April 1967, just before Abrams was named deputy to Westmoreland. Palmer said, "Despite some deep misgivings about the U.S. strategy being pursued . . . I enthusiastically supported the missions assigned to IIFFV by MACV. I confided my misgivings to only a very few persons; one of those was General Abrams. Although he listened carefully, Abrams seemed unimpressed." The second discussion was after Abrams became deputy. "His reaction was that it was too late to change U.S. strategy. As for any major changes within MACV, the pattern was set in concrete."[2] But after Abrams took over as COMUSMACV, he would indeed introduce a new strategy.

Abrams spoke often and emphatically in his meetings with commanders and staff about his "one war" concept, both with the Marines and Army. He said that pacification was not "the other war" as it had been called, but part of a unified strategy which had security for the people in the hamlets and villages of Vietnam as its centerpiece, thus making it possible for them to be won over to the South Vietnamese government.

"'The enemy's operational pattern is his understanding that this is just one, repeat one war,' stressed Abrams. 'He knows there's no such thing as a war of big battalions, a war of pacification, or a war of territorial security. Friendly forces have got to recognize and understand the one war concept and carry the battle to the enemy, simultaneously in all areas of conflict.'"[3]

Abrams was absolutely correct in that the enemy had always fought one war. Ho Chi Minh had begun the war against the French in late December1944 with Giap's attack by only a platoon with a two-fold mission—fight and proselytize. From then on it was one man, one woman, a few men and women, fighting the French and proselytizing the people. The military was hitting them, withdrawing, striking again, withdrawing. Danger was ever present. One never knew where the next strike would be. This went on continually—guerrilla and small unit actions while bigger units were raised, trained and then utilized. As the larger units attacked, the smaller conjoined military and political operations did not stop. They continued everywhere. In the villages and cities. In the countryside. Vietnam was like a rash that would pop out in spots here, there, and here again, there again. There was no rest from the concern about what would happen next, and where. The proselytizing never stopped: meetings, surprise visits in the night, posters stuck up, pamphlets handed out, discussions, recruitment, oaths of loyalty, of secrecy. When Americans came into the war and fighting reached the scale of Tet '68, the low- and mid-level efforts, military, political, and psychological, were simultaneous with division-size attacks, and it was all one war for one goal—to win.

General Frederick C. Weyand, who had been one of Westmoreland's 25th Division then IIFFV commanders, said, "The tactics changed within fifteen minutes of Abrams' taking command."[4]

Would that it had been so.

The problem with Weyand's statement that the tactics changed is that they did not. Not essentially. If any American general could have "won" the war, Abrams would have been the one to do it. He was the very best that America had to offer. Abrams was a great soldier, a man of prodigious energy and keen intellect. I, and many others, had then, and have still, the utmost admiration and respect for him. But the fact is that pacification and Vietnamization, two core aspects of the one war concept, continued to be seriously short-changed by the orders and actions of Abrams' subordinate commanders. For reasons I still ponder because of his forthright style of leadership and high standards, they continued with search and destroy. Large numbers of troops were committed to missions in terrain and circumstances which favored the enemy, as during Westmoreland's command.

That this was so has been demonstrated by several credible historians, one of whom is Andrew F. Krepinevich who said, "Even though General Abrams okayed the adoption of [MACV's Long Range Planning Task Group's] "one war" approach, the effect on the units in the field was minimal."[5]

I can attest to the minimal effect. From mid-July 1968 to January 1969 I served as S-3 Plans and Operations Officer, then Executive Officer of 11th Armored Cavalry Regiment under Colonel George S. Patton—the two senior staff positions. From January to mid-July 1969 I was Commanding Officer, 1st Squadron, 4th Cavalry, 1st Infantry Division under Major General Orwin C. Talbott. Since 11th Cav was a IIFFV unit I sometimes got to listen to Abrams and his IIFFV commander, and also to brief Abrams on 11th Cav operations. Then, in 1st Division as a battalion-level commander, because of the helicopter I could be with the division generals doing the directing and, only a few minutes later, be down among my soldiers doing the fighting and dying. Until mid-1969, with 1st Division having only months left before withdrawal from Vietnam, it continued essentially as a search and destroy unit, as did the other American divisions.

The War and a Prediction

During my last year of teaching at West Point, 1966-67, I had volunteered for Vietnam. I kept a copy of my request to the Adjutant General of the Army: *I desire as low level command or staff duty with a U.S. unit as possible in Vietnam.* I was sent instead to Command and General Staff College.

The first man from my West Point Class of 1956 to be killed in action was my companymate Raymond Celeste who died in November 1965 as an advisor to an ARVN unit. Before I got to CGSC, eight more classmates had been killed to include my Beast Barracks roommate, Robert Stewart, an Air Force pilot, number one in order of merit in our class. In May 1967 Bob did not return from a mission. His body was never recovered.

At CGSC I began to keep a journal. This entry I made almost two weeks before anybody had ever heard of Tet '68: *19 Jan 68: "Laos about ready to topple, negating all our efforts [there] – yet almost no concern in the press. Three horrendous practical blunders: (1) decision to commit U.S. ground troops in Vietnam after failure of military aid mission, (2) failure to call up Reserves in '65, (3) decision to leave Haiphong open and other targets untouched. Within a year this country will have suffered its greatest humiliation – it does not have the physical strength to expand the Vietnamese operation to Laos and Cambodia; therefore, it will lose both as neutrals; Thailand will be pressured to come to terms with Communists in its government; and the U.S. will be fought and frustrated to a standstill in Vietnam, forced by world opinion to withdraw. This series of developments will greatly encourage the South American Communists and drive the U.S. into a period of isolationism. Better heads should, however, prevail, and we will not see S. America go Communist. What does this mean for the longer term? Probably a detente with Russia, an expansion of Communist China's influence to the south, a greater sense of moral outrage at such fiascoes as Vietnam."*

My predictions on the course of world events turned out to be quite accurate, from which I take no satisfaction. I had wanted the South Vietnamese people to choose their own destiny. On 30 January 1968, after I made the journal entry, the Tet Offensive astonished the world. It led to riots in our country and demands around the globe for getting out of Vietnam. I had been off in my withdrawal prediction by half a year. The first unit to return to the United States left in early July 1969, just as I was finishing my Vietnam service.

With Colonel Patton and 11th Armored Cavalry Regiment

Instead of being assigned to a combat unit as I had requested, I got orders to Headquarters, U.S. Army Vietnam, the huge administrative and logistical arm of MACV. I was glum, knowing I would end up at USARV as a junior lieutenant colonel in some obscure office, shuffling papers. But on 18 July 1968 I landed at Bien Hoa Airbase, and at the Long Binh replacement depot was astounded to discover that my orders had been abruptly changed. I was to join 11th Armored Cavalry Regiment, the famed Blackhorse regiment. Colonel George S. Patton, who had been my company tactical officer as a captain at West Point, and whom I had not seen or talked to since then, had taken command of 11 ACR only a few days earlier. He had seen my orders and prevailed upon USARV to get me assigned to his command.

General Abrams had been one of the elder Patton's battalion commanders, leading the counterattack of Third Army at Bastogne. Abrams, a tough, courageous, highly intelligent fighter, was awarded two Distinguished Service Crosses and two Silver Stars for valor. President Johnson had given Abrams the mission of improving Vietnam's armed forces. During his year as deputy to Westmoreland he did what he could for Vietnamization, with the goal of equipping and training Vietnamese forces so they could take over the war.

I flew to regimental forward headquarters at Lai Khe where a captain met me and took me to see Patton. "Goddamn, Bill, I've got work for you!" he greeted me, clapping me on the shoulder. This was the energetic, profuse, profane Patton I knew from cadet days twelve years earlier, only with graying hair and lines in his face, son of Old Blood and Guts. "Come on," Patton said, "here's what's going on." He propelled me into what turned out to be the briefing tent and began slapping a pointer onto the operations map. In maybe five minutes of fast talking he covered several weeks of cav affairs in actual time, bringing me up to the present. Then Patton rushed me into his helicopter and we were off to check on units. We overflew some positions as Patton gave me a detailed run-down on our units, the terrain, and enemy. Then we landed at other units where I had a chance to talk with some of the men. We were airborne again and just about to land at another troop position when Patton got a call to come to Division for a meeting of brigade commanders. We landed back at Lai Khe, headquarters of 1st Infantry Division as well as our regiment, and Patton dashed off. Thus began an unforgettable six months with Colonel George S. Patton in combat.

The highlights of my experiences in Vietnam, I believe, are important as a reflection of the whole war, its instances of what appeared to be American successes, and its failures, which were not so apparent at the time. We were plowing what seemed like new ground, hopeful of a good harvest, but in fact these fields had been almost entirely ruined by what had happened earlier, and very little good could grow there.

In these first hours with Patton I realized that being inserted into a war was not an entry into history; it is a step into the unknown, and you either create everything around you or it is created for you. As the senior staff officer at regimental level and later a commander at battalion level I should have had a better understanding of what I was doing in terms of the larger construct, but I didn't. Instead, I quickly learned the specifics of what was going on around me and took my place in the action. Each event that cropped up was something new and had to be dealt with in terms of the conditions of the moment, not something that had happened to the Chinese a thousand years ago, or to the French twenty years earlier, or even to our own unit yesterday. And if I, with briefings and maps, felt this immediacy, and my most urgent duty was to react to the circumstances of the moment, act to meet them, and plan for the next, what was it like for our troopers—a driver in an ACAV or a tank who knew only that he was the first vehicle in column on a treacherous dirt road and that his track commander would tell him when to turn left or right into jungle so dense he would often lose sight of an adjacent vehicle?

> *Letter to Sandra, 21 Jul 68. I've been at the command post at Lai Khe now for a little over 24 hours and, needless to say, have been very busy. The responsibility is awesome; we have over 4600 men, hundreds of armored vehicles, and thousands of pieces of major equipment. In terms of sheer firepower, the regiment is the most powerful ground combat unit in Vietnam.*

Organic to the regiment were the Headquarters and Headquarters Troop, Air Cavalry Troop, Aviation Platoon, and 1st, 2nd, and 3rd Squadrons (battalion-size). Attached, and fully integrated into our operations were several companies: engineer, medical, supply and service, military police; and detachments: postal, public information, military history, chemical, transportation, signal, military intelligence, radio security, and psychological operations. In addition we had liaison teams from the Air Force, division artillery, and sometimes Free World liaison detachments from Korean, Australian, and South Vietnamese sources.

Each of the three squadrons consisted of three troops (company-size) of ACAVs (armored cavalry assault vehicles), a tank company of M48A2 or A3 tanks mounting 90 mm guns and machineguns, and a howitzer battery of 155 mm armored self-propelled tracked vehicles. Each squadron had an aviation section of four helicopters: UH-1C or D ("Hueys"), and OH-6A Light Observation Helicopters (LOHs or "Loaches").

The Air Cavalry Troop was the most versatile and valuable component of our combat power, usually making the first contacts. It had three elements: aeroscouts with OH-6As; AH-1G "Cobra" gunships; and an aero rifle platoon (ARP) with Hueys – 28 helicopters in all. Adding regimental headquarters helicopters and its aviation platoon, we had about 50 helicopters and over 400 tracked armored vehicles, an enormous combat force. In sum, an armored cav regiment was a magnificently organized, equipped, and trained instrument of war.

For World War II. And for facing the Soviets in Europe during the Cold War.

Through necessity and innovation, though, we did things that seemed impossible. But we were indeed very heavy, very loud, we ate up enormous resources, and we damaged the countryside just by our movements, to say nothing of the results of our enormous firepower. That has to be weighed while considering our overall contribution in the very complex Vietnam War.

The regiment never operated as a pure cav regiment. Rather, dependent upon mission, it was divested of some of its elements such as one or more squadrons or ground troops, and it acquired others – one or more U.S. infantry straight-leg or mechanized battalions and an ARVN Ranger battalion, in a flexible system called operational control, or opcon. Sometimes our organic, attached, and opcon or direct support strength approached 6,000 men.

More so than most post-WWII armor officers because of his heritage, Patton had studied and practiced armor operations of that war. When he commanded a tank company in the Korean War he regretted that the mountainous terrain would not allow him to employ his tanks against the enemy as he wanted to, in fast, decisive movements. In Vietnam, writing a 2 July 1968 memo on his second day at 11ᵗʰ Cav, he had exhibited his traditional training: *This is basically a reconnaissance war keyed to the meeting engagement.* Soon he learned that this old concept was way off the mark, except perhaps for our air cavalry troop. The enemy would not cooperate by using outdated conventional methods of warfare, and neither would the jungle or swampy terrain or the villages and hamlets containing enemy who were everywhere. Patton adjusted his thinking.

Also, higher headquarters was not cooperating. Patton could not employ his regiment en masse. The regiment's Operational Report for the quarter ending 31 July 1968 reflects a problem that was to bedevil Patton and our squadron and troop commanders: *Operations were characterized by a parceling out of squadrons and troops at various times to the 1st and 9th Infantry Divisions, to the 101st Airborne Division, to the 199th Light Infantry Brigade, to the 1st Australian Task Force, and to the 5th, 25th, and 18th ARVN Divisions. In addition, troop size units were OPCON to IIFFV and Capital Military Assistance Command (CMAC).*

Our regiment had been in country since September 1966, assigned to II Field Force Vietnam (IIFFV), the corps-size headquarters which was responsible for all American forces in Cochinchina from the northern outskirts of Saigon, north and west to Cambodia, and east to the South China Sea. When I arrived, the regiment was opcon to 1st Infantry Division and remained that way for the six months I was with Patton. Although we had the bulk of two of our cav squadrons under our control, one squadron was habitually assigned to security of our Blackhorse Base Camp, 40 miles east of Bien Hoa near Xuan Loc, and it conducted largely independent operations in that area.

In the Bien Hoa/War Zone D area which was our primary regimental tactical area of responsibility (TAOR), in addition to the remainder of the regiment we usually had two infantry battalions from 1st Division and an ARVN Ranger battalion under our control. We conducted both armored cavalry and infantry-type operations, to include many air assaults. Our operations covered a huge area, essentially not to change during my time with the regiment. It went all the way from Xuan Loc (about 50 miles east of Saigon) west to Long Binh/Bien Hoa, north on both sides of critical Highway 13 almost to An Loc (about 60 miles from Saigon), and sometimes included a large portion of War Zone C to the west of Highway 13. Infamous War Zone D was in our area of responsibility, consisting of rugged farmland which turned into dense jungle as it went farther to the east of Highway 13 and Lai Khe. Even when some of our units were under operational control of other headquarters and thus distant from us, we kept in radio contact and supported them administratively and with maintenance and some logistics. Patton and I flew to visit them when we could, and our Tactical Operations Center (TOC) received and recorded their daily reports of action.

Assisting the regimental commander in planning and controlling all regimental tactical operations was the tactical operations center (TOC), or Command Post (CP). As Regimental S-3, I was in charge of it. Basically, it was manned by personnel from our staff sections S-2 (Intelligence); S-3 (Plans, Operations, and Training); Communications; and also liaison personnel from 1st Infantry Division, Division Artillery, Air Force, and Vietnamese units. During the day I would have about three dozen or so people in or close around it at any one time, and at night about a dozen, more when we had contact with the enemy. In these early days I flew with Colonel Patton every day and quickly got to know a lot about our units, personnel, area of operations, and enemy. My assistant S-3s and Operations Sergeant Major Paul Squires performed admirably at the TOC when I was out with Patton.

Letter to Sandra, 21 Jul 68. Let me say something once and not again. This is not an easy job, and it is not a particularly safe job. But you must see those troops in the field to appreciate how I feel. They are kids in their late teens and early twenties, by and large. They are being asked to do things beyond the imagination of most people. They need and deserve every ounce of devotion and care I can give them.

Clear and Hold?

I had heard that Abrams wanted a change from 'search and destroy' to 'clear and hold' tactics, and that small unit ambushes and patrols were preferable to large assaults into deep jungle. In reality, though, there was not a complete switch to clear and hold away from jungle sweeps, at least not in 11th Cav, and, as I was soon to discover, also not in other units of 1st Infantry Division. When I first met Abrams a week or so into my tour, I agreed with 'clear and hold.' But I saw that in fact, following Division orders, we were deep into search and destroy, and we continued that way. Patton's motto, known to all troopers, was "Find the bastards and pile on." We were trying to do that even in the jungle, and Abrams knew this and did not correct us. IIFFV, 1ˢᵗ Infantry Division, and other divisions and brigades continued with search and destroy, obviously with Abrams' tacit, if not direct, concurrence.

I wrote letters and sent audio tapes to my wife, confined to non-upsetting, funny and nice things. The combat operations and their often gruesome outcomes I recorded in my journal which, except for a few extracts in my books, *One Hell of a Ride*, and *Danger's Dragoons*, I never shared with anyone, especially my family. My journal was for my eyes only.

Journal, 22 Jul 68. So many killed and wounded for no visible gain. We go into The Catcher's Mitt, busting jungle and losing men without killing many enemy. "The Catcher's Mitt" was in War Zone D, northeast of Saigon and east of Lai Khe, south of the Song Be River. An outline of its territory looked like a mitt on the map. Busting jungle – crashing through it with our 50-ton tanks and 14-ton ACAVs – was almost always a loser. We all hated jungle busting, and from my earliest days with the Cav I strove for ways to reduce our casualties and yet accomplish our given missions in this terribly hostile territory. The enemy would have to have been stone deaf not to hear us and see the trees shake as we pushed up against them, knocking down on us nests of red ants that bit like hell and, in jungle defoliated with Agent Orange and other toxins, creating a shower of dust and debris from dead leaves and branches that would choke us and decades later give us the cancers that many of our men and I contracted. The enemy would try to place some mines where they thought we would pass, or wait at the edge of small clearings – which we always tried to avoid – to fire RPGs at us. Most often we did not know where the enemy was, but they knew where we were. We were worse than an enormous mass of elephants shoving and trumpeting through dense growth. In such places the advantage was always with the enemy, and our losses were greater than theirs. We "threw tracks" – the tracks would come off the sprockets – and our crews busted torsion bars and their knuckles in horsing the tracks back on – and we cussed and endured. Jaubert back in 1945 had told Leclerc that the marshy Mekong Delta was no Sahara where he could maneuver his armored forces. Well, The Catcher's Mitt in War Zone D was certainly no Sahara either. But those were our orders from 1st Division – sweep – as inept a term as has ever been devised for armor operations in jungle – sweep, search and destroy. There was no Abrams' clear and hold in the jungle of War Zone D. Little to clear, and nothing to hold.

Strategic Hamlet

On 28 July I recorded in my journal, *At dawn flew out w/Col. to see how the resettlement operation was progressing. It was pathetic to look at the village and see the kids scurrying around, see the people in their activities, and know that we were going to level the place* [by Division orders].

At the time, I wondered how this Strategic Hamlet policy could possibly result in "winning hearts and minds," a simplistic term I disliked and never used. The policy was a short-range expedient with dramatic long-term negative results. Should we ever have wondered that the displaced people would hate us and the ARVN for doing this to them?

On my third trip to National Archives in 2002 to recover original documents, I found a 1st Division Memorandum for Record dated 16 July 1968 documenting the plans for resettlement of three hamlets: Bo La, Binh My, and Binh Co in War Zone D at the edge of the jungle, and thus favorite spots for VC infiltration and logistics operations. As it turned out, Bo La was the only one we actually razed, the one we had visited that day. Binh Co, I found, would play a profound role in my Vietnam experience and my life.

Briefing Abrams

On 31 July I was in the TOC when Patton thrust his head in and bellowed, "Haponski, get your ass over to the briefing tent! Abrams is landing in zero two [two minutes]. Give him a briefing."

No sweat. With eleven days on the job, I was going to brief the commander of ground forces in Vietnam. Abrams later was to make several visits to us in both our headquarters and wherever we were in field operations.

Actually the briefing should be no sweat, I thought. I had learned our units well from having visited them, studied the maps, talked to the commanders and men, and knew how they fit into the overall mission. By now I had planned some of what they were doing and gone on a mission or two with units.

No sweat. Except that this was an enormously hot day under the canvas, and everyone was sweating profusely. I had grabbed a pointer and barely finished checking the latest grease pencil markings on the acetate overlay of the operations map which showed the current friendly and enemy situations when Patton barked from the briefing tent entrance, "Atten- *shun*!"

A rumpled man with a baseball cap sporting four black stars, and with a fat, half-smoked cigar thrust into the corner of his mouth, clomped in and sat down, then Patton beside him. Abrams physically was a direct opposite of the tall, spiffy Westmoreland. "A reporter once described Abrams as looking like 'an unmade bed smoking a cigar,' a characterization that delighted Abrams."[6]

I started by briefing the general on the enemy situation in our area of operations, normally the S-2's job, but today I was the whole show. At first the general appeared interested enough, but after a couple minutes and no questions from him, just after I had gotten into the friendly situation, his eyes glazed, no longer seeing the map. Then his chin dropped, and his head began bobbing slightly. In another minute, Abrams' chin was on his chest, cigar still clamped in his mouth. I thought he was going to set himself on fire.

Patton's steely blue-gray eyes were staring straight into me. Most certainly *he* was wide awake. Nothing to do but to go on with the briefing, making a mental note of where I was when the general nodded off. I toned down and droned on at a decibel level I figured would not awaken him.

I had gotten through perhaps eight or ten minutes of elapsed time when Abrams suddenly looked up squarely at me. I instantly picked up the briefing where he had dropped off into his snooze. He listened briefly, looked at his watch and broke in, "Thanks, but from where you stand, how do you see 11ᵗʰ Cav's operations?"

"We're doing well, and we're going to do better, sir." (A good, safe answer.)

"Is that right, George?" Abrams asked, turning to Patton beside him.

"Damn well is, sir," Patton responded enthusiastically.

Abrams grunted toward me, "Good job," and got up to leave.

Patton saw him off and came back into the briefing tent. His eyes were fixed directly on me as he strode up and stopped, uncomfortably close.

He thrust his head forward and barked out fiercely, "I would have fired your ass if you'd awakened him, you know that?"

"I know, sir."

Patton stared ominously at me, as if he were going to draw his pistol and kill me on the spot. Then he broke into a broad toothy grin, clapped me on the shoulder and said, "Damn good job, Bill. Just don't ever try that shit on me."

Gratuitous Brutality

On the evening of 8 August, 3ʳᵈ Squadron cordoned the village of Chanh Luu, eight kilometers southeast of Lai Khe. This village had shown itself to be extremely hostile, so it was no surprise when a battle erupted on the next day. Unlike other contacts we had, this was almost entirely a tunnel fight, with our opcon 36ᵗʰ Vietnamese Ranger Battalion engaging the enemy while 3ʳᵈ Squadron kept the village sealed.

Patton, some others, and I had landed at Chanh Luu that morning and watched our 36th Rangers at work. In late afternoon Patton and I returned to the TOC to plan and coordinate follow-up actions. While there, I observed the first prisoners being brought in, and late in the evening of 9 August, dead tired though I was from the day's exertions, in considerable detail I recorded several events in my journal.

Journal, 9 Aug 68. Fear in a sack: the man was dark and powerfully built. His arms were tightly bound by cords, a burlap sack over his head. . . . Col. Patton said he had been severely handled by our ARVN Rangers and had refused to talk. . . .The man was not young, perhaps in his late forties. He was in shock, hardly perceiving what was happening. He was bare except for blue shorts, and he was partly covered with caked mud, whether from the tunnel he hid in or the treatment he received I don't know. . . .Our Vietnamese interrogator appeared and began to question him. He became desperate, pleading, though never quite losing dignity. Tears welled in his bloodshot eyes, and his face seemed to flatten even more. The interpreter was not satisfied with the response, took his fist and harshly raised the man's chin. Then he stepped down on his knee, and I started to intervene but there was no further mistreatment. The man insisted he was an innocent civilian, that his eldest son had joined the VC four years ago and his second son had been killed by a helicopter gunship. The VC had taken his papers, he said, and he had gone to province headquarters to get more. The officials, not believing him, had jailed him for fifteen days, then sent him back to Chanh Luu without his papers. When we cordoned the village last night he had gone into hiding, afraid since he had no papers.

[Recorded later] *Have now found out how the man was earlier interrogated by our ARVN Rangers: tied down flat in his own yard, gauze mask put over his mouth to hold it open and water poured into it off and on for two hours ["waterboarded"] – that and beating. Now the ARVN have him again.*

This was bad. Brutality by Americans was worse:

Journal, 4 Sep 68. A clean-cut American boy brutally beats a scrawny, cleft-lipped, ignorant farmer.

I threatened this American that I would get his ass if he laid so much as a finger on another prisoner. I informed his likewise clean-cut lieutenant, who directed the proceedings, that I'd do the same to him.

The creature was pitiful, his cleft lip showing teeth rotted to the gums. His head bled from a beating he had gotten earlier from ARVN. He hunched, a dwarf-like thing caught in the corner of a tent where men beat him.

I thought that maybe in a few weeks the fair-faced soldier would return to a comely young girlfriend. But he would leave behind him a scarred, ill-begotten cast-off creature, afraid of ARVN, maybe afraid of VC. Perhaps he was VC. If not before, he probably would be now. I directed that his head be stitched and I watched him being led away, gently this time, by a medic. Nagging me, though, was the suspicion he might soon again be in the hands of ARVN who would resume the beating, only harder because an American lieutenant colonel who understood nothing about war had interfered.

That evening at the briefing, I stood and outlined what had happened and said there would be no more treatment of prisoners like this, and everybody had better get the word. I was only a staff officer, looking squarely at squadron commanders, senior to me. Patton sat there. I didn't know if he concurred, but I didn't care. I was steaming.

Regimental Pacification Operations

Between the edge of the vast jungle that was War Zone D and Colonial Route 13, which ran north out of Saigon to the Cambodian border, was a large stretch of farm land with many farming hamlets and villages. Dirt roads, mined in places the VC and locals knew but we didn't, connected the hamlets. The terrain was gently rolling, containing several small streams and rice paddies. Small and large growths of trees and brush sheltered VC in groups, usually of not more than squad size. As part of our ongoing pacification operations I planned and helped control seal and search operations in several of these hamlets and villages, such as the large operation at Chanh Luu.

A cavalry regiment was a lousy unit for hamlet pacification. In the first place, just traveling across the farm land and dirt roads to get to a hamlet caused damage even though we tried to minimize it. Then too, commanders of tanks and ACAVs in a contact naturally would spur their drivers to move quickly and make sharp turns with no thought other than to kill the enemy and keep themselves and their crews from becoming casualties. Additionally, for moving between buildings and engaging VC, tankers with 90 millimeter cannons and .50 caliber machineguns were far less useful than grunts with M16 rifles. If a tank gun fired, the damage would be enormous—not the best circumstance in our effort to convince the people to feel good about their government.

Protecting Saigon, the capital, always had first priority in MACV plans, and this led to a density of American units more or less in a ring out from the center of the city, a concentration not experienced by other major cities farther north along the seacoast. In addition to 11th Cav, the cavalry squadrons of three U.S. infantry divisions – 1st, 9th, and 25th – were within striking distance of Saigon, and all of them had played major roles in counterattacking the enemy during Tet '68, rushing into enemy formations and blasting them with ground fire and air attacks. I later learned that Abrams often stressed in his Saturday briefings at MACV headquarters how important it was to keep the enemy and their rockets out of Saigon, and he told us the same in our TOC. If people in the capital itself feared for their safety, how could anybody trust their government? Although 11th Cav was a great mobile reserve for protection of Saigon, we were way too bulky and powerful to be a good pacification instrument. But here we were, and we would give pacification our best. With any units not out on search and destroy, we set night defensive positions (NDPs) right up against the edge of several hamlets. During the day, troops would work inside a hamlet and patrol out from it, and at night they would set out listening posts and ambushes to interdict enemy which had to use the inhabitants to support them with food and information on our activities.

Our regimental efforts at pacification were hindered by the district chief who had no interest in it and would not send his RFs and PFs out to the hamlets. Also, our ARVN 36th Ranger Battalion commander, Captain San, was no help. Mostly, we treated him just like one of our

American unit commanders. We gave him orders and he more or less carried them out—not really what Vietnamization was supposed to be all about: training the Vietnamese to conduct their own war. I learned that San was more adept at victimizing his countrymen than he was at fighting the enemy. At various places along the roads in his area he set checkpoints to extract a fee from any civilian who wanted to pass. U.S. advisors in all areas and at all levels were constantly working at this problem – without much success. Patton was trying to overcome this coercion – with no discernable effect.

This whole pacification effort in our area was askew. It seemed to us that to be effective, the impetus ought to come from the Vietnamese, not the Americans. But here we were, trying to do what we could whereas the district chief could care less and the Ranger commander profited from the war, no doubt giving the district chief his cut.

A Little Girl in Binh Co

The 1st Division summary of operations of 16 September stated that our 1st Squadron *continued reconnaissance in force operations and night ambush patrol operations* in its area of operations. "Reconnaissance in force" was not a new type of operation, just another way of saying "search and destroy." What was theory and sounded good at MACV headquarters and was received enthusiastically in Washington as a better way of going about business—Abrams' "One War"—was not what was happening in 11th Cav's Tactical Area of Operations. Yet we did not get corrected by Division, IIFFV, or Abrams himself during his visits. Indeed, we were complying with Division orders.

An event of the night of 15/16 September 1968 would greatly impact our future regimental operations. Alpha Troop sealed the tiny farming hamlet of Binh Co which was right up against the edge of the jungle of War Zone D. During the night the troop received small arms fire and four RPG rounds which caused minor damage to two ACAVs and wounded six troopers, who were dusted off. The search after daylight yielded only one RPG round and two men classified as VC. I learned there was a little eleven year old girl in trouble in Binh Co. When Alpha Troop had received the probe, two houses – huts, really, with baked mud walls and thatched roofs – had caught fire from one of our defective illuminating rounds, and the houses had burned to the ground. One house was that of the little girl. I heard she was huddling away from everyone, in tears.

Having to escape from her burning house, with shooting going on only yards away was not, however, the worst thing that had happened to her. I learned later that the pilot of a helicopter gunship, quite likely from 11th Cav back in April before Patton or I had arrived, had looked down and seen a man on a road. He was leading his two old oxen from Binh Co to Binh My to try to trade them for a younger pair. It was the middle of the afternoon on a clear day. He was wearing black pajamas—like almost all farmers of the area. The gunship attacked, repeatedly, killing the man and his two oxen. The man's wife was now a widow with four girls, the oldest 18, the next 11, and the two little ones, nine and eight.

That eleven-year-old girl from Binh Co, whose name I found out later to be Nhan, reminded me of my eleven-year-old Maura. The hamlet of Binh Co was to become important in our regimental pacification efforts, and Nhan and her three sisters were to become profoundly important in my life.

The next day, in an audio tape I began telling Sandra and Maura about Binh Co. I explained that it had almost no male population since they were either ARVN or VC, quite certainly mostly the latter. The VC used this hamlet and others like it in the vicinity as supply points, so the people were caught in the fighting between our forces and the VC. Until our units arrived, the VC came in from the jungle any time they wished, collected taxes from the inhabitants, propagandized, sometimes helped them, other times harassed them, and paid or forced them to do labor and otherwise aid them. Binh Co had perhaps seventy-five or so houses and maybe three hundred people, just a farming hamlet.

The small houses with hard-packed, immaculately clean earthen floors were furnished with the barest living essentials: board pallets to sleep on, things that looked like sawhorses for seats, a pot for cooking, and a minimum of other household items.

Patton told our S-5 civil affairs officer, Captain Lee Fulmer, to pick out from regimental stocks some canned goods and a few other things we thought might be useful to the family. I added a couple gifts I had my driver pick up in the PX, and we flew to Binh Co. This would be a pathetic offering, but maybe it would be a start.

When we arrived, upon our interpreter's query an old woman motioned toward out a girl hugging a wall, trying not to be seen. This, I was to find, was Nhan. I pointed my movie camera and took a few feet of film before she saw me and fled around the corner of the house, terrified. Much later I learned that she had never seen a camera and thought I was pointing a gun at her. Our interpreter finally convinced her to face us and come forward. Trembling, she made a few little steps toward us. When I gave her a doll and dress she was speechless at the gifts, unlike anything ever seen in Binh Co. That night, in my van I entered in my journal, *I'm sure that the house we'll build for them will be better than the one we destroyed.*

Within a day or two of the illumination round accident, Binh Co had become the center of our pacification efforts. After a few weeks, during which we built two new houses for those that had burned, added a new school, paid for a schoolteacher, put in a playground, and helped the inhabitants develop other projects, Abrams came to visit and liked what he saw. We quickly expanded our pacification efforts to other hamlets. Unfortunately the province and district chiefs visited only for the ceremonial opening of the school and took no action to provide permanent RFs or PFs.

I came to love the four Binh Co girls, especially Nhan, the 11-year-old, and they provided considerable relief from many difficult and sordid events. The fact was, though, my visits to them were always fleeting since I had so much to do.

Haponski with Nhan (holding hands) and her younger sisters Tuong (front left) and Luong (right) in Binh Co, October 1968. (Collection of author)

Elsewhere, other aspects of the war continued. We kept on jungle busting toward objectives that 1st Division wanted searched, and we helped select B-52 targets for War Zone D. On several occasions I landed in the strike zone immediately after B-52 strikes to conduct bomb damage assessment (BDA). On some days I found pieces of bodies hanging in trees. On most other days, though, there was nothing much except evidence we had hit a long-vacated site or nothing at all – just jungle. Meanwhile, a myriad of small engagements continued.

Our engineers had finished their construction projects in Binh Co. The new school was a very plain looking building, simply boards with an earthen floor and a tin roof. I said in a letter to Sandra and Maura, *It's much better than any of the buildings currently in Binh Co. The old school next to it had so many shell holes in the roof it couldn't keep the rain out, so I hope this one will fare better.* I told them that after we visited the school we went to the new house of the mother with the four children. It was a rather large wooden building with a tin roof. We asked her how she liked her new house, and she said she liked it. The earthen floor was just being put in. She was using a decrepit hoe and leveling the dirt. Inside there were already two bunkers built, that is, holes in the floor which every house in Vietnam had because of the war, and in which the family, as soon as they heard any hostile activity, immediately tumbled. Nhan was suspicious of me and hung back behind her mother.

A week later I wrote of going out to Binh Co again: *Colonel Patton and I saw the crippled schoolmaster in the stained white pullover shirt in which I'd seen him every time. Large gaps showed here and there in his mouth, and his few teeth were betel nut stained. He was writing an assignment on the board, which consisted of just that – a board. He had some kind of scratchy chalk and no slate at all.*

Colonel Patton had worked hard at getting the Vietnamese government officials interested in this place, but except for the school opening, the district chief hadn't visited the hamlet. He had written it off as totally VC. We looked at Binh Co as one of the marginal hamlets which, if he were to take an interest in it, would perhaps come around. We found that when this district chief spoke at the school opening several days earlier he had told the people they couldn't go to Tan Uyen, the large village to the south. They needed to go there to market their farm products and buy supplies, they protested, but he said no. In a letter I told my family, *That's the kind of person we have to deal with. He's responsible for this entire district and has very little interest in seeing that anything proper is done about it. This is what's so discouraging. There are many good government officials I am sure. We've met some of them. But there are also many who are interested only in what they can get out of the war. This little bandy-legged bastard is one of those. So that's what the people of Binh Co face.*

"Find the Bastards and Pile On"

In September and October I went on as many missions with our aerorifle platoon as I could. First Division expected us to carry out sweeps in the jungle, and Patton's motto was our guide: "Find the Bastards and Pile On." The enemy in the open farmland were so well integrated with the populace that there was no possibility of a big fight there. Both by division orders and Patton's nature we went searching in the jungle of War Zone D. Patton had other business one day so I had his command and control helicopter. We had flown for some time when we heard that one of our scout helicopters had been shot down in the jungle. Flying quickly to the scene we found the wreckage. Circling, providing covering fire as well as we could, we were shot at, the second time sounding as if we had been hit, but it was a near miss. Then another scout chopper was hit and crash landed. We flew immediately toward it.[7]

Major Doc Bahnsen, the air cav troop commander, said, "We had already called a medevac and it was settling down about this time. Gray and the door gunner were still laying down suppressive fire, as was Bill Haponski's aircraft as it orbited overhead. Just a few days earlier, my troopers saved Haponski's life, and he returned that favor by helping save ours while we recovered [the lieutenant] and his crew chief."

The reference was to an incident when I had accompanied Doc with his aerorifle platoon into a wooded area in farmland and we engaged a squad of VC in thick undergrowth. I was between two aerial rifle platoon soldiers (ARPs) and filming the action as we advanced on line, engaging the enemy. Suddenly a VC popped up directly in front of me with his AK-47 pointed at me, and the ARP next to me instantly fired and dropped him at my feet. Doc and his ARPs were legendary. They would go anywhere, do anything to fulfill Patton's desire to find them and pile on. I was thankful that day they were such tough, courageous fighters, and quick on the trigger.

The Hoi Chanh (Rallier) from Binh Co

In a late October audio tape to Sandra I told her about recently talking with a Hoi Chanh, a rallier from the VC who for four years had lived in the jungle of War Zone D and who previously had been a resident of Binh Co. He knew the people in Binh Co, to include the family of girls. As a result of the first visit Colonel Patton and I had made to the hamlet and the subsequent work we had done, his wife had encouraged him to rally. By now, Nhan had become my little friend, and the next day at Binh Co she saw me coming, dashed up to me and began smiling, an enormous change from the first fearful looks I had gotten five weeks earlier. She was wearing a new white blouse, perhaps purchased with some of the money I had given the mother. I wrote to my parents, *She put her arm around me and hugged me the whole time I was there. I bent down and kissed her, and we went arm in arm to the school.*

At the new school I found that the schoolmaster we had hired had a blackboard which Lee Fulmer had gotten for him, the kind we used in our briefing tent. He had written their lessons on the board, so there had been improvement since the last time I had seen the school.

Our PIO lieutenant gave me a note with data I had requested. School enrollment was eighty students, and approximately thirty children from Binh Co did not attend because their families were too poor. The teacher was being paid thirty to forty piasters per month for each student, or about thirty to forty cents per student. With thirty children not attending because their family could not afford forty cents each, for about twelve dollars a month those thirty children could go to school. There were, in addition to the eighty children from Binh Co, thirty students who walked to school from Binh My each day, three kilometers distant. We intended to build a new school in Binh My as soon as we could get the material, and we would try to fund more children in Binh Co. In the meantime I would pay for the thirty children.

In French times Binh My was known as a Viet Minh headquarters for resistance. Like its nearby sister Binh Co, until a month or so earlier it had been VC controlled. Now the VC mostly, but not entirely, had to bypass it because our troops at the adjacent NDP had changed the situation. The villagers of Binh My very much wanted the school we were going to build, and indications were that we would succeed as in Binh Co. The problem, of course, was how long we could remain in the area. We were continuing our efforts to get the province and district officials interested enough to position ARVN troops or RF/PFs there. It was crucially important to extend the GVN influence to these places if there was to be any lasting hope for them. We were having great difficulty in getting the lumber and funds for the school projects, but many agencies were now interested (maybe due to Abrams' interest in our project?), and we were determined to succeed. Many of the young men of these hamlets were VC, probably living in the jungle close by, and we hoped that our actions would influence them to rally to GVN. The larger problem was to convince the government officials to do the right things for their people, and even more, to get the inhabitants of the hamlets interested in and capable of doing things for themselves.

I wanted to find out how the rallier was doing. He had been flown out to Binh Co earlier in the day so he could move his family to the Chieu Hoi center in Phu Loi. Hoi Chanhs could not stay in their home hamlets for fear of VC reprisals. The same man who had sat happily in my van on the preceding evening was in his house when I entered. He was crying, his wife was crying; they were having a family argument. Apparently his wife, after having encouraged him to rally, had reconsidered. She did not want to leave her home, and she didn't know what to do because her husband would have to go to Phu Loi, a strategic hamlet. She was confused, and he was confused. Perhaps fear of the VC had more than a little to do with the whole matter. It was heartbreaking. I made a quick check with Lee Fulmer and told her we would bring her husband back in another few days after she had a chance to think about it. I promised her we would take her goods, animals and all, and put them on a truck and move them and her to their new home in Phu Loi, which would be about an hour and a half's drive away. So we left it at that.

In a tape I told my wife I felt like shit.

The Gruesome Costs of War

In my journal I wrote, *Many times I have flown over the hamlet and seen the child's house, but have had no opportunity to stop. Today I went back, being sick of what had happened, and desperately needing solace. I did not find it; my sweet child was ill with a cold. She hugged me, and I patted her cheek, kissed her, and asked a medic to check her.* What had happened was that very early that day I had been headed to Binh Co, and near the hamlet we had flown over an ACAV just as it hit a mine. Some munitions inside it had exploded. Landing and running toward it I saw two men helping a third who was staggering, groping and moaning, covered with blood. One man was lying on the ground, dead. Several others were wounded and as I approached, one of them shouted, "We're okay." The man being helped, though, was not okay. He had taken the blast in his face and his eyes were gone, blood and gore running down his face and body.

In my journal I later noted that I grabbed the first aid kit from my chopper and put a compress on his face, the gore slipping through my hands. I thought at first he was black, but later had doubts – I saw that his legs were white through his ripped trousers. Only the top part of his body was black, charred from the explosion, the skin peeled and bare flesh showing beneath. We loaded him onto my helicopter as he gasped for water. We lifted off and I poured him a cup and put it in his bloody hand. He held it, the gore from his face falling into the cup. Desperately thirsty he sucked at the cup and was drinking his own blood. I tried to comfort him, shouting above the helicopter noise that he would be all right. He spoke, and I had to put my ear close to his mouth to hear him. He was asking me who I was, telling me he could not see me. I recorded in my journal: *'I'm Colonel Haponski; we're only a few minutes out from the hospital,'* and he gasped, *'Thank you, Sir.'*

Sir! – Unthinkable! A man in such shape calling me 'Sir.'

When we landed and got him onto a stretcher I then saw his arm – a huge slice had been cut above the elbow as neatly as a piece of meat in a butcher shop. After we deposited him on the operating table I left the operating room, the gore clinging to my fingers, burned flesh all over me. I literally tasted the smell and

I puked onto the floor. I found the latrine and threw up some more and tried to wash the mess off but it clung and reeked. I gagged and retched and retched until, exhausted, I went out and slumped into a chair. An hour or so later, back at our base camp I was able to wash and change clothes and try to get away from the smell and taste and feel of burned, gory flesh.

Abrams and the Pacification Disconnect

I had learned from listening to General Abrams how important pacification was to him. Other than that, though, at the time I had no idea of his prior beliefs. I much later learned that, as Vice Chief of Staff of the Army in 1966, he had approved a detailed plan, "Pacification and Long-Term Development of South Vietnam," abbreviated PROVN. It was written by a special staff of mid-level officers in the Pentagon, all of whom had been province or district advisers in Vietnam. Chief of Staff, General Harold K. Johnson, had "told this group to develop an alternative concept to Westmoreland's strategy of attrition." The group defined 'victory' as "bringing the individual Vietnamese, typically a rural peasant, to support willingly the GVN."[8] This definition of 'victory' was closer than any previous pacification plan had come to what was needed. Unfortunately, these officers so eagerly presented their case at the Pentagon they had alienated senior officers, and although Abrams had approved the study and Westmoreland and his staff had studied it, practically speaking it had gone next to nowhere.

General Davidson, Westmoreland's J-2 (Intelligence), strongly supported his boss and believed that most of his decisions, efforts, and results were good ones. He did, however, fault Westmoreland's "order of priorities." He said, "In 1966 and 1967, and for that matter throughout his commandership in Vietnam, Westmoreland viewed pacification as a stepchild. While he pontificated about pacification, he devoted his energies and interests to operations like Cedar Falls and Junction City, not to clearing and holding the insignificant hamlets and villages around

Saigon. And—as an old military axiom goes—whatever the commander emphasizes gets done well by the staff and subordinate commands. So it was in Vietnam. The MACV staff and the American units emphasized big-unit military operations."[9]

In 1968 I probably had not heard of William Colby, who progressively was CIA Chief of Station in Saigon, Chief of the CIA's Far East Division, and at the ambassador level, head of Civil Operations and Rural Development Support – CORDS. Nor had I heard of Robert Komer (Colby's predecessor), or National Security Action Memorandum 362 of May 1967. In this directive, President Johnson had formalized new arrangements to make pacification a priority for American action. From that time forward, MACV would reassert its responsibility for pacification which it had been given in 1964, marking a significant shift away from the 1965-67 confusing, often haphazard, mixed civilian and military control of those efforts.

Part of the pacification package was the appointment of Komer, a civilian with new rank of ambassador, as Westmoreland's deputy for pacification.[10] Komer was a hard-driver who, according to Colby, insisted "to startled American generals that his position as Westmoreland's Deputy (and the rank of Ambassador that Johnson gave him) put him at four-star rank with the three other Deputies, his limousine equaling theirs in size with four stars on its front. He was meticulous in his subordination to Westmoreland, who gave him full support."[11]

After the Tet '68 offensive "Blowtorch Bob" Komer had wished to push pacification out into rural areas where the villages and hamlets were VC or contested. Whereas Komer wanted pacification expanded—now!—President Thieu wanted to wait. Thieu told the new Secretary of Defense, Clark Clifford, "that only after the government consolidated its grip on the cities and their environs and on the areas where South Vietnamese forces were already stationed would he propose moving into contested zones."[12] Abrams was not ready to embrace a U.S. pacification offensive so soon after Tet had significantly set pacification back, and he was not fond of Komer's aggressive style.

Shortly after Abrams took over, two months or so before Patton or I arrived at 11 ACR, Abrams got the same PROVN group together to present the study again, this time at MACV with Abrams' corps and division commanders and high-ranking staffs in attendance. Again the enthusiastic young officers alienated their audience. General Davidson, said, "The bulk of the comments of the senior officers was virulently negative. Abrams, now angry, got into the discussion forcefully . . . . That stifled further dissent, but it left the generals unhappy and unconvinced." Davidson continued, "Even those who disagreed with the concept dutifully, if unenthusiastically, gave it their full support. . . . Every general in Vietnam knew that Abrams held the power of life or death over his career."[13]

There is a disconnect between Davidson's statement that Abrams' subordinates "gave it their full support," and what was actually happening in the field, then and later – which was more American search and destroy by divisions than pacification. In fact, Davidson acknowledged as much. He pointed out that, "Almost immediately the news media began to push the story that Abrams was abandoning Westmoreland's large-unit search and destroy tactics in favor of security operations by smaller forces. This was untrue. Abrams made no abrupt and voluntary change of operational strategy. As Bob Komer said later, 'I was there when General Abrams took over. . . there was no change in strategy whatsoever.'" Davidson continued, "I was J-2 MACV when General Abrams took over and I can confirm what Komer said. I talked daily with Abe about the enemy situation and every Saturday conducted the Weekly Intelligence Estimate Update . . . a gathering which Abrams used (as Westmoreland had before him) to discuss operations with his principle commanders and staff. In 1968, Abrams never spoke of any new strategy nor did he voice any dissatisfaction with large-unit search and destroy operations. What did happen in mid-1968 was that the war itself changed. . . . By mid-1968 Troung Chinh had secured Politburo approval for his concept of returning to guerrilla-type small-unit action, and in accordance with Troung's concept, the Communists scaled down their operations. Abrams reacted to the enemy operations with increased small-unit patrols and raids of his own, but he kept maximum pressure on the VC and NVA in his own war of attrition. . . . It was not Abrams who changed the American strategy for the ground war, but Giap and Truong Chinh."[14]

"His own war of attrition?" Abrams would not have liked that characterization. It may help to look at the forces Abrams had at the time for making his one war concept a reality. His combat divisions of course wanted to focus on enemy main and regional forces. That was where the big military plays were to be found, if at all. Armies want to fight other armies. Generals want to defeat other generals. But the situation after Tet had made this, at least temporarily, almost impossible because the bulk of enemy main and regional forces in the South needed recuperation. What was left for Abrams was to use his MACV advisory structure and CORDS in an innovative, much more vigorous way. After the enemy's Fall Offensive of August and September 1968 petered out, Abrams was now ready to move on pacification. But Thieu still was not, and it took a lot of prodding by Abrams to get him to announce a supposedly Vietnamese initiative which Komer had actually drafted, the Accelerated Pacification Campaign (APC), which would run from 1 November 1968 through 31 January 1969.

At 11 ACR we had already heard from Abrams himself the gist of the upcoming APC and were well into the essential part of it, security for hamlets and villages, before it was officially launched. But such high level dealing as a new country-wide pacification campaign changed our daily activities not much. Following mission guidance, I was still planning and helping to conduct operations according to the "pile on" concept. I was also trying to improve the lot of the people of Binh Co, especially my family. I wanted to get a mechanical sewing machine so the oldest of the four Binh Co girls could learn to sew and the family could make a living. *Somehow or other*, I wrote to Sandra, *they have to learn how to do that.*

By now the tenuous nature of American attempts at pacification had become clear to me. The local enemy never gave up their efforts to win over the people by persuasion or otherwise. In an audiotape to Sandra, 5 Nov 68, I told her, *Something is very definitely wrong in Binh Co. It has changed drastically in the last few days.* Nhan, instead of holding my hand and skipping along with me as in the past, wouldn't come anywhere near me as we walked.

I learned that about four or five nights earlier, VC had gotten into the hamlet and informed the people that if they continued to cooperate with the Americans there would be reprisals. Four young women, three of them Binh Co residents and one a prostitute who had drifted in, were abducted, warned not to have anything to do with the Americans, then released. So now my "adopted"family was caught between Americans and VC. We would continue taking military and civic action to try to assure the people of Binh Co they were secure, but the very fact that the VC had eluded the nightly ambush our NDP unit put out demonstrated that absolute security was impossible. Was the mother of the four girls now afraid to accept our help?

Vietnamization in 11th Armored Cavalry Regiment

President Johnson had given Abrams a two-faceted mission, pacifica-tion being one part, and Vietnamization the other. The president had "specifically charged him to improve South Vietnam's forces."[15] In late November Patton appointed me as executive officer, XO, a job I told him I did not want. But he was insistent. I turned from tactical planning and operations to overseeing all aspects of the regiment's performance in support of those operations – administrative, logistical, medical, main-tenance, engineer, aviation, Blackhorse base camp at Xuan Loc – every-thing. Patton and I had experience first with the 36th Ranger Battalion, and then when they were replaced, with the 51st Ranger Battalion. For some time Patton engaged in a tugging match with the 51st's com-mander, Captain Thoung. The captain wanted to do what he wanted to do, and Patton of course wanted Thuong to do as Patton wanted him to do, so the two of them were at loggerheads. I wrote to Sandra, *Both of them will flatter one another – Patton pats Thuong on the back, tells him what to do, and Thuong smiles and says, 'Yes sir, Roger, Roger.' He can do anything, and he will do anything that Patton wants, he says, but when it comes to doing it, he doesn't, and he has lots of excuses.*

Thuong filed a complaint that went all the way up to the Vietnamese III Corps headquarters, then over to IIFFV and back down to us. I invested considerable time and staff resources in preparing a draft response for Colonel Patton. Thuong had said that the Americans were ordering him to do things, weren't even informing him of what he was expected to do, and that wasn't the way it was supposed to work. We should have been "cooperating" with him. Thuong had come to us with a good reputation for field operations, but we weren't seeing it fulfilled. He also had other reputations, one of which was that he had three wives and many girlfriends. My draft of our reply read, *And of course it's difficult to get him in the field at night with all of this activity going on, with his travels back and forth to Bien Hoa and Saigon.* Patton cut that part out.

Thuong, however, had a point. We had gotten no guidance from higher headquarters on Vietnamization, and in retrospect it must have been treated by them and by us as an afterthought. The Vietnamization concept required the sponsor unit to provide training, but basically we were using his battalion, or rather, trying to use it, as just another unit in our overall operations. I believe we must have been either too busy with combat operations and didn't want to be slowed down by a recalcitrant Ranger unit commander, or there was not enough higher command interest in providing anything that could be called training except what they got "on the job."

Then we had more trouble with the battalion. I received a report of a survey of 91 people who lived in the area that the battalion was responsible for pacifying. It was highly negative, relating many instances of thievery and abuse. *Thirty-seven respondents reported that they were afraid to remain in the surveyed area because of the Rangers, but that they had property in their hamlets and could not move. . . . Respondents noted that the district chief also fears the Rangers and despaired that they [villagers], humble people, could do anything to alleviate the situation.*[16] The villagers listed many things the Rangers stole on their periodic sweeps, from chickens, fruits, and vegetables to radios and money. They severely beat one man and stripped his house bare of anything of value.

When we confronted Thuong with these and similar accusations he laughed them off as fiction and was offended we would even be interested in such things. "You do not understand," he said. "Vietnam is different from America." When we reported villager grievances through province channels we got assurances that the matters would be looked into, and that was the last we heard of them. Vietnamese Ranger, Marine, and Airborne units were said to be the best forces in GVN, and maybe most were. If so, our two battalions in 1968 seem to have been the exception. Both had been a trial and, I suppose in retrospect, we were much like other American units with a lot to do on their hands—impatient. We had gotten no guidance from higher headquarters on Vietnamization and done little on our own that would enable the Rangers to be more capable within a truly viable South Vietnamese army.

The Accelerated Pacification Campaign

In 11th Cav we were ahead of the game in the Accelerated Pacification Campaign (APC), which was to run from 1 November 1968 to 31 January 1969. We had been into pacification from the time Nhan's house had burned down in September. Our campaign goal was to raise the three hamlets in our area of operation from their V (VC) or D, E status (contested) to C, B, or A (GVN controlled), according to the Hamlet Evaluation System (HES) of the APC. By the time I left 11th ACR in January 1969, we rated one of them as C, Binh Co. The other two were still D and E. Patton kept trying to get the province chief interested enough to provide RF/PFs for the hamlets and failed. The province chief spent one night in Nhan's new house to demonstrate GVN's confidence in security. (We had the hamlet heavily guarded.) Her mother was highly honored and refused to accept the compensation we tried to give her. The province chief left and never returned, nor, so far as I know, did the obnoxious district chief. Without continuous, effective GVN presence we knew that our efforts would be for naught when we left the area, and that is what happened. While I was in Vietnam I had arranged a means of sending money to the Binh Co family after I returned stateside. I failed to get it to them. The 11th ACR had moved, and the hamlets went back to the VC and remained that way until the end of the war.

During my six months in 11th Cav we had done what we could for pacification, both working in the hamlets and trying to secure them. We conducted search and destroy operations into the base camps of the Dong Nai Regiment in War Zone D and had minimal success while taking a lot of casualties. From all causes, in my six months with the regiment we lost 64 men killed in action who were on our rosters, plus a number unknown to me of killed in our opcon units: U.S. infantry and mechanized infantry battalions, armored cavalry troops, and in our ARVN Ranger battalions, and other GVN units. I am not sure whether anything we did improved the fighting qualities of the two Ranger battalions we had under our control. We certainly had a difficult time getting them to do what we wanted done. I do know, however, that they were detrimental instead of helpful to our pacification efforts.

But that was the whole problem. They were *our* pacification efforts, not *theirs*. We tried to get them to do what *we* wanted done. That reflects the overreaching dilemma throughout South Vietnam: the people who presumably were the ones most interested in ensuring civilian loyalty to the government should have been the source of pacification ideas, planning, and implementation—the Vietnamese themselves. Instead, all the way from Westmoreland's 1964 HOP TAC program, which he named and planned, through Abrams' 1968-69 APC program, which Komer planned and which Abrams strongly urged President Thieu into implementing, and beyond, it was the *Americans* who were mostly the inspiration, mostly the planners, and a mainstay of the forces which provided security, such as it was. One historian said, "The American ground strategy created a paradox: The U.S. Army was fighting on behalf of an army and a government that it tended to treat as irrelevant."[17]

Major General Talbott and 1st Infantry Division

On 13 September 1968, 1st Division's commander, Major General Keith L. Ware, was killed in action, and Major General Orwin C. Talbott replaced him. Talbott "explained that the division was going to move battalions from region to region and mission to mission rather than to leave them for a long time in a single assignment. This method of operations was meant to increase a sense of flexibility and aggressiveness within maneuver units."[18] Possibly good for 1st Division units, but likely bad for South Vietnam. The two main missions as directed from Washington were pacification and Vietnamization, both of which would benefit from American units staying in place as much as possible. Yet, over three years since our first combat units came ashore, we remained committed to the massive firepower and movement tactics of World War II.

The country-wide Accelerated Pacification Campaign "called for maintaining security in secure hamlets and restoring it to contested ones. The government wanted 1 million persons enrolled in the PSDF [People's Self Defense Force] and two hundred thousand weapons distributed, with one self-defense group of fifty members in each target hamlet. RF [Regional Force] companies would conduct mobile operations on the perimeters of relatively secure (A, B, and C) hamlets, while the militia [PSDF] (supported by PF [Popular Force] platoons) operated inside the . . . contested and enemy controlled (D, E, and V) hamlets. . . while regular ARVN forces and the RF [Regional Forces] would provide security. In enemy-controlled areas, ARVN and RF were expected to conduct search-and-destroy operations to disrupt enemy logistics and troop movements. . . . The Phung Hoang [controversial Phoenix] part of the APC called on each [Vietnamese] corps, province, and district to

15

attack the [Viet Cong] infrastructure in concert with pacification and tactical operations."[19]

At Corps level, "In January 1969 . . . [Lieutenant] General Walter T. 'Dutch' Kerwin, the [IIFFV] commander, gave subordinate commanders an ultimatum to meet their APC goals, which were rooted in the HES [Hamlet Evaluation System]. This requirement moved inexorably down the chain of command to the 2d Brigade of the 25th Division, whose commander . . . warned battalion commanders they would lose their jobs if any enemy-controlled hamlets remained in their areas of operations at the end of the APC."[20]

Since the HES was a highly subjective report, it was most unlikely that many enemy-controlled hamlets would remain.

CHAPTER 12

Inside a U.S. Unit at Squadron (Battalion) Level, 1969

✳   ✳   ✳

ON 5 JANUARY 1969 IN Di An, seven miles northeast of the northern edge of Saigon, I took command of 1st Squadron, 4th Cavalry, 1st Infantry Division. Throughout Vietnam, the Accelerated Pacification Campaign still had almost a month to go. Hating war, with years of service in armor and cavalry from platoon through battalion level and regimental combat experience I was well trained to wage it, and I would give it my best. My goals in commanding 1-4 Cav were to hurt the enemy as much as possible, save as many of my men as I could, and help the South Vietnamese people.

Early Days in Command

Instead of operating directly under division control in accordance with Army's design of divisional cav squadrons, my task force was initially placed under operational control of Colonel John T. Carley's 2nd Brigade of 1st Division. I was responsible for an area of operations (AO) on the northern outskirts of Saigon – all of Di An District (pronounced Zee-On) and a portion of Lai Thieu (Lie Tyu) District. In an audiotape to Sandra I said, *It's quite a challenge – fifteen villages including thirty-four hamlets, and lots of industry, large power plants, sugar factories, many other things I don't even know about yet – a very different area from the totally rural and jungle area in which 11th Cav operates north of Bien Hoa.* Additionally I had ready reaction responsibility for major bridges over the Saigon

River as well as the huge Newport Bridge over the Dong Nai River leading into Long Binh and Bien Hoa from Saigon.

I was pleased at the prospect of working with Nguyen Minh Chau,
the Di An district chief who had a sterling reputation among Americans.
Chau was a Vietnamese Marine Corps major who had been seriously
wounded four times and partially paralyzed as a result of the third
wound. His fourth wound occurred only two months earlier, just outside
the gate of Di An Base Camp, when he was shot at night riding in his
jeep. He barely survived the assassination attempt and carries the bullet
in his lung to this day. The 2nd Brigade's operational report for the period
1 Nov 68 – 31 Jan 69 pretty well summed up the enemy situation as I
inherited it and as it played out in the next few weeks: *VC/NVA forces did
not conduct any major ground attacks or attacks by fire during this reporting
period. Enemy initiated activity in the Brigade AO remained at a low level,
consisting of mining of roads, harassing fire with mortars, and terrorism by
assassinating six innocent civilians and pinning notes to the bodies of the victims
as US/GVN agents. Capture of key reconnaissance and high level staff personnel has compromised existing enemy plans.*

This "low level" of activity, as so often happened, turned out to be
one of those periods in which the enemy was planning and preparing
for a high point, in this case, the 1969 Winter-Spring Offensive with,
as always, its ultimate target Saigon if the planned early attacks north
of the city proved successful. On the day after my assumption of command, my task force was to play the central role in discovering what
these "existing enemy plans" were. It would be a case of astonishing
beginner's luck which would resonate all the way to the top, to General
Abrams himself.

Flying out to my units, at 1200 hours I got an urgent call to land
at brigade headquarters. At every level the VC had an equivalent to the
GVN political structure. An informer had told Chau he knew where the
VC district chief, Bay Phuong, was going to hold a meeting. The killing
or capture of Bay Phuong would be a blow to the VC infrastructure and
its operations in the district.

Chau had not just a professional reason for wanting to get Bay Phuong, such as the 17 October 1968 terrorist bombing of the crowded Di An marketplace which killed people for whom Chau felt a deep responsibility: three children, an old man, and four women, one of whom was pregnant. Thirty others were wounded, fifteen of them seriously. Chau also had a personal score to settle. On 20 October, three days after the marketplace carnage, it had been Bay Phoung's men who had tried to assassinate Chau.

Partially paralyzed and not yet fully recovered from the assassination attempt, Chau walked unsteadily with a cane. Nevertheless he went out into his district every day to help his people. He had a mission this day: Get Bay Phuong. Chau and I would conduct a combined operation, with my troops cordoning the hamlet and Chau's RFs/PFs searching it. By long-standing SOP, the American commander was always in charge, which, of course, was a major impediment to Vietnamization.

We captured not Bay Phuong, but a lieutenant, as our prisoner claimed. Ultimately he was revealed to be a lieutenant colonel, a prestigious rank indeed in an army which gave similar responsibilities to officers two or three grades lower than in our army.

Lieutenant Colonel Nguyen Sau Lap[1] was a senior planner for COSVN's military operations. He had been in Saigon for several days, planning the attack on Saigon for the 1969 Winter-Spring Offensive, and was on his way back to COSVN when we captured him. He ultimately revealed details of his plan, to include dropping the massive Newport Bridge. Lap's information was key to Abrams' ability to quite easily defeat the enemy's offensive.

Pacification in Di An/Lai Thieu Districts

Our primary mission in the Di An/Lai Thieu area was pacification. The Task Force QuarterCav pacification program under APC was already progressing well when I arrived, and I shifted it into high gear. A bright and shining spot of our effort was our S-5, civil affairs officer.

I had come from 11th Cav thinking I would never see the equal of its S-5, Captain Lee Fulmer. I was wrong. Captain Tom Witter, a Pennsylvania National Guard officer, matched Lee in zeal and competence. There was nothing Tom would not do or try in order to make life better for the Vietnamese.

In Di An District, Chau in fact was the prime mover of the pacification program, unlike in every other district I knew where the American advisor was de facto in charge. Chau and his small staff collected and analyzed the intelligence, did the planning, and executed the plans. His RF and PF, although small in number, were doing a fairly decent job of providing nighttime security in the hamlets. I gave Chau my enthusiastic support. My troops were ready to do whatever would help him.

I met with Chau a few times a week and we planned joint operations, with me supplying security while he did the spade work in the hamlets. Tom worked closely with Chau, supporting his civic action efforts. Taking great risks, Tom was out many nights with our movie program, very popular in the hamlets. I often accompanied Tom on these missions. He and his sergeant, one helper, and an interpreter were the team that knew which strings to pull, whether to get pigs for a farm, tools for digging a well, or a bus to take children to the Saigon Zoo. The kids had never seen anything like it, and on one occasion, some little boys had to be taken off the bus where they tried to stow away in order to get a second trip. That was the sadness of it all – despite my going after and receiving the highest civic action budget in the division, two thousand dollars a month, and doing the most with it in our area, there was never enough money, there was never enough time, and there was never enough of Tom Witter and his three assistants to go around.

Tom worked closely with Captain Steve McGeady, our equally tireless, courageous, and competent doctor. Steve and his medics traveled throughout our area to do what they could about both minor and serious ailments. Meanwhile, my Viet Cong Infrastructure (VCI) platoon under highly competent Lieutenant Walt Kurtz kept probing, trying to find the VC who controlled enemy activity within the villages.

Years later, in an email Tom Witter told me that of all the active duty assignments he had in the Pennsylvania National Guard, his combat tour with QuarterCav was the most rewarding. "I sought to bring my squadron commander's concepts to our program and I believe we had one of the best programs in the country." Indeed we did, as Division acknowledged not just verbally and in writing, but in the monetary and other support they gave us.

Colonel General Tran Van Tra, the COSVN deputy commander and later commander, said in his unfinished memoirs, "During [early 1969] . . . . many infrastructures were lost and many comrades were lost, especially in the areas adjacent to cities and the highly populated areas which were important strategically."[2] Our task force contributed to their loss.

Apparent Pacification Successes

Country-wide, the APC seemed generally successful. If the Hamlet Evaluation System were to be believed, the goals were met, raising 1,000 hamlets out of the VC or contested levels. Additionally, the People's Self Defense Force seemed to offer improved security. One of my pleasant duties in relatively quiet Di An District was to go to the hamlets where a few PSDF civilians would be lined up, rifles at their sides, and Major Chau and I would "inspect" them—proud, almost all rather old men, some handicapped—in front of a small crowd of mostly women and children, and I would shake the hand of each member and present him with a certificate which Chau provided, indicating completion of a basic course in how to defend his village.

The enemy, of course, shifted gears as the APC and its follow-on was ongoing. While main force units in jungle base camps and in sanctuaries across the border were rebuilding, the VC infrastructure actually was significantly increasing its number of liberation committees. Also, assassination squads remained busy in villages. I had seen what the Viet Cong had done to some villagers in Major Chau's district, one of the most thoroughly pacified in all of South Vietnam. The villagers' "crimes" were to be the parent of a son in ARVN, or the pregnant wife of an RF or PF. On two occasions, at daylight I saw mutilated bodies laid out on a road after a night's work.

All Vietnamese Corps areas, I, II, III, and IV, reported gains in pacification, and in reality, overall there were gains. II Corps was the largest of the four in area and perhaps the most successful. In a post-war book the foremost pacification research expert, Richard A. Hunt, who earlier had a tour in Vietnam as an officer with MACV, reported on activities of Major General Charles Stone who commanded 4th Infantry Division, the largest U.S. unit (Army) in the II Corps area. Stone employed a mobile defensive-offensive concept to fulfill his pacification mission. Hunt wrote, "Stone deliberately decided to defend the strategic points in his area of operations—the cities, the CIDG camps, the critical terrain, and the population—by blocking the [enemy's main force] avenues of approach. He chose this course rather than scouring the remote and sparsely populated jungles of the central highlands for an enemy that seldom massed his forces for a large-scale fight. Stone's comment 'I have everything the enemy wants and he has nothing I want' pithily summed up his philosophy. He refused to fight the Communists on their terms or chase them through outlying areas. To make any headway in II Corps, the enemy was almost compelled to attack the 4th Division's strong points. Close cooperation between American and ARVN units made it more difficult for the enemy to single out South Vietnamese installations for attack without exposing its forces to the risk of heavy losses from counterattacking American firepower. Joint operations and a concern with defending the population centers severely curtailed enemy access to the people."[3]

Despite obvious gains throughout South Vietnam as a result of the APC, though, some Americans at the top were dubious of long-term results, Hunt reported. "Even boosters of the accelerated campaign conceded that the government's performance needed further improvement to defeat the Communists."[4]

Pacification Problems at Squadron (Battalion) Level

I had no time to fly back to Binh Co to see Nhan, and I missed her. I heard that her mother had learned to sew on the treadle machine we had finally been able to get her. My next project was to replace the oxen, but they were very expensive, $400 each in 1969 dollars.

I was out early every day with my driver Sergeant Bob Towers and interpreter Sergeant Chu, either taking a VR (visual reconnaissance) by helicopter, driving the roads in my jeep, or riding my command ACAV while accompanying a unit on a mission. We were trying to make the people healthier, more secure, prosperous, and contented with their lives under the South Vietnamese government. But in doing so, in our sweep missions and convoy escort duties we were unavoidably causing damage to their crops, roads, and sometimes homes and people. We tried hard to get our armored vehicle crews to be much more careful where and how they drove, but when push came to shove and their safety was at stake, they naturally protected themselves and their buddies. This often meant a quick swerve or burst of speed that endangered or hurt civilians, or took out a row of vegetables or fruit trees or resulted in road accidents.

Support units in our AO also were causing problems with defoliation agents sprayed from trucks into copses outside hamlets. The spray would drift over onto crops, wilting them. Sometimes Tom Witter and I would enter highly defoliated areas – one as a result of an accidental massive spill from an Air Force aircraft – in order to make solatium payments to affected villagers. We did not know that the Agent Orange and other toxic sprays were endangering villagers and ourselves, a dreadful fact to become evident both to them and us years hence. Our very presence and what we deemed were necessary activities often were causing damage and providing the enemy with support and recruits among the population.

Preparing for Major Combat

As we were moving out of the 90-day APC period I began requesting a more appropriate mission from General Talbott. The enemy main forces were up north, and there is where I thought we should be employed, using our firepower and mobility against them in areas where we could maneuve.

My gut instinct was that the Di An honeymoon would not last, and we needed to toughen up. Virtually none of my men had seen major combat, having arrived after Mini-Tet of 1968. The line troops at least were getting out on day and night missions, but much of the headquarters company and the squadron staff rarely left the base camp and therefore had no real idea of what the men on the tracks were experiencing. Consequently I put the headquarters in the field, operating out of our armored command center tracks, and we essentially conducted training in real combat situations, minor though they were.

Division and Brigade ordered us to set out what they called nighttime mounted ambush patrols (MAPs). Using half of a cav platoon for a MAP equated to putting out five armored vehicles, about 135 tons of steel, sticking up to 13 feet above ground, to intercept walking men armed with RPGs who were being guided quietly through the dark by locals. On my first night MAP on top of my command ACAV I envisioned what my track must look like through the eyes of an enemy some twenty or thirty yards distant. It was not a pretty image, ripe for an RPG. I also relearned how noisy an armored vehicle is, even while sitting with the engine off and radios turned down to barely audible levels. Any steel on steel contact such as an unintended bump of an M16 against a hatch cover while trying to silently fight off mosquitoes sounded like a fire alarm going off on a still night. That our MAPs did not get blown away was not so much due to our skill in placing them, or in putting out listening posts around them, or in remaining almost motionless for hours during long nights, as it was to the enemy's discipline. During my time in command, although on occasion the enemy would stumble into a MAP and there would be an exchange of fire, we did not have a single incident in which the enemy deliberately attacked one. The enemy was always out there, but they were moving to accomplish some specific mission and would not be deterred, thankfully, by finding such sitting ducks as a half cav platoon on mounted ambush patrol, then blasting it with RPGs.

The II FFV Periodic Intelligence Report for 5 January 1969, the day I assumed command, had stated: *The enemy local force units* [in 1-4 Cav area of operations] *are the C63 Lai Thieu Company and the Di An Platoon, believed to have a strength of 30 personnel each.* After I had been in Di An area for awhile, could anyone not appreciate my frustration at having a cavalry task force of dozens of armored vehicles and hundreds of men facing only 60 local force VC and a few transients? We had enormous firepower, and it needed to be used where it could be effective—against main force units located where we could maneuver. I asked General Talbott to allow me to put my command section in or close to Lai Khe, the division headquarters, where I could work with his G-2 Intelligence and G-3 Plans and Operations, utilizing my task force under division control throughout the entire division area. My proposal was not approved.

The Gathering Storm: Enemy Winter-Spring Offensive, 1969

Our Di An area of operations began heating up. In late January 1969 the task force received urgent missions from Brigade which resulted in night seals and subsequent daytime searches of hamlets. We killed a few VC and captured others. Tet '69 was approaching, most of my armored cavalry troops were now under my command, and my area of operations was extended. I now had my squadron consolidated. This was due not at all to my oral and written pleas for more effective employment of the squadron but to the enemy's planned offensive. I was also given another infantry company and an infantry battalion's recon platoon. We had a potent armored cavalry task force, now closed in on what the enemy called the inner defensive ring around Saigon. We were ready.

Tet arrived on 16 February with dragons dancing in the streets, colorful banners and parties, but no attack yet. Even though the enemy knew his plans had been compromised by our prisoner of 6 January, MACV believed that COSVN basically would attempt to follow through with those plans. To make sure that Saigon was secure for Tet 69, Abrams had pulled 1st Cavalry Division down from the Central Highlands and deployed it to the north and northeast of 1st Infantry Division. This defensive act was somewhat surprising, given Abrams' well known offensive spirit, but understandable in view of how much he had invested in pacification. Unless Saigon itself was secure, he said, the whole effort would be a failure. My task force had been directly affected by this caution. For the first time I had my entire squadron together, reinforced to make a powerful task force, with a mission of preventing the enemy from taking Saigon from the north.

On 22 February 1969 I wrote Sandra: *Things have been very quiet in Di An for several weeks.*

Within hours, the enemy attacked.

This began a very busy period for us as we sealed and searched hamlets, sent ready reaction forces to adjacent units in contact, and had a few minor brushes with the enemy. But nothing significant developed in our area. Essentially, we were a lot of combat power, moving and communicating, but not shooting much. To our north, east, and west the enemy was fiercely shelling and attacking, but the Di An area was an exception. South of us Saigon received a few rocket rounds that did little damage, and not much else happened near us.

In a few days the activity to the north of us subsided. Division kept us in place, still poised for defense of Saigon. During the lull in attacks, in Di An/Lai Thieu area the effects of COSVN instructions to enemy guerrilla units to increase terrorism during the offensive were apparent. On 10 March I recorded in my journal, *One body lies in the sun. We drive past, remarking more on the children who are gathered across the road from it than on the corpse. My men had killed two terrorists, but one had a family who had carried him off. I was told that the wife and his children were wailing. A third was also dead, an innocent woman caught in the crossfire. Three dead, one of whom was innocent, and innocent children mourning. What do they care that their father was VC? They only care that he was their father.*

Dramatic Change in Mission

On 16 March 1969, the course of the war changed for the task force in a manner not seen since Tet 1968, over a year earlier. A buildup of NVA main force units was taking place about 25 miles north of Di An in the Michelin Rubber Plantation area, both in the rubber itself and in the jungle surrounding it. MACV and IIFFV had determined that Saigon was under no immediate pressure, and here was an opportunity to strike the enemy before they got any closer. I had been in several plantations, though not the Michelin, and I knew that armor could be deadly there because we could maneuver. Going down the lanes with tanks and ACAVs was easy. Going across them not so easy but possible by knocking down some trees on the move.

Lieutenant General "Dutch" Kerwin, Commander of II Field Force Vietnam, ordered a three-division operation with mission to search out and destroy 7th NVA Division forces and supporting units. Operation Atlas Wedge, as conceived and executed, would turn out to be the largest and most effective such operation of 1st Infantry Division's post-Tet '68 years. For once, search and destroy was the right tactic for the occasion. We didn't have to search much—we knew the enemy was there. We only had to destroy.

My mission would be *an armored RIF* [reconnaissance in force – another term for search and destroy] *west into Objective 7*, an ellipse drawn by Division on the map of the Michelin. On the way, we were to take intermediate objectives in the Long Nguyen Secret Zone, a vast jungle location for enemy base camps which, historically, the French and later the Americans knew not much about. It was where in 1967 1st Division had sent Lieutenant Colonel Terry Allen with part of his 2-28 Infantry Battalion, consisting that day of two companies and his battalion command group, on a search and destroy mission. The dense jungle had been infested with enemy who knew the terrain well, and the battalion was caught in a disastrous ambush, losing 59 dead, 77 wounded, and 3 missing presumed dead – later confirmed. My West Point classmate Major Don Holleder was among the dead. The battle should have resulted in an investigation into inept leadership and instead was hailed as a victory by the then commanding general, Major General John H. Hay, who insisted it was not an ambush, but a "meeting engagement." Westmoreland picked up on the term, and MACV pronouncements led a wire service to call the battle a "victory."

I had learned in 11th Cav that civil affairs missions were best accomplished on an area basis. We often allowed squadron S-5 sections to remain working in a familiar area when the squadron itself departed. This could not always be accomplished, but when it could it meant continuity of operations that was highly beneficial to the pacification effort. Consequently, I decided to leave Tom Witter's S-5 civil affairs section in Di An to help Major Chau since there were no hamlets where the squadron task force was headed, just jungle and rubber plantation.

For the upcoming mission my command headquarters would be my two ACAVs, with me riding on top of my ACAV, HQ 16. I had learned from division intelligence that we might find large numbers of enemy in the jungle on our way to the Michelin, our final objective, but no one knew for sure. On the night of 17 March when I was back in Di An, late in the evening, keyed up from two days of intense planning and preparation, I wrote in my journal, *Tomorrow we go into the dense jungle in search of the enemy. It will be difficult, crashing through with tanks. Supposedly the 7th NVA Division and the 34th Artillery Group are in there.* We had been doing pacification work in the Di An area for the two and a half months

I had been in command, and now we were to be employed in the role I had been advocating all along, combat against main force units in terrain favorable to our deployment. At least it should be favorable when we reached the rubber plantation.

My journal continued, *Today as we flew low over the area I could see some evidence of heavy traffic. It will be no picnic. I trust that I will bring out as many as I take in.*

This was not to be.

Our role in Operation Atlas Wedge had begun, part of a corps-size search and destroy effort in an area where we could maneuver. Although I did not know it, we would never again travel the relatively quiet roads of the Di An area, poking around backyards looking for tunnels. This was the real thing.

The Long Nguyen Secret Zone

From our line of departure paralleling Route 13, ahead of us looking west were miles of jungle, and beyond that, the huge rubber plantation. It was terrain rich in history, most of it violent. I radioed my TOC at Lai Khe, and the operations clerk dutifully transcribed what I said: *Beginning jungle busting move now.*

One of my great troopers, Terry Valentine, told what it was like as a crew member on a tank while jungle busting: "Dense jungle, thorny vines, termite mounds that even tanks could not knock down, trees and bamboo that had hives of ants in them (very vicious ants at that). Vines were so intertwined that I have been pulled right off my tank when I got tangled up in them."

From the time we left Route 13, we were in for one hell of a ride.

I was my own command and control center with no staff at my elbow except a radioman and an interpreter while I busted jungle with my troops during the day, and at night caught a few hours sleep inside my sweltering ACAV on the twelve-inch wide bench cushion placed on top of a row of .50 caliber ammo boxes that lined the insides of the hull. I could choose to sleep on my left side or my right, but not on my back because the cushion was too narrow. I never slept soundly. I was always subconsciously aware of the intermittent traffic from the radios around me, turned down to the lowest possible volume. Swatting mosquitoes was a waste of time. We slopped on the repellant which became part of the obnoxious mixture of our sweat and jungle grime, and just mucked it out at night, trusting to the yellow tablet that turned our skin a strange orange color and was supposed to keep us from getting malaria, which it sometimes did not.

Atlas Wedge was to become a test of our endurance. I learned some things about young men, and about myself, that I could have learned in no way other than to be down there with them in the Long Nguyen Secret Zone and other such exotic places. I am profoundly grateful for having had that privilege.

The Michelin Rubber Plantation

Having had only one contact with an enemy squad at night in the jungle and finding only deserted base camps (small wonder – they heard us coming), on the fifth day my task force entered the rubber. I had requested but got no helicopter (a LOH)[5] so I climbed onto my command track and moved out with my two ground units. For the first time we were in the rubber itself. The 11th Cav had had some sharp engagements with elements of 7th NVA Division a few days earlier, marked by the stench of rotted corpses.

As we moved north the plantation floor became overgrown, in some places shoulder-high, evidence of not being recently worked, but the overgrowth was no hindrance. We could move quickly down the lanes of the immense plantation, unlike through the jungle.

On 23 March the 11th Cav was ordered to withdraw and resume its former mission far to the southeast. My task force now was left with the entire Michelin responsibility. We were to attempt to regain contact with the 7th NVA Division, deny them use of the plantation for base camps, and destroy any units we encountered. To support this action I acquired command of Fire Support Base Doc which 11th Cav had hastily established at the edge of the plantation.

For two more days we continued to work the northern portion of the plantation and had only minor contacts. On the morning of the fourth day, 25 March, we had gotten into the edge of a newly constructed, unoccupied enemy base camp and discovered enough bunkers for 1500 men, a huge complex. In the afternoon, before we could complete destroying the bunkers, and after discovering another large, freshly-prepared base camp, we were ordered by Division to leave the rubber plantation by dark to allow it to fill up again with enemy. I got a new mission: after we cleared out and took position in and around FSB Doc, when I believed the time to be right I was to attack.

Knowing that the enemy customarily went back into areas which U.S. forces had just exited, I thought that they would not be long in filling the vacuum left in the plantation by our withdrawal. Before we moved out to Doc, though, an incident occurred which will never leave me. The squadron daily journal entry of 1527 hours recorded my report, *Engaged three VC moving south along stream*, and at 1600 hours, *3 VC KIA*. Additionally I reported two of my infantrymen wounded, one very seriously. I had spotted three enemy and jumped off the top of my ACAV and run toward them, trying to fire my AR-15 but it jammed. Green tracers from an AK ripped past me just above my shoulder, and I killed one, perhaps all three, of the enemy with grenades. Their clothing and documents revealed them not as VC but as NVA reconnaissance troops.

It was long after dark when we carefully made our way into FSB Doc. Earlier in the day I had had little time to feel the effects of killing the man before he killed me. But now, as I sat on top of my ACAV in the night, I felt like hell. Many times previously I had fired on the enemy, but from the air or at a distance on the ground I did not know the results. And I had often ordered fire to be brought on the enemy while directing my troops. But now I myself had killed a man, maybe three. I was miserable. I had learned first-hand what my troops had to endure.

A Mobile Defensive – Offensive Battle

FSB Doc was an open area covered with shoulder-high elephant grass and clumps of dirt left when the village of Thi Tinh had been razed years earlier in Diem's strategic hamlet program. Huge anthills and some copses of brush and trees dotted this wasteland. Only three quarters of a mile to the west, seeming even closer at night, lay the edge of the Michelin plantation, and from less than a half mile to the north and east, dense jungle reached ominously toward our small circular perimeter. More relatively open wasteland lay to the south. On the night of 27/28 March I knew in my head and could feel in my gut that we were in for an attack.

I think that on that night I must have been regretting once again the manner in which too many mounted forces had come to be employed in Vietnam. In fire support bases and fixed installations such as the division headquarters base at Lai Khe, ACAVs and tanks were not much more than pillboxes – not even as good, especially considering the crews which had to expose themselves to fire the machineguns on top of their vehicles. Like the French years before, American units in Vietnam had given up too much of their mobility in favor of fixed defenses, too much of their offensive power in favor of protecting their logistical assets. But this was not for me to sort out. Especially not that night. My defense of this fire support base would be as mobile as I could make it. One of my cav platoons would wheel the perimeter and cut up any attack as it came in.

Much later I wrote in my journal, *On the night of the 27th I could feel the danger in our situation. We occupied the fire support base closest to the 7th NVA Division, battle-tested troops. We were totally alone, reinforcement consisting only of air-lifted troops to be landed at night, a difficult undertaking. Before dark I reviewed contingency plans with the infantry, artillery, and cavalry commanders.*

As I walked the perimeter, checking positions, I again thought through my Michelin attack plan which I might launch on the 29th, depending on what intelligence I could get. Everything was ready. But this night would be the enemy's turn.

At 0210 hours, hell erupted. Fierce mortar, rocket, and RPG bombardment, and machinegun and small arms fire of a reinforced battalion blasted into our firebase. The first horrendous concussions had been sheer terror. My ears rang so loudly from the instantaneous din that in the flashes of explosions I saw mouths of men near me shouting, but at first I couldn't hear them or the screams of my wounded. My radioman next to me in the hatch was wounded, but not seriously. He shouted he was okay, kept flipping dials and monitoring. Then quickly the powerful ground assault struck. The cav platoon outside the perimeter had cranked up and were soon in among the enemy. Because of the circling platoon and the return fire from our artillery and tanks, ACAVs, and infantry bunkers inside the base and, somewhat later, from air cav rockets and Air Force miniguns, the NVA struck hard against but never penetrated our perimeter.

Their sporadic attacks during the remainder of the night were weak, easily defeated. Under the light of flares, the cav platoon roaming the area outside the base was still blasting everything that moved. At one moment I was seeing by the light of those flares; in the next it seemed that Sergeant Bob Towers was beside me saying, 'Dawn,' and as if Bob had just then created it, it was dawn, and I was seeing by its light. A radio somewhere suddenly came to life and blared a cheerful wakeup call, "Gooooooooooooooooooooooooooooooo ooooooooood *mor*-ning Vietnam!"

To the heroic strains of the Star Spangled Banner, Armed Forces Vietnam Network from its comfortable studio in the Brinks Hotel, Saigon, was cheerfully welcoming the new day.

Once again, in a kind of mini-repeat of Tet '68, when the enemy chose to attack, a mobile defensive-offensive tactic in trafficable terrain caused them big trouble. Unfortunately our daybreak counterattack was unsuccessful in making more than minor contacts with a rear guard. By dawn the enemy had withdrawn into the jungle, leaving blood trails and dead behind them but taking many wounded and dead with them.

Haponski at edge of FSB Doc at noon
after the battle. (Collection of author)

When the division damage assessment team flew in after daylight they found that three 107 mm rockets had hit just outside our perimeter and one 122m rocket inside it, 150 mortar rounds had impacted close to and inside the perimeter, and about 250 RPGs had been fired, some impacting within and others outside it. There could be no count of the thousands of rounds of automatic weapons fired into us. All of our armored vehicles had been scarred with rounds or shell fragments, and debris covered the tops of our vehicles.

The 7th NVA Division history says, "In spite of the enemy's superior numbers and fire-power advantage. . . . on 28 March 6th Battalion/165th Regiment, led by Battalion Commander Minh Ho and Political Officer

Tran Van Duc, daringly attacked a concentration of American vehicles at Thi Tinh, inflicting heavy damage on two troops of armored personnel carriers and killing many soldiers."[6]

The historian blew some wind, as usual. For one thing, our numbers were not superior. I had one troop, not two, and part of a tank platoon, an infantry company, and another infantry platoon, and the artillerymen. Given the evidence of enemy histories, their organizational strengths as indicated in their training documents, and our intelligence estimates derived primarily from POWs, their strength numerically was probably equal to or somewhat greater than ours.

Regarding firepower we certainly had the advantage, especially when I chose to use it in as mobile a fashion as possible. However, we were at a significant disadvantage in occupying an isolated position with a high concentration of men and vehicles within a circle only about 100 meters in diameter, making an ideal target.

Relative to the statement that they daringly attacked us, that is for sure. It took guts beyond imagination to take on an armored unit on the perimeter and an infantry company in bunkers plus artillery tubes available for direct fire if I had called for it. Add the firepower from the mortars within Doc and the artillery from our adjacent artillery fire support bases, and then add the firepower we got from the air, and the result was awesome.

Battalion Commander Minh Ho was a courageous man. He and his men did well indeed. Even after having taken a terrible beating in the initial assault they bravely tried to continue the attack, then covered their withdrawal with one company. I found from studying the enemy history that back in August 1968 at Loc Ninh, Minh Ho's battalion had inflicted severe casualties on an 11th Cav troop in an ambush, and I confirmed it with 11th Cav records. The battalion had been decorated as a heroic unit, a high honor. This NVA unit had well lived up to its reputation and proved to be a dangerous foe.

Where the enemy account went way wrong was in its statement of "heavy" damage inflicted. We had one ACAV destroyed and two tanks moderately damaged by mortar rounds. The many other vehicles hit suffered only light damage. The RPGs and mortars had peppered us with shrapnel but did not penetrate armor plate.

The enemy report of the battle said they killed *many soldiers*. We lost six men killed and two dozen wounded and evacuated by dust off. Other wounded, to include Doctor McGeady and my radioman, were treated by our medics on site and returned to duty.

The enemy historian claimed a victory on their "beloved soil of Thi Tinh." In a sense he was right. I was certainly willing to allow that any losses at all of my fine young men was a victory for them.

Attack into the Michelin

On the day after we had pulled out of the rubber to let it fill up again with enemy, General Kerwin, IIFFV commander, had said in a memo: *The 1st Inf Div and the 25th Inf Div should go back into the Michelin possibly this weekend, timing dependent upon enemy activity.*

The attack into the Michelin which I had been planning since we were ordered out of the rubber had been delayed by the enemy's assault on us in Doc, and it needed to be launched, soon. My task force's strike would be a major attack, the only one by 1st, 25th or 1st Cav Divisions. We would be the whole show.

Our attack into the bunkered enemy base camp would be with two cavalry troops, a tank company minus one platoon, and infantry platoons riding on the armored vehicles. Doctor McGeady later said in his journal, "The Colonel wanted to put the AVLB [Armored Vehicle-Launched Bridge] across at the base camp & Charlie would find us in his lap before he knew what had happened."

This was our primary attack plan. Our alternate plan, in case we could not get the AVLB across the stream bordering the enemy base camp[7] was to cross at a ford in the northern Michelin and attack south. I much preferred the primary plan because in our earlier foray into the rubber we had found that the enemy, relying on what they thought was the security of the streams, had built their bunkers with their gun ports facing north. If we could get in from the south behind them instead of facing them from the north, we would have an easier time.

We did not know the enemy strength, but based on our recent experience in the rubber, and remembering the unblown bunkers in the extensive base camp capable of holding multiple battalions, I expected a big fight. Division intelligence indicated that much of the 7th NVA Division could be in the rubber or surrounding jungle.

I did not know it at the time, but one of my tank commanders, Sergeant Mike O'Connor, had no intercom or commo in his tank and should have stayed at Doc to get it fixed, but he was determined that his platoon was not going to go without him.

On 30 April at 0545 hours, the 13th day of Atlas Wedge, all vehicles began moving out, to include O'Connor's, still with no commo. An hour and 42 minutes later my air scouts went in low and reported the base camp loaded with enemy. The air cav immediately engaged, followed by fighter bombers that had been circling. A daylong fierce battle had begun. Our attempt to get the bridge across into the enemy camp had been met with fire, and we lost three men killed and several wounded in the fight. Also, the engineers said that the span was too great by a couple of feet so we immediately switched to the alternate plan, racing north to the ford. After we crossed the ford, striking into fleeing enemy, we turned south on line and were met with determined resistance from the first bunker line.

The North Vietnamese commander at LZ X-Ray and Albany had told his subordinate commanders to "grab them by the belt, and thus avoid casualties from the artillery and air."[8] This was the common tactic our enemy tried at first, then many of them fled from our assault. We had an enormous opportunity here, and I cut off their retreat with heavy artillery fire, helicopter gunship runs, and air strikes which served also to pin them in their bunkers. While one cav troop supported with its frontal cannon and machinegun fire, I swung the other troop into the flank of the bunkers, and the troop assaulted them one after the other from their weak flank. Then the other troop moved through to finish the job. We fought all morning and into late afternoon as our fighter bombers with napalm and high explosive, gunships with rockets and machinegun fire, and artillery pounded the bunker complex, coordinated with our ground attack. My helicopter was fired on by a heavy antiaircraft machinegun, and a fighter bomber took it out with bombs. As darkness approached, C Troop of my task force finally emerged on the other side of the enormous base camp, now smoldering. My – Troop, though, did not get all the way through and had to remain overnight (RON) within the enemy position as darkness fell.

B Troop had been the hardest hit by RPGs, losing six men killed and several wounded within less than a minute. O'Connor, still without commo, had managed to command his 50-ton tank, firing his 90 mm cannon and .50 caliber machinegun himself, in the thick of the fight, taking out several bunkers and enemy. Among the – Troopers was Platoon Sergeant Chuck McGrath, acting platoon leader, his arm and chest bandaged from his tank getting hit by the initial RPGs, his driver and back deck man dead. His platoon was also the hardest hitting as he led his men in the fighting. Years later he had no recollection of any of his actions which earned him the Silver Star. His men hazily remember some of what happened. They recall taking courage from him. In shock themselves over their terrible losses of friends, responding to his orders, they went about their work, some on the ground, some on their vehicles, taking bunker after bunker. Gene Raynes, an ACAV crewman, said, "The first bunker that I throwed a grenade in had a NVA in it and the medics went in and brought him out on a stretcher but he died while being moved to evacuate and they dumped him."

Gene doesn't remember what he was doing just before dark in the RON position. Whatever it was, he came across McGrath, bandages stained with blood, sitting with his back propped against a rubber tree, his hands hanging loosely at his sides, palms up on the ground. Raynes lit a cigarette and stuck it between McGrath's unmoving lips. Raynes said, "I seen him just sitting there and I thought he might need a smoke.

At first the cigarette just stuck there, then he moved it with his lips and took a drag, and then he chewed me out, 'Damn it Raynes, I can light my own cigarettes.' I noticed though he smoked it."

At dusk I walked among my C Troopers and talked with them. It's always the eyes that tell you what men have been through. Many young men had become old this day. Early in the morning the enemy had "grabbed us by the belt" and tried to hang on in a classic example of their favorite technique, causing close-in, vicious fighting, but our tank cannon and .50 caliber machinegun fire blasted them and penetrated their bunkers which were then grenaded or run over and collapsed by our tanks with trapped enemy inside, crushing them to death. As the count of my dead rose, I had had a kicked in the gut feeling all day long.

The clearing on the stream bank as darkness fell was strangely peaceful, and the C Troopers could bathe. Most, though, were too exhausted, too heartsick at the losses of their buddies. From early in the morning until just before dark we had lost twelve wonderful young men KIA, and about three dozen dusted off. Another three dozen were patched up and continued the fight.

This was one of those battles which demonstrated that when the enemy left jungle base camps and exposed himself to attack in terrain where a mobile force could maneuver, he was in dire straits, as in Tet '68. We learned from captured prisoners and documents that he expected the Michelin plantation to be a safe haven. It was off limits to B-52s because the South Vietnamese economy was heavily dependent upon rubber, the next most important crop to rice. When we found him in the plantation, though, such rules of engagement no longer applied, and I used all the firepower I could bring to bear, from the air and on the ground.

During the night, base camp survivors and any other nearby units had made off into the surrounding jungle. Starting at first light we methodically swept the battle area, taking and air-evacuating six terribly wounded prisoners and finding many bodies, weapons and other munitions.

The physical destruction was immense. Huge swaths of the plantation had been bombed and burned out. Trees were in shreds. Gaping holes marked where 500 and 750 pound bombs had impacted, scattering body parts. Long, narrow swaths blackened from napalm canisters revealed bunkers into which flaming jelly had penetrated, incinerating everyone inside. The smell of burned and rotting flesh in 100 degree heat was nauseating. My young men and I were exposed to sights, sounds, and smells that will never leave us.

The French called latex "white gold." They might better have called it "white blood." The rubber trees that were still standing were dripping latex from the topmost shredded leaves and broken limbs down the trunks, leaving white trails of tears all the way to the ground where they congealed in dirty gray puddles. It seemed as if every living thing had been scarred, desecrated with the wounds of bullets, grenades, RPGs, rockets, canister, artillery, bombs, napalm. It was as if the whole wretched plantation was weeping at the terrible madness. For the rest of the war the plantation would be the scene of more fighting, but nothing to approach this scale. We had certainly stirred up a hornet's nest, striking into battalions of two regiments.[9] They had fought fiercely to protect the 165th's regimental headquarters at the very southern tip of the huge base camp. A captured document said that units in the Michelin had been ordered to fight to the death. They certainly did.

The Division after action report states: *Contact in the area of operation* [after the enemy attack on FSB Doc on the 28th] *was negligible again until 30 Mar when Task Force Haponski engaged in one of the most significant contacts of Atlas Wedge.* This is an understatement. Our battle turned out to be not only the single largest battle of Atlas Wedge with more enemy KIA than any other, but it was the biggest fight in all of Vietnam on that day and for many days to come. At best, a dubious honor. At worst, an everlasting shame at the folly of men. We all tried to do our best that day. I know that we fought like hell for ourselves and our buddies. They in the NVA 165th and 209th Regiments did the same.

Like most battles at this stage in the war, post-Tet '68, it went virtually unnoticed by all except those on both sides who fought it. From our start in Di An as a pacifying force with only a troop of cavalry and some infantry, we had become by far the most powerful tested and proven ground combat force in the division. During the remainder of my tenure we were not to relinquish this distinction. General Talbott had finally discovered a proper role for his armored cavalry task force: to move, shoot, and communicate in terrain where we could severely punish the enemy.

A bright side of the battle was that we captured tons of rice, many bicycles, and some household-type items. I always sent useful war booty back to my Binh Co family and other residents on my resupply helicopters after they had delivered their loads to us. Against regulations, no doubt, I had Tom Witter sell some of the rice to get enough money to buy two young cattle, one male and one female, and deliver them to the girls' mother in Binh Co as replacements for the two oxen lost when their father was killed. With a treadle sewing machine and a team of oxen my family would be able to get along, and hopefully do better than that.

In a subsequent, much smaller fight in the Michelin we killed 11 NVA in fierce, close-in fighting. Documents from the bodies confirmed that they were from one of the units in bunkers we had overrun on the 30th. I was amazed that after the pounding we had given this battalion, they were still in business, still a dangerous foe. One of the documents contained the unit's oath to fight to the death. Once again I felt renewed respect for our enemy.

Kill Ratio

Shortly after Atlas Wedge, Lieutenant General Julian J. Ewell succeeded Lieutenant General Kerwin as commander, IIFFV. I had known Ewell well when in 1956 I was one of the three cadet battalion commanders in his regiment of cadets at West Point, meeting frequently with him for command guidance. He was then a heavily combat-decorated colonel, which he had been since age 24 when he commanded a 101st Airborne regiment that jumped into Normandy on D-Day. As a cadet I was impressed with Ewell. In Vietnam, though, I heard that as a division commander he had the reputation of being a body count man, especially concerned with the kill ratio of units – that is, the number of enemy killed as compared to the number of men lost KIA.

General Abrams, with all of his emphasis on "one war," with pacification at the core of it, had picked Ewell for his new corps commander, a man he knew well, a man who found body count and kill ratio statistics so important he later wrote a book on it as one in the Army's official Vietnam Studies series.[10] Earlier, Ewell as commander of 9th Infantry Division in the Mekong Delta, was reported by Hunt to have said: "'I had two rules. One is that you would try to get a very close meshing of pacification. . . and of military operations.'" This was a strange choice of words, depicting the two as distinct entities. Hunt continued, "Ewell contended that maximum pressure on the enemy boosted pacification more than anything else. 'The only way to overcome VC control and terror is by brute force.'"[11]

I found that this new emphasis on kill ratio was to have a powerful effect on 1st Infantry Division's operations. In order to increase the ratio, ambushes directed by Division and Brigade became a higher priority, and my armored cavalry task force was not exempt. This ineffective use of our combat power as ambushers handicapped us in doing other things we could do well, especially, as I was to find out, in our later operations along Route 13.

Convoy Under Attack

From my journal, recorded soon after the event: *I saw the burning, snarled wreckage of the tanker trucks, ammo trucks, and helicopters, and then I took command of the ambush area.*

This day, 28 April 1969, was a strange one. My task force had grown considerably, and I had an enormous area of responsibility. But it most definitely did not include Route 13 north of Lai Khe. However, at midday I got a call from Brigadier General Albert H. Smith who was acting division commander while General Talbott was on R&R. Breathlessly he told me that the convoy going north on Thunder Road (Route 13) had been ambushed and he needed me up there immediately to take command. He said there were burning vehicles, two helicopters had been shot down, and the convoy was stopped and receiving fire in the ambush zone and nobody seemed to know what to do. Prior to his call I had no responsibility for the convoy or the area it was in, and I had no unit close to the spot. I was in the air 25 miles south of it, and had only a LOH with one operational FM channel. Before I had a chance to inquire why I was to command, Smith was nervously asking me how soon I could get there. After several more calls from him, at last I had the ambushed convoy in sight, and indeed it was a mess. Flipping channels back and forth I found out who was under me and was able to get a counterattack going. I got control of the artillery and air strikes, ordered actions to protect the convoy itself, and told a lieutenant below me to use an armored personnel carrier to push enough of the burning vehicles off the road to get the blocked portion of the convoy moving again. I got Smith to give me a nearby unengaged mechanized infantry company to move to a position where I wanted it to interdict the enemy who was by now withdrawing into the jungle, and I air assaulted a straight leg company into another position. Finally the blackened, smoldering ambush site was quiet.

The losses were awful: Four POL tankers, one 5-ton truck, one armored personnel carrier, one armored car, and two helicopters destroyed. Three 1st Infantry Division soldiers were dead, two in a helicopter and one from a mechanized platoon. Six division soldiers were wounded, and another five from the transportation and MP units. Eleven enemy bodies were left behind and we took one prisoner.

This convoy attack shook Division. The quarterly operational report stated that the 28 April ambush *was the first convoy ambush on Hwy 13 in the 1st Infantry Division TAOI since prior to the 1968 Tet offensive.* Nothing except rescue of prisoners had higher priority than securing road convoys. As the lifeline of all units, the main supply routes had to be kept open and free from interdiction. The result was that by that evening, Task Force Haponski had an expanded mission: I retained responsibility for fire support base and Rome plow security in multiple areas while convoy security was added to the list as the main mission. I would be responsible for Route 13 from Lai Khe north to An Loc and then Route 303 to Quan Loi. From a meager beginning in early January when I had one troop and one infantry company under my command in a largely pacified district, I found myself in "Indian Country" with up to ten company/troop size maneuver units, an air cav troop, nine fixed installations to include fire support bases and semi-permanent NDPs, several artillery batteries, and a few dozen odds and sods of combat and combat support units under my control. The area was huge and my mission usually included not just convoy security on Thunder Road from Lai Khe north to Quan Loi, a distance of 32 miles, but also two other main supply routes of 38 miles, a total of 70 miles of bad road. The only way to accomplish my road security mission, given the paucity of forces I had to support it, was to "blitzkrieg" the sides of the roads with half of a cav platoon, moving swiftly, hitting into any ambush position before it could cause convoy casualties.

Thunder Road Counter-Ambush, and Other Missions

After the failure of the 1969 Winter-Spring Offensive, COSVN realized that attacking Saigon again would be impossible and instead shifted to achieving as many battlefield "victories" over U.S. forces as possible in order to strengthen their hand in the Paris Peace Talks.

I was ordered to continue the wasteful mounted ambush patrols in the jungle. Consequently much of my armored cavalry would not be available for the critical mission of convoy security. On 2 May the enemy struck again. My journal summarizes: *Flying from the south, I saw the smoke billowing hundreds of feet into the sky. The convoy had again been ambushed and was a tangle of burning trucks and men.*

The immediate problem was that there was no ground counterattack going and the convoy was taking heavy fire. I ordered my tank company and cav platoon to race to the ambush site, turned the air support over to the air cav commander, and told the platoon leader of the mech infantry platoon that was interspersed in the convoy to get between the convoy and the ambushers, which he more or less did. But he was not attacking, and I lost communication with him. This situation required my immediate presence on the ground. *Journal, cont'd. As I landed and climbed on* [an armored personnel carrier—APC] *to attack, an ammunition truck blew up behind us, just after we had left the spot. Close call.*

At first it was nip and tuck with me commandeering one of the infantry APCs and directing part of the mech platoon to attack. My ready reaction force soon arrived and within an hour we had driven the enemy back into the jungle. The sight on the road, though, was appalling. Killed were two infantrymen and two truck drivers.

Some serious business had to be addressed with higher authority. In order to do the Thunder Road job properly, I needed area command of the entire road from Lai Khe north so I could task whatever units were in it for reinforcement when necessary. Additionally, I needed to have the convoy commander and internal convoy security unit integrated into my command so I could immediately and directly control all security forces. These and other of my needs were partially met by Division.

The enemy tried to ambush the convoy again the next day. We surprised them in their ambush positions, and they paid a terrible price: 35 dead and captured out of the 80-man ambush force, with many of the remainder no doubt wounded and carried off into the jungle.

In addition to road security on three routes, I was given responsibilities for securing land clearing operations by Rome plows in several locations, and for armored RIFs and air assaults of infantry companies elsewhere: search and destroy. We had contacts and hit mines almost every day, and sometimes several times a day. At night we regularly took mortar and rocket rounds in our locations, and sometimes also in the daylight hours. The enemy never let up. Main forces could be elsewhere preparing for further combat, but local units and individuals were always at it.

Division issued orders which took my cavalry, tank, and infantry units into the jungle. Hardly a day would pass that I did not air assault an infantry company into a jungle corridor habitually used by the enemy to infiltrate toward Saigon. On most occasions, the infantrymen found only old base camps, but sometimes they would have a brief contact. The jungle was so dense that sometimes we had to use a jungle penetrator for dustoffs, a bullet-shaped metal cage that would be lowered through the treetops by a medevac helicopter.

My Rome plow mission cost the lives of two men and several more wounded. Rome plowing the jungle with intention to impede the enemy was fruitless. The enemy was accomplishing his objective of inflicting casualties without in return suffering significant losses.

I had put my combat headquarters in one of the fire support bases on Thunder Road where I could control the counter-ambush mission. On 20 May I had written to my wife: *The rains have started during the day as well as night, so the monsoon season is getting into full swing.* The water level inside our bunkers rose and we were sloshing in mud. The 1st Division's Lessons Learned report for this quarter ludicrously stated: *Below-ground bunkers are impractical during the rainy season. . . . The intense rainfall causes underground bunkers to fill with water even after considerable engineer attention to drainage.*

But that's where we were existing. During this same quarter, according to the Division's Operational Report, *"considerable engineer attention"* was given *in the Commanding General's Villa area,* to providing the division commander a concrete sidewalk from his quarters to the Division TOC. Also, *Construction is currently in progress for a protective cover over the CG's trailer. A latrine-shower facility for the Visiting Officers Quarters-VIP area is also in progress and a service road has been constructed to that facility.* Trying to keep my soldiers and myself from getting trench foot, I thought of the division engineers, and especially of their Rome plows fruitlessly plowing jungle when they could have been used for drainage control. But division headquarters had priority on engineer resources as the water rose higher and higher in my firebases and our vehicles sank deeper and deeper into the mud while my troops and I wallowed in it, performing our exhausting missions during those long monsoon season days and even longer nights.

The Horrific Ben Chua Mission

On 21 May I was alerted that in addition to all other missions, I would send some of my task force into the jungle south of the Michelin as part of a division force reacting to a reported enemy buildup. Our portion of Operation Bushwhacker would be a tough, dangerous mission. The tough part would be the jungle busting to conduct bomb damage assessments (BDAs) from B-52 strikes, just as we had done back in March on our way toward the Michelin. The dangerous part was the location. The area we were to penetrate was known for units taking casualties from VC who knew the extensive trail network, having operated there for years, and who were now guiding NVA units.

Our Thunder Road mission was over three weeks old, and we had learned a lot about what to do and not to do. I knew that my executive officer could handle it well, so I elected to lead the other mission, using my headquarters ACAVs once again as task force command unit. The operation was well named: *bushwhack—to make one's way through woods by cutting at undergrowth.* If making our way through untouched jungle was difficult, as it always was, the terrible scarring of the landscape in the objective area by countless B-52 strikes, air strikes, and artillery barrages made the job many times more formidable. We had to push through trees that had been knocked over from the earlier blasts and shove aside brush from the limbs and tops of trees that had dropped to the ground. Our drivers had to be especially alert so that our armored vehicles didn't pitch off into bomb craters before the track commanders knew they were at the edge of the gaping holes. And, as always, we had to fight off the red ants that dropped down from the branches along with the poisonous defoliation dust that we ingested. We were headed for a recently bombed area just north of a village that was anathema to Americans and South Vietnamese, Ben Chua.

We finally emerged from jungle onto a mined road – more a miserable track than road—leading south along the Saigon River. We mineswept the road ahead of us and used our AVLBs to cross streams. Slow as this was, it was faster than busting jungle to get to our objective area. In 1949 the French lieutenant, Jean Delaunay, had lost most of his right hand to a booby trap on this road, and he had later rebuilt one of the bridges the Viets had blown on the spot where we now laid down an AVLB. By late afternoon we were getting close to Ben Chua, only two miles north of Ben Suc, the village that had been razed in Cedar Falls. Years earlier the Ben Chua villagers had fought the French and survived, and they remained bitter about the American/ARVN destruction of their nearby sister village, Ben Suc. We began to discover for ourselves why this place had such a bad reputation. Along a stream we found one mine and blew it in place. We were not so lucky with the next mine, and just at dark, a tank hit it, wounding three men.

For the next few days we continued to bust jungle, doing our BDAs, and we continued to hit mines. One day while my pilot and I were flying over the bomb-cratered jungle in a LOH, he announced a sudden drop in oil pressure and we had to land immediately, not a nice prospect in this God-forsaken place. Fortunately we spotted some of my vehicles through the canopy and dropped into a small clearing near them. The helicopter had to be air-lifted out. The next day, not far from the bulldozed land that had been Ben Suc, my LOH received machinegun fire that came close, close, but did not hit us. This place was a curse. We knew that any unit taking on Ben Chua was virtually certain to sustain casualties, and we did. We hit more mines and had more wounded. The following day my LOH again was shot at. The atmosphere was tense, as if a dark, foreboding cloud hung over the village. The few peasants working the fields close in to Ben Chua were extremely hostile and uncooperative as we questioned them.

Late in the afternoon, Division ordered us to seal the village for a search by ARVN the next day. As we put in the seal, a horrendous explosion lifted one of my 50-ton tanks several feet into the air and filled the sky with dirt and debris. The tank commander, his gunner, and his driver were lying on the bank of a stream about 150 feet away where they had been blown out of the tank. Miraculously not dead, but grievously wounded, they were later evacuated to Japan. SFC Merrill Barnes, the tank company mess sergeant who had been riding on the back deck with his marmite cans of hot food for his troops, was buried in mud with only his head showing, horribly wounded. One of the tankers in his company and a medic dug the unconscious Barnes out of the muck, and the medic directed artificial respiration until Barnes died. Our engineer search team had not detected the 500 pound bomb dug into the stream bed right where we had put an AVLB bridge across. The bridge above the bomb was blown to bits, the tank destroyed.

The effort to dig a dud bomb that huge out of the earth and transport it to this spot, bury it under the mud in the bottom of the stream, and wire it so it could be command detonated boggled our minds. How long had it lain there while the VC in charge of detonating it waited for his or her chance – days – weeks – months? This man or woman – no doubt one of the "farmers" we had observed around the village—had selected a likely spot in the stream, then chosen a well-camouflaged location some 100 meters or so away in which to lie in wait. Time was no problem for this Ben Chua VC. He or she had plenty of it, and would wait.

During the night we were probed, RPGd, and mortared. Shortly after daylight the ARVN were landed by cargo helicopters to begin their search. Children were always the most reliable indicator of the condition of a village. By this time in Vietnam I had planned and participated in probably two or three dozen village seals and searches. In almost all of them, as soon as it became daylight the children would cautiously approach the ring of vehicles on the edge of the village. They knew better than to come running and clamoring for handouts, so they would wait, digging their toes in the ground and kicking clods of earth or studying the sky until the inevitable happened: a bored G-I would gather up some things, commonly C-rations, hop down from his vehicle and go to them. He would soon be mobbed with kids trying to get at the goodies until a sergeant would yell at him to get back on his vehicle. Then the kids would wait some more, and sooner or later they would be rewarded with visits from other soldiers in the seal force. Not in Ben Chua. There were no kids waiting for handouts in Ben Chua. Instead, the few that we saw clung sullenly to their mothers or grandmothers, avoiding looking at us. Old men indifferently looked on. Ben Chua was devoid of young men, unquestionably VC. As Viet Minh the village had defeated the French; as Viet Cong it was continuing the fight which had caused us several casualties while we caused none in return, and it seemed to me as if Ben Chua would fight us forever.

Unknown to us and virtually everyone else in the world, as I was directing my unit while trying to save my men, Dr. Henry Kissinger was meeting with Le Duc Tho in Paris about a U.S. offer of total troop withdrawal from Vietnam.

Mother of All Ambushes

For some time, MACV, II Field Force, and Division intelligence staffs were all reporting an expected Summer Offensive: *The primary objective [is]. . . to gain a favorable position at the Paris Peace Talks.* Division-size attacks were expected in the An Loc and Quan Loi areas, places on our Thunder Road convoy route.

My blitzkrieg search tactics along the route were continuing to be all shot to hell by Bushwhacker requirements. Now I had not nearly enough mounted units even to blitz selected areas along Route 13.

The first mortar rounds in our division area impacted during the night of 5/6 June at an ARVN compound in Chon Thanh on Thunder Road between my FSBs Thunders II and III. Thereafter, virtually all 1st Division and ARVN fire support bases and base camps from Phu Loi north were hit during the darkness with mortars, RPGs, rockets, recoilless rifle fire or a combination, and two were struck with ground assaults.

Given the enemy attacks during the preceding hours of darkness, I wanted at least some kind of ready reaction force at hand to protect the ARVN convoy headed for Quan Loi. Instead, I was ordered to commit a cav troop to jungle search and destroy. My air cav did not spot anything amiss in the desolate four and a half mile stretch of road just south of An Loc. I flew over the convoy, swooping down low to fly ahead of it, zig-zagging back and forth across the road to the edge of the wood line, 150 meters to each side. I was down so low on the west side of Thunder Road that our rotors were blasting the elephant grass in waves as we passed over. I do not know which happened first – whether or I saw them or they fired the RPG at the convoy – the two actions were so close together.

I had been leaning out of my low-flying helicopter, watching intently below me. Our downdraft had suddenly blown the camouflaged cover off a pit that held three or four men, and instantly blew off another lid and another. About 20 feet off the ground, I was looking behind me at startled NVA faces that were looking up and then gone in an instant as we passed. The door gunner on my side began lacing down the side of the road as we rushed over it. On my order my Cobra gunships came in and began work. Division artillery had just finished firing a salute to celebrate 1st Infantry Division's successful D-Day landing at Normandy, 25 years earlier on this day, and now, with the artillery tubes still warm from the tribute, they were firing in support of us. As the situation developed in the next several minutes, I realized the immensity of the area of contact—over three miles long. The kill zone itself appeared to be nearly 2 miles long, on both sides of the road. I had never heard of an ambush of this size during American times.[12] We had an enormous opportunity here. So far, only one truck had been hit, we had put fire on the enemy before he could deliver any more against the convoy, and fighter bombers were only minutes out.

Earlier in the morning I had explained to Division that I had no available reaction force in case of ambush, and had gotten permission to break off just one platoon of cav from its jungle-busting mission and start it toward Thunder Road.

Now I needed that close-by cav platoon immediately. Under a platoon leader so new he had not yet been in a fight, the platoon broke out of the jungle and into the ambushing force. The enemy was hit hard as the platoon's armored vehicles fired their way through their ambush position while artillery and air strikes supported our ground attack.

We learned later that our enemy was the reinforced 101D Regiment with strength in the ambush position of about 800 men. Eventually I had on the ground my whole – Troop and an 11ᵗʰ Cav troop with their accompanying infantry, around 200 or so men, but with our mobility and firepower from many sources, and especially with room to maneuver – 150 yards of Rome-plowed strips on each side of the road to the edges of the jungle – we had an enormous advantage. As on 3 May, again we had surprised them, and we were pounding them hard.

With a raging battle below, things were also hot in the air. I had told my pilot to orbit at 1,000 or so feet, and as we made a pass to the east side of the highway, suddenly he violently swerved our chopper and then told me that radar had locked on us.[13] After we evaded for a couple more passes, our aero scouts spotted the antiaircraft position in a jungle clearing and their gunships eliminated it. Even more unusual was the next event. Several times I had had AK and machinegun fire directed at my helicopter, as it was during this day, but never RPGs. On one of our orbits I watched in amazement as not just one or two but about two dozen RPG rounds came shooting up at us simultaneously, as if several RPG teams had been coached to attack aircraft en masse. I leaned out and watched the rounds approach from below, shoot on past us, then arc back earthward and explode. It happened again on the next pass, although with fewer rounds this time. Later I learned that although individual RPGs occasionally had hit and brought down helicopters at quite low altitudes, nobody had ever heard of such a salvo. Perhaps the enemy had been experimenting with radar-controlled antiaircraft fire and RPG salvoes. If so, thank God he had negative results to report for this day.

The enemy initially had to fight in position, then tried to flee into the nearby jungle. I was putting artillery in to the west to deter their escape, and any time they appeared in an opening, either I, the air cav, or the forward air controller (FAC) in his OV-10 observation plane would spot them and call in gunships, air strikes, and artillery. One of the enduring images I have of Vietnam is looking down from my helicopter just before dark on 6 June and seeing enemy below me crossing jungle clearings, still trying to escape to the west as we pounded them from the air and with artillery.

The enemy evacuated their dead and wounded as well as they could, but they left behind 57 bodies, and we took two prisoners. The additional dead and wounded carried off must have been frightful. We captured a lot of weapons and ammunition to include mortars and recoilless rifles. The 101 D Regiment had not been able to employ many of them because it had been so quickly overrun. One of our prisoners told of utter confusion as his unit was suddenly struck with armored vehicles.

By dark on 6 June two of my ACAVs had hit mines in the ambush site and were combat losses, and one ACAV was damaged by an RPG. In the ARVN convoy, one truck had been destroyed. Five of my men and two ARVN were wounded, thankfully not seriously. Once again, armored cavalry had inflicted heavy losses on an enemy against which it could maneuver.

Despite these losses, as after the Michelin battles, the enemy was resilient. The 101D Regiment licked its wounds and within two weeks struck a unit farther north, out of my area. The enemy we fought in and around the Michelin and on Thunder Road survived severe losses and lived to fight another day. They were extraordinary soldiers, in for the long haul.

The 7th NVA Division history says: *The soldiers of 7th Division can never forget the challenging and brutal year of 1969.*[14] Our task force shared a measure of credit for making their lives miserable.

*   *   *

I had taken care of my Binh Co family as well as I could back when we had the pacification mission in Di An area, going to Binh Co a few times and having the girls to my base camp. But when we went north to fight main force units, I was unable to visit them. Because of the intense fighting, on only one occasion was I able to return to Di An by invitation of Major Chau to celebrate the opening of a district school and a building for sewing classes. I got an hour to myself to fly over to Binh Co and was terribly disappointed to find that Nhan had left a day earlier to visit her older sister in another village. Her mother said that ever since I had left, after her long day of chores was finished Nhan would go to what had been our landing pad at the edge of the hamlet and look into the sky to see if I would be coming.

CHAPTER 13

American Withdrawal and Vietnamization, 1969 - 1972

*   *   *

1969: Setbacks for Our Enemy

Nineteen sixty-nine, as General Tra had acknowledged, had been a tough year for our enemy in South Vietnam. Their battlefield losses of main forces, local forces, and VC infrastructure in the hamlets and villages had seriously depleted their full spectrum of strength.

Things generally were going well for President Thieu and GVN. The official Communist history *Victory in Vietnam* states: "By the end of 1969 the enemy had retaken almost all of our liberated areas in the rural lowlands of Cochin China. We were only able to hold onto our bases in the U Minh Forest, the Plain of Reeds, and a number of isolated liberated base spots."[1] The decent performance of GVN's armed forces during Tet '68 had given them spirit, and the general mobilization after Tet had seemed to go reasonably well. Also, the enemy's revered Ho Chi Minh died on 2 September 1969. Gone was the hallowed figure who had so inspired generations of Vietnamese, North and South, to fight for independence and unification.

But the North responded to these setbacks as it always had – with greater resolution. The history relates: "To increase forces available to attack the enemy, the Central Military Party Committee and the High Command sent many units with full TO&E strength to South Vietnam. At the same time, the main force units on the battlefield were reorganized to conform to our supply situation and to the new situation and responsibilities of each local area, especially in the key theater: eastern Cochin China [IIFFV area]."[2]

That the enemy was able to reorganize, recruit replacements, resupply, retrain and be ready to fight again was a testament to how they had been able both to modernize their armed forces at all levels yet retain their historic readiness to do battle. Even given how tough 1969 had been for them, they still were able to use main forces to attack us, as evidenced by the wide-spread February attacks and the later battles my task force and other units fought.

The enemy admitted, though, in its official history that by the end of 1969 the population of their liberated areas had shrunk, that GVN had retaken control over several important contested areas and had established a significant number of new outposts. In some areas, the history acknowledged, hamlet guerrilla forces suffered severe casualties, and recruitment in the hamlets dropped. Supply of units was increasingly difficult, some soldiers deserted, and some defected to GVN. The history went on to say:

"Reviewing this situation, the 18th Plenum of the Party Central Committee [in January 1970] stated clearly that. . . in 1969 the enemy made some progress because our efforts to counter his actions were not timely, the operations of our main force units and our guerrilla warfare actions were not very effective, and we did not devote a sufficient level of attention to the need to attack the enemy's pacification program."

The history continued with the difficulties of troops stationed along the Ho Chi Minh Trail: "For three solid months, from June through September 1969 . . . 6th Engineer Battalion . . . ate sycamore berries, roots, and weeds in place of rice, and they were forced to burn straw and eat the ashes in place of salt."[3]

The enemy's main forces and infrastructure alike had been sorely stressed by Tet '68, mini-Tet '68, Fall Offensive '68, Winter-Spring Offensive '69, and the Summer Offensive of 1969. Conditions from late 1969 into early 1972 led some American participants and subsequent historians to believe that victory for the South could have been achieved. Pacification and Vietnamization had made some gains. Tests to determine how sustainable were the gains lay just ahead.

The 1970 Operation in Cambodia

Westmoreland and Abrams had long wanted to interdict the Ho Chi Minh Trail and its Laotian and Cambodian bases with sizable ground forces. The Trail—actually a huge network of trails—went from North Vietnam through Laos and Cambodia, then fed into South Vietnam at multiple points. Also, although only a relatively minor amount of supplies made their way into RVN clandestinely by sea on the eastern coast, much more arrived in the Cambodian port of Sihanoukville, then were trucked eastward. Huge supply and munitions depots lay a tantalizingly short distance across South Vietnam's western border in Cambodia and Laos. Some small cross-border operations had indeed been conducted secretly, such as a brief raid into Laos in late February 1969 by a unit of U.S. Marines in the A Shau Valley. Additionally, MACVSOG sent patrols across the borders both to interdict and report on activities, but with limited success. Continuous air strikes also failed to stop the flow of goods and troops into the South.

In March 1969, with an eye on speeding up the Paris Peace Talks, President Nixon had authorized secret bombing of Cambodian bases near the Vietnam border. During our Operation Atlas Wedge some of the B-52 strikes actually in Cambodia were reported as strikes in support of us in the Michelin area. But it was not until May 1970 that a cross-border operation big time was ordered by Washington. According to Westmoreland (then Chief of Staff of the Army), during a meeting of the Joint Chiefs, the Secretary of Defense, and the Commander in Chief on 1 May, Nixon "was ebullient. He was, he said again and again, going to 'clean out the sanctuaries. You had to electrify people with bold decisions,' he said. 'Bold decisions make history,' he exclaimed, 'like Teddy Roosevelt charging up San Juan Hill.'"[4]

Striking into Cambodia was a "bold decision" indeed, and when it became known, it certainly did electrify people. Congress and the people of the United States were shocked. Universities were rocked with demonstrations, and at Kent State four students were killed by rifle fire of National Guard soldiers. *Why!* many demanded, would Nixon spread a losing war into another country?

The goals of the "incursion" as it was called, were elimination of huge base areas, destruction of COSVN, disruption of the supply operation from the port of Sihanoukville in Cambodia, punishment of enemy main forces, and, importantly, a test of Vietnamization. Could RVNAF plan and conduct a large operation against enemy main forces? Just as pacification was at core an American idea, not Vietnamese, the move into Cambodia was an American test of Nixon's relentless emphasis on Vietnamization as a means of exiting Vietnam "with honor."

President Thieu tasked his two best field commanders with the major RVNAF thrusts. Lieutenant General Nguyen Viet Thanh, commander of IV Corps, was to head the southernmost strike, while Lieutenant General Do Cao Tri, commander of III Corps, would lead the northern thrust into "the Parrot's Beak" area of Cambodia. IIFFV would send a powerful force of American ground units and air cavalry west from vicinity An Loc/Loc Ninh.

While I was in 11th ACR I had met the nattily-dressed paratrooper Tri who seemed to me to exude a confidence matching his reputation among American advisors as an aggressive, highly capable commander. And Thanh, unlike many South Vietnamese leaders, was capable and well-liked by his men. He was a casualty on the first day about 10 miles across the border when his helicopter collided with a U.S. Cobra gunship in midair, and all on both helicopters plunged to their deaths. While Tri, dubbed "the Patton of the Parrot's Beak" in the U.S. press, was doing an excellent job commanding in Cambodia, back in Saigon some of his adversaries were accusing him of corruption.

RVNAF's performance was spotty – very good to very bad—but, overall they did reasonably well in encountering and combating NVA formations and completing their missions. However, the Vietnamese units still had U.S. advisors who connected them with heavy American air, airlift, and artillery support, so this was not a true test of Vietnamization which could prove their abilities to fight without that support.[5]

How was the Cambodia incursion viewed by South Vietnamese military leaders? Not long after the war ended, the U.S. Center of Military History sponsored a series of monographs, one of which was by Brigadier General Tran Dinh Tho, J-3 of the Joint General Staff. In the section on "The Cambodian Incursion" he first treated some of the real successes of the RVNAF while acknowledging the important role of U.S. advisors and the crucial U.S. support they provided.[6] Then he concluded, "Despite [the incursion's] spectacular results, and the great contribution it made to the allied effort, it must be recognized that the Cambodian incursion proved, in the long run, to pose little more than a temporary disruption of North Vietnam's march toward domination of all of Laos, Cambodia, and South Vietnam. . . . There was no [US/RVNAF] plan to return to the border areas to conduct operations of value to Cambodia, or to keep the enemy base areas cleared out. In the absence of any such long-range repeat operations, it is not difficult to explain the temporary nature of the advantage accruing to the US/RVNAF war effort from the Cambodian incursion. To incapacitate North Vietnam, and end the war on our terms, it would have been necessary to bring that country completely to its knees. But that was a different and much larger problem."[7]

In his memoir, *No More Vietnams*, Nixon asserted that Cambodia 1970 was "the most successful military operation of the entire Vietnam War."[8] A senior U.S. commander had another opinion. Lieutenant General Bruce Palmer had been IIFFV commander, then Westmoreland's deputy in Vietnam. Later as a four-star, he was the acting Army Chief of Staff during the several months between the Westmoreland and Abrams tenures in that office. He said, "Looking back, the Cambodian incursion of May 1970 was the second major turning point in the war, in my view. Tet 1968 ended any hope of a U.S.-imposed solution to the war, while

Cambodia 1970 fatally wounded South Vietnam's chances to survive and remain free. Consider how the gains from Cambodia boomeranged:

(1) The loss [of Cambodia's Sihanoukville port] forced Hanoi to rely entirely on cross-country routes from the North for maintenance of its forces in the South. In effect the Ho Chi Minh Trail became the jugular vein for the NVA effort in all South Vietnam. As a consequence Hanoi expanded its initially primitive routes into a wide network of all-weather roads and way stations that could handle even tanks and other heavy equipment. In the end, this logistical capability enabled Hanoi to overrun the South with massive conventional assaults. . . .

[Palmer might have added here that the enemy also constructed a modern pipeline with branch lines for transporting fuel to the southern battlefield.]

(2) Although NVA capabilities against the heavily populated areas of [all of the IIFFV zone, the Saigon area, and south to the southernmost tip of Vietnam] were greatly reduced, the nature of ARVN was such that Saigon could not take advantage of this development by shifting some ARVN troops northward. ARVN was a territorial based and supported army. The families of ARVN soldiers lived near their home stations and were partially sustained by local ARVN resources—housing, for example. Historically ARVN regiments and divisions [except the elite Airborne and Marine divisions based in the Saigon area] had not performed well when deployed any great distance from their families. In the Vietnamese culture, particularly in the South, family ties were stronger than loyalty to ARVN or the government, and if the families needed help when so separated, the soldiers simply deserted."[9]

One of the effects of increased pacification and Vietnamization efforts in 1969 was to prompt the NLF into creating the Provisional

Revolutionary Government (PRG) in June of that year under President Huynh Tan Phat. Now there was a second national government in the Republic of Vietnam's geographical territory. The new PRG offered a formal but structurally loose southern headquarters over the many lower level "shadow" governments, from hamlet level up. Truong Nhu Tang, the boy who had been so much influenced by Ho Chi Minh when he met Ho in France so many years ago, became its minister of justice. He said, "The [Thieu] administration's effort to portray the Saigon regime as an autonomous, legitimate government would now be answered by another Southern government fighting hard in every international forum to establish its own claim to legitimacy."[10]

Tang said the PRG set up its headquarters south of the NLF (military) headquarters in the jungle near Tay Ninh, with COSVN located at that time not far to its north. All three headquarters were only a few miles away from U.S. and ARVN units, and they continued to avoid intensive MACV efforts to locate and destroy them. He said, "This jungle dweller's life was to be mine for the next six years. . . . We lived like hunted animals. . . . wariness and tension were the companions of every waking moment [as – -52 raids got closer and closer]. Elephants, tigers, wild dogs, monkeys—none of these were strangers to our cookpots. . . . All of this was a far cry from the carefully prepared dining my mandarin upbringing had taught me to enjoy."[11] NLF fighters trained nearby, and their class time featured "current news, political and military issues, and the history of the revolution—all intended to strengthen their determination. . . . Marxist subjects were never touched on. Instead, instructors would devote their attention to elaborating Uncle Ho's great nationalistic slogans: 'Nothing is More Precious than Independence and Liberty'; 'Unity, Unity, Great Unity!' . . . around which would be woven the themes of patriotism and the sacred duty of expelling the Americans."

"After the war," Tang reflected in a footnote, "one American writer declared that the average guerrilla couldn't have told dialectical materialism from a rice bowl. By and large, this was true. As far as most Viet Cong were concerned, they were fighting to achieve a better life for themselves and their families, and to rid the country of foreign domination—simple motives that were uncolored by ideological considerations."[12]

He also spoke of espionage: "By this time the shattered Saigon networks [as a result of Tet '68] had been rebuilt, and we had been successful in inserting people into the Thieu administration at all levels and into the Southern army as well."[13]

Tang told how, in the winter of 1969-70, they solved the problem of transportation other than by foot. "Quite often the peasants would get their bikes [and motor scooters] from the local Saigon army forces—in our case the ARVN's 5th and 18th Divisions. . . . Eventually our Finance Department was able to set up regular supply channels directly between these divisions and the Front, forgoing the peasant middlemen. From that point on we had a regular supply, not just of Hondas, but of typewriters, radios, cigarettes, and a variety of other goods. Before long, there was a thriving business between senior officers of these ARVN divisions and the Front in weapons and ammunition as well." Tang implied that they could have gotten American M16 rifles, but the troops preferred their AK-47s from China. "Among the most popular items," he said, "were grenades and Claymore antipersonnel mines. More than a few American soldiers were killed with these mines bought from their ARVN comrades."[14]

I had had a 5th Division battalion opcon to me in jungle not far from the PRG's headquarters. The first three men I lost in our attack into the Michelin were killed by an American claymore fired by enemy protecting their regimental command post. Is it possible that someone in this ARVN battalion sold that claymore to its enemy, and mine?

1970: Colby Sees Pacification as a Success

Colby, the head of CORDS, said that by late 1969 basic security for most of the population had been achieved. Now, in 1970, it was time for a new, improved plan. He said, "The word went out to the American advisers at the national and local levels that the plan should be written and worked out by the Vietnamese, the Americans to be as helpful as they could but not to dominate the planning process—as they certainly had in the APC and the 1969 phase."[15]

Colby outlined many improvements that had occurred, and then, to highlight his point that pacification was successful, he said, "By year's end I was staying overnight in areas that had been 'Indian Country' the year before, driving on local roads or going up canals where prudence had dictated no penetration earlier. I especially enjoyed an uneventful trip with two jeeps through a central Vietnam province. My last trip over that road had generated an armored cavalry escort organized by the local American unit to be certain that nothing happened to the Ambassador [Bunker] and General Abrams's deputy [Colby]."[16]

Reflecting on events of 1970, General Davidson said that the pacification improvements were impressive, "But with all these gains in pacification, the loyalty of the bulk of the South Vietnamese peasants remained neutral between the GVN and the Viet Cong. The hold of the Viet Cong had been broken, but loyalty to the GVN had not replaced it. The villagers liked their new authority, but with typical peasant skepticism realized its limitations, and they were right. The same corrupt and incompetent civilian officials remained at district level and above. The military officers remained politicized, and the soldiers undisciplined and piratical. While things changed at the village level, at upper levels they did not, and short of a respite of many years, could not."[17] While this statement seems to skirt the fact that the leaders of the Viet Cong, and many of the fighters of the VC, were not peasants but middle and upper class people from various backgrounds, and the fact that many GVN soldiers were courageous and competent and loyal, there remains much to think about in his assessment.

Colby entitled Part Six of his book, VICTORY WON. President Thieu was enthusiastic about the forthcoming 1971 Plan. Colby said, "The fact that the stated goals were reasonable and real produced confidence that at last, a winning strategy to end the war's agony had been found." He stressed that the 1971 Plan was Thieu's, but in discussing it he reveals how much American influence was still at work when he says such things as "I initially worked out these improvements. . . . I had observed a practice that we now inaugurated in the Vietnamese villages. . . . We moved in another new direction. . . . The Plan we worked out. . . ."[18]

I, and *We*—Americans—not Thieu?

Colby tells of a lengthy motorbike ride which he and John Vann[19] planned, going alone, in the Mekong Delta. Then, surprisingly, he undercuts its significance when he adds, "Although we were both sure we would make it, John arranged for a couple of helicopters to be on alert to respond to our radios if trouble did arise."

Colby stated, "We had deliberately given the Delta the priority for pacification," and he was pleased to find some roads that he could drive over in a jeep with no escort. He admitted, though, "On some of my overnight visits to the region, the morning jeep transit to the local airstrip to meet the aircraft to take me back to headquarters in Saigon still produced what we called the 'pucker factor,' a tightening of the nether sides in anticipation of what might erupt from a mine placed in the road by a Communist sapper squad during the night, despite the sandbags carefully placed in the jeep floor against just that possibility."[20]

Helicopters on alert to rescue them? Pucker factor? VC sapper squad? No such squad was necessary. Not much training was needed to plant a mine, as witnessed by the many local women, old men, and young people who did it well and often. Was this Security with Fingers Crossed? And what about Vietnamization?

1971: A Semi-Test for Vietnamization, Lam Son 719

Operation Lam Son 719 was the South Vietnamese portion of a combined US/RVNAF operation between early February and late March 1971 to move into a huge base area in Laos and disrupt the North Vietnamese interdiction and supply system, causing as many enemy casualties as possible. A revised Cooper-Church Amendment of 5 January 1971 prohibited U.S. ground forces and advisors from crossing the border. Abrams determined that the U.S. role would be to secure a staging area up against the border for RVNAF. Additionally it was to provide air support over Laos, and artillery support up to the range of the weapons emplaced near the border. U.S. helilift, air cavalry, tactical air, and B-52 support were crucial elements of the overall plan.

Under a mediocre I Corps commander, Lieutenant General Hoang Xuan Lam, RVNAF seemed cursed from the beginning. Terrible weather severely curtailed air support and turned roads and trails into a quagmire, and helicopters ran into heavy antiaircraft fire. After early successes, Lam found that the NVA was much stronger in the objective area than anticipated. Instead of melting away, they put up a fierce defense which was soon reinforced. After two weeks it was obvious that General Lam could not handle the situation, and President Thieu ordered General Tri north to take command. On the way, Tri was killed in an aircraft accident and the situation for the South Vietnamese continued to deteriorate. Although some units performed well, at least initially, even some of the elite airborne and Marine units ultimately panicked and broke, not having U.S. advisers with them to control air support. According to General Palmer, Abrams was furious at Thieu for not reinforcing, "and never quite forgave him. [Thieu] believed that the heaviest offensives from the north were yet to come, early in 1972, and that he could not afford the severe casualties that were implicit in a prolonged campaign in Laos."[21]

President Thieu declared the operation a resounding success. One of his generals had another view. Major General Nguyen Duy Hinh had served in several high level staff and command assignments, including division command. He said, "The picture of ARVN soldiers hanging on the skids of a helicopter which evacuated them from lower Laos, and other equally dramatic photographs showing battered I Corps troops returning back across the Laotian border, caused grave concern among

South Vietnamese, military and civilian alike. . . . Popular sentiment seemed to be aroused by the dramatic accounts and personal feelings of the I Corps troops who returned from Laos. Almost without exception they did not believe they were victorious."[22]

General Hinh thought that in many respects RVNAF had done well, but pertinent to the question of Vietnamization, he said, "Credit should be duly given to the role performed by U.S. Army aviation, U.S. Air Force, and U.S. Naval air, for without them Lam Son 719 could hardly have been possible."[23] And that was the problem with Vietnamization: American planning and support, in essence, dominated the process. Colonel Vu Van Uoc, Commander, Air Operations Command VNAF, said after the war, "ARVN completely lost the notion of being an independent army."[24]

In a television address to the American people on 7 April, after the RVNAF withdrawal, President Nixon proudly proclaimed, "Tonight I can report that Vietnamization has succeeded."

If Lam Son 719 were to be graded as an exercise in Vietnamization, by most standards other than Nixon's, it was a failure.

1972: "Nguyen Hue Campaign," or the Easter Offensive[25]

Thieu's rationale for breaking off battle during Lam Son 719 and withdrawing his battered troops from Laos had been to preserve as many of them as he could for what he foresaw as a much greater trial ahead, a heavy enemy offensive in 1972. He was correct in predicting that offensive. The North's official history stated, "In May 1971, the Politburo decided to 'develop our strategic offensive posture in South Vietnam to defeat the American 'Vietnamization' policy, gain a decisive victory in 1972, and force the U.S. imperialists to negotiate an end to the war from a position of defeat."[26]

Beginning on 31 March, the equivalent of about thirteen enemy divisions plus several independent regiments and supporting units struck successively on three major fronts in a coordinated, conventional assault, assisted as always by regional and local forces, first in I Corps, then III Corps, then II Corps.[27] Their armor and heavy, long-range artillery were used to back up the infantry in vicious assaults that over-ran initial objectives. In I Corps, the enemy battled for a month, captured Quang Tri and then advanced on Hue. In II Corps they tried to split South Vietnam in half by taking Kontum in the west, then advancing east toward the sea. The III Corps critical target was An Loc, which, if taken, would open the gateway[28] for a 60-mile surge down a much upgraded, now-paved Route 13 to the heart of South Vietnam, Saigon.

The South Vietnamese were now fighting without the aid of American ground combat units but still had some U.S. advisors who controlled crucial air support. Earlier, North Vietnamese forces under General Tran Van Tra had been successful in taking and holding the jungle area to the northwest of Loc Ninh, so when the NVA launched its offensive, called the Easter Offensive by the Americans, the village of Loc Ninh northwest of An Loc became an important target. Loc Ninh, like the province capital An Loc, were large villages in Binh Long Province. The province chief, Colonel Tran Van Nhut, was both an excellent administrator and combat leader.

Two years earlier, 1st Infantry Division had been withdrawn to the States. This left our old Task Force 1-4 Cav area of operations along Route 13 north of Lai Khe to the South Vietnamese, primarily ARVN's 5th Division whose units had sometimes worked with my task force in 1969.

In early 1972, major units of 5th Division and reinforcements from 18th Division were located at and around Loc Ninh and An Loc as a bul-wark against three nearby NVA divisions plus supporting units, num-bering ultimately some 35,000.

After deception attacks around Tay Ninh in the first few days of April, the NVA stuck hard at Loc Ninh. Most ARVN troops initially defended well, then some units broke and panicked. On 8 April Loc

Ninh fell, as scattered 5th ARVN troops tried to retreat to An Loc. The 209th Regiment of the 7th NVA Division, which we had first fought in our 30 March 1969 Michelin battle and again in May 1969 in its ambush positions on Route 13, distinguished itself by ambushing the retreating ARVN forces, inflicting severe casualties. The 7th Division then pushed south, occupied Route 13 all the way from what had been our 6 June 1969 counter-ambush area, south to our old Thunder III FSB, then farther south to six miles north of Lai Khe, headquarters of 5th ARVN Division. The NVA 7th Division's mission was to prevent ground reinforcement from reaching An Loc, the only access road being Route 13. Now the NVA with its Soviet-made T-54 tanks "owned" this area where, only three years earlier I had been "King of the Road."

Local VC and the people assisted the NVA in many ways, one of which was to secure food supplies, especially canned and dried food, from hamlets around An Loc.[29] Ultimately major units of three enemy divisions—5th, 7th, and 9th—would attack An Loc and ARVN units which were dug in around it.

In a helicopter above the battles raging below was Major General James F. Hollingsworth. He commanded Third Regional Assistance Command, what was left of the former IIFFV after virtually all of its combat units had been withdrawn to the U.S. In this position he was both adviser to III Corps commander, Lieutenant General Nguyen Van Minh, and commander of the remaining American advisors in III Corps. In World War II Abe and Holly had been two of the very best tank battalion commanders under Old Blood and Guts. Profane, brash, with numerous valor and Purple Heart awards from three wars, Hollingsworth was a fighter. Abrams told Hollingsworth to give full support to General Minh in defending An Loc. Hollingsworth, being Hollingsworth, took this as a call for him to fight this battle, and fight it he did. Day and night he flew over An Loc, programmed B-52 strikes, brought in tactical air to hit troops and tanks on the ground, constantly encouraged his advisors with the An Loc defenders to hang in there, and helped them coordinate the ground and air support they needed.

Inside An Loc was advisor James H. Willbanks who wrote the definitive book, *The Battle of An Loc.* He coordinated and fought until wounded and evacuated several weeks later. Willbanks quoted Hollingsworth's statements to *Newsweek* reporters: "'Once the Communists decided to take An Loc, and I could get a handful of soldiers to hold and a lot of American advisors to keep them from running off, that's all I needed.' He told the advisors in An Loc, 'Hold them and I'll kill them with airpower; give me something to bomb and I'll win.' General Abrams chastised Hollingsworth for this statement because he thought Hollingsworth had given the impression he was taking over what should have been a South Vietnamese-run show. In fact he would do just that because the ARVN corps commander was not prepared to handle a battle of this magnitude. It was just what the American general had prepared for his whole life."[30]

After the initial enemy assaults, An Loc was reinforced by air-landing the equivalent of five infantry regiments, an extraordinary feat in and of itself.[31] The defenders took positions within and on high ground around the village and fought against vicious attacks. Their enemy had not mastered the tactics of combined armor-infantry assault or urban fighting, and many of their tanks were destroyed by defensive fire on the ground and from the air.

For two and a half months the North Vietnamese pounded An Loc with artillery in support of infantry-armor attacks which cost them heavy casualties. Surprisingly enough to skeptics, Colonel Nhut's lowly RF/PF and PSDF proved especially heroic and effective in the ground defense. The South Vietnamese had perhaps their finest hour of the war to date. The regional and local forces who, until Abrams' times, had been poorly supported by their government and the U.S. aid mission, had been equipped and trained to a level that made them credible fighters. These men fought tenaciously to defend their homes and families.

With enemy tanks in the streets, the defenders used LAWs – light anti-tank, shoulder-fired weapons—against the unsupported tanks with devastating effect. The American advisors played a heroic and crucial role, providing the necessary ground communication for Hollingsworth's overhead direction of air support.

In an effort to lift the siege of An Loc, the ARVN 21st Division struggled to move north from Lai Khe to clear Route 13 of the 7th Division and a regiment of the 9th which had been committed to support the 7th. For weeks the ARVN pushed against heavily dug-in enemy which included the 165th and 209th Regiments, battalions of which we had fought in 1969 in the Michelin and along this road. Now they were dug in at and near what had been our FSBs Thunder I, II, and III. The ARVN were beaten back time after time despite intensive American and South Vietnamese air support. The enemy defending the route was facing the same kind of bunker problems we endured in the same locations during the monsoon season three years earlier. The 9th Division *History* reports, "This was now the middle of the rainy season. Our fighting fortifications, bunkers, and trenches were constantly flooded. . . . The earth had been pounded to dust [by American and VNAF bombing and artillery] and the rains turned the dust into mud, which greatly hindered the movement of our forces, our efforts to send food and water out to our fighting positions, and the transportation of our dead and wounded back to the rear."[32]

The 21st ARVN was reinforced by elements of the 25th ARVN Division and they finally linked up with the southernmost defenders of An Loc. When the smoke of battle finally lifted over An Loc, the RFs, PFs, PSDF and ARVN were standing as victors.

Virtually all RF/PFs in the An Loc battle lived in the An Loc/Quan Loi/Loc Ninh area, and many of the 5th Division soldiers had their homes just south of it. The ultimately successful defense of An Loc demonstrated that when South Vietnamese were defending their home turf, under command of a few good leaders such as Colonel Nhut, and with the lives of their families at stake, they could fight like tigers. As a test of Vietnamization, however, there was no reliable gauge since again

ARVN had advisors which brought them reinforcement and enormous air support, to include crucial logistic resupply by landing helicopters and C-123s on the small airstrip, and when antiaircraft fire was too intense, by airdropping equipment and supplies from C-130s. A general much respected by Americans, Lieutenant General Ngo Quang Truong, who commanded I Corps, wrote a treatise about the Easter Offensive in which he praised various forms of U.S. support, obtained through the advisers. He was especially thankful for B-52 support which was used several times as tactical air, striking concentrations of enemy close-in to An Loc as they launched their attacks. After praising the leadership of Colonel Nhut and the resilience and effectiveness of the soldiers on the ground, he wrote, "The enemy's back had been broken and An Loc saved only because of timely B-52 strikes."[33]

By late September 1972 the enemy had been pushed back from their advanced positions in all three Corps zones. However, some terrain in the battlefield areas remained under enemy control. Truong Nhu Tang, the PRG's minister of justice, and a perceptive commentator on the war, said "For all the verbiage that has been spent on these events, what had happened was very simple. Practically the entire North Vietnamese army was now inside South Vietnam—to stay."[34]

Of huge significance in terms of the viability of Vietnamization was its present—1972—and its near future. It had been severely tested ever since the 1967 decision of the Politburo to conduct war with "big battalions" in "big battles." With support of the Viet Cong infrastructure, guerrilla activities, and small unit battles continuing as always, the emphasis for the North continued to be on its general offensive/general uprising strategy. In the face of this strategy, the question was, could the South go it alone?

President Nixon, in his book *No More Vietnams* published ten years after Saigon fell, had declared the Cambodian incursion of 1970 a success of Vietnamization, coming on the heels of his declared success of pacification. Carrying this mindset into the 1972 Easter Offensive, he was not going to let Vietnamization now fail, so he had ordered an all-out effort by the remaining U.S. forces to support the Vietnamese, not allowing himself to see that if such an effort were necessary, it in itself would proclaim the failure of Vietnamization.

A 10 June 1972 transcript of a briefing by General Abrams and his staff painted a more realistic picture. It demonstrated then, and in the later analyses, that the South could not go it alone. The transcript stated, "A dramatic increase in the Free World Military Forces' tactical air capability has been realized since the enemy offensive began. At that time forces consisted of 16 United States Air Force squadrons, 10 navy squadrons on two aircraft carriers, and 9 VNAF squadrons. Since 30 March [the opening of the offensive] tactical air forces of the United States Air Force, Navy, and Marine Corps have deployed to Southeast Asia from the continental United States, Hawaii, Korea, Japan, Okinawa, and the Philippines. The Seventh Fleet carrier force has been increased to six ships capable of tactical strike operations."[35] The U.S. Navy in fact played one of its most significant roles in the war when its large-caliber guns pounded the enemy in I Corps, then added an amphibious attack to slow the enemy advance. Naval air struck in South Vietnam and in North Vietnam up to a 30-mile buffer zone along the Chinese border. "For the first time in the long Southeast Asian conflict, all of the Navy's conventional resources were brought to bear on the enemy [now also with 8-inch guns and aerial-delivered mines in harbors]."[36]

The Abrams briefing continued, "Our available forces now consist of 30 United States Air Force squadrons, 30 Navy squadrons, 5 Marine Corps squadrons, and 9 VNAF squadrons, an overall increase of 39 squadrons."[37] In other words, a significant portion of the U.S. Air Force, Navy, and Marines responded from wherever they were based in the world to answer Abrams' call for maximum effort to defeat the offensive.

General Truong, the South's best field commander, acknowledged this massive U.S. support. He wrote, "Among other things, the United States substantially increased its air and naval fire support and provided South Vietnam with as much equipment and supplies as were required. Furthermore, this support was coordinated with an increased bombing campaign in South Vietnam, increased interdiction of supply lines in Laos, renewed bombing of North Vietnam, and the blockade of major North Vietnamese ports, all in a remarkably successful effort to reduce the effect of the enemy offensive. . . . Quang Tri city certainly could not have been retaken, nor could ARVN forces have held at Kontum and An Loc had it not been for the support provided by the U.S. Air Force."[38]

By November, Nixon said that because of his intensive bombing of North Vietnam, "We succeeded in crippling North Vietnam's military effort."[39] Nixon's assessments were—well, Nixon's.

Pacification had taken a severe beating during the enemy's 1972 offensive. South Vietnam's General Tran Dinh Tho wrote, "For all its efforts, the GVN was still a long way from solving the social and economic problems that plagued Vietnam, especially in the context of a war in which the enemy always held the initiative and had the capability to wreck any achievements any time he chose. This happened in 1968 [Tet Offensive] and again in 1972 [Easter Offensive], when a few months of attacks undid years of hard toil. Unless South Vietnam was free from North Vietnam's military threat, pacification or any nation-building task remained a hopeless proposition."[40]

Situation, Late 1972, early 1973

Both sides were exhausted from fighting and needed replenishment in manpower, supplies and equipment. The South Vietnamese had the advantage due to the enormous help, ready at hand, of the Americans. But their enemy had made inroads that would take great effort, time, and casualties to try to overcome.

The North had been stopped from attaining their ultimate objectives in all four Corps areas, but they retained important advantages for further action. The bulk of their units, several of them severely battered, were still in South Vietnam or just across the border in Cambodia or Laos. As had been their practice from the earliest times of the French

war, while they recuperated, resupplied, re-equipped, took in replacements, and retrained for the next missions, they kept fighting to the best
of their ability. The NVA and ARVN sparred to grab land before the
anticipated final Paris Peace Talks in order to enhance their positions
at the bargaining table. The guerrilla war continued while NVA main
force units exerted pressure and in many places scored tactical victories.

Near the end of 1972, from the Demilitarized Zone in the north
NVA offensive actions had opened a corridor relatively free of ARVN
interdiction all the way south from I Corps down the western reaches
of South Vietnam through II Corps to III Corps north and northwest
of Saigon. The danger to the South's capital was palpable. Except for
garrisons at An Loc and Chon Thanh on Route 13, the NVA controlled
all of Binh Long Province. Barely northwest of An Loc and its ARVN
garrison, which did not patrol much beyond its defensive perimeter wire
and bunkers, the PRG headquarters was so secure that in the spring of
1973 Loc Ninh became its temporary capital. The ARVN 5th Division
was hard-pressed in trying to keep Route 13 open from Lai Khe for supply of the garrisons, and aerial resupply soon became the only means to
enable their existence. Additionally, NVA units were positioned to cut
off access to critical objectives in adjacent Phuoc Long Province to the
east and north of An Loc. In IV Corps south of Saigon to the southern
tip of South Vietnam, unlike farther north, enemy units did not focus
so much on terrain objectives as on continuing pressure throughout the
whole area with guerrilla and small regional force actions.

The geographical control situation throughout much of South
Vietnam was recognized by both the North and the South as one which,
on a map, in many areas looked somewhat like leopard spots. North
Vietnamese strongpoints were the black spots separated by their encompassing enemy. In some places, the situation was reversed. The Southern
troops were the leopard spots, hard-pressed by their enemy.

In their well-used talk-fight strategy, North Vietnam stalled on negotiating a final peace agreement, perhaps to buy time for highlighting for
the world Thieu's profound intransigence: he adamantly would not sign

an agreement that would leave the North's troops in South Vietnam and hand them other advantages. In essence the draft agreement included: an in-place cease fire, withdrawal of U.S. forces; exchange of POWs; prohibition of sending additional troops to Vietnam, equipment replacement only on an item-for item basis; international commissions to ensure compliance, and an international agency to organize free elections in South Vietnam.

Ominously for the South, the draft agreement did not require the withdrawal of all of the North's troops. President Thieu adamantly had insisted all along that the agreement must guarantee removal or he would not sign. The spectacle of Nixon bullying Thieu to sign left no doubt in many quarters that America had pulled the strings from the beginning. Enraged at the North's delaying tactics, to show them he really meant business Nixon ordered Linebacker II, the "Christmas bombing" of North Vietnam in December 1972. This time the air assault would be primarily with the big stuff: B-52s in concentrated attacks. He told Admiral Moorer, chairman of JCS, quite certainly in more vulgar language than he included in his memoirs, "I don't want any more of this crap about the fact we couldn't hit this target or that one. This is your chance to use military power effectively to win this war, and if you don't I'll consider you responsible."[41] The goal of the bombing was to take out the remaining military and other facilities in the Hanoi/Haiphong area which supported the North's war effort— power plants, industrial buildings, electric works, railroads, bridges—a devastating blow not just to the military but to the nation's economy. To get the recalcitrant Thieu in line, Nixon sent General Haig to him with an ultimatum: sign or all aid will be cut off immediately.

Thieu was finally forced into acquiescence by Nixon's threat, and the North quickly resumed talks. Nixon said, "Militarily, we had shattered North Vietnam's war-making capacity. Politically, we had shattered Hanoi's will to continue the war."

An agreement was signed.

Nixon proclaimed in his book, *No More Vietnams*, written 10 years after the war had ended when only an alien from Mars would not have known that North Vietnam had won the war, "On January 27, 1973, almost twenty years after the French had lost the first Vietnam War, we had won the second Vietnam War."[42]

Well!

The "Sustainability Quotient"

Nixon's statement deserves the derision which it received, but the circumstances which led up to it went to the very core of American participation in this war.

Mathematicians define "quotient" as the result of dividing one number by another. The term has also come to have much broader meanings. Sociologists, psychologists, and business consultants speak of other quotients such as moral, emotional, adversity. These quotients include the capacity to analyze and to act.

War inevitably damages both sides. I believe that America collectively-- its people, its Congress, its president—has what may be called a sustainability quotient in conducting war. It is an ability to sense how long America can engage without further pervasive damage to itself, and an ability to act upon that feeling.

Tet 1968 vividly revealed that America had reached the limits of its sustainability quotient. A sense of what the U.S. could and should do was central in two key addresses by the US presidents who led most of the American effort in the Vietnam War, Lyndon B. Johnson and Richard M. Nixon.

Two months after Tet, Johnson said in his 31 March 1968 address to the nation that his administration had offered 30 previous peace initiatives "that we have undertaken and agreed to in recent years." If the war were to continue, he said, "Armies on both sides will take new casualties. And the war will go on. There is no need for this to be so. There is no need to delay the talks that could bring an end to this long and this bloody war."

The war continued.

Nixon began his 23 January 1973 address, "I have asked for this radio and television time tonight for the purpose of announcing that we today have concluded an agreement to end the war and bring peace with honor in Vietnam and in Southeast Asia."

Johnson did not live to hear Nixon's address. He had died on the previous day.

The American war in Vietnam had been building since 1945 when the U.S. supported the French Expeditionary Force. This was nearly 23 years before Johnson spoke, and 28 when Nixon definitively proclaimed that America was getting out. By contrast, America's World War II had lasted three years and seven months. For America, that global war was far shorter than the "limited" Vietnam War. When faced with the necessity for survival during World War II, the sustainability quotient was simply the duration of the war, whatever that might turn out to be. America knew that the war had to be fought until resolution, and fiercely supported the effort. But after many years of war in Vietnam, America ultimately concluded that its survival did not depend upon "victory." An acceptable duration had been exceeded.

Part Three: The Vietnamese War—
The Result

*   *   *

Haponski's question:
"Were you afraid of the VC? of the Americans?"
The answer of the four women from Binh Co—Nghanh,
Nhan, Tuong, Luong:
"We were not afraid of them. But we were afraid of
and didn't like the ARVN."
Phu Cuong, April 2010

*   *   *

CHAPTER 14

A South Vietnamese - North Vietnamese War, 1973-1974

∗   ∗   ∗

THE SIGNING OF THE PARIS Peace Accords on 27 January 1973 marked the beginning of a radically new type of Vietnam War—no more U.S. advisors, no more U.S. artillery, naval gunfire, or air support. Pacification, as the Americans and South Vietnamese had attempted to practice it, was virtually dead. CORDS ceased to exist on 27 February 1973 when a tiny fraction of its capabilities was transferred to an office under the U.S. ambassador. Vietnamization was on its last legs.

Old Training and The New Face of the War

After the war, North Vietnamese Colonel Bui Tin reflected on the American army and its Vietnamization attempt: "In my opinion, the organization and equipment of the American forces were formalistic and cumbersome, and therefore totally unsuitable for contending with conditions on the ground in Vietnam, its climate and above all the nature of a struggle that was rooted in the people. The same was true of the Saigon army. Under American influence, its organization and weaponry lacked any flexibility. Even its uniforms were too heavy as I discovered in 1975 when I met many high-ranking Saigon officers and we compared the weight of our respective equipment including boots and rucksacks, only to conclude that what had been supplied by the Americans and before them by the French was unsuitable for jungle warfare or the heat of the lowlands."[1]

There is more than a little truth in his statement, as borne out by photos of diminutive Vietnamese under American steel helmets which produced massive headaches and seemed to swallow the individual. We saw many Vietnamese units solve the problem by wearing only the light helmet liners, even during contact with the enemy. After all, was the reasoning, the enemy wore light pith helmets, jungle hats or caps, usually not steel helmets. Much more troublesome than their equipment, Bui Tin said, was that "the Saigon army only knew how to fight American-style. It had forgotten its basic roots and lost its self-confidence."[2]

Interestingly, our U.S. military schools and colleges not only short-changed American officers by not teaching to the war we were fighting and projecting ahead to those we might have to fight, but Vietnamese officers ironically felt that "[Vietnamese] commanders given U.S. schooling got very little benefit from it. . . . What little they did learn did not apply to the situation in Vietnam, where the enemy and the terrain required a different type of warfare than that taught at American defense colleges."[3]

Our enemy had learned from necessity how to fight a people's war. They had organized in different configurations to meet specific needs, from local fighters, recruiters, and administrators at the hamlet and village level up to division-size forces, and they had gained years of experience in doing so. Contrasting with the people's war strategy of the enemy in which the people supported them through compassion or compulsion or some combination of the two, the South Vietnamese never were able similarly to fight a people's war. Nguyen Ba Can, Speaker of the House in Thieu's government and, near the end of the war, briefly Prime Minister, said, "It is important to consider that there were two categories of people in [South] Vietnam. One category had to fight for the other category—I mean the armed forces. Only the armed forces had the responsibility to fight the war, in the opinion of the people. The people remained outside of this. They were not involved in the fight.

It was the opposite of a 'people's war.' The way we conducted war, we should have realized that in the long run we had to lose it. . . . To sum up, the war was lost from its inception."[4]

MACV was disestablished on 29 March 1973 and replaced by a Defense Attaché Office, Saigon. It had only a small contingent of military staff. Except initially for certain replacement supplies and equipment— and by congressional action that too would soon be severely curtailed— South Vietnam would be on its own.

Of course, neither the South nor the North respected the Accords. Both sides continued a land grab begun in late 1972. Armed clashes and political proselytizing by both sides among the South Vietnamese people continued.

The International Commission

The Accords provided for an International Commission of Control and Supervision (ICCS) which had many duties, among them to supervise the cease-fire and compliance with other restrictions on actions. It was to report on how the Accords were being followed. Two Communist countries, Hungary and Poland, and two non-Communist nations, Canada and Indonesia, were its members. Canada resigned after five months, citing continuous squabbling, lack of cooperation, and the enormous number of violations which made the Accords ineffective. It was replaced by Iran, at that time, politically a U.S.-leaning, non-Communist country under the reign of Shah Pahlavi.

The ICCS consisted of various field teams from all sides of the war, each of which comprised representatives of all four ICCS nations. These teams had diplomatic status and were to have freedom of movement in order to carry out their tasks.

The establishment of ICCS headquarters at Tan Son Nhut airbase on the northwestern edge of Saigon set up an interesting coincidence. South Vietnam's enemies from Hanoi and from the PRG of South

Vietnam now set up offices in the capital which they had tried and failed to take by revolutionary violence.

Since the U.S. was the only signatory more or less trusted by the North, and since it had a multitude of aircraft ready at hand in South Vietnam, initially it was American aircraft and their crews which flew team members into Saigon and to various places in Vietnam where they needed to travel to execute their duties. Ironically in ICCS there was a strange mingling of former enemies within South Vietnam, basically no longer shooting at one another.[5] Except verbally, and there was a lot of that.

General Tran Van Tra had been Deputy COSVN Military Commander in 1969 when my task force had fought against his units. Then he was commander of the 1972 Easter Offensive attack on Loc Ninh-An Loc, the crucial northern gateway to Saigon. He said, "In January 1973, at the Regional Command Headquarters, in a bunker in the middle of a jungle base area [near Loc Ninh I was told that] the Central Committee had appointed me head of the military delegation of the Provisional Revolutionary Government of the Republic of South Vietnam to the Four-Party Joint Military Commission in Saigon. . . . My beloved Saigon! For a long time, during the era of the French colonialists, I had lived, engaged in seething revolutionary activities, won victories, and tasted defeat there. I had been away from the city fighting for decades, and was now returning in full view of the people and my comrades, and within the thick encirclement of the enemy. . . . Like everyone else, I had never used my real name, but had habitually used a code name, which I had changed now and then to make it difficult for the enemy to monitor me and maintain secrecy for our operations. . . . Now, faced with a new mission, I would meet the enemy face to face and would of course have to choose a name. Almost without thinking, I took the name "Nguyen Viet Chau," the name of a younger brother with whom I had been very close and who was killed in 1969 when he was presiding over a meeting of the party committee of Can Tho City. My brother and I had lived in Saigon, had participated together in secret revolutionary activity there during the period of French domination, had been released from a French prison at the same time, had partici- pated together in the August 1945 uprising, and had left our beloved Saigon to take part in the resistance war."[6]

General Tra said that during a meeting of his Regional Command in early 1973, "We promised that we would be worthy of being represen- tatives of the heroic people's armed liberation forces of the South in the middle of the enemy's capital and in the bosom of our beloved compa- triots." A pickup of the general and his small staff was arranged for the air strip at Loc Ninh where Colonel Patton and I had landed in August 1968 to check on our squadron which had been engaged in heavy combat during Tran Van Tra's attacks in the final phase of their 1968 Offensive.

Tra wrote, "On 1 February 1973, at the appointed hour, a flight of U.S. helicopters commanded by an American lieutenant colonel who was accompanied by a puppet officer, and flying along the course and at the altitude we had designated, made a circle around Loc Ninh, one after the other, from the northern end of the air strip. While they were circling around they had clearly seen the air strip, the town and, more importantly, the large number of anti-aircraft positions and tanks, deployed in many perimeters around the town, which were prepared to respond if they tried any funny business. On that day the town of Loc Ninh was like a large festival. Revolutionary flags few everywhere."

Tra described the festive atmosphere of the cheering crowd which had gathered from Loc Ninh and surrounding hamlets to see him off: "A quick, seething, and spirited rally was held beside the waiting American helicopters." Then, "Our delegation members waved to the people, then the comrades, two abreast, solemnly boarded the helicopters, amidst the affection of the people and the forest of flags and flowers. The U.S. major commanding my helicopter was very polite, carefully inspect- ing my seat, then stepped down, stood at attention and saluted, invited me to board the helicopter, fastened my safety belt, then sat down in his seat. The helicopters took off in an orderly formation, circled once above the airfield, then headed straight for Saigon along Route 13. The large number of people at the airfield were not the only ones seeing us off: nearly everyone, people traveling along the road, standing in their yards and on the streets, or working in the rice paddies and potato fields around Loc Ninh stopped work to wave at us. That was an extremely moving, very peaceful scene in an area scarred with the devastation of war."

Tra flew over An Loc which in 1972 he had tried so desperately to take, and which I remember so well from my convoy duties and two postwar visits. He said, "The flock of helicopters followed Route 13 past Binh Long, Tau 0, Chon Thanh, Bau Bang, Lai Khe, Ben Cat. All of those places had been the location of many fierce battles between us and the American and puppet troops over the course of many years. I looked down at the jungle, which previously consisted of thick growths of large and small trees but was now denuded and desolate. There were many bomb craters on the surface. Many long scars of devastation caused by B-52 carpet bombing succeeded one another and crisscrossed one another in the devastated jungle."[7] The general flew over what had been my Thunder III, II, and I fire support bases. He and I had both lost men in battles on and along that road, he many more than I.

Tra continued, "The helicopters landed in the military part of the airfield [Tan Son Nhut]. Our delegation thanked the crew members and shook their hands. Looking neat in the tidy insignia-less liberation army uniforms, we formed into an orderly line on the runway. The officers carried briefcases and wore revolvers. The enlisted men wore floppy jungle hats and carried backpacks and AK rifles. Everyone wore the famous rubber sandals. I [didn't] know whether the Americans and their puppets understood the significance of that or not, but the many Vietnamese and foreign reporters who were present at the airfield that day were very observant. They photographed us with movie cameras and still cameras. I smiled with delight when I noticed them photographing our rubber sandals. They said, 'Wearing simple, proud rubber sandals, they set foot on Tan Son Nhat.[8] They entered Saigon, capital of the Republic of Vietnam, in the same rubber sandals they wore during Tet of 1968.' (UPI, 1 February 1973). The reporters told the truth. Those rubber sandals had left their proud imprints on the streets of Saigon, at many important objectives, and even at Tan Son Nhat airfield, as well as all the other towns, cities, and municipalities in South Vietnam during Tet [1968]."[9]

General Giap gloated over the consternation of the South when northern and Viet Cong members of the Control Commission were later observed going about their business in Saigon: "People in Sai Gon were in a complex state of mind. The puppet army and administration were anxious and in disarray when Viet Cong officers and fighters appeared in the streets. Some people guessed that the Viet Cong would take over Sai Gon once the Americans had [completely] left."[10]

Tran Van Tra took part in the incriminations and re-incriminations that was the history of the ICCS. As the Commission was arguing, guns on both sides were firing. Tra of course, and the other delegates on his side, blamed everything on the American "puppets," Thieu and his regime. He said, accurately, though, "The most important aspect of the agreement, and the first matter that had to be implemented, was the ceasefire. Articles 2 and 3 of the agreement and the protocol on the ceasefire made clear and specific stipulations about the complete cessation of hostilities, the forces remaining in their original positions, etc. But after 28 January 1973, the day on which the ceasefire took effect (and until 30 April 1975), it was ironic that there was not a day on which the guns fell silent on any of the battlefields in South Vietnam."[11]

The pending departure of almost all Americans from Vietnam came to a head in March. Tra reported, "In the morning of 15 March 1973 USARV, the U.S. Army Command in Vietnam, conducted a flag-folding ceremony and [hurried] out. In the afternoon, MACV, the U.S. Military Assistance Command in Vietnam, actually the U.S. GHQ which commanded all U.S. troops, the vassal [Allied forces] troops, and Thieu's army and the imposing U.S. aggressive war apparatus in Vietnam, the Tan Son Nhat headquarters of which had been dubbed the 'Pentagon of the East' by the press, also pulled down and folded its flag. Whether by accident or by clever design, the next day the military delegations of the DRV and the PRG of the RSVN drove into the courtyard of that 'Pentagon of the East.' The two delegations got out of their cars and advanced directly into the reception room, past two rows of American MP's who stood at attention and saluted, in order to attend a party organized by the major general who headed the U.S. delegation. We laughed, drank American whiskey, and talked about the weather and peace in Vietnam, in the 'Pentagon of the East.' Thus the U.S. troops also got out. But . . . they left behind all kinds of weapons, military bases, and even officers in civilian clothing, to prop up the Thieu regime."[12]

Saigon's Decisions and Actions

To many observers in late 1972 and early 1973, it seemed that GVN had emerged from the Easter Offensive in better shape than their enemies. In fact, South Vietnamese General Tran Van Don (who in the last weeks of the war rose to become Deputy Premier and Minister of Defense) said of the period right after the Paris Accords were signed, "Strangely enough . . . our military situation at that time was probably the best it had ever been, including the time of maximum buildup of U.S. forces in our country. . . . In fact, at that time, we had the best control over our highways, roads, and other lines of communication that I can remember since the relatively safe days right after the 1954 Geneva Accords. The situation was so secure that Senator Ton That Dinh and I, accompanied by a group of ten staff assistants, drove from Saigon to Hue (about 750 miles) and back to assess the overall military situation, which proved quite good. We spent about ten days on the road, traveling openly with no armed escort whatsoever and had not the slightest difficulty. The countryside was as peaceful as it had been in 1954. The two opposing sides tried their best to influence peacefully as much of the population as they could. In general, we were able to control all province and district cities, but Communists had many of the small villages and hamlets which contained the bulk of the people."[13]

General Don was correct in that the enemy was sorely stressed. At the time, the effective combat strength of South Vietnam's main forces was much greater than that of the PAVN and Viet Cong. In addition they still had many of their RFs, PFs, and PSDFs whereas their enemy's regional and local forces had suffered much more. Hanoi's official history acknowledged: "After many years of ferocious, continuous combat, our local armed forces had suffered rather serious attrition. The enemy's efforts to conduct pacification, gain control of the civilian population, draft troops into their army . . . caused us a great many difficulties. On a number of battlefields we were even forced to send main force troops, cadre and soldiers who were natives of North Vietnam, down to serve as local cadres and guerrillas."[14] General Tran Van Tra confirmed, "In 1973 our cadre and men were fatigued, we had not had time to make up for all our losses, all units were in disarray, there was a lack of manpower, and there were shortages of food and ammunition."[15] Contrary to that situation, in late 1972 just before the Peace Accords came into effect, the Americans had kicked into high gear their programs called Enhance, and Enhance Plus, which loaded GVN with replacement equipment—in fact, as became evident, more than it could train soldiers to maintain and operate.

RVNAF had been helped for years by the U.S. Vietnamization program. No good deed goes unpunished? Vietnamization had done virtually everything to help the Vietnamese military except to remove U.S. advisors from Vietnamese high level staffs and combat units and in their place send liaison personnel, just as was the case with Allied units and is normal in joint combat operations. Had this been done, the Vietnamese would have been forced to use their own artillery, airlift, logistical and tactical air support for troops in contact. They would have had to exercise fully their own planning, command and control. Unfortunately, there never had seemed to be a right time to do that. ARVN performance had always been so demonstrably questionable that no one in sufficient authority, South Vietnamese or American, was willing to risk the losses that might have resulted from battles without the support U.S. advisors brought. But in early 1973, with U.S. advisors no longer on the scene, there is scant evidence that Thieu prepared his forces to solve that critical problem of self-reliance.

What he did do was to institute "the Four No's": No territory or outpost would be given up to the enemy; there would be no coalition government; no further negotiation with the enemy; and no tolerance for Communist or neutralist political activity. This strategy, if it can be called such, was meant to stiffen the resolve of the South Vietnamese to build a secure nation which would resist and repel their enemy.

Hanoi's Decisions and Actions

On the Communist side, the most encouraging aspect of the situation for them in the early months of 1973 was that whereas General Don could report accurately that travel along the coastline was quite safe for ARVN, the situation inland was different. PAVN units could move relatively securely from Hanoi south through a corridor along the Annamite Chain all the way down to positions near Loc Ninh. All headquarters of the DRV "conducted a general review of the situation and goals of the first six months of 1973." The result, taking only one instance of actions around Quang Tri, is representative of many that occurred throughout South Vietnam. In the region around the nearly defunct Demilitarized Zone, "the Military Region Command used provincial and district local force troops, supported by guerrilla forces, to hold our front lines directly in contact with enemy forces. This enabled the Military Region's main force units to be gradually withdrawn from the defense lines in northern Quang Tri and pulled back to base areas for reorganization and consolidation. . . . They strengthened their combat posture and stayed ready to advance into the lowlands when an opportunity presented itself."[16]

Creation of Four Corps Headquarters, and Improvements to Roads and Pipelines

Two major events revealed the North's determination to finish the war. They created four corps headquarters, and they made vast improvements to their roads and fuel pipelines to the South.

The 1968 Tet Offensive, 1970 Cambodian incursion, 1971 Lam Son 719 operation, and 1972 Nguyen Hue Campaign (Easter Offensive) showed that the lack of NVA corps commands had greatly decreased the effectiveness of combat actions. Trying to coordinate so many individual infantry divisions and separate regiments, plus regiments and brigades of air defense, armor, artillery, engineer and many smaller technical and support units across such widely dispersed areas had led to confusion on the battlefields. The solution was to create, successively, four corps headquarters, 1st, 2nd, 3rd, 4th, similar to what the South Vietnamese had long possessed. By doing so, the North came into line with other modern armies..

The order of battle (organization) for their 1st Corps gives an idea of the magnitude of the PAVN forces: three infantry divisions, an air defense division, a tank brigade, an artillery brigade, an engineer brigade, and a signal regiment, plus specialty troops such as transportation and medical. Almost all 1st Corps units had participated in the Dien Bien Phu campaign, the 1971 Laos campaign (Lam Son 719), and the Quang Tri campaign (northern element of Easter Offensive). The other three corps were similarly organized, and almost all units had extensive combat experience.

The official history stated, "The formation of these Corps marked a new step forward in the maturation of our army in terms of the scale of its organization and forces and represented a qualitative change in our army after almost 30 years of force building and combat. With several combined-arms corps with rather powerful equipment and considerable assault power, a high level of mobility, and the ability to conduct continuous, sustained combat operations, our army was now able to launch large-scale offensive campaigns using combined-arms forces in several different strategic theaters in order to bring the war to an end."[17]

Although General Giap had long been out of the business of being a battlefield commander, from his position as Defense Minister and Chairman, Central Military Party Committee, no doubt he felt great satisfaction in bringing PAVN to this point—formation of four modern army corps from its meager beginning: his command as "general" of that little band of 34 comrades at Pac Bo in 1944.

Increasing the effectiveness of the main forces, though, was not the whole show. Although since Tet '68 the fate of the war's outcome seemed to hinge primarily on the fortunes of the main forces, the Northern leaders never forgot what needed to be done at the lowest levels. The history continued, "As we centralized and expanded mobile strategic reserve main force troops and main force elements at the military region level, the Central Party Military Committee, the Ministry of Defense, and the headquarters of the military regions also devoted a great deal of attention to the development of local force and guerrilla militia forces. . . . All battlefields implemented a variety of measures to increase the personnel strength and raise the fighting capabilities of local armed forces, and especially of the province-level local force battalions and village guerrilla teams to move deep into the rural lowlands, areas temporarily under the enemy's control, to work with local cadres to expand our guerrilla and secret self-defense forces and to strengthen and expand our sapper-commando forces. With additional troops provided by higher levels, a number of provinces organized local force regiments."[18]

The second major event which revealed the North's intentions was the improvement and expansion of its logistics and communications networks within the South. Unfettered now by American air attacks, not only did the army greatly improve the Ho Chi Minh Trail on the western (Laotian-Cambodian) side of the Annamite Mountains range, but it also began construction of a new parallel, wide road on the eastern side, inside Vietnam itself, all the way down into

Cochinchina. Dubbed "Ho Chi Minh East," this road enabled delivery of equipment and supplies directly to fighting units. Additionally, "paralleling the strategic transportation and troop movement corridor was a petroleum pipeline network [over 1,000 miles long, of which 800 miles was built] during 1973 and 1974."[19] Before the end of the war, North Vietnam's pipeline complex reached from its border with China, where five four-inch lines fed it,[20] all the way down to Phuoc Long province, northeast of An Loc. A defensive array of NVA main force units protected road and pipeline work from ARVN units to the east while air defense units engaged Thieu's air force which tried to disrupt it.

Saigon remained the primary objective for future attack, and the isolated ARVN post of Tong Le Chon within Communist-controlled Tay Ninh Province to the northwest of the capital city was a problem for the NVA, impeding travel southward. The NVA partially solved the problem in March 1973 by establishing a year-long siege of the post, preventing patrols and any offensive action emanating from it. During 1973 Saigon itself was well protected by heavy ARVN concentrations and the strategic reserve of airborne and Marine units positioned around and within the city. Having interior lines, building logistical and combat unit strength was easier for the South than the North. Ominously, Thieu's forces were following his orders to dig in and defend its terrain— A Maginot Line syndrome?—while his enemy was building for highly mobile offensive action.

Relative to North Vietnam itself, work progressed to repair the damage of American air attacks and naval actions which had ceased at the end of 1972, anticipating the signing of the peace accords in January. During 1973, production facilities were rebuilt, harbors cleared of mines (largely by the U.S. Navy), and port facilities repaired. Total economic production surpassed that of 1965 when America committed its ground forces, rice production was high, the numbers of youths entering military service was up, and after they were trained they were sent south in large convoys. For forces in both North and South Vietnam, the Politburo and COSVN prescribed training sessions of three to six months for political cadre and military units.[21]

During 1973, while Thieu was strengthening his defense capability and having some success in driving back NVA units that were investing his ARVN strongpoints and threatening lines of communication, Le Duan was overcoming serious problems that could inhibit his push to end the war. Many of the difficulties were associated with his two patron states, China and the Soviet Union. Tensions between those two Communist nations dated back to the 1920s as a result of ideological differences on how world Communism should develop, as well as pragmatic problems with the long border between the two countries. Minor border disputes had existed for decades, but in early 1969 these had erupted into a Sino-Soviet border conflict with significant casualties on both sides. The other world powers were concerned that the hostilities might even develop into a nuclear confrontation since China now had the atom bomb. The situation simmered down after several months, though, when negotiations settled some of the thornier border issues.

Ho Chi Minh had been highly successful, generally, in sensing how far his competitive patrons would go in supporting his independence movement, and consequently he got significant military and economic assistance from both. China had often encouraged Ho and then Le Duan to maintain pressure on the Americans in South Vietnam, and not to give up the revolution. This was fully in accord with Le Duan's intentions. But long-established relationships and modes of doing business have a way of reversing themselves with changing conditions. China's difficulties with the Soviet Union had forced a reevaluation of its own economic and military needs, and its Vietnam policies. In mid-1973, Premier Zhou Enlai was encouraging Le Duan to "'relax' and stop fighting in the south for five or ten years."[22] As usual, the North Vietnamese cordially listened and then proceeded to do what they wanted—make plans to end the war as quickly as they could.

Contrasting Sides in the Story

Whereas earlier in this book the story played itself out largely at the levels of the people and the fighters themselves, now it necessarily focuses on what happened at the very top within Vietnam: on the one hand Nguyen Van Thieu alone; and on the other, Le Duan among a bevy of high-ranking officials who planned carefully, consulted often, and arrived at conclusions based on long experience.

The South Vietnamese side of the story is virtually that of Nguyen Van Thieu. Whereas Chairman of the Joint General Staff, Cao Van Vien, and his office provided necessary staff work, it was Thieu himself who set their agenda and shaped the process toward the final decisions which he made. One can be certain that every major decision on the South Vietnamese side that affected the outcome of the war was now entirely his, from conception to proclamation. Crucially, the commands which went out to his four corps and his strategic reserve during the vicious fighting which was to come were not shaped in any meaningful way by his highest level staff. They were his, and his alone.

The situation on the North Vietnamese side was very different. Whereas no one doubted that Le Duan would have the final say, the careful, progressive work of the Politburo, the Central Party Military Committee, and its two senior generals, Vo Nguyen Giap and Van Tien Dung, were very much integral to the decision process. In 1973 both generals were members of the Politburo and the Military Committee. In addition, Giap served as Minister of Defense, and Dung as Chief of the General Staff. They had been together for a long time. If Giap was miffed when Dung, as his deputy, went over his head directly to Le Duan to plan the 1968 Tet offensive, by 1973 he seemed to have gotten over it, and they were working together in relative harmony.

Giap begins his book, *The General Headquarters in the Spring of Brilliant Victory*, with reflections on the military headquarters situation just before the 1972 "Christmas Bombing." He found the once-again stalemated peace talks in Paris depressing. "For several days on end, Van Tien Dung and I had been returning home late from our Headquarters, where we often worked until midnight." On 18 December the first B-52 bombs of Linebacker II struck Hanoi, aimed at military targets but some strayed and caused civilian casualties. After a suspension ordered by Nixon for Christmas Day, on the next night, Giap reported, "At times, the solid command post [bunker] of the Army Headquarters shook like in an earthquake."[23] Giap was getting a taste of what it was like for the French in their command post bunker at Dien Bien Phu, and for Viet Cong and NVA troops in bunkers during B-52 raids in South Vietnam.

Sixty days after the signing of the Accords, the Politburo met, and then the Military Committee concluded they should continue to combine main force actions with those of the guerrilla units, and continue operations to win over the southern population. Giap said that immediately after the meeting the Committee "sent a telegram to the various battlefields, making clear that our military actions were to include initiating attacks and counterattacks, not merely defensive operations."[24] On 24 May the Politburo met again, and in speaking to the membership Giap used information obtained from spies in both General Cao Van Vien's office and Thieu's office, including the South's "urgent pacification plan from March to August 1973, the three-year pacification plan (1975-1977), the five-year plan for the building of the puppet army (1974-1979), the eight-year economic plan (1973-1980)."[25]

Considering espionage within the President's office and that of the Joint Chiefs of Staff which resulted in delivery to the North of such high level plans, and the infiltration of so many spies into other military units and political agencies in the South, there was not much the North didn't know about what to expect. This situation continued to the end of the war. Colonel Bui Tin said that when he entered Independence Palace on the morning Saigon fell he found himself the senior officer on the scene and as such encountered Big Minh and staff waiting in the president's office. Bui Tin said he tried to calm everyone's nerves by making small talk, asking Big Minh about his orchid collection and asking a staff member "why his hair was so long since he had vowed to wear it short for as long as Nguyen Van Thieu remained president. . . . At this Big Minh laughed and said it was no wonder we had won the war because we knew everything."[26]

Rehabilitation Operations by the North, 1973-1974

Greatly concerned over not just personnel losses during the 1972 offensive, but also of equipment during this period of reduced patronage by China, General Giap and his staff and combat commanders made prodigious efforts internally to rebuild. "During 1973-1974 all units of the armed forces conducted a general inventory of property and finances and organized the retrieval, collection, and repair of equipment, thereby partially resolving some of our logistics and technical support problems."[27]

Units were told to reduce their expenditure especially of large-caliber ammunition, and to repair and use captured equipment. At upper echelons, great efforts were made to produce needed equipment, to move damaged equipment to the North for repair, to substitute low-caliber ammunition which was in good supply for larger caliber, to send repair teams with specialty tools to the battlefields to make on-site repairs, and to train many more technicians. At the same time, combat units on the battlefields were ordered to assist engineers in improving the road and pipeline networks needed for large-scale movement of equipment and supplies to the South. As a result, the North was able greatly to increase the flow of materiel to their units.[28]

The result of these rebuilding efforts was that in early 1974 PAVN units began increasing the number and strength of attacks on ARVN forces, and this continued throughout South Vietnam during the year. Even more ominously for the survival of South Vietnam's government, as it would turn out, some of its generals and civilians in high positions were beginning surreptitiously to contact the PRG about whether some kind of coalition government would be possible.[29]

The Thieu Government and Corruption

In June 1973, the North's Military Committee reported that "Quantities of weapons recently poured in by the United States fell into the hands of the Liberation Army."[30] Quite certainly most of this was not the result of capturing weapons during battle, but dealings with corrupt South Vietnamese officials.

In my research I had found no evidence of this kind of corruption for personal gain on any significant scale in North Vietnam so I asked Merle Pribbenow, the CIA expert on Vietnam, to comment. He agreed, saying in an email to me: "There were reported problems of pilfering of supplies at Haiphong harbor during the war, but I do not recall anything indicating that there was high-level corruption or that the problem was as serious and widespread as it was in South Vietnam. However, during the war the North was definitely not free of corruption; it was just that there wasn't the vast amounts of money floating around North Vietnam that there was in the South."

Many South Vietnamese high-ranking officials commented on how damaging corruption was to their efforts during the last years of the war. General Cao Van Vien, South Vietnam's ranking soldier, had been commander of the elite airborne brigade, and commander of III Corps. Vien was respected by all MACV commanders. In a post-war monograph written in the United States he said that several high-ranking military officers to include province chiefs and two corps commanders—plus Thieu's assistant for security!—were publicly charged with corruption. The two corps commanders were temporarily removed from command, but Thieu took no action on his security assistant. By 1971, Vien said, corruption had become widespread in RVNAF.[31]

General Vien reflected on the period 1973-75: "Finally, after many years of continuous war, South Vietnam was approaching political and economic bankruptcy. National unity no longer existed; no one was able to rally the people behind the national cause. Riddled by corruption and sometimes ineptitude and dereliction, the government hardly responded to the needs of a public which had gradually lost confidence in it."[32] Vien spoke gently, as was his custom, and his words painted a sad, wishful, respectful, and therefore rosier picture than actually existed.

Other high-ranking generals were less kind. The United States was still providing some military aid to South Vietnam. General Tran Van Don, Thieu's Minister of Defense in the last stage of the war, said, "With a team of young, but dedicated, technicians I determined that the greatest problem with the administration of the aid we did get from the United States . . . was with the organized system of corruption at all levels of our administration. [It was there during the Diem regime] but the situation was no better under his successors."[33] Don said, Nguyen Van Ngan, one of President Thieu's closest aides . . . . in 1974 . . . talked influential Democratic members in South Vietnam's Congress into alerting Thieu to corrupt officials from the central down to the district levels. . . . Of sixty generals and two hundred full colonels, fewer than one-third were 'clean.' A two-star general in the First Corps, Vietnam's most exposed area . . . illegally sold rice to the Communists. . . . in the Highlands military region [Second Corps] . . . . All positions of command from district to provincial levels—even that of regimental commanders—were 'purchasable.' . . . . Ngan told me that until 1973 President Thieu was relatively honest, but he changed after the signing of the Paris Peace Agreements. . . . he shut his eyes to what his family was doing."[34]

Don stated, "One thing that deserves close scrutiny by historians [is] . . the incredible 'clout' exerted on our powerful leaders by their wives. There were a thousand ways, both legal and illegal, of making money in war-torn Vietnam. And the wives of our leaders mastered all of them."[35] Don cites examples of Mrs. Thieu acquiring wealth. Several other high-ranking military and civilian officials had similar stories to tell, and one wonders where the story tellers themselves may have fit into corruption schemes.

Giap said, accurately, of the 1973 U.S. withdrawal, "The U.S. troops had completely pulled out. . . . Business circles regretted the 'fortune-making' time when U.S. troops were present. The wives of puppet

soldiers no longer worked for Americans, polishing shoes or selling cigarettes around U.S. garrisons. Rice in the six western provinces no longer flowed to Sai Gon in the same high volume as in the past. Imports
were reduced. Unemployment was rampant. Money was devalued very
quickly. Prices increased by leaps and bounds. Corruption prevailed at
all levels without exception. The army abounded with 'ghost soldiers.'"[36]
Such soldiers did not actually exist. Their names were included in army
lists for wages that were supposed to be paid automatically to their families but were instead raked off by scheming military and civilian officials.

∗   ∗   ∗

President Nixon in late 1972 had secretly promised President Thieu that
the U.S. "would take swift and severe retaliatory action" against North
Vietnam if it violated the Peace Accords. Again in a meeting with Thieu
at San Clemente in April 1973 he emphasized that if South Vietnam
needed assistance, "we would act as the situation required." Nixon did
not doubt he could do as he promised. Months earlier the American
people had given him the largest margin of victory in a presidential election in history. And he could manage Congress. He was Nixon. But in
May, the House cut off funds for financing directly or indirectly U.S.
combat activities in, over or off the shores of North Vietnam, South
Vietnam, Laos or Cambodia. Also, by June, Watergate revelations were
cutting closer to Nixon himself and he was far more concerned with
Nixon than with South Vietnam. Then too, Congress proved to be far
more resistant than Nixon believed and on 7 November 1973 overrode
the president's veto and passed the War Powers Resolution (Act). This
put further restrictions on the president's ability to conduct war without
Congressional action.

Thieu and others of his administration had taken Nixon at his word.
They were bitter and later denounced America for betrayal. How could
a country not do as its leader had promised? They could not fathom,
given their type of government, and indeed that of many countries in

the world, that a U.S. president had no right to make such promises without the backing of Congress.

PAVN 's Creation of a New Offensive Posture, 1974

By May 1974 PAVN had regained its strength throughout most of Vietnam. Whereas the United States had earlier supplied more equipment and other war materiel than the South could use, the Soviet Union and China, apparently with the exception of artillery rounds, had essentially done the same for the North.

*   *   *

An ominous development for South Vietnam was that there would be no repeat of Enhance and Enhance Plus type aid of late 1972. For FY 1973 Congress had appropriated $2.27 billion in military aid; In FY 1974 it decreased to $1.1 billion, cut to $700 million in September 1974.

*   *   *

During late spring and continuing through the summer and fall of 1974, PAVN units struck at many spots near the coastal cities of Da Nang, Chu Lai, and Quang Nai in II Corps zone. Farther north, in I Corps, they attacked just south of Hue. ARVN was able to hold them out of Hue, but the ring around the city was closing.

As it turned out, the attacks in III Corps zone north of Saigon were the critical successes for PAVN, although Giap and the Military Committee did not at first recognize this. Early in April, General Tran Van Tra's 7th Division overran the fire support base at Chi Linh on the Song Be River. This opened up an avenue for attack on Chon Thanh on Route 13, the critical compound south of the An Loc outpost. Tra had been heavily pounding Tong Le Chon on the upper reaches of the

Saigon River southeast of An Loc for weeks, and by mid-April his troops overran the heroically-defended outpost. The loss of this post and of others at Tay Ninh opened up the routes to Dau Tieng and the Michelin Plantation. The 7th and 9th NVA Divisions were in position to sweep south. Critical positions along Route 13 which led into Saigon were now threatened all the way from An Loc south to Ben Cat. Then an NVA attack swept south along the Saigon River through Ben Chua, which had given us so much grief, and down into the Iron Triangle. Another arm of the attack went west to An Dien where I had had troops defending the bridge into Ben Cat. If these attacks had succeeded, ARVN to the north on Route 13 would have been cut off, and the road south would have been open to Phu Cuong, the last major ARVN position north of Tan Son Nhut on the northwestern edge of Saigon. But they did not succeed. ARVN counterattacks had given Thieu's forces breathing time.

Political Generals, and the Nature of GVN Military Forces

President Thieu, a general who had come to power in one of the coups after Diem's assassination, like Diem carefully crafted both civilian and military promotions, often down to district and battalion levels. Politics trumped merit. It was more important for a president to remain in power, even to the point of stationing his trusted elite reserve units close by as "palace guard" than to chance a strictly merit promotion. Earlier, in a few extreme cases, he had had to remove political favorites and replace them with more competent men. In October 1974, though, considerably upset that his top commanders had lost terrain to the enemy's strategic raids—the cardinal point in his four no's was not to give up positions— he relieved three of his four corps commanders, retaining only Ngo Quang Truong of I Corps. Gone was General Thuan, commander of III Corps, who, as a Thieu favorite and former 5th Division commander, had been most unimpressive when he worked with our 11th Armored Cavalry and 1st Infantry Division.

Thieu was soon to need all the competence and courage he could get from his commanders. Whereas ARVN had regained many of the positions it had lost, with the winter dry season already started, the enemy was in a greatly advantageous position. In an arc centered on Route 13 only 60 miles north of Saigon, General Tran Va Tran was building his combat capability by training his units and receiving considerable amounts of fuel, weapons, ammunition, and other war materiel from the nearby terminus of a main branch of the Ho Chi Minh Trail and pipeline.

After the war, General Don proposed reasons for the defeat of GVN. For one thing, "We did not adopt correct military strategy to deal with the inexorable Communist steamroller. We spread our forces too thin, trying to maintain a presence in and defend each province town, an ambition clearly beyond our capability. Although by this time we had an armed force of over one million men, such a method of defense did not have a chance for success."[37]

Don also said that the nature of GVN's military forces was that families often lived in or near the defensive positions, thus virtually precluding mobility in response to an enemy attack. A soldier's natural inclination was to protect his family and this interfered with his ability to fight with his unit or to withdraw so they could fight another day. I recall in particular two instances of this family situation while in Vietnam. In 11th Cav I visited our Ranger battalion NDP at the edge of Bien Hoa Airbase and witnessed the desperate living conditions of families. They had built hovels from any scrap material available. One soldier, his wife and two children lived in a piece of culvert about four feet in diameter, twelve or fourteen feet long. This soldier had no choice but to fight if attacked since there was no place to which his unit could withdraw. They were already on the edge of the greater Saigon area, the refuge of last resort. In another instance, I had responsibilities for the Song Be bridge next to the hamlet of Phu Giao which the 209th Regiment had attacked in May 1974. This was the regiment of which my task force had fought elements in the Michelin and along Route 13. The RF defenders of the bridge had built small huts into the superstructure of the bridge itself where they lived with their families. The wives and children peddled soft drinks, grapefruit, and other snacks to civilians and military as they crossed the bridge. These soldiers had to fight to the death in order to keep the bridge, their huts, and their families from being dropped into the river, and they succeeded for awhile in repulsing attacks. Soldiers in units elsewhere which could withdraw, however, had decisions to make: fight the enemy, or try to scramble away with their families, or, as many did, desert with their families before fighting erupted.

The North Plans for the Dry Season, 1974-75

Giap and his Central Military Committee (or Commission, as he called it) had worked during the summer of 1974 on plans for the coming dry season when good trafficability would favor mobility in the attack. The plan contained guidelines for continuing operations in 1975-1976 and was approved by the Politburo in a meeting starting on 30 September 1974, running into October. Giap commented on the need for conserving resources in certain areas: "Heavy guns and tanks must be used thriftily; since the signing of the Paris Agreement, both the Soviet Union and China had stopped dispatching artillery to us."[38] Many meetings had preceded the Politburo's conference, and all high-level cadre had had a chance to contribute to the plan through its many revisions before Le Duan and the Politburo approved it—and the plan would continue to be tweaked as events developed.

Giap reported that on December 13, 1974 the Phuoc Long Province campaign began. Dong Xoia, a village we had secured in 1969, was "liberated," resulting in capture of a large store of artillery, shells, and rifles. A relieved Giap said, "The concern over a shortage of shells, which had been weighing heavily on my mind for some time, was now alleviated!" The province headquarters town of Phuoc Binh (Song Be) fell on 31 December. "For the first time in the South, a province—one near Sai Gon—had been entirely liberated."[39]

Phuoc Long Province was the ultimate test of Vietnamization. Giap noted that the South had fought back entirely using its own resources, and lost. He could not know it at the time, but the victory was to have far greater significance. Almost five months earlier, President Nixon had resigned in order to avoid impeachment for Watergate crimes, and now, President Gerald Ford did not counter with an American attack, as Nixon had promised to Thieu if such a thing were to happen. This signaled that the South indeed would be on its own for the rest of the war.

*   *   *

A patter of criticism of Ford for not supporting South Vietnam failed to take into account both the War Powers Act and the realities of any American military response. Congress would not have sanctioned such a move, and even if it had, the Phuoc Long situation did not lend itself to the quickest form of American reintervention, B-52 bombing. The North Vietnamese units around Phuoc Long were not massed and therefore not susceptible to the kind of bombing that had saved An Loc in 1972, and a timely insertion of sufficient U.S. ground forces would have been logistically and tactically an impossibility. Above all, the American people, profoundly thankful to be out of Vietnam, would not have supported such an attempt. Three weeks later, at a press conference [21 January 1975], a reporter asked, "Mr. President, are there circumstances in which the U.S. might actively reenter the Vietnam war?" The president replied, "I cannot foresee any at the moment."

How much did U.S. withdrawal from the war and subsequent cuts in aid to the South Vietnamese determine the outcome to a decades-long war? Not much. On 31 December 1974 when Phuoc Long fell, the hour was late. Ho Chi Minh long ago had tapped into the two thousand years of resentment against foreign domination. Not his Communism, but his nationalism, his beliefs and conduct as a revolutionary, allowed him first to inspire, then shape and ultimately control a Vietnam-wide movement that would never give up on its idea of independence and union.

*　　*　　*

Success in Phuoc Long kicked Giap's Military Committee and the Politburo into high gear. The official Communist history *Victory in Vietnam* states, "During the final days of 1974, after hearing reports from our battlefield commanders . . . the Politburo foresaw that a strategic opportunity might appear earlier than anticipated. For this reason, in addition to the basic two-year plan for 1975-1976, the Politburo ordered that another plan be drafted so we would be ready to seize any opportunity to liberate the South during 1975."[40]

Historically, Ho and Giap had fought their war taking time—lots of it—to prepare carefully and ensure that to the best of their abilities whatever they undertook would be successful. This was the Confucian way, the Viet Minh way. When Le Duan became powerful in the late 1950s, he was of a different mentality. He wanted to finish off the war in the South. Now, at the end of 1974, having met with a huge, relatively unexpected success quite quickly and easily in "liberating" Phuoc Long Province, not only Le Duan but Giap and others of the Politburo and Military Committee smelled blood in the water and were circling for the kill.

CHAPTER 15

Revolutionary Violence, the Final Act, 1975

*   *   *

GIAP SAID, "THE CORE BELIEF of the current Central Committee Plenum was that the revolution in the South must continue its march along the path of revolutionary violence."[1] That term, "revolutionary violence," had been central to the ideology of Communist parties ever since Lenin. Marx and Engels, in *The Communist Manifesto*, never used the term, but stated, "The Communists openly declare that their ends can only be attained by the forcible overthrow of all existing social conditions." Lenin, embroiled in an actual uprising of the proletariat, took this belief to its logical conclusion, asserting in "The State and Revolution" that revolutionary violence was the sole means of achieving overthrow of the bourgeois state since its leaders would not give up power in any other way. From early in his rise in the Party, Le Duan had enthusiastically advocated that concept. In his 1956 treatise, "Tenets of the Revolution in South Vietnam," he had proclaimed that the road to victory was that of revolutionary violence. And here, in early January 1975, with the Phuoc Long Province victory, the end was in sight.

Crucial Ban Me Thuot

For some months before that victory, the Military Committee and Politburo had made many revisions to their overall plan for 1975-1977, and always they came back to the Central Highlands as the critical area to strike in their march on Saigon, and in particular the large village of Ban Me Thuot, 100 miles north of Phuoc Long on Route 14. On 10 March 1945 this was where Lieutenant Jean Leroy and his small detachment had escaped into the jungle on the day after the Japanese coup. Also, General Leclerc had recognized its importance in controlling access to points east and south, and had it seized in his northward sweep in Cochinchina in late 1945. Because of its advantageous position as the crossroad of trade routes, by 1975 Ban Me Thuot in the western Central Highlands had grown larger into what might be called a small city, and a strong South Vietnamese garrison had long been stationed there. As a result of the 1974 strategic raids, NVA units were relatively close to the city. Capture of it could lead to control of Route 14 to the south to Phuoc Long Province, and Route 21 east which intersected with strategic Route 1 on the coast. Route 1, called The Mandarin Road in colonial times, ran all the way south along the coast from Hanoi, across the Demilitarized Zone, then down to Nha Trang, Cam Ranh, Phan Rang, and Phan Thiet, all large cities heavily defended by Thieu's forces. Thus it was possible that capture of Ban Me Thuot would result in cutting South Vietnam in half, trapping all forces north of Nha Trang, and opening up Route 14 all the way south to Chon Thanh on Route 13 below An Loc. If Ban Me Thuot were to fall, Saigon would be in great danger.

The official history stated, "Throughout the years of the resistance war against the French and on through the resistance war against the United States, the Central Highlands had always been a strategically important battlefield for both ourselves and the enemy. It was an area suitable for mobile operations and could support combat operations by main force units in Vietnam and throughout the Indochinese Peninsula. . . . On orders from the General Staff, between late December 1974 and February 1975 reinforcement units for the campaign began arriving at their designated assembly positions."[2]

Senior General Van Tien Dung, who for some time had been working in reasonable harmony with Giap, was sent down from Hanoi by the Politburo to take charge of the campaign. Dung said, "I bid farewell in turn to Vo Nguyen Giap [and others] of the Central Military Committee. We were in agreement. We didn't say much to each other as we parted, but those who went to the battlefield and those who stayed at home were agreed on one thing: This time we must effect a change quite different from those of any previous campaign."[3]

Dung said that their enemy at the beginning of 1975 had 1.3 million troops, including 495,000 main force men, 375,000 regional force (RF) troops, and 381,000 civil guards (PF and SDF troops). That information as well as the positioning of those troops was based on reports from spies in Thieu's office, his general staff, and the offices of other high-ranking officials. The numbers generally accorded with what South Vietnamese officials later acknowledged. In addition, Thieu had a significant air force whereas the North had relatively few planes and they did not factor into the battle except in some minor instances. Thieu had a significant advantage in numbers but had caused a terrible handicap when he insisted that his commanders must not yield ground. Dung had many fewer fighters in all categories, but he would fight using highly mobile forces. He had the initiative—attack—whereas Thieu, by fixing his units in place, would defend. It would be an uneven fight from the beginning.

Ban Me Thuot was an area that could be expected to be friendly, or at least not hostile, to Dung's forces. It was the traditional Montagnard capital in that part of the Central Highlands. On 19 September 1964, five Montagnard CIDG camps near Ban Me Thuot had revolted against the South Vietnamese government. Ten days later the uprising ended, but only after U.S. advisors acted as intermediaries between the tribes and GVN. In early 1975 Dung could expect some assistance from the Montagnards, or at least apathy rather than resistance.

Dung set up his headquarters west of Ban Me Thuot in forest that was tinder dry. He had problems with forest fires burning communication lines, and with elephants pulling down branches on which the lines were strung. Because he concentrated his forces in that area he had an advantage over Thieu's men 5 to 1 in infantry; in tanks and armored cars he was slightly superior, and he had twice as much artillery. Dung told his staff what they already no doubt knew: "In the final phase of revolutionary war, in conditions where we are stronger than the enemy, we definitely must carry out annihilation attacks and liberate the towns and cities. . . . For the attack on Ban Me Thuot we are in a stronger position than the enemy." He pointed out that he had three divisions whereas the enemy had only one main force regiment and some RF/PF security forces. "The battle for Ban Me Thuot is the key opening battle of the campaign." he exhorted them.[4] Early in March he was ready, and he issued orders.

The Battle for Ban Me Thuot

Dung wrote, "On the night of March 9 we sat at headquarters and continued to follow the situation and wait for 'H' hour. None of the staff cadres could hide their joy and excitement as the momentous hour came nearer. For a soldier in battle, the night spent waiting for 'H' hour is like waiting for midnight on New Year's Eve. From the highest ranks to the lowest, we had been waiting years for this New Years Eve." Although this night in the Truong Son mountains was peaceful, tens of thousands of soldiers were moving toward their objectives.

At 2:00 A.M. artillery and rockets poured down, and small arms and RPG fire added to the din. "Tanks, armored cars and troop transports roared in toward town from all directions." Soldiers of Thieu's 23rd Division fought back fiercely as fighter bombers supported them in counterattacks, but by mid-morning on 11 March the division headquarters and all major defensive positions had been overrun. The next day the South Vietnamese strongly counterattacked, and at the height of it, communications failed at Dung's headquarters. Elephants again. He wrote, "Disturbed by the bombs and shells of the battlefield, a herd of elephants started 'evacuating' past our headquarters, headed for the Vietnam-Cambodian border." The rush threatened to flatten the headquarters, but the elephants just missed it and the only casualties were broken telephone lines.[5]

By 12 March, most of the fighting around Ban Me Thuot was over, the city had fallen, and NVA formations were thrusting eastward toward the sea. Le Duan commented in a Politburo meeting, 24 March 1975, "Our victory is bigger than we expected. Ban Me Thuot marks a turning point and the beginning of a great general offensive to liberate South Vietnam. The current victory cannot be separated from the victories we have won over the past ten years. This is the culmination of so many previous victories. The general offensive has begun; the Central Highlands opened the door. We will follow up by attacking Danang. Finally, we will liberate Saigon."[6]

As General Dung was attacking Ban Me Thuot, PAVN forces throughout South Vietnam were attacking almost everywhere. For example, the Dau Tieng-Michelin Plantation area had been assaulted by the 9th Division beginning 4 March, and they now occupied the base camp area we had battled through six years earlier. North of Ban Me Thuot, all was in chaos. PAVN was attacking hard-pressed ARVN units, and the ARVN counterattacks were not succeeding.

Thieu Abandons His "Hold at All Costs" Strategy

Shortly after Ban Me Thuot fell, President Thieu was forced to confront the failure of his absolute "no"—no giving up terrain. He quickly formed a new plan of defense which, according to some of his top generals, was the fateful decision which caused the ultimate collapse. He ordered that Ban Me Thuot be retaken and a final defensive line established in an arc roughly from the sea just north of Nha Trang to just north of Ban Me Thuot, then southwest the entire length of the border with Cambodia. Enclaves were to be established and held north of that line around Hue, Da Nang, Chu Lai, Quang Nai, and Tuy Hoa. When the situation stabilized, the enemy already within the final defensive line in the south, such as in Phuoc Long Province and Dau Tieng, would have to be driven out. To accomplish this, Thieu at first ordered withdrawal in I and II Corps to the enclaves on the sea, and the release of the elite airborne division from I Corps to be used in driving the enemy out of Ban Me Thuot.

General Vien, Chief of General Staff, wrote, "President Thieu's decision to switch strategy from 'hold at all costs' to 'hold as you can' was inevitable; he had no other alternative. The unfortunate thing was that this alternative was implemented too late and without appropriate planning and preparations. Therefore this sudden decision came as a hard psychological blow, with all the undertones of defeat."[7]

No other instance shows more clearly the disastrous effect of Thieu running a one-man show all those years. He would not trust his General Staff and corps commanders with studying options and devising contingency plans a year or so earlier because he knew everything better than anyone else. There must be no yielding of positions or even contingency plans drawn. In contrast were General Dung, Giap, the Military Committee, and Politburo who had planned together for years, sharing the single-minded goal of unifying the country under socialism and working as a team toward that end.

General Dung Orders Attack—Go, Go, Go

General Dung ordered attack—attack without delay. His troops had to forget the traditional manner of using time to carefully prepare their moves. He told his commanders, "The old ways of thinking, organizing, and acting ran counter to the demands of the newly developing situation. . . . It was not as if the enemy were organized., waiting for us with defenses prepared; they were disorganized, falling apart, yet when we attacked we still demanded full discussion."[8]

General Quang Van Thi said that rumors of Thieu ordering that all of I Corps and part of II Corps be abandoned, and that a new line be established intersecting the sea at Nha Trang to the south led to panic in I and II Corps. "These rumors were in part responsible for mass desertions in certain units as officers and soldiers asked themselves: 'Why do we have to fight to defend Danang and Hue while it has been agreed that the new line would lie somewhere [south]. . . between Ban Me Thuot-Nha Trang'"?[9]

General Dung bemoaned the loss of even one day when they waited until dark to move on the roads to avoid the South's air attacks. These strikes were at high altitude, no doubt because of the antiaircraft fire, and he said, "when they dropped their bombs their aim was not precise, yet we still did not send our troops into battle during the day—waiting, late, wasting time."[10] No more Confucian patience here. The general had to tell his commanders to go, go, go. They responded and they went, during daylight and darkness, slowing only sometimes to scarf up enormous quantities of abandoned equipment, munitions, fuel, vehicles, even aircraft. Before the battles, Giap had worried about having enough artillery and shells since the Chinese had stopped supplying them. No worry once battle was joined. They had more of everything than they could use, captured from their enemy or, in the case of food, mostly given to them by the people.

Disastrous Withdrawal

Thieu's withdrawal orders caused disaster. The forced withdrawal is the most difficult military maneuver to conduct effectively. Unless withdrawals are planned carefully, they usually start from a crisis situation, an inability to hold a position which negatively affects the mind and the performance of units. Maintaining contact among units is difficult, and an unexpected enemy thrust can cause a rupture that can lead to chaos.

Even before orders went out to South Vietnamese units to withdraw, soldiers' families and civilians were fleeing the oncoming destruction, clogging roads and impeding the withdrawal. Panic spread as shells struck in and around groups as I and II Corps units tried to move back to assigned positions. Hue fell, the imperial capital of the Nguyen Dynasty, causing psychological shock, and Route 1 south, the old Mandarin Road, was a mess of vehicles, soldiers, and civilians fleeing. Da Nang was next, and so on down the coast as columns of PAVN troops made their way through throngs of desperate people, past bodies, pushing aside destroyed vehicles to open the road ahead.

General Lam Quang Thi had been commander of I Corps Forward and at times acting commander of the corps. He said, "By March 25, the situation was rapidly approaching chaos. A city of 300,000 people, Danang was suddenly overcrowded with 2 million refugees [from Hue and other cities to the north]. Soldiers deserted to take care of their families. Police desertions mounted and bands of armed stragglers roamed the streets. Shooting incidences between soldiers and police were reported. Food and water were running short and people panicked when they saw the evacuation of U.S. personnel and Vietnamese employees of the U.S. consulate. Civilians and soldiers fought to board commercial and American ships to flee the city. The airport was invaded and military aircraft seized by panicking soldiers. Bands of hungry, thirsty children wandered aimlessly in the streets, demolishing everything that happened to fall into their hands. Danang, before its fall, was seized by the convulsion of collective hysteria."

Thi's wife arrived in Da Nang from Hue that same afternoon by military aircraft. "The next day I flew my wife to the airport. She and the family of Brigadier General Khanh . . . boarded one of the last military flights out of Danang [headed for Saigon] under heavy MP escort."[11] As the enemy entered the city, Thi and other generals fled by whatever means, air and sea. Thi's helicopter made it to an LST offshore at night. I Corps commander General Truong and another general separately swam out to sea and were picked up by a U.S. Navy ship. The commander of 1st Division and some of his staff were shot down in their helicopter, and all were killed. Thi and his aide later flew in their damaged helicopter to Saigon where he was reunited with his family.

*   *   *

As Da Nang was falling, a White House memo on 25 March shows that President Ford was meeting with Henry Kissinger, Secretary of State; General Frederick Weyand, Army Chief of Staff; and Graham Martin, Ambassador to the Republic of Vietnam. The president told Weyand that he and the ambassador were going to Vietnam, post-haste: "Fred . . . . We want your recommendation for the things which can be tough and shocking to the North. I regret I don't have authority to do some of the things President Nixon could do."

*   *   *

By 2 April the coastal cities of Qui Nhon, Tuy Hoa, Nha Trang and Cam Rahn were taken, with only some isolated spots of defenders still holding out. All of I Corps and II Corps essentially had collapsed. By mid-April, Cambodia and Laos were on the verge of falling to the Communist forces of their countries. Worse for the South Vietnamese, Phan Rang, the last major defensive position on the coast, had fallen. Thi said, "The fall of Phan Rang was a fatal blow to President Thieu's concept of [establishing] a new South Vietnam [behind the defensive arc that Thieu had ordered held]. It was also a fatal blow to his morale as ARVN units, before leaving the town, bulldozed and leveled the graves of his ancestors as the ultimate expression of hatred and anger."[12]

General Dung, commanding the massive PAVN movement southward, told of his logistics chief coming upon a broken-down truck and finding two sloppily-dressed drivers repairing it. This officer asked, "'Say, what unit are you from? Don't you think that's a ridiculous, inappropriate way for victorious troops to dress?' The drivers answered, 'Sir, we're POWs.' At this time over the whole battlefield, and in all units, our soldiers were using people who had previously been in Saigon's armed forces to drive and repair all kinds of vehicles.. . . . In our advancing columns American M113 armored [personnel carriers], M-48 and M-41 tanks, 105mm and 155mm artillery pieces, and PRC-25 radios began gradually to make their appearance."[13]

I Corps and II Corps had been lost, and to the south in III Corps, the situation was critical for the South Vietnamese forces. Tran Van Tra's 9th Division, having taken Dau Tieng, cut Route 22 south of Tay Ninh and fought off ARVN counterattacks. Tay Ninh Province was now isolated from Saigon. An Loc and Chon Thanh on Route 13 were evacuated as the NVA moved in and now owned the terrain on which our Thunders III, II, and I FSBs had stood. The northern gateway to Saigon that we had kept closed was about to be burst open.

On 3 April General Dung was driven to Loc Ninh where cheering throngs received him. He was a short distance to the west at COSVN headquarters on 8 April when a motorcycle approached and Kissinger's nemesis at the Paris Accords, Le Duc Tho, got off. He brought the invigorating news that the Politburo had approved a plan for the liberation of Saigon. Dung was to command the campaign to be named in honor of Ho Chi Minh, and Tran Van Tra was to be one of the two deputy commanders. Le Duc Tho told the assembled commanders and staff that the Politburo said everyone must be focused on victory: "They have five divisions. We have fifteen divisions, not to mention our other strategic reserve forces."[14]

Politics and Corruption

With the fall of Phan Rang, General Thi and several other senior generals were arrested for unauthorized abandonment of positions. Thi believed the accusation to be unjust since Thieu had ordered the evacuation of Hue, and General Truong had ordered evacuation of Da Nang. More plausible, Thi said, since he had been a long-time supporter of Air Marshal Ky, "was that President Thieu, increasingly concerned about a possible coup d'etat, was determined to neutralize politically unreliable generals by putting them under house arrest under the pretext of having withdrawn without authorization."[15] According to some South Vietnamese generals and top-level civilians, even in Thieu's positioning of the reliable Airborne and Marine divisions in the last weeks, the intent was not so much to stem the NVA advance as to guard against a coup.

General Cao Van Vien, GVN's most senior general, was respected by the three MACV commanders during his 10-year service as chairman JCS, a man who had loyally served both President Diem and President Thieu. In his analysis of leadership in South Vietnam, Vien believed that in the last months, then weeks of the war, Thieu's initial decisions not to yield terrain were prominent in the final collapse. However, more to the point, he found inherent problems in national and military leadership dating back to the Diem assassination which, as it turned out, fatally weakened the South's ability to survive. He wrote, "Of the flaws and vulnerabilities that military leadership in the RVNAF might have demonstrated, the most detrimental were perhaps political-mindedness and corruption. The November coup of 1963 had changed military leadership so completely that the RVNAF were never the same again. . . . Politics had been so ingrained among senior commanders that it was impossible for them to relinquish it and return to military professionalism. The Thieu regime, in fact, feared not so much the enemy from the outside as those who had once been partners and comrades-in-arms. And that explained why, one by one, the politically ambitious ones had to go, but political rivalry still persisted. . . . As to corruption, although it was not directly accountable for the collapse of the nation, its effect certainly debilitated professional competency and, by extension, the war effort. The regime eventually accepted corruption as an inevitable vice because, as Vice President Huong had tragically admitted, 'we would be left with practically no one to fight the war if all corrupt commanders were to be prosecuted and relieved.'"[16]

The Beginning of the End

On 9 April the final thrust began principally with a massive attack on Xuan Loc near what had been Blackhorse base camp where, seven years earlier, I had joined 11th Cav. The official Communist history, *Victory in*

Vietnam, reported, "Xuan Loc was an important gateway to Saigon. . . . The 7th Division made the main assault."[17] Destruction of elements of this division had been Task Force QuarterCav's objective in our 30 March 1969 attack into the Michelin. The 7th Division's history said, "The 165th [Regiment] would lead the primary attack [on Xuan Loc]."[18] That regiment's command post at the southern edge of the base camp in the Michelin had been what our enemy that day fought so fiercely to protect. The 5th and 6th Battalions of the regiment were the strike forces at Xuan Loc. The 5th Battalion, the major unit we had hit as we turned south in the rubber was designated as the main attack element at Xuan Loc. The 6th Battalion, the one that had struck us so hard in FSB Doc on 28 March 1969, was the secondary attack element at Xuan Loc. Meanwhile, the 209th Regiment cut Route 1 east of Xuan Loc. A part of this regiment was one of the units we had attacked in their bunkers in the Michelin and then later in May 1969 in their ambush positions along Route 13. The South Vietnamese defenders at Xuan Loc fought a fierce battle and inflicted heavy losses on 7th Division. When I was in 11th Cav in 1968 I had attended a ceremony and luncheon at the province chief's villa on the edge of the attractive market square. At the end of the 1975 fight, a newsman wrote, "Xuan Loc's once bustling central market is now a pile of rubble about two feet high."[19]

*   *   *

General Weyand returned from Vietnam and told reporters that there might be a chance for the South Vietnamese to hold a small piece of Vietnam as a bargaining chip, but they would need military aid immediately.

While the desperate battle at Xuan Loc was taking place, on 10 April the nation watched on TV as President Ford addressed Congress on a host of foreign policy issues. Turning to Vietnam he said, "I have received a full report from General Weyand, whom I sent to Vietnam to assess the situation. He advises that the current military situation is very critical, but that South Vietnam is continuing to defend itself with the resources available. However, he feels that if there is to be any chance of success for their defense plan, South Vietnam needs urgently an additional $722 million in very specific military supplies from the-United States. In my judgment, a stabilization of the military situation offers the best opportunity for a political solution."

But at this very late date, with the enemy in Xuan Loc ready to move on Saigon, the U.S. could do little except plan for evacuation of remaining U.S. and selected South Vietnamese personnel, which it did. Congress would provide funds only for evacuation efforts.

$$* \quad * \quad *$$

On 21 April President Thieu resigned, transferring power to Vice President Huong. During a TV address to the South Vietnamese people he bitterly, tearfully read from Nixon's 1972 letter pledging "severe retaliatory action" if North Vietnam threatened the South. Thieu said, "The United States has not respected its promises. It is inhumane. It is untrustworthy. It is irresponsible."

A few days later Thieu and his family flew out to Taiwan.[20]

On 23 April President Ford addressed the convocation audience at Tulane University. He said, "We, of course, are saddened indeed by the events in Indochina. But these events, tragic as they are, portend neither the end of the world nor of America's leadership in the world. . . . Today, America can regain the sense of pride that existed before Vietnam. But it cannot be achieved by refighting a war that is finished as far as America is concerned."

This, a week before Saigon fell.

$$* \quad * \quad *$$

On the 23rd, the U.S. evacuation of Saigon began. General Don said that by the 26th, "Sixteen enemy divisions equipped with armor and heavy artillery were tightening their ring around Saigon."[21] General Dung had moved his advance headquarters down from Loc Ninh to the Long Nguyen Secret Zone just west of Chon Thanh near the spot where my task force had turned west to attack toward the Michelin Plantation six years earlier.

On the 27th, President Huong stepped down in favor of General Duong Van Minh ("Big Minh") who appealed for a cease fire and was ignored. On the 28th and 29th, PAVN forces were shelling Saigon and Tan Son Nhut. On 29 April, Merle Pribbenow, the CIA officer who helped so much in producing my books by translating enemy histories and providing invaluable insights, caught one of the last helicopters out. Ky and General Ngo Quang Trung took off by helicopter and landed on an American aircraft carrier. Generals Vien, Thi, and families were evacuated by the Americans. Big Minh and his wife bravely stayed behind, Minh futilely believing that he could negotiate an acceptable government with their conquerors.

The ARVN IV Corps commander and his deputy committed suicide, as did the ARVN 7th Division commander. The 5th Division commander shot himself in his headquarters at Lai Khe, which had been our 1st Infantry Division headquarters and one of QuarterCav's logistics and maintenance locations after we moved north out of Di An.

The official Communist history *Victory in Vietnam* states: *The Campaign Headquarters decided to attack Saigon from five directions: northwest, north-northeast, east-southeast, west, and southwest.* Of the five, my men and I had fought in the first three. In the northwest, the NVA 3rd Corps was to strike from the Tay Ninh-Dau Tieng area to seize Tan Son Nhut and the South Vietnamese General Staff Headquarters. From the north-northeast, 1st Corps was to target Phu Loi and destroy the 5th Division at Lai Khe and Thu Duc. The thrusts from the east and southeast would employ two corps, the targets of which were Binh Hoa and Independence Palace in Saigon.

The End for Di An District

On the 29th of April the Lai Khe base was heavily shelled during the night, Ben Cat District Town was under attack, and National Route 13 was interdicted between Phu Cuong, the province capital, and Lai Khe. Phu Cuong was penetrated by NVA sappers who set up blocking positions at some places.[22] The fighting had reached Di An District. Nguyen Minh Chau, my friend, the incredibly brave, capable Marine who had been promoted to lieutenant colonel, described his last days:

"The situation at that time was extremely tense. The district government and the district military headquarters were hurriedly working on a defense plan against enemy tanks.

"I had to stay with my soldiers and the people until the end. The situation in the district was still very quiet. Absolutely nothing had happened; there had been no Communist ground or artillery attacks, but some of the soldiers were worried and shaken because they heard of the evacuation of one location after another, and how some people had taken their families onto ships or boats and sailed out to sea, and others were being evacuated by American aircraft from Tan Son Nhut Airbase. My in-laws were worried about their grandchildren so they took all my children down to Saigon to stay with them, leaving me free to carry out my duties. My wife, however, refused to leave and stayed at the base to give me moral support. Seeing this, the soldiers and the local civilians felt more at ease and less worried. . . .

"All my RF soldiers, PF soldiers, and all the district, village, and hamlet officials obeyed their orders and were determined to remain at their posts to fight to the end. However, on the night of 29-30 April, we were abandoned and left helpless because we lost all contact with the Bien Hoa Province Military Headquarters. We did not know whom to look to for our orders. East, west, north, or south, there was no one to help us, and a North Vietnamese regiment accompanied by T-54 tanks had moved down from the direction of Tan Uyen to the [northern part of] Di An district and was sitting there, waiting."

I discovered many years later that my Binh Co family was directly in the path of NVA forces rushing on Saigon and could have been in great danger during fighting. General Giap said, "Division 312 (Army Corps 1) made preparations to attack Binh Co and Binh My."[23] The battlefield commander of NVA forces, General Dung, said, "It was the first time in the decades of resistance [in this part of South Vietnam] that trucks of the regional logistics section and the logistics departments of all the zones could come down from the east . . . all the way to Binh Co and Binh My north of Tan Uyen."[24] But as NVA units bore down on the two hamlets, great good fortune seems to have intervened. The ARVN units evacuated. During my 2010 visit there, my girls from Binh Co, now grown women with families, told me that the night after ARVN left, they had been on their sleeping mats, eyes wide open, holding one another close as they heard the tanks clanking and grinding and trucks passing harmlessly by during the night.

Chau continued, "Our only choice was to fight as long as we could. We did not know whom we could rely on for help, so all we could do was entrust our fates to God. It was a night filled with terror and anxiety. Everyone, from officers and officials down to privates, had an anti-tank rocket, a machinegun, or a rifle in his hand and waited up the entire night for the enemy to approach our perimeter. We heard the sound of artillery and tank cannons, both ours and the enemy's, echoing up from the direction of Hau Nghia and 25th [ARVN] Division's base camp at Cu Chi [to the northwest]. We watched the flares drifting through the night sky all along the western horizon, and when we looked toward Saigon we could see the lights of helicopters landing and taking off. We guessed it was the Americans evacuating their people. We were all very shaken. We had no idea what would be the final fate of Di An district and of all of South Vietnam. We longed for dawn. Then we could decide what to do.

"However, as dawn neared, a reconnaissance team in a forward outpost called back by radio to the District Military Headquarters to report that the tanks had changed direction. They had turned onto the [Di An Base Camp] perimeter highway and driven from the direction of Lai Thieu straight toward Saigon. The next morning at 10:00 we heard the voice of General Duong Van Minh over Saigon Radio ordering all units to lay down their weapons and surrender. This news hit everyone, from officer to private, like a bolt of lightning, and the entire compound where the soldiers' families lived and the local population all burst into tears. I immediately used my radio to order all soldiers and district, village, and hamlet officials to destroy all documents and leave their units, wishing them and their families well and saying a few words of farewell, with my heart full of such sadness and bitterness that I could not stop my tears. 30 April 1975 ended my military career, a career that had lasted exactly 21 years, because I had joined the army in April 1954."[25]

The End for South Vietnam

The 312th NVA Division, famous for Dien Bien Phu and replicated to produce the 7th Division, drove into Phu Loi and Thu Dau Mot (Phu Cuong). After the fierce fighting of Xuan Loc, the NVA 7th Division's 141st & 165th Regiments had attacked westward and were now mopping up in Bien Hoa Airbase which had been our forward CP of 11th Cav, and its 209th Regiment had taken up blocking positions on Route 13. The bridges for which my Task Force 1-4 Cav had had ready reaction force responsibilities over the Saigon and Dong Nai Rivers were all taken. Finally, with PAVN forces closing in on Saigon from multiple directions, as the official history relates, *At 10:45 A.M., the lead tank . . . crashed through the palace gates and roared into the grounds of Independence Palace. A number of cadre and soldiers. . . marched into the Palace conference room and took puppet President Duong Van Minh and his entire cabinet prisoner. At 11:30 A.M. on 30 April 1975, the flag of the Revolution was raised in front of the main building of the Independence Palace complex.*[26]

North Vietnamese tank entering smashed-down gate
of Independence Palace, 30 April 1975. (Getty)

*   *   *

Addendum

After the Fall of Saigon

When General Tran Van Tra's International Control Commission
duties were finished in 1973 he had gone back from Saigon to Hanoi and
then down south again as COSVN commander. As a deputy to General
Dung during the final campaign, on 30 April 1975, the day Saigon fell,
he was at the command headquarters in the Long Nguyen Secret Zone
just west of Chon Thanh, very near where we had turned west off Route
13 for our attack toward the Michelin. Tra said, "Suddenly a cadre

gleefully brought in a tape recorder and placed it on the table: it was the voice of Duong Van Minh announcing his unconditional surrender over the radio and ordering the puppet troops to throw down their weapons and surrender. Everyone gathered around, listening silently. Everyone jumped with joy. Le Duc Tho, Pham Hung, and Van Tien Dung, who were very moved, hugged and kissed one another and firmly shook hands. "[27]

General Dung also described what it was like at the command headquarters when they got the news of surrender. "We wept. Yes, those tears were reserved for this day of total victory which so many generations had fought for with all their devotion and with all their passion, committing their lives to it. . . . Our thought, our first thought in that first moment of victory was of our beloved Uncle Ho. . . Uncle's arm was still beckoning affectionately, calling us to his embrace . . . beating time for us as we sang." The song was one which Ho was especially fond of leading groups in singing—Ket Doan—"Unity."[28]

The next day, Tra received word that the Politburo had appointed him chairman of the Military Management Committee of Saigon-Gia Dinh, and he quickly departed for Saigon. He said, "Our convoy left the command headquarters [and] passed through the Dau Tieng rubber plantation [the Michelin]."[29] In doing so, he drove through what had been our Fire Support Base Doc six years earlier where we had lost men and had killed many more of his in a fierce night battle. Then he crossed the ford we had bridged for our attack into the Michelin to strike into units of his 7th Division, resulting in the largest battle ever fought in the historically bloody plantation. A few days later General Giap flew down, and he and General Dung hugged in shared jubilation.

∗   ∗   ∗

General Creighton Abrams, MACV commander, had said at his WEIU briefing on 29 August 1969, a few weeks after I returned home: "In the whole picture of the war, the <u>battles</u> don't mean much."[30] He was in charge. He was right. But during my command of Task Force 1-4 Cav, we lost 43 men either directly under my command, or in fights over which I had command authority. Twenty-one of them were killed in "battles," the big ones to which Abrams was referring. It is hard, very hard, to acknowledge that Abrams was right. I have long known I would have an agonizingly tough time answering parents or wives on what their loved one died for if they asked me. I do know they were courageous, fine young men who died while doing what their country asked of them as they were looking out for one another, and that is the best answer I could give. I believe that many combatants in that very long, heart-rending war—French, French Union, American, Free World Forces, South Vietnamese, North Vietnamese—might say the same.

CHAPTER 16
You Cannot Kill an Idea With Bullets

*   *   *

"You know, you never beat us on the battlefield."
Colonel Harry G. Summers, Chief, Negotiations Division,
Four Party Joint Military Team
Hanoi, a week before the fall of Saigon

*   *   *

"That may be so, but it is also irrelevant."
Colonel Nguyen Don Tu, Summers'
North Vietnamese counterpart

*   *   *

THE VIETNAMESE WERE CONDITIONED BY two thousand years of revolt against foreign occupiers. When they lost, as most often they did, they prepared for another try, time after time. The leaders of the few times they won were legends, revered down through the centuries.

Our story has been one of events *within Vietnam* and the people in that country who in large measure caused the events or took part in them. The high level politics of Washington, Paris, Beijing, and Moscow – well revealed in many histories of the Vietnam War-- provided a framework within which our exploration progressed. The Vietnamese leaders of both North and South, contrary to frequent accusations, were not mere puppets of the foreign powers which supported them, but strong-willed leaders who sought and accepted outside help and advice, but who ultimately danced to their own tune, often to the frustration of their supposed masters.

Independence. Unity. Two words, a single concept. How to convey it to the masses in order to create a nation?

Much of it did not have to be conveyed. A deep yearning was already there.

The Beginning—the French War

During French times, several separate Vietnam independence parties rose. All were nationalists. In the 1920's the nationalist VNQDD party was the strongest of all. But at that same time, another nationalist, Ho Chi Minh, was coming to believe that the Lenin socialist revolution was the example to follow, more in tune with true nationalism because it fostered a party of the people. And he was not the only one. Many other young Vietnamese, some of whom had been in France, in China, in Russia had the same belief. Ho rose to prominence among these early Communists and from abroad gave them guidance. They worked in the Viet Bac, north of Hanoi, to spread their views and gain followers. Communists and Nationalists shared a single goal and competed for adherents.

By 1930 both were secretly proselytizing in many places throughout Vietnam. During the world-wide Depression, exploited workers in the South listened to fellow workers who were Communists and rose up in demonstrations, brutally quashed. Fifty colonial soldiers at their garrison of Yen Bai just north of Hanoi were influenced by the nationalist VNQDD party, mutinied, and were guillotined. The French were just too strong.

Until World War II. Then the Japanese—Orientals—subjugated the French. It could be done!

At Pac Bo in 1944 Ho told a small group of revolutionaries, "Everything because of the people; everything for the people. People first, guns last. If we have the people on our side, then we will have guns. If we have the people, we will have everything.'"

A year later came atom bombs and the August Revolution. It was a new age in Vietnamese nationalism. On 2 September 1945 Ho Chi Minh stood on a balcony in Hanoi addressing a huge crowd, proclaiming the independence of Vietnam – not North or South Vietnam, but Vietnam – in his mind and the minds of many, one country, a nation of Vietnamese people.

Ho's consuming inspiration came from the American Revolution. He began his address by quoting the Declaration of Independence: "All men are created free and equal." Then in ringing phrases he added precepts of the French Revolution – liberté, égalité, fraternité. When much later asked to confirm that he was a Communist and a graduate of the Moscow school of revolution he laughed and said he learned about revolution not in Moscow but in Paris, capital of Liberty, Equality, and Fraternity.

Ho briefly had experienced the promise of America in New York and Boston, and he and his country had been exposed to things French for a very long time. Wonderful things – an enlightening educational system, culture. Terrible things – suffocating dominance, cruelty.

Relatively few in Ho's crowd in front of that balcony were Communists, primarily just the cadre of the fledgling Viet Minh units which had marched down from the Viet Bac to celebrate this historic moment. Many of those cadre were indeed Communists, as were most of the others who sat and stood behind the speaker. Not Soviet or Chinese types of Communists, but Vietnamese Communists. These prominent people had not been primarily peasants but mid-level professionals, business people, and intellectuals. The man in front of them had made all this possible – he and American atom bombs. With the Japanese occupiers due soon to disappear from the scene, that left only the French. Just days after Japan announced its surrender, Emperor Bao Dai had appealed to President Charles de Gaulle, "We would be able to understand each other so easily and to become friends if you would stop hoping to become our masters again."

Quite certainly most of those in the crowd in front of the speaker knew Communism only as a word that at the time didn't mean much. And it didn't mean much later to the bulk of the Vietnamese people. But independence did – *doc lap*—which melded with unity, or unification, into one idea – independence of a nation of one people. To resist foreign domination was to be patriotic. That is how the United States of America was born.

Although in 1945 their cause seemed hopeless in the face of an expeditionary force coming to reclaim colonial rights for France, the North Vietnamese leaders had many things going for them in addition to their fervor: the shaky ground on which post-war colonialism stood, the great distance of France from Vietnam, the extremely poor state of the French economy. Working against them was the fact that America in the Truman administration was the leader of free nations in a global effort to contain Communism. The French Expeditionary Force arrived in uniforms, carrying weapons, and driving combat vehicles that America had supplied France during the war just concluded. At its head was the first of the French generals to be Supreme Commander of French Union forces, four-star Leclerc, the best man for the job. Leclerc's force was organized, trained and equipped (not well, but equipped) to fight the conventional war they had left behind them in North Africa and Europe. They quickly adapted to the new environment and conditions, but they never had enough troops to do all the things they knew had to be done. The terrain and climate were inhospitable, the enemy formidable. With every guerrilla killed or every civilian harmed they created new recruits for their enemy. Leclerc soon came to realize that the fervor for independence was so strong it could not be quashed. His opponents—fighters in the bush, innocent-looking men and women in the rice paddies and fields—would fight forever. After eruption of all-out war in Tonkin, Leclerc concluded, "You cannot kill an idea with bullets." He told his government to "make a deal, make a deal, make a deal, at all costs."

But the French government was under enormous pressure internally and externally. Loud, powerful voices cried out that the reputation of France was at stake. Moreover, France was seen by many other free nations as a finger in the dike holding back a flood of global Communism. There was no deal.

Over two years ground on as Viet Minh forces grew to regimental size while guerrillas and local forces kept up the fight in and around the villages throughout all three parts of Vietnam, and political cadre drew more and more people to support them. Then in 1949 the face of the war changed profoundly with the Red Chinese victory. This created a new, huge Communist nation on the border of North Vietnam, enabling a profound increase in support for the North Vietnamese, to include an advisory mission, CMAG. That America responded with its own MAAG and other aid for the State of Vietnam which dwarfed Chinese and Soviet support spurred Giap along his path to develop main force divisions. His 1950 Border Campaign along with a simultaneous campaign in the South showed that a new stage had been reached in the war: division-size attacks at the same time that smaller actions were ongoing throughout much of Vietnam. The almost total destruction of several of France's very best units along Colonial Route 4 thoroughly shocked the French people. The war had been going on for five years and the people of France were war weary and war poor. Casualties of French Union dead, wounded, missing were 36,000. Street demonstrations included mothers crying for sons lost, demanding an end to the madness.

Pressures on governments to stay the course are extreme. Would all of that money, so much needed at home, have gone down the drain? Would all those brave men and some women have died in vain? UN forces were at war against Communists in Korea. France was needed both in NATO and Indochina, and the U.S. pressed strongly to keep them in the fight against Communism.

So would France quit in Indochina? No.

Instead, France went all in with General de Lattre, its most senior general, one who had an encompassing view of French interests. He assumed the dual post of High Commissioner of Indochina and Supreme Commander of French Union forces. He was the best. If anyone could win, it would be de Lattre, *le Roi Jean*.

De Lattre built a defensive line around the Delta and formed powerful mobile groups. He spoke forcefully to Vietnam's youth and got more of them into the fight. De Lattre turned back the enemy each time Giap struck with his divisions, and he kept Ho from fulfilling his promise of being in Hanoi by Tet. Ultimately, though, the combination of death of his soldier son and cancer accomplished what Giap could not do – put this fabled soldier out of action.

A year and half passed with yet more jostling of the top French civilian and military positions in Indochina, and prime ministers in France. The French people were even more sick of the war, and France itself was in greater need of the funds being drained from it. By now the prevailing notion in the French government was to exhibit sufficient military strength in Vietnam and create conditions good enough to enable the government to enter peace negotiations from a position of strength. In mid-1953 General Navarre was sent over to Indochina with more hope behind him than conviction by his government that he could do this.

One facet of the Navarre Plan was to use the existing plan for a *base aéroterrestre* at Dien Bien Phu, prepared by the departing General Salan. The air-ground base at Na San had drawn Giap to attack it, and French air, artillery, and counterattack had done just as Salan had predicted – caused significant enemy casualties with minimal friendly losses. And when the base no longer was useful it was evacuated, no problem. A similar base at Dien Bien Phu should be able to draw even more enemy to it, and they would face the same fate. But, by incredible feats of movement of units across great distances, supported by an amazing rudimentary system of logistics created seemingly out of the sheer will to succeed, Giap was able to encircle, then fiercely attack the French Union defenders.

Since the advent of the new Eisenhower administration in early 1953, Secretary of State Dulles had been drumming for more American support for the French, and getting it. Over eighty percent of military and economic expenditure was coming from the U.S. As the potential fall of DBP turned into likelihood, then virtual certainty unless the U.S. intervened, Eisenhower weighed options. In the Joint Chiefs of Staff, only its chairman, Admiral Radford, was in favor of intervention while most of the rest of the Eisenhower administration as well as Churchill and other allies, with good reason, were against it. The moment passed, and Giap overran DBP.

The epic battle highlighted the best in the opposing armies – On the French side, the dogged courage and professionalism of defenders such as Marcel Bigeard, Geneviève de Galard, and the volunteer Vietnamese paratroopers who jumped into the fight on the last two nights in a desperate attempt to do what they could in a cause they knew was lost – On the Viet Minh side, the hundred thousand or more civilians who formed the incredible logistics chain which kept the army supplied, and the tens of thousands of soldiers who fought so courageously during fierce battle, going at it again after being repulsed with heavy casualties, and again and again for 55 days and nights until they triumphed.

During the Geneva Conference, Ngo Dinh Diem became prime minister of the southern Nation of Vietnam. The ensuing Accords resulted in two independent Vietnams, North and South. Diem refused to sign, believing that the negotiators had run rough-shod over South Vietnamese interests. Since the U.S. also did not sign, what to do now, America?

The Middle—the American War

After a slow start in 1945, two presidents, their administrations, and an uninformed or largely pliant American public had increasingly become alarmed at Cold War developments and favored supporting the French. With the collapse of Dien Bien Phu, Eisenhower's administration believed that America was so far committed in containing Communism in Indochina it needed to do all in its power to bring about new circumstances which might result in eventual success. It would not sign the Geneva Accords of 1954; it would urge the French to regroup its forces in the South and hold them there as long as possible; it would strongly support the man of the hour, Prime Minister Diem. Reflecting on the issue of nationwide 1956 elections proposed in the Conference Final Declaration, Eisenhower thought, along with many others, that if elections were held, 80 percent of the Vietnamese would vote for Ho, and there would go America's hope for keeping the dominoes from falling. Diem pre-empted the issue in 1955, at least in his mind and in that of the American administration, by holding his own elections in the South in which a questionable vote brought him the presidency of the new Republic of Vietnam. In 1956 French forces departed Vietnam, leaving a formidable situation for an American embassy and MAAG mission to face.

After Geneva the North had been weaker than the South which was spared much of the physical devastation and bloodshed. Nevertheless, in the Politburo were "South-firsters" who urged completion of the war by moving units south before the Americans could get ground combat troops to Vietnam. The "North-firsters," those who wanted first to build the economy, refurbish the military forces, and solidify socialism in the North, held sway. For a time. By 1959, though, when Diem had launched a potent offensive against Communists in the South and incurred widespread discontent among the Southern people for his oppressive methods, a new power in the North had taken over – Le Duan, now First Secretary of the Party, a fervent "South-firster" and proponent of revolutionary violence as the path to take in the South. Ho Chi Minh, who had made all this possible, had been edged aside into primarily a diplomatic role even as he remained the inspiration for the people.

The years 1960-62 in the South were marked with increasing gains for the Viet Cong through a powerful combination of terror and proselytizing. Nineteen sixty-three was a terrible year with Viet Cong at Ap Bac thoroughly whipping a larger South Vietnamese force and killing three of its American advisors. Then Buddhist protests against the harsh Catholic-dominated Diem regime turned into riots and self-immolations, much televised around the world. Near the end of the year, Diem and his brother were assassinated, launching an era of coups which brought to power the first in what was to become a succession of generals as heads of state. But there was no stability in their governments—in fact, just the opposite. After President Kennedy's assassination, President Johnson immediately pledged continued support, saying he would not go down in history as the president who lost Vietnam.

Nineteen sixty-four was even worse, with widespread guerrilla attacks and Viet Cong domination of more territory than that controlled by the South Vietnamese government. The crisis required new American leadership in Vietnam, resulting in President Johnson's selection of General Westmoreland as commander of MACV and General Taylor as ambassador. Westmoreland's first major act was to launch a pacification program he and his staff designed, HOP TAC. This was to set an unfortunate pattern of Americans planning and to a large degree conducting pacification, an enterprise that should have been a South Vietnamese priority. South Vietnam was in crisis. After years of military and economic aid which clearly had failed to stem the tide, the prestige of the United States was at stake. Would America call for negotiations and withdraw? No. Johnson, pressured by advice, politics, and his own determination not to fail, in early 1965 decided to commit ground troops. America now owned the Vietnam War.

Like all active duty U.S. military officers, Westmoreland was the product of a command culture stemming from World War II. The armed forces were organized, equipped, and trained to fight the Soviet Union and Eastern Bloc in Europe should that become necessary. Although President Kennedy had taken steps to produce a counter-insurgency capability by promoting the Green Berets and other special forces, essentially the military was wedded to massive conventional warfare and not well suited for other types of conflict. When the first U.S. ground units came ashore in Vietnam, Westmoreland in effect took off his advisor's cap, relegating pacification to the back burner, and put on his combat commander's helmet, ready to engage the NVA. His strategy would be attrition; his tactic, search and destroy.

The first major battles of the American war in the Ia Drang had revealed operational differences that were to prevail to the end. As a result of Westmoreland's tactic of search and destroy, many battles were fought in the jungle where the enemy had the terrain advantage and the initiative. The enemy most often chose where, when, and how to fight, and when to break off fighting, withdraw and regroup to fight another day. Later battle studies showed that the enemy usually initiated the engagement. In those instances in which Americans took the initiative in planned operations and American firepower was applied massively in attacking base areas, the enemy was not hurt as badly as one might think should have been the case. This applied to both ground and air attacks. Junction City, the largest allied ground operation of the war, did not succeed in decimating large enemy units or in crippling COSVN. Intensive bombing of North Vietnam did not put the North on its knees. At all levels of conflict one wants the initiative. The side which has it and maintains it is likely to be the victor. The jungles of Vietnam, though, brought another dimension to large-scale battles. The enemy needed the jungle for cover and concealment, and when he was attacked there he had the advantage. However, when he left it to attack the cities, or as at Khe Sanh, a large defensive position, he exposed himself to massive firepower. During Tet '68 when the enemy launched surprise attacks throughout South Vietnam they were hurt badly when met by mobile defenses employing massed artillery, air strikes, and strong counterattacks. Westmoreland conceded that his greatest successes came when the enemy exposed himself.

When General Abrams arrived in Vietnam as deputy to Westmoreland he had come with a mission from President Johnson, "Vietnamization," an effort to provide better equipment and training in order to enable the South to go it alone in the war. The most dramatic improvement was in providing the M16 rifle, a weapon which could compete with the AK-47, and Vietnamese were trained in how to use and maintain it and other new equipment. However, a problem not well addressed at the time was the advisory system. It put planning and support of large operations almost exclusively in U.S. hands, and this did little to promote competence and self reliance in the echelons of South Vietnamese command and control. This problem persisted throughout the American war.

Not long after the Marines had arrived in 1965 they found Westmoreland's search and destroy tactic faulty. Marine General Karch said that the real war was among the people and not in the mountains. The war, he said, could only be won when the people were protected. If the people were for you, you would triumph in the end. If they were against you, the war would bleed you dry and you would be defeated.

General Walt agreed and endorsed a Combined Action Program (CAP) which placed small Marine units in hamlets along with RF/PF soldiers with a mission to work among the people and protect them from the VC. The program came reasonably close to being effective, but Westmoreland insisted on search and destroy, and this hurt Marine pacification efforts.

In 1966 Buddhists were protesting against their government, this time that of Ky and Thieu. Ky responded to the most violent of the protests in and around Hue and Da Nang with his air force and elite Marine units. For a time, South Vietnamese units were fighting pitched battles against one another as the VC and NVA kept score. More widespread civil war in the South was narrowly averted, but the spectacle did little to enhance America's confidence in the South Vietnamese government, and it did much to strengthen the enemy.

Search and destroy remained the predominant U.S. tactic. The largest search and destroy operations of the Vietnam War, Cedar Falls and Junction City, in retrospect revealed a major reason they were so unsuccessful despite Westmoreland's claims. The enemy knew about both before they were launched. Enemy espionage throughout the war was highly effective, with agents planted in the highest offices of the military and civil administration to include General Vien's and President Thieu's offices and staffs. Dinh Thi Van had suffered weeks of torture during five years of imprisonment but she managed to establish a network that among other accomplishments secured the Junction City plans, lifted from General Vien's staff. Espionage penetrated most aspects of the South's military and government and was a major contributor to enemy success.

In 1967, Thieu won election as president, with a bitter Ky as vice president. Despite this discord, the U.S. administration hoped for and in fact found more stability. In mid 1967, though, General Weyand, an excellent division commander, on condition of anonymity had told a reporter, "Westy just doesn't get it. The war is unwinnable. We've reached a stalemate, and we should find a dignified way out." Near the end of 1967 Westmoreland, like French General Navarre before the Dien Bin Phu disaster, discounted enemy gains and proclaimed there was "light at the end of the tunnel."

Then Tet '68 struck, a cataclysmic event in the war. It was the main contributor to Johnson's surprise announcement that he would not be a candidate for another term, and to Westmoreland's departure from Vietnam. Although American peace proposals had been offered in 1966 and 1967, not until May 1968, four months after the start of the Tet Offensive, did U.S. and North Vietnamese envoys meet informally in Paris. The Johnson administration could accept portions of the ensuing North Vietnamese proposal, but not that section prescribing that the NLF would establish the program for settling South Vietnam's internal affairs without foreign interference. The war went on.

A new MACV commander might be able to restore confidence in America's role in the war and capitalize on the huge blow militarily that the enemy had suffered. Abrams was America's best general. When he became MACV commander in mid 1968, he announced a new strategy, "one war," pointing out that the enemy had always fought only one war, a coordinated military effort with a span from single guerrilla up to main force divisions which was wholly integrated with political and psychological campaigns among the people to gain and hold their allegiance.

Could Abrams' concept be translated into action? Pacification initially would be at the center of his plans, with focus on providing real security for the people in order to give them opportunity to bond with their government and aid in the fight against the enemy. But Abrams' most senior subordinates, despite professed agreement, did not much employ the new strategy. U.S. units to include 11th Armored Cavalry Regiment and 1st Infantry Division continued to put most of their efforts into search and destroy—"Find the bastards and pile on."

Also, pacification continued to be more an American than South Vietnamese concern. Our 11th Cav pacification effort in Binh Co, for example, lacked the central ingredient—GVN support. The district chief was an impediment, so we never got RF/PFs into our hamlets. Additionally, the actions of our two successive Vietnamese Ranger battalions alienated the people. In our area, pacification was coming from us, in planning and execution. The Vietnamese province and district officials and our Rangers were not only not involved, but their actions among the people were detrimental. Nearing the end of 1968, Abrams got an initially recalcitrant President Thieu to buy into a three-month Accelerated Pacification Campaign (APC), announced as a Vietnamese plan. Unfortunately, it was not Vietnamese. It had been devised by the head of CORDS, the U.S. pacification agency. Its reporting mechanism, the Hamlet Evaluation System, immediately became suspect for producing subjective, optimistic results.

Earlier in the Pentagon, Abrams had approved a plan called "Pacification and Long-Term Development of South Vietnam," abbreviated PROVN. Then while APC was ongoing, he had the staff which developed PROVN present it in Vietnam at one of his weekly briefing sessions. Abrams' senior commanders and staff derided it, enraging Abrams. Although the plan became MACV policy it was not effectively followed. Search and destroy prevailed.

My main mission when I took command of 1st Division's armored cavalry task force in January 1969 was pacification. However, such a force was much too powerful to remain in a pacification role, and after two and a half months we went north to engage NVA main force regiments. Atlas Wedge was a corps-planned search and destroy operation aimed at the NVA 7th Division which had been located in the Michelin Rubber Plantation and surrounding jungle. As we attacked west, busting jungle in the Long Nguyen Secret Zone, we were as ineffective as our 11th Cav squadrons had been in the jungle of War Zone D. However, when we reached the plantation we could maneuver, and search and destroy was the right tactic for engaging the enemy. Their night attack on our fire support base was met with our mobile defense. That and our following attack into the Michelin showed that when American units operated in terrain conducive to maneuver, our firepower was devastating.

The same held true during our following route security mission. We could maneuver in the Rome-plowed swaths on both sides of the roads, and we pounded the enemy hard in their ambush positions. But when we went back into the jungle during our Ben Chua mission, we took casualties and inflicted none.

In mid-1969 the first U.S. units were withdrawn from Vietnam. President Nixon wanted Vietnamization to produce a South Vietnamese military that could defend the country when all Americans had been returned stateside so he could claim "peace with honor" as a result of the ongoing negotiations. American units were directed to work closely with the Vietnamese and to train them as much as possible.

A partial test of Vietnamization was the 1970 incursion into Cambodia. The Vietnamese in fact played a significant role in the planning, overseen by MACV which would commit U.S. ground units and air support as part of the operation. South Vietnamese performance was spotty—some units did well, others not so well. And this was with all units having their U.S. advisors with them to coordinate the artillery and close air support they got. So despite Nixon's excited proclamations that Vietnamization had worked, this was not a true test, the question being unanswered as to how well they would have done had they been on their own.

The test of Vietnamization in the 1971 Lam Son 719 operation in Laos was somewhat more valid in that uproar over Nixon's 1970 incursion across the border into Cambodia had resulted in Congressional prohibition of U.S. advisors or ground forces from crossing Vietnam's boundary. However, there was no prohibition involving airspace. During the operation, U.S. artillery shells looped westward, helilift and air cavalry supported the Vietnamese, and tac air and B-52s struck enemy forces. Some South Vietnamese units did well, at least initially, but then an almost general panic set in as the enemy strongly counterattacked. The televised images of soldiers desperately clinging to helicopter skids to be lifted out, and the condemnations by many soldiers of their leaders, greatly affected the confidence and morale of the South Vietnamese military and people. In the United States, Nixon's triumphant pronouncement that Vietnamization had succeeded was largely met with derision.

In the 1972 Easter Offensive the enemy struck full force in all four corps areas, as he had done in Tet '68, using all military assets from guerrillas to divisions. There were virtually no American ground combat forces remaining in Vietnam; however, many Vietnamese ground units still had their U.S. advisors. Nixon ordered full support. Offshore navy craft provided their heaviest shelling of the war. Intensive bombing of the North resumed, as well as mining of its harbors. In South Vietnam the fighting was fierce and went on for weeks. Of most concern was the situation at An Loc since it was only a short distance north of Saigon. If it fell, the northern gateway to the city would be burst open. But due to the fine leadership of the province chief and the courage of his RF/PF, PSDF, and ARVN soldiers, supported through their U.S. advisors with enormous tac air and B-52 strikes, An Loc held. Again, throughout South Vietnam the performance of RVNAF was spotty, but a multitude of acts of heroism by individuals and units was uplifting to the South's spirits. Several South Vietnamese generals, though, including the best field commander, General Truong, said that RVNAF could not have held at such critical places as An Loc and Kontum without advisors bringing massive U.S. air support.

Near the end of 1972 the North's representatives at peace talks in Paris were stalling in their classic talk-fight stratagem, and a furious Nixon ordered the "Christmas Bombing." When the North came back to the table and in January 1973 signed the peace accords, Nixon proclaimed victory, saying that almost twenty years after France had lost the first Vietnam War, we had won the second Vietnam War. True by hardly any other reckoning than Nixon's.

The End—The Vietnamese War

The January 1973 Paris Peace Accords marked the beginning of an entirely Vietnamese war. No more U.S. advisers. No more U.S. Army ground units, Navy, Marines, or Air Force. Ominously, the bulk of the North's army was still in South Vietnam, but for awhile the Southern forces were in better shape than their enemy, who had taken a beating when they exposed themselves to enormous firepower. As usual, though, the North went back at it, slowly rebuilding the full spectrum of their strength from guerrilla to main force, and continuing their proselytizing. Additionally they greatly improved their logistical network with enhancements to the Ho Chi Minh Trail and a new modern road reaching from the Demilitarized Zone down through western South Vietnam to Loc Ninh. This road network plus new pipelines greatly enhanced their combat strength. The South set about rebuilding their pacification structure, and for a period in some places it provided more security than in the past. But their enemy never let up, always doing what they could with guerrillas, small tactical units, and political cadre working among the people to increase the number of supporters.

As 1973 turned into 1974 it became quite certain that a showdown was approaching between two very large armies. Guerrilla war and small battles were ongoing, but the major decisions in both Hanoi and Saigon were now focused on corps and divisions. In one sense the South had the advantage in having a significantly larger army and navy. It had a modern air force that far outclassed the North's much smaller, largely defensive air force. But the South's logistics were a major problem. The U.S. Congress cut appropriations, seriously affecting Nixon's promises that the U.S. would support South Vietnam with military aid for as long as it took. By mid-1974, the huge amounts of equipment left over or shipped by the Americans had become, or was becoming, useless through lack of spare parts. Fuel and ammunition of all kinds were in short supply, and strict rationing of them was in effect. To the contrary, North Vietnam, with some exceptions, continued to be supplied by China and the Soviet Union, as well as their own northern factories. Corruption in the South was a greater problem than ever, and that, combined with continued politicization of civilian and military appointments, caused morale among both the people and their military to suffer.

The North decided it was time again for major revolutionary violence, and they laid plans for a 1975-76 campaign. Their December 1974 quick conquest of Phuoc Long Province north of Saigon, though, surprised them, and they immediately went into high gear. Thieu's insistence on defending terrain at all costs set the stage for disaster as the enemy employed mobile blitzkrieg tactics. From Ban Me Thuot in early March until late in April 1975 it was one victory after another for PAVN until on 30 April a tank crashed down the gate of Independence Palace and the North had won the war.

Reflections

Our story has been an exploration from the point of view of a combatant, a soldier-scholar who needed to know what the war in which he fought and lost soldiers killed and wounded was about—really about. During years of research and reflection on my own participation, and study of many primary and secondary sources, I found that the story had to focus on people and events *within Vietnam* where the war was fought, among the leaders and combatants who fought it, the people North and South who lived it

The history of Vietnam was rooted in its heroes, women and men who were idolized for their tenacious efforts to deliver their homeland from centuries of foreign domination. The Vietnamese wanted independence. And they wanted one country, one Vietnam, not one of three parts or two parts.

Why couldn't the Americans contain Communism by assisting the South Vietnamese? Basically, the North could govern, the South could not. The North had a leader they admired and would follow, the South did not. The Americans fashioned the South Vietnamese armed forces along the same lines as their own, neither of which was organized, equipped, or trained to fight a war against men and women who had learned how to conduct theirs from the ground up across two decades and more. Americans planned and conducted pacification, which should have been a Vietnamese endeavor. As for Vietnamization, the South Vietnamese needed to learn how to plan, launch, and support combat operations all by themselves. But their dependence on American advisors sapped their self-reliance.

Our enemy generally were tough fighters, used to hardship and danger. I marveled at the little men we pulled from holes and tunnels in the jungle. Some of them had been existing there for years. They smelled terrible, like the jungle rot that was their life. Some had had terrifying B-52 strikes hit among them. A few of them chieu-hoi'd, but others fought until captured, often wounded. I was astonished at the bravery of individuals and units. It took guts to attack armored cavalry in a fire support base, but they came at us; and it took guts to stand up in lanes of rubber trees to fire RPGs and AKs at our attacking armored vehicles, but that is what they did. As we were killing and wounding them, they killed and wounded us. When their unit was badly hurt they would retire to a base camp and fill the vacant ranks with recruits, some of whom had just arrived from North Vietnam. They would regroup, retrain, and come back at us on another day in another place.

In my 2005 visit back to Binh Co I discovered that the only thing remaining from our rebuilding of the two houses and the school in 1968 was the tin roof of my adopted family's house. It now was on the new house of Luong, the youngest of the three girls. The termites had loved our American-supplied lumber and had eaten the two houses and school down to the ground. Perhaps that could be taken as a metaphor for the whole American effort were it not for the several cattle I saw behind Luong's house. They turned out to be the offspring a few generations later of the young bull and heifer I had Tom Witter deliver to them in 1969. These livestock and a treadle sewing machine had given the family a decent chance of surviving the hardships of the war.

The French could never have won. It was too late, the world had shifted too much against colonialism, and the enemy was too much strengthened by an inbred idea of independence and unity. General Leclerc said, "You cannot kill an idea with bullets." "Make a deal, at all costs."

We Americans could never have won. Our character, world opinion, and the likelihood of China coming into the war—perhaps resulting in a nuclear World War III—would never have allowed what would have been required: a brutal crushing of North Vietnam by invasion supported by massive area bombing as in World War II, followed by occupation of long duration. General Abrams concluded, "In the whole picture of the war, the battles don't mean much." He was right. Colonel Summers said to his North Vietnamese counterpart, "You know, you never beat us on the battlefield." Colonel Tu replied, "That may be so, but it is also irrelevant." Colonel Tu was right.

The South Vietnamese could never have won. They needed foreign troops to ensure their survival; they were plagued by corruption and favoritism in political and military appointments; they failed to offer their people a cause around which they could rally; and their forces too often victimized the people they were charged with protecting. When I returned to Vietnam and found the four women from Binh Co, one of my questions was whether they had been afraid of the VC? Of the

Americans? Their answer was, "We were not afraid of them. But we were afraid of and didn't like the ARVN." Their response speaks volumes about the South Vietnamese failure to win.

*   *   *

Some have said the war was lost because America left the war and Congress cut appropriations for the South Vietnamese. Others believe the causes went far deeper and have asked how much longer the U.S. should have stayed; what number of names on the Vietnam Wall beyond the 58,307 should we have accepted; how much more than three-quarter trillion dollars should we have spent; how much longer should we have supported a government that could not gain the support of its people; how much longer should we have supported a military which had superior numbers of personnel and equipment but could not defeat its enemy? How long? Years? Decades? How long?

According to authoritative U.S., French, and Free World sources, other losses for the Indochina and Vietnam wars were: French Union forces 89,797 dead and missing; RVNAF 220,000; Free World 35,282; Viet Minh, Viet Cong, and PAVN 1.1 million. How many civilians in North and South Vietnam, and in Cambodia and Laos were killed, wounded, disabled? No reliable figure can be given, but probably two to three million.

Vietnamese had fought foreigners for two thousand years and our enemy was determined to fight for as long as it took. The lengthy mural that Hal Moore had seen in Hanoi showed only a couple inches as America's portion in the history of the Vietnamese struggle for independence. Had America not pulled out, would another inch or two, or a foot or more have brought victory in Vietnam?

To me, and to many Americans, Vietnam was a tragedy beyond comprehension. We wanted the South Vietnamese to survive and prosper. Many South Vietnamese were courageous, giving, loving, industrious people. We had made friends, and we and they had suffered. Bonds are deep, and wounds are painful.

No general—French, American, South Vietnamese—could ever have brought victory. The war in Vietnam was lost before the French Expeditionary Force fired its first round, before the South fielded its first soldier in the National Army of Vietnam, before the first U.S. advisor set foot in country.

An idea—independence and unity—would triumph over bullets.

*   *   *

The "Idea" is Not Forgotten

On 30 April 2015, at the 40-years celebration of the end of the war, marked by parades and speeches, "Prime Minister Nguyen Tan Dung praised 'the great victory in 1975' for ushering in 'an era of independence and reunification . . . '"

(USA Today, 8A, May 1, 2015)

NOTES

Preface:

1 Sharp, *Strategy for Defeat*, 271.

2 General Curtis E. LeMay directed and led hazardous bombing missions over Europe in World War II, became commander of Strategic Air Command (SAC), Vice Chief then Chief of Staff of the Air Force during Indochina and Vietnam War years 1957-65. As a member of Joint Chiefs of Staff, he had direct access to and influence upon Secretary of the Air Force and Secretary of Defense, and sometimes the President. LeMay, an advocate of massive bombing, in 1968 wrote in retirement, "Sharp, swift air blows of maximum strength in 1965 could have ended the war in days." (*America is in Danger*, 306).

Senator Barry M. Goldwater was the 1964 Republican candidate for President opposing Lyndon B. Johnson. His statements on using nuclear weapons and quickly ending the growing war in Vietnam greatly helped the Democrats win a landslide victory. In his 1978 memoir he said, "In Vietnam we fought a twelve-year war which could have been ended in twelve weeks." He stated that during the presidential campaign, on TV he was asked about interdicting the supply routes from Red China. He said he replied, "Defoliation of the forest by low-yield atomic weapons could well be done." (*With No Apologies* pp. 12, 202)

3 Born Philippe François Marie, with title comte de Hauteclocque.

4 Vézinet, 239. see Map 1.

5 Moore and Galloway, *Soldiers Still*, 20.

6 Ibid., 25.

7 Ibid.

Chapter 1:

1 That of 1ˢᵗ Infantry Division to the north and northeast of Saigon. See Map 2.

2 Gardner, 11.

3 Colby, 16. See Map 3.

4 Rusk, 433.

5   Ball, *Past Has Another Pattern*, 364-67.

6   Palmer, Bruce, 24.

7   Rusk, 442.

8   Eric Schmitt, "In Battle to Defang ISIS, U.S. Targets Its Psychology," *New York Times*, December 29, 2014, 1.

Chapter 2:

1   PBS Transcript, "Vietnam: A Television History," 3.29.05.

2   Bain, 88-89.

3   Ferry, 199-201, 210-11, 215-18.

4   "He took the name Nguyen Tat Thanh at age ten, in keeping with Vietnamese custom." (Brocheux, 2).

5   Duiker, *Communist Road to Power*, 14.

6   Bui Tin, *xi*.

7   Lieutenant General Dong Van Khuyen, "The RVNAF," in Sorley, ed., *Vietnam War*, 67.

8   Fall, ed., *Ho Chi Minh on Revolution*, *vii*.

9   Website, Library of Congress.

10   Fall, *The Two Vietnams*, 91.

11   Pike, *History of Vietnamese Communism*, 1.

12   Fall, *The Two Vietnams*, 93-94.

13   Some sources say one or two million died.

14   The "Red Earth" referred not only to the natural color of the soil at his plantation but the blood it soaked up.

15   Tran Tu Binh, 12.

16   Ibid., 19, 21.

17   It was in such country that Viet Cong and North Vietnamese Army (NVA) formations established their base camps.

18   Pribbenow, trans., *History of the Dau Tieng Rubber Workers Movement*, 11, hereafter called *History*. Vietnamese language book, available at Texas Tech U, Vietnam Archives, Haponski Special Collection.

19   Ibid., 31, 32.

20   Ibid., 38.

21   Fall, ed., *Ho Chi Minh on Revolution*, 131.

22   Pribbenow, trans., *History*, 48.

23   D'Alzon, et al., *La Presence*, 25, Annexe 6.

24   Marr, 91.

25   Ibid., 174.

26   Pribbenow, trans., *History*, 49.

27   Currey, 60.

28   Duiker, *Communist Road to Power*, 71.

29   Brocheux, 79-80.

30   Duiker, *Ho Chi Minh*, 268.

31   Shipway, 39.

32   Giap, *Military Art of People's War*, 67-68. Also see *The 30-Year War*, Vol.1, pp. 3-9.

33   Duiker, *Ho Chi Minh*, 283. Also see Brocheux, 86-87, and Patti, 57.

34   Duiker ibid., 287.

35   Fall, *Ho Chi Minh on Revolution*, 138-39.

36   It played a role in the NVA attack on my fire support base in 1969.

37   Currey, 80.

38   Giap, *How We Won the War*, 7.

39   Currey, 80.

40   *The 30-Year War*, Vol.1, p. 9. Also see Currey, 82-83.

41   Pribbenow, email to author.

42   Tran Van Don, 1-2.

43   Bui Diem, 13, 17, 20, 21, 24.

44   Marr, p. 110.

45   Patti, 58.

46   Ibid., 83-84.

47   Currey, 88.

48   Ibid., 91-93.

49   Patti, 129.

50   Marr, 361.

51 Currey, 94-95.

52 A large religious sect with armed forces which had their temple at Tay Ninh.

53 Marr, 481.

54 Ibid., 521.

55 Later Army Minister, Defense Minister, and Prime Minister of France.

56 Marr, 480.

57 Patti, 196-99. The new government at this time was still provisional and would become official on 2 September 1945 when Ho proclaimed it at the ceremony in Hanoi.

58 Ibid., 200.

59 Ibid., 246. There are questions about how extensively Ho had visited the United States. A Marxist American journalist and member of the U.S. Communist Party, Joseph R. Starobin, visited Ho in his jungle headquarters in 1953, and wrote, "His English was very good. . . . Ho spoke of his travels to the Western Hemisphere. Yes, he had visited New York; he remembered Harlem and the Statue of Liberty; and his eyes lighted up as he agreed with me that San Francisco was among the most beautiful cities of the world. Starobin, *Eyewitness in Indo-China*, 110.

60 Vézinet, 233.

61 Dunn, 21.

62 Patti, 250. Some reports are of a flyover of two U.S. aircraft, taken by the crowd as evidence of U.S. support for Ho's new nation: "The dramatic effect was heightened when a couple of American fighters flew low over the celebration, their white-starred insignia visible. The Viet Minh wasted no time declaring that this was proof that the U.S. Government supported the new DRV" (Dunn, 21- 22). Marr, 537 has a similar statement. In a later radio interview Patti said the American fly-over was entirely accidental (Marr, 537, fn 259). That Patti does not mention it in his book seems to imply that he did not want to own any portion of this mistake.

63 Marr, 463-64.

64 Dunn, 134.

65 Ibid., 22.

66 Ibid., 152.

67 McAlister, 50.

68 Dunn, 202-203 (emphasis by author). Several historians point to a later date, 19 December 1946, in Hanoi as the start of the war when the Viet Minh attacked in force. The many combatants on both sides who died from September 1945 forward to that date would not have agreed.

69 Dutrone, 52. All translations from French by author unless otherwise specified.

70 *The 30-Year War*, Vol. 1, 1945-1975, vii-viii, 33.

Chapter 3:

1   Vézinet, 288.

2   Ibid., 238-39. "Classic type" refers to Gallieni or Lyautey's "oil spot" technique of combating insurrection.

3   Bradley, 392.

4   Vézinet, 239.

5   Or "Pacha," a Turkish title meaning captain or skipper.

6   Bernier, 7.

7   Ibid., 15-22.

8   Ibid., 32.

9   Ibid., 33.

10 Ibid., 36.

11 Ibid., 40.

12 *Historia*, Vol. 2, p. 164.

13 Bernier, 50.

14 Salan, *Memoires*, Vol. 1, p. 185.

15 Massu, *Sept Ans*, 224.

16 French higher headquarters commonly named task forces after their commander, just as did the Americans. In Vietnam, 1st Division reports commonly referred to my unit as Task Force Haponski. Massu, a legendary tough commander, went on to become a general who commanded the French paratroops dropped into Suez in 1956 and who later used his troops to overthrow the French government in Algeria and bring de Gaulle back into power.

17 Ibid., 238.

18 *Coups de Massu*, December 1945, 14.

19 To my knowledge, this tactic was not much used during the American war in South Vietnam. It was highly labor intensive and counterproductive in the sense that the local people could be resentful, having better things to do than to be digging trenches which ultimately would be filled back in by a bulldozer or easily spanned by a mobile bridge. During the earliest stage of the French war, the Viet Minh did not yet possess enough land mines as an alternative to the intensive digging, but in time they developed this capability.

20 Massu, *Sept Ans*, 244-45.

21 Leroy, 28.

22 Ibid., 41.

23 Ibid., 85-87.

24 Guiberteau, 43-44.

25 Bernier, 66-68, 70.

26 Ibid., 73.

27 Leroy, 89.

28 Guiberteau, pp. 58, 71. (In 1968 Colonel George S. Patton commanded 11th Armored Cavalry Regiment when I was his senior staff officer. He told of his first tour in Vietnam, in 1962. He was inspecting an H-13 helicopter unit and was shown two helicopters down for repair. Each had an arrow sticking into the bubble, shot by some irate Montagnard tribesmen.(Sobel, Brian M. *The Fighting Pattons*. Westport, CT: Praeger, 1997, 106.)

29 Ibid., 64.

30 Bernier, 69.

31 Before Massu died in 2002 he publicly apologized for having tortured prisoners in Indochina and Algeria, just as the opposing forces had tortured his men.

32 Suzanne (Torres) Massu, *Un Commandant Pas Comme Les Autres*, 74. She later married Jacques Massu.

33 Vézinet, 240-41.

34 Salan, *Memoires*, Vol. 1, p. 175.

35 *Le General Leclerc: Vu par ses compagnons de combat*, 295-96.

36 Massu, *Sept Ans*, 252-53.

37 Ibid., 248-49.

38 Pribbenow, trans., *History*, 10

39   *The 30-Year War*, Vol. 1, p. 61.

40   Pike, *History of Vietnamese Communism*, 77.

41   Fall, *Two Viet-Nams*, 107.

42   Giap, *Banner of People's War*, 12.

Chapter 4:

1   *The 30-Year War*, Vol.1, 42-43.

2   Ibid., 45.

3   *Journal Officiel le 22 août 1945.*

4   http://www.itnsource.com/shotlist//BHC_FoxMovietone/
     1946/06/17/X17064601

5   Tonnesson, 36.

6   The French had leased coastal territory in South China in 1898 and had conces-
     sions in Shanghai and other cities.

7   Vézinet, 247.

8   Ibid., 252.

9   Tonnesson, 39-40.

10   Vézinet, 265.

11   Lacoutre, *Ho Chi Minh*, 119.

12   In an interview of Salan in 1982 by Will Brownell, "[Salan] did concede that
     great crimes had been done against [Giap]. The torture was conceded 'tho Salan
     tried to shirk it a bit by noting that it was carried out by Vietnamese auxiliaries
     and not done by Frenchmen....[General Massu] conceded the same to me in an
     interview.'" (Currey, 25, 45).

13   Salan, *Memoires*, Vol. 1, p. 367.

14   Ibid., 380.

15   *The 30-Year War*, Vol.1, p. 380.

16   Vézinet, 272.

17   Tonnesson, 74.

18   Zhai, 11.

19   Ibid., 12.

20   Ibid., 13.

Chapter 5:

1   Currey, 125-27.

2   Bui Diem, 46.

3   Currey, 129.

4   Shipway, 235.

5   Schoenbrun, 232-35.

6   Fall, ed., *Ho Chi Minh on Revolution*, 196

7   *The 30-Year War*, Vol.1, 82.

8   Truong Nhu Tang, 11-16.

9   Leroy, 106, 115.

10 Shipway, 235.

11 Ibid., 251.

12 *Ibid.*, 251-52.

13 *The 30-Year War*, Vol.1, p. 91.

14 Lacoutre, *Ho Chi Minh*, 174-75.

15 *The 30-Year War*, Vol.1, p. 91.

16 Giap, *Fighting Under Siege*, 14.

17 Fonde, 311-12.

18 *The 30-Year War*, Vol.1, p. 100.

19 Giap, *Fighting Under Siege*, 12.

20 Vézinet, 278.

21 Ibid., 277-83.

22 Giap, *Fighting Under Siege*, 34-35.

23 Vézinet, pp. 285-86. Also, *Pentagon Papers*, Gravel Edition, Vol. 1, p. 23.

24 *Pentagon Papers*, Gravel Edition, Vol. 1, p. 24.

25 Lacoutre, *Ho Chi Minh*, 179.

26 Vézinet, 286-90, and *20 Siecle* I, 41.

27 Or, "Negotiate, negotiate, negotiate, at any price." Fonde, 344.

28 *20 Siecle*, I, 41.

29 Kalb, 56.

30 *Unités Combattantes Indochine* – Official Publication of Ministry of War listing all French and French Union combatant units, headquarters locations, and periods

of service in Indochina. Available at Texas Tech U Vietnam Archives, Haponski Special Collection.

31 Giap, *Fighting Under Siege*, 62-63.

32 Ibid., 82.

33 Ibid., 81.

34 Ibid.

35 *The 30-Year War*, Vol.1, p. 117.

36 Leroy, 126.

37 Chaumont-Guitry, 32, 35-36.

38 Ibid., 56.

39 Ibid., 68-69.

40 Ibid., 75, 78-79.

41 Ibid., 154. This did not change during the American war.

42 Giap, *Fighting Under Siege*, 62-63.

43 *20 Siecle* I, 46.

44 *The 30-Year War*, Vol. 1, p. 128, says the old man was shot dead, but Giap's memoirs do not say this.

45 *Historia* Vol. 1, p. 77.

46 *The 30-year War* Vol. 1, p. 134.

47 Giap, *Fighting Under Siege*, 143.

48 *Historia*, Vol. 1, pp. 1, 78.

49 *The 30-Year War* Vol. 1, p. 135.

50 Giap, *Fighting Under Siege*, 170.

51 Ibid., 153.

52 Ibid., 154-155.

53 General Don, page 39, claims that he and an associate were the ones who proposed that flag. This seems highly unlikely since he was only a captain at the time.

54 Hammer, 221-24.

55 Bui Tin, 10-11.

56 Giap, *Fighting Under Siege*, 161.

57 Leroy, 141.

58 Ibid., 146.

59 Nguyen Thi Dinh, 12-13.

60 Delaunay's experiences sound familiar to 1-4 Cav troopers, but we would add the enemy's RPGs as deadly weapons not possessed by Delaunay's enemy, although they had some bazookas.

61 Napalm bombs were first used in Vietnam in 1950.

62 Emails to author.

63 Bui Diem, 60.

64 Ibid., 65, 68.

65 Ibid., 70.

66 *20 Siecle* I, 66,

67 Ibid., 72-73.

68 Giap, *Military Art of People's War*, 88.

Chapter 6:

1   Zhai, 16-18.

2   *Pentagon Papers*, Gravel ed., Vol 1, p. 179.

3   Kalb, 62.

4   Fall, ed., *Ho Chi Minh on Revolution*, 183.

5   Zhai, 24.

6   *Historia* Vol. 1, p. 167.

7   *20th Siecle* I, 77.

8   *The 30-Year War*, Vol. I, 195, and *Historia* Vol. 1, p. 167.

9   *Historia*, ibid., and 20 *Siecle* I, 79.

10 *Historia* Vol. 1, p. 167.

11 Fall, *Two Viet-Nams*, 115.

12 Bui Tin, 14-15.

13 Pribbenow, trans., *Military Encyclopedia of Vietnam*, 102-103.

14 Pribbenow, trans., *The Resistance War*, 181.

15 *Pentagon Papers*, Gravel ed., Vol 1, p. 36.

16 *20 Siecle* I, 81.

17 Fall, *Two Viet-Nams*, 115.

18 Gras, 368, and 20 Siecle I, 80.

19 Gras, ibid.

20   *Historia* Vol. I, 168-173, and *20 Siecle* I, 79-89.

21   Giap, *The Road to Dien Bien Phu*, 167.

22   Bergot, *Indochine 1951*, 141.

23   Giap, *The Road to Dien Bien Phu*, 176.

24   *Historia* Vol. 1, p. 177.

25   Gras, 367.

26   Ibid.

27   Pike, *History of Vietnamese Communism*, 83-85.

28   A Dinassaut was a relatively large riverine force usually of about 10-12 boats mounting a mixture of machine guns, mortars, or howitzers, and carrying infantry. Sometimes, as in this case, it was larger with a cruiser and LSTs in support.

29   Bergot, *Indochine 1951*, 23.

30   Fall, *Two Viet-Nams*, 117.

31   Bergot, *Indochine 1951*, 178

32   Ibid., 141.

33   Simonin, 15, 17. Tirailleurs—light infantry from French colonies.

34   Ibid., 26.

35   Ibid., 114.

36   Ainley, *In Order to Die*, 211.

37   Ibid., 29-30.

38   Ibid., 42-43.

39   Ibid., 46.

40   Ibid., 146.

41   Ibid., 221-22.

42   Simon, 30.

43   André. 48.

44   United States Department of State / "Foreign Relations of the United States, 1952-1954. Indochina" (in two parts); (1952-1954, Part 1, p. 6.

45   Bergot, *Indochine 1951*, 189.

46   United States Department of State / Foreign relations of the United States, 1952-1954. Indochina (in two parts), (1952-1954, Part 1, p. 23.

47   State Department policy study report, 11 February 1952.

48   Cable 12 February 1952, Ambassador to France David K. E. Bruce to Department of State.

49 U.S. National Intelligence Estimate, 3 March 1952. Use Internet search term: 3 March 1952. Secret. NIE 35/1.

50 Tran Van Don, 6.

51 Bui Tin, 15.

52 Ibid., 40.

53 Currey, 81.

54 Lanning and Cragg, 88-89.

55 Fall, *Ho Chi Minh on Revolution*, 228.

56 Giap, The Road to Dien Bien Phu, 356.

57 Ibid., 385.

58 Haponski, "Toward Dien Bien Phu: The Historical Context," in *The Angel of Dien Bien Phu*, 9.

59 Salan, Vol. 1, 31-34.

60 Pribbenow, trans., "The Glorious History . . . " 107-109.

Chapter 7:

1   De Galard, 17.

2   Ibid., 22-29.

3   Ibid., 30.

4   Ibid.

5   Haponski, *The Angel of Dien Bien Phu*, 10.

6   Windrow, *Last Valley*, 205-206.

7   Haponski, *The Angel of Dien Bien Phu*, 10.

8   Windrow, *Last Valley*, 217.

9   Haponski, *The Angel of Dien Bien Phu*, 11.

10 Ibid.

11 Windrow, *Last Valley*, 46.

12 Lawrence and Logevall, eds., 218.

13 Bigeard, *Pour une parcelle*, 134.

14 Ibid., 135.

15 Windrow, *Last Valley*, 206.

16 Ibid., 242.

17 Ibid., 281.

18 Haponski, *The Angel of Dien Bien Phu*, Appendices – and D, 149-52, 155-56.

19 De Galard, 50.

20 Americans probably were more parochially focused on the McCarthy anti-communism hearings, then underway.

21 Two other French women were briefly at DBP before the fighting got intense. Brigitte Friang, a magazine news reporter, member of the Resistance and concentration camp survivor, jumped in on 22 November, the 3rd day, with 5th BPVN. She was a qualified military parachutist and made six combat jumps in Indochina. At DBP she went out with troops on reconnaissance in force missions and then made another jump to join a linkup force from Laos. Colonel de Castries' secretary was evacuated before the 13 March assault, and Cogny declared there would be no other French women allowed to stay overnight. Two mobile field brothels of Algerian and Vietnamese women were there, and some performed heroically in helping care for the wounded. Geneviève, trapped, was the lone French woman after the enemy struck.

22 Then when she got back to Paris she received an offer for a movie that would star Leslie Caron as Geneviève. She ignored it.

23 Giap, *Dien Bien Phu*, 128-130.

24 Fall, *Hell*, 366.

25 Windrow, *Last Valley*, 497. As one who earned my paratrooper wings during peacetime training, including night and equipment drops, I find the prospect of anyone making his first jump into a desperate combat situation at night to be terrifying, and yet these men volunteered to do just that.

26 Fall, *Hell*, 373.

27 De Galard, 83.

28 Ibid., 84.

29 Bigeard, *Pour une parcelle*, 188.

30 De Galard, 93.

31 Giap, *Dien Bien Phu*, 134.

32 Windrow, *Last Valley*, 624.

33 Fall, *Two Viet-Nams*, 116, 122. (Translation of Navarre by Fall).

Chapter 8:

1   Lam Quang Thi, 72.

2   Ibid., 81-82.

3   Fall, ed., *Ho Chi Minh on Revolution*, 245.

4   Duiker, *Ho Chi Minh*, 456-57.

5   Ibid, 459.

6   Geneva Accords. For text see https://www.mtholyoke.edu/acad/intrel/genevacc. htm. For Final Declarations, see http://vietnam.vassar.edu/overview/doc2.html. For Unilateral U.S. Declaration, see Sagar, *Major Political Events in Indo-China 1945 – 1990*, p. 190.

7   Pike, *History of Communism*, 115 and 163n.1.

8   Bui Tin, 66.

9   U.S. Department of State Bulletin, November 15, 1954, pp. 736-37.

10   CD, BACM Research, *Pentagon Papers: The Complete Report, Unredacted*, IV.A.3.ix (16 Dec 54).

11   Ibid., IV. A. 3.ix (19 Dec 54).

12   Jacobs, 22-23.

13   Ibid., 32.

14   Ibid., 71-72.

15   Ibid., 86-89.

16   Fall, *Two Viet-Nams*, 319.

17   Lam Quang Thi, 88.

18   Lien-Hang T. Nguyen, 45.

19   Nguyen Thi Dinh, 13.

20   Ibid., 49.

21   Ibid., 49-50.

22   Ibid., 62-63.

23   Ibid., 66-67.

24   In an email to the author Merle Pribbenow said, "I have never seen it used as a unit of area, but the word 'cong,' which means 'to work' or 'to labor,' is also used as a unit of work, meaning the amount of work that one person can do in one day. In this case, it probably means the amount of land that one person can till in one day,

meaning that they gave her enough land that it would take one person three days to till, plant, harvest, etc."

25 Nguyen Thi Dinh, 84-85.

26 Ibid., 87. This was the infamous Decree 10/19 which restored the guillotine as executioner's tool.

27 Pribbenow found in *History of the COSVN Military Command (1961 – 1976)* that Nguyen Thi Dinh was a deputy commander of Military Command Headquarters, COSVN (Central Office South Vietnam) who was assigned responsibility for militia operations, that is, guerrilla warfare. Pribbenow said in an email to the author, "As a major general, she was not, however, in the military actions chain, but probably dealt with politics and propaganda."

28 Nguyen Thi Dinh, 100.

29 Brigadier General Tran Dinh Tho, "Pacification," in Sorley, ed., *Vietnam War*, 235.

30 Truong Nhu Tang, 50.

31 Ibid., 77-78.

32 Ibid., 100.

33 Lien-Hang T. Nguyen, 5.

34 Ibid., 49.

35 Pribbenow, trans., *Ministry of Interior, General Department 1, Political Security Department III*: "Anti-Reactionary Forces: Chronology of Events (1954-1975)," 131, 133-35.

36 Bui Tin, 54-55.

37 Corn, 162.

38 There is some question about the order of who was the first or second killed. See discussion on the Vietnam Wall on internet.

39 Brigadier General Tran Dinh Tho, "Pacification," in Sorley, ed., *Vietnam War*, 222.

40 Palmer, Dave, 37-38.

41 Pribbenow, trans., *Victory in Vietnam*, 153.

42 General Cao Van Vien, "Leadership," in Sorley, ed., *Vietnam War*, 275.

43 Sorensen, 658-59.

44 Lawrence, 77.

45 Davidson, 371.

46 To my knowledge, the full list was never revealed.

47 Davidson, 369-377.

48 Sorley, *Honorable Warrior*, 322 n12. As taken from Tom Johnson, "Notes of President's Meeting with General Wheeler, JCS and General Creighton Abrams, March 26, 1968, Family Dining Room," LBJ Library.

49 Gavin, *Crisis Now*, 128.

50 Sorley, *A Better War*, 134. Illness confirmed by William G. Seiber, National Archives staff, in phone call to author, 17 August 2012. See Sorley, *Thunderbolt*, 178-95 for a comprehensive discussion of the selection process and results.

51 Westmoreland, *A Soldier Reports*, 42.

52 Ibid., 63.

53 Davidson, 314.

54 Taylor, Maxwell, 330-31.

55 Bui Tin, 41, 42.

56 Pribbenow, trans., *Victory in Vietnam*, 124-26.

57 Pribbenow email to author: "Tri-Thien Front (also called the B4 Front) originally consisted of the two northern provinces of South Vietnam, Quang Tri and Thua Thien."

58 Moore, *Soldiers Still*, 46.

59 Lien-Hang T. Nguyen, 28.

60 PAVN official histories make no distinction of "VC" divisions. All are listed as PAVN divisions. In fact, the original "VC" divisions became more and more "PAVN" as NVA individual soldiers and units took positions within them either to strengthen them or replace casualties.

Chapter 9:

1   Westmoreland, *A Soldier Reports*, 35.

2   Palmer, Dave, 55.

3   Zaffiri, 106.

4   Westmoreland, *A Soldier Reports*, 38.

5   Ibid., 68.

6   Ibid., 75.

7   Ibid., 75-76.

8   For a limited time and scope, cross-border operations were later authorized.

9   Attended by President Johnson's top advisors—Secretary of State Dean Rusk, Secretary of Defense Robert McNamara, (then) Ambassador to Vietnam Henry Cabot Lodge, General Maxwell Taylor, CIA Director John McCone, and others.

10   Westmoreland, *A Soldier Reports*, 82.

11   Ibid., 83.

12   CD, BACM Research, *Pentagon Papers: The Complete Report, Unredacted*, IV C. 8. iii.

13   Ibid., IV C. 8. ii.

14   McNamara, *xi*.

15   Taylor, Telford, 189.

16   Taylor, Jay, 31.

17   http://www.archives.gov/research/military/vietnam-war/casualty-statistics.html. Other official sources somewhat differ.

18   Subsequently, this report was called into question and later deemed false.

19   http://www.history.com/this-day-in-history/us-marines-land-at-da-nang

20   McNamara, 179.

21   Ibid., 181.

22   Bui Diem, 338.

23   Zhia, 169-70.

24   Lien-Hang T. Nguyen, 76.

25   Pribbenow, trans., *Victory in Vietnam*, 182.

26   Westmoreland, 83.

27   Palmer, Bruce, 45-46.

28   McNamara, 237, 239.

29   Palmer, Dave, 117.

30   Within hours of my July 1968 arrival in Vietnam I encountered War Zone D where our 11th Armored Cavalry units were on search and destroy missions in the deep jungle..

31   Moore, *We Were Soldiers*, 10. "Jumpin' Joe" Gavin – Chief of Army Research and Development.

32   Ibid., 26-27.

33   Ibid., 33, 36-37.

34   Ibid., 49-51.

35   Ibid., 55.

36   Ibid., 57, 60.

37   Ibid., 51.

38   Ibid., 62.

39   Ibid., 84.

40   Ibid., 192-93, 199, 200.

41   Gwin, 129-30.

42   Ibid., 155.

43   Ibid., 165.

44   Westmoreland, *A Soldier Reports*, 157.

45   Gwin, 165-66.

46   Sorley, *Westmoreland*, 262.

47   Moore, *We Were Soldiers*, 339.

48   Sorley, *Westmoreland*, 95.

49   Palmer, Bruce, 212n22.

50   Ibid., 43.

51   Westmoreland, *A Soldier Reports*, 130.

52   Ibid., 135.

53   Ibid., 144-45. Emphasis by author.

54   Palmer, Dave, 64.

55   Westmoreland, *A Soldier Reports*, 145-46.

56   Ibid., 145.

57   Murphy, 7.

58   *Krulak, 180, 186.*

59   *Ibid.*, 194.

60   Shulimson, 13.

61   Caputo, *xix, xviii-xix, xix-xx.*

62   Ibid., 229.

63   Ibid., 305-06.

64   Ibid., 336.

65 Walt, 112, 114.

66 Caputo, 333.

67 Ibid., 334.

68 General Cao Van Vien, "Leadership," in Sorley, ed., *Vietnam War*, 293-94.

69 Walt, 105-106.

70 Goodson, *viii*. Some teams were larger and more diverse than Goodson's.

71 Ibid., 17.

72 West, 325-28.

73 Westmoreland, *A Soldier Reports*, 194.

74 Brigadier General Tran Dinh Tho, "Pacification," in Sorley, ed., *Vietnam War*, 262.

75 Nolan, 43-44, 53.

76 Ibid., 57.

77 Dragoons: originally mounted infantry but the term evolved into a common name for cavalry. In Vietnam my generic call sign was Dragoon 6, the squadron commander.

78 Nolan, 62.

79 Ibid., 73.

80 Ibid., 93.

Chapter 10:

1 Rogers, 15.

2 Ibid., *v*.

3 Ibid., 19.

4 Ibid., 19-24.

5 Ibid., 30, 34-35, 37.

6 Ibid., 63-64.

7 Ibid., 38, 39.

8 Ibid., 58-59.

9 Ibid., 46.

10 Ibid., 74.

11 Ibid., 50-54.

12 Ibid., 74-78, 158.

13 Ibid., 83, 84.

14 Palmer, Bruce, 56.

15 Pribbenow, trans., "The Secret Intelligence General."

16 Dinh Thi Van, 3.

17 Ibid., 43-44.

18 Ibid., *123*.

19 Ibid., 153-54.

20 Ibid., 207, 211.

21 Ibid., 224.

22 Ibid., 227-36.

23 Pribbenow, trans., *The Ten-Thousand Day Journey*, 200 ff.

24 Ibid, 202-44.

25 Rogers, 103-109, 113-114.

26 In addition to its organic Regiments 1, 2, and 3, the 16th Regiment was attached to 9th Division.

27 Ibid., 121.

28 Ibid., 127.

29 Ibid., 149, 151.

30 Sharp/Westmoreland, *Report on the War*, 137.

31 Pribbenow, trans., *Victory in Vietnam*, 197-98.

32 Sharp/Westmoreland, *Report on the War*, 137.

33 Rogers, 155-159.

34 Corn, 134, 135.

35 Ibid., 171-172.

36 Shultz, 49.

37 Ibid., 8.

38 Ibid., 83.

39 Ibid., 90, 348.

40 Lien Hang T. Nguyen, 90-91.

41 Ibid., 102.

42 Giap, *Banner of People's War*, 77.

43   Haig, 176.

44   Ibid., 178-79.

45   Palmer, Bruce, 58.

46   Westmoreland, *A Soldier Reports*, 315.

47   Pribbenow, trans., *Victory in Vietnam*, 224.

48   Sorley, ed. *Vietnam Chronicles*, 66.

49   Westmoreland, *A Soldier Reports*, 335.

Chapter 11:

1   Sorley, *A Better War*, 17.

2   Palmer, Bruce, 63.

3   Sorley, *A Better War*, 18.

4   Ibid., 17.

5   Krepinevich, 254.

6   Sorley, ed., *Vietnam Chronicles*, photo caption.

7   The complete story is in John (Doc) Bahnsen's book, *American Warrior*, with input from all troopers involved, 184-192.

8   Davidson, 409.

9   Ibid., 430.

10   Hunt, 88.

11   Colby, 208.

12   Hunt, 150.

13   Davidson, 614.

14   Ibid., 571-72.

15   Hunt, 87.

16   11 ACR Quarterly Pacification Report, available NARA.

17   Hunt, 61.

18   Wheeler, 500.

19   Hunt, 158.

20   Ibid., 186.

Chapter 12:

1 Not his real name, disguised to protect him if he is still alive. Merle Pribbenow told me that after our enemy regained control over prisoners of war they often treated them severely under the presumption they had revealed information.

2 Tran Van Tra, 76.

3 Hunt, 178.

4 Ibid., 202.

5 OH-6A Light Observation Helicopter (LOH or "Loach").

6 Pribbenow, trans., *7th Division: A Record*, 90.

7 Because of the need for secrecy we could not do a ground reconnaissance. Our hasty look, necessarily from a distance in the air in order not to alert the enemy, indicted we could span the creek with the AVLB.

8 Moore, *We Were Soldiers*, 269.

9 8th Battalion of 209th Regiment and 5th Battalion of 165th Regiment. The 6th /65th Battalion which had attacked us in Doc was now in a jungle base camp to the west, recuperating, receiving replacements, and beginning to train for new missions.

10 Ewell, *Vietnam Studies: Sharpening the Combat Edge*.

11 Hunt, 61, 189.

12 Viet Minh had staged bigger, longer lasting ambushes in French times.

13 Only the second recorded incident of enemy radar use at this time in the division area.

14 Pribbenow, trans., *7th Division: A Record*, 89.

Chapter 13:

1 Pribbenow, trans., *Victory in Vietnam*, 246 .

2 Ibid., 243.

3 Ibid., 246-50.

4 Westmoreland, *A Soldier Reports*, 388.

5 As part of IIFFV's thrust, 11th Armored Cavalry dashed into the rubber plantation at Snoul and found a massive cache of munitions. In doing so, LTC Grail Brookshires' 2nd Squadron also rescued General Delaunay's cousin, the director of the plantation, just as he was about to be taken away as a prisoner by the enemy.

6   Brigadier General Tran Dinh Tho, "The Cambodian Incursion," in Sorley, ed., *Vietnam War*, 532, 545.

7   Ibid., 548.

8   Nixon, *No More Vietnams*, 149.

9   Palmer, Bruce, 102-103.

10   Truong Nhu Tang, 147.

11   Ibid., 156, 158.

12   Ibid., 164, 166.

13   Ibid., 172 .

14   Ibid., 160.

15   Colby, 277-78.

16   Ibid., 288.

17   Davidson, 635.

18   Colby, 295, 298, 301.

19   John Paul Vann, deputy for CORDS in III Corps zone, then IV Corps, then senior American advisor II Corps, killed in a helicopter crash, 1972.

20   Colby, 304, 311.

21   Palmer, Bruce, 112-13.

22   Major General Nguyen Duy Hinh, "Lam Son 719," in Sorley, ed., *Vietnam War*, 592, 595.

23   Ibid., 594.

24   http://ehistory.osu.edu/vietnam/essays/theend/0023.cfm, p. 23.

25   As was common, North Vietnamese campaigns were named after Vietnam heroes, in this case an 18th century emperor, Nguyen Hue, whose conquests resulted in an independent and unified Vietnam until the French colonization of the 19th century.

26   Pribbenow, trans., *Victory in Vietnam*, 283.

27   The GVN Corps Tactical Zones had been re-designated in 1970 as Military Regions 1, 2, 3, 4, north to south, but the old terminology sometimes was still used.

28   Gateway: A North Vietnamese term for critical points around Saigon which ARVN and Americans controlled, blocking a move on Saigon. Task Force QuarterCav first controlled the Di An/Lai Thieu gateway on Route 13, then the Lai Khe/Ben Cat gateway farther north on Route 13.

29   Lieutenant General Ngo Quang Truong, "The Easter Offensive of 1972," in Sorley, ed., *Vietnam War*, 654.

30   Willbanks, 65-66.

31   Sorley, ed., *Vietnam Chronicles*, 869.

32   Pribbenow, trans., "*9th Division*," 238.

33   Lieutenant General Ngo Quang Truong, "The Easter Offensive of 1972," in Sorley, ed., *Vietnam War*, 660.

34   Truong Nhu Tang, 207.

35   Sorley, ed., *Vietnam Chronicles*, 872.

36   Marolda, 326-45.

37   Sorley, ed., *Vietnam Chronicles*, 872.

38   Lieutenant General Ngo Quang Truong, "The Easter Offensive of 1972," in Sorley, ed., *Vietnam War*, 663-64.

39   Nixon, *No More Vietnams*, 113.

40   Brigadier General Tran Dinh Tho, "Pacification." in Sorley, ed., *Vietnam War*, 246.

41   Nixon, *Memoirs*, 734.

42   Nixon, *No More Vietnams*, 120, 124.

Chapter 14:

1   Bui Tin, 57.

2   Ibid., 61.

3   Hosmer, et al., 89.

4   Ibid., 56-57.

5   Predictably there were some hostile incidents, and a few ICCS members were killed or wounded.

6   Tran Van Tra, *History of the Bulwark B-2 Theatre*, 7-9.

7   Ibid., 9, 12-14.

8   Instead of the Americanized "Nhut" the spelling used by many Vietnamese is "Nhat."

9   Ibid., 15, 17.

10   Giap, *General Headquarters*, 50.

11   Tran Van Tra, *History of the Bulwark B-2 Theatre*, 11.

12 Ibid., 25.

13 Tran Van Don, 229.

14 Pribbenow, trans., *Victory in Vietnam*, 346.

15 Tran Van Tra, *History of the Bulwark B-2 Theatre*, 33.

16 Pribbenow, trans., *Victory in Vietnam*, 336.

17 Ibid., 342-44.

18 Ibid., 339, 346-47.

19 Ibid., 349.

20 Zhai, 203.

21 Pribbenow, trans., *Victory in Vietnam*, 350-53.

22 Zhai, 207.

23 Giap, *General Headquarters*, 1, 13.

24 Ibid., 35.

25 Ibid., 44n1.

26 Bui Tin, 85.

27 Pribbenow, trans., *Victory in Vietnam*, 347.

28 Ibid., 347-50.

29 Truong Nhu Tang, 232.

30 Giap, *General Headquarters*, 46.

31 General Cao Van Vien, "Leadership," in Sorley, ed., *Vietnam War*, 298-99.

32 Ibid., 826.

33 Tran Van Don, 232.

34 Ibid., 235-37.

35 Ibid., 237.

36   Giap, *General Headquarters*, 50.

37 Tran Van Don, 230.

38 Giap, *General Headquarters*, 106-07.

39 Ibid., pp. 117-118.

40 Pribbenow, trans., *Victory in Vietnam*, 359.

Chapter 15:

1 Giap, *General Headquarters*, 56.

2 Pribbenow, trans., *Victory in Vietnam*, 362-63.

3   Van Tien Dung, 34.

4   Ibid., 44, 48-49.

5   Ibid., 62-63, 83.

6   Pribbenow, trans., (email to author): *Comrade Le Duan's Comments in a Politburo Meeting Held 24 March 1975, After our Victory at Ban Me Thuot*, 213.

7   General Cao Van Vien and Lieutenant General Dong Van Khuyen, "Reflections on the War," in Sorley, ed., *Vietnam War*, 873.

8   Van Tien Dung, 87.

9   Lam Quang Thi, *The Twenty-five Year Century*, 357.

10 Van Tien Dung, 87.

11 Lam Quang Thi, *The Twenty-five Year Century*, 360, 361.

12 Ibid., 377.

13 Van Tien Dung, 142.

14 Ibid., 158.

15 Lam Quang Thi, *The Twenty-five Year Century*, 379.

16 General Cao Van Vien, "Leadership," in Sorley, ed., *Vietnam War*, 316.

17 Pribbenow, trans., *Victory in Vietnam*, 406.

18 *The 7th Division: A Record*, p. 290, as quoted in George J. Veith and Merle L. Pribbenow II, "'Fighting is an Art': The Army of the Republic of Vietnam's Defense of Xuan Loc, 9-21 April 1975," *The Journal of Military History*, Vol. 68, No. 1. (Jan., 2004), 163-213.

19 Nicolas C. Profitt, "Escape from Xuan Loc," *Newsweek*, 18 April 1975, p. 22, as quoted in Veith and Pribbenow, 208.

20 They flew on to London where they lived quietly for a number of years until they moved to Boston where he died in 2001.

21 Tran Van Don, 249-50.

22 Van Tien Dung, 239-240.

23 Giap, *General Headquarters*, 242.

24 Van Tien Dung, 174.

25 Nguyen Minh Chau, "Happy and Sad Memories of a Time of War" [Ky Niem Vui Buon Trong Thoi Chinh Chien], *KBC Hai Ngoai*, Issue 18, June 2003, pp. 59-66, translated by Merle L. Pribbenow, Jr..

26 Pribbenow, trans., *Victory in Vietnam*, 420-421.

27 Tran Van Tra, 199-200.

28 Van Tien Dung, 247.

29 Tran Van Tra, 200.

30 Sorley, ed., *Vietnam Chronicles*, 59.

BIBLIOGRAPHY

Indochina holdings are available at Texas Tech University,
Vietnam Archives, Texas Tech Item Number: 25620000000,
Finding Aid for the William Haponski Collection.

*   *   *

Acheson, Dean. *Present at the Creation: My Years in the State Department.* New York: Norton, 1969.

Ainley, Henry (pseudonym). *In Order to Die.* London: Burke, 1955.

Allen, George W. *None So Blind: A Personal Account of the Intelligence Failure in Vietnam.* Chicago, IL: Dee, 2001.

Amicale des Planteurs d'Hévéas. *Planteurs d'Hévéas en Indochine 1939-1954.* Brou, France: LG Comp, 1996.

----- . *Les Planteurs d'Hévéas en Indochine de 1950 a 1975: Contre vents et marées, souvenirs, récits et témoignages.* Panazol, France: La Vauzelle, 2006.

André, Valérie. *Ici, Ventilateur!* Paris: Calmann-Levy, 1954.

Bahnsen, John C. ("Doc"). *American Warrior: A Combat Memoir of Vietnam.* New York: Citadel Press, 2007.

Bain, Chester A. *Vietnam: The Roots of Chaos.* Englewood Cliffs, NJ: Prentice-Hall, 1967.

Ball, George W. *The Past Has Another Pattern, Memoirs.* New York: Norton, 1982

----- . *Vietnam and the Rethinking of Containment.* Chapel Hill, NC: University of North Carolina Press, 1991.

Bass, Thomas A. *The Spy Who Loved Us: The Vietnam War and Pham Xuan An's Dangerous Game.* New York: Public Affairs, 2009.

Bergot, Erwin. *Bataillon de Corée: Les volontaires français 1950 – 1953.* Paris: France Loisirs, 1983.

----- . *Commandos de Choc en Indochine: Les Héros oubliés.* Paris: Bernard Grasset, 1975.

----- . *Gendarmes au Combat: Indochine 1945 – 1955*. Paris: Presses de la Cité, 1985.

----- . *Indochine 1951: Une Année de victoires*. Paris: Presses de la Cité, 1987.

Bernier, Jean-Pierre. *Le Commando des Tigres: Les Paras du Commando Ponchardier, Indochine 1945-1946*. Paris: Jacques Grancher Éditeur,1995.

Bigeard, Marcel. *Lettres d'Indochine*. Paris: Editions 1, 1998.

----- . *Pour une parcelle de Gloire*. Paris: Plon, 1975.

Bodard, Lucien. *The Quicksand War: Prelude to Vietnam*. Boston, MA: Little Brown, 1967.

Bradley, Omar N. *A Soldier's Story*. New York: Henry Holt, 1951.

Brocheux, Pierre. *Ho Chi Minh, A Biography*. Cambridge: Cambridge University Press, 2007.

Bui Diem. *In the Jaws of History*. Bloomington, IN: Indiana University Press, 1987.

Bui Tin. *Following Ho Chi Minh: The Memoirs of a North Vietnamese Colonel*. Honolulu: University of Hawaii Press, 1995.

Caputo, Philip. *A Rumor of War*. New York: Holt, 1977.

Chaumont-Guitry, Guy de. *Lettres d'Indochine*. Paris: Alsatia, 1951.

Chen Jian. *Mao's China & the Cold War*. Chapel Hill: University of North Carolina Press, 2001.

Colby, William. *Lost Victory: A Firsthand Account of America's Sixteen Year Involvement in Vietnam*. Chicago, IL: Contemporary, 1989.

Coleman, J. D. *From America's Chokehold on the NVA Lifelines to the Sacking of the Cambodian Sanctuaries*. New York: St. Martin's Press, 1991.

Cook, John L. *The Advisor: The Phoenix Program in Vietnam*. Atglen, PA: Schiffer Military History, 1997.

Cooper, Nicola. *France in Indochina: Colonial Encounters*. New York: Berg, 2001.

Corn, David. *Blond Ghost: Ted Shackley and the CIA's Crusades*. New York: Simon and Schuster, 1994.

Cosmas, Graham A. and Terrence P. Murray. *U.S. Marines in Vietnam: Vietnamization and Redeployment 1970-1971*. Washington, DC: U.S. Marine Corps, 1986.

Coups de Massu. A series of booklets produced by Groupement Massu during Indochina conflict 1945-46, available only at Texas Tech University, Vietnam Archives, Haponski Special Collection

Croizat, Victor. *The Brown Water Navy: The River and Coastal War in Indo-China and Vietnam, 1948-1972.* New York: Sterling, 1984.

Currey, Cecil B. *Victory at Any Cost.* Washington, DC: Potomac, 1997.

D'Alzon, Claude Hesse, et al. *La Presence Militaire Française en Indochine 1940 – 1945.* Vincennes: Publications du service historique de l'Armée de Terre, 1985.

D'Argenlieu, Thierry. *Chronique D'Indochine 1945 – 1947.* Paris: Albin Michel, 1985.

Davidson, Phillip B. *Vietnam at War, The History: 1946-1975.* Novato, CA: Presidio, 1988.

Decoux, Jean. *À la Barre de* l'Indochine 1940-1945. Paris: Librarie Plon, 1949.

De Galard, Genèvieve. *The Angel of Dien Bien Phu.* Introduction, sketch maps, appendices by William C. Haponski. Annapolis, MD: Naval Institute Press, 2010.

Devillers, Philippe and Jean Lacouture. *End of A War: Indochina 1954.* New York: Praeger, 1969.

Dinh Thi Van. *I Engaged in Intelligence Work.* Hanoi: Gioi, 2006.

Duiker, William J. *Ho Chi Minh.* New York: Theia, 2000.

----- . *The Communist Road to Power in Vietnam.* Boulder, CO: Westview, 1996.

----- . *Vietnam: Revolution in Transition.* Boulder, CO: Westview, 1995.

----- . *Vietnam Since the Fall of Saigon,* Updated Edition. Athens, OH: Ohio University Center for International Studies, 1989.

Dulles, John Foster. *Present at the Creation: My Years in the State Department.* New York: W. W. Norton & Company, 1987.

Dunn, Peter M. *The First Vietnam War.* London: C. Hurst, 1985.

Dutrone, Christophe. *Le Viet-Minh: de l'Indochine au Vietnam.* Paris: Éditions Les Indes Savantes, 2009.

Echenberg, Myron. *Colonial Conscripts: The Tirailleurs Senegalais in French West Africa, 1957 – 1960.* Portsmouth, NH: Heinemann, 1991.

Eisenhower, Dwight D. *Mandate for Change 1953-1956.* New York: Doubleday, 1963.

----- . *Waging Peace 1956-1961.* New York: Doubleday, 1965.

Ewell, Julien J. and Ira A. Hunt, Jr. *Sharpening the Combat Edge: The Use of Analysis to Reinforce Military Judgment.* Washington, DC: Department of the Army, 1974.

Fall, Bernard. *Hell in a Very Small Place: The Siege of Dien Bien Phu.* Philadelphia, PA: J. B. Lippincott, 1967.

----- . *Ho Chi Minh on Revolution: Selected Writings, 1920-66.* New York: Signet, 1967.

----- . *Last Reflections on a War.* New York: Schocken, 1972.

----- . *Street Without Joy.* Harrisburg, PA: Stackpole, 1964.

----- . *The Two Viet-Nams: A Political and Military Analysis.* New York: Praeger, 1965.

----- . *Viet-Nam Witness 1953 – 66.* New York: Praeger, 1966.

Fergurson, Ernest B. *Westmoreland: The Inevitable General.* Boston: Little, Brown, 1968.

Ferry, Jules François Camille. "Speech Before the French Chamber of Deputies, March 28, 1884," *Discours et Opinions de Jules Ferry,* Paul Robiquet, ed. Paris: Armand Colin & Cie., 1897. Translated by Ruth Kleinman in Brooklyn College Core Four Sourcebook (Internet).

Fonde, Jean-Julien. *Traitez a Tout Prix . . .* Paris: Édition Robert Laffont, 1971.

Gardner, Lloyd C. *Approaching Vietnam: From World War II through Dienbienphu.* New York: W. W. Norton, 1988.

Gavin, James M. *Crisis Now.* New York: Random House, 1968.

----- . *War and Peace in the Space Age.* New York: Harper & Brothers, 1958.

Gelb, Leslie H. *The Irony of Vietnam: The System Worked.* Washington, DC: Brookings Institute, 1979.

Giap, Vo Nguyen. *Banner of People's War, the Party's Military Line.* New York: Praeger, 1970.

----- . *Big Victory Great Task.* New York: Praeger, 1968.

----- . *Dien Bien Phu.* Hanoi: Foreign Languages, 1984.

----- . *Fighting Under Siege.* Hanoi: Gioi, 2004.

-----. *General Headquarters in the Spring of Brilliant Victory (Memoirs).* Hanoi: Gioi, 2013.

----- . & Van Tien Dung. *How We Won the War.* Philadelphia: RECON Publications, 1976.

----- . *The Military Art of People's War.* Stetler, Russell, ed. New York: Monthly Review Press, 1970.

----- . *People's War, People's Army.* New York: Bantam, 1962.

----- . *The Road to Dien Bien Phu.* Hanoi: Gioi, 2004.

----- . *Unforgettable Days.* Hanoi: Foreign Languages, 1975.

Goldstein, Gordon M. *Lessons in Disaster: McGeorge Bundy and the Path to War in Vietnam.* New York: Holt, 2008.

Goodson, Barry L. *Cap Mot: The Story of a Marine Special Forces Unit in Vietnam 1968-1969.* Denton, TX: University of North Texas Press, 1997.

Gras, Yves. *Histoire de la guerre d'Indochine.* Paris: Plon, 1971.

Gravel, Mike ed. *The Pentagon Papers. The Defense Department History of United States Decisionmaking on Vietnam.* Vol. 1. Boston: Beacon, 1971.

Guiberteau. Yannick. *La Dévastation: Cuirrasse de Riviére.* Paris: Albin Michel, 198

Gurney, Gene. *Vietnam: The War in the Air.* New York: Crown, 1985.

Gwin, Larry. *Baptism: A Vietnam Memoir.* New York: Ivy Books, 1999.

Haig, Alexander M., Jr. *Inner Circles: How America Changed the World, A Memoir.* New York: Worldwide Associates, 1992.

Halberstam, David. *The Best and the Brightest.* New York: Ballantine Books, 1969.

-----. *The Making of a Quagmire.* New York: Random House, 1965.

Hammer, Ellen J. *The Struggle for Indochina.* Stanford, CA: Stanford University Press, 1954.

Haponski, William C. *Danger's Dragoons, The Armored Cavalry Task Force of the Big Red One in Vietnam, 1969.* Wheaton, IL: First Division Museum, 2014.

Head, William and Lawrence E. Grinter, eds. *Looking Back on the Vietnam War: A 1990s Perspective on the Decisions, Combat, and Legacies.* Westport, CT: Praeger, 1993.

Herring, George C. *America's Longest War: The United States and Vietnam, 1950 – 1975,* 2nd ed. New York: Knopf, 1979.

Hickey, Gerald Cannon. *Village in Vietnam.* New Haven, CT: Yale University Press, 1964.

Historia, Hors Serie 24. *Notre Guerre d'Indochine.* Vol. 1. *La Piége: Mars 1945-Julliet 1951.* Paris: Librarie Jules Tallandier, 1972.

-----. Vol. 2. *Le Duel: Aout 1951-Octobre 1955.*

History of the Dau Tieng Rubber Workers Movement (1917 – 1997)[Lich su' Phong Trao Nhan Cao su Dau Tieng]. Ho Chi Minh City: Workers Publishing House, 2000. Selectively translated for the author by Merle Pribbenow. Vietnamese book available in Vietnam Archives, Haponski Special Collection.

Hoang Ngoc Lung. *The General Offensives of 1968-69.* Washington, DC: U.S. Government Printing Office, 1981.

Ho Chi Mi~~ ~~ *On Revolution: Selected Writings, 1920-66.* Ed., Bernard Fall. New York: Sign~~~~ 967.

Hoope~~~~ ~~dwin B. et al. *The United States Navy and the Vietnam Conflict,* Vol. I. ~~ing~~ton, DC: Department of the Navy, 1976.

Ho~~~~ Stephen T. et al. *The Fall of South Vietnam: Statements by Vietnamese Military* ~~d~~ *Civilian Leaders.* New York: Crane Russak,1980.

~~~~t, Richard A. *Pacification: The American Struggle for Vietnam's Hearts and Minds.* Boulder, CO: Westview, 1995.

~~c~~obs, Seth. *Cold War Mandarin: Ngo Dinh Diem and the Origins of America's War in Vietnam, 1950-1963.* Lanham, MD: Rowman & Littlefield, 2006.

Johnson, Lyndon Baines. *The Vantage Point: Perspectives of the Presidency 1963-1969.* New York: Holt, Rinehart, Winston, 1971.

Kalb, Marvin and Elie Abel. *Roots of Involvement: The U.S. in Asia 1784-1971.* New York: W. W. Norton, 1971.

Kellen, Konrad. *Conversations with Enemy Soldiers in Late 1968/Early 1969: A Study of Motivation and Morale.* Santa Monica, CA: Rand Corporation, 1970.

Koburger, Charles W., Jr. *The French Navy in Indochina: Riverine and Coastal Forces, 1945-54.* New York: Praeger, 1991.

----- . *Naval Expeditions: The French Return to Indochina, 1945-1946.*Westport, CT: Praeger, 1997.

Krepinevich, Andrew F., Jr. *The Army and Vietnam.* Baltimore: Johns Hopkins, 1986.

Krulak, Victor H. *First to Fight: An Inside View of the U.S. Marine Corps.* Annapolis, MD: Naval Institute Press, 1984.

Lacouture, Jean. *Vietnam: Between Two Truces.* New York: Random House, 1966.

----- . *Ho Chi Minh: A Political Biography.* New York: Vintage, 1968.

Lam Quang Thi. *Autopsy: The Death of South Vietnam.* Phoenix:: Sphinx, 1986.

----- . *The Twenty-five Year Century: A South Vietnamese General Remembers the Indochina War to the Fall of Saigon.* Denton, TX: University of North Texas Press, 2001.

Langguth, A. J. *Our Vietnam: The War 1954-1975.* New York: Simon & Schuster, 2000.

Lanning, Michael Lee and Dan Cragg. *Inside the VC and the NVA: The Real Story of North Vietnam's Armed Forces.* New York: Faucett Columbine, 1991.

Le General Leclerc: Vu par ses compagnons de combat. Paris: Alsatia, 1948.

"La Route Coloniale 13 entre Paksé & la Route Coloniale 9," *Indochine*, 8 Sep 1941, (pages unnumbered).

"La Route Coloniale 14, Saigon à Tourane par les Plateaux Mis," *Indochine*, 1. b 1943, 11-12.

Lawrence, Mark Atwood and Fredrik Logevall, eds. *The First Vietnam War: C. Conflict and Cold War Crisis*. Cambridge, MA: Harvard University Press, 20 l.

Le Gro, William E. *Vietnam from Cease-Fire to Capitulation*. Washington, DC: U Army Center of Military History, 1981.

Leroy, Jean. *Fils de la Rizière*. Paris: Éditions Robert Laffont, 1977.

Lien-Hang T. Nguyen. *Hanoi's War: An International History of the War for Peace in Vietnam*. Chapel Hill, NC: University of North Carolina Press, 2012.

Logevall, Fredrik. *Choosing War: The Lost Chance for Peace and the Escalation of War in Vietnam*. Berkeley: University of California Press, 1999.

MacCarrigle, George L. *Taking the Offensive: October 1966 to October 1967*. Washington, DC: CMH, 1998.

Mann, Robert. *A Grand Delusion: America's Descent into Vietnam*. New York: Basic Books, 2001.

Marolda, Edward J. *The U. S. Navy in the Vietnam War*. Washington, DC: Brassey's, 2002.

Marr, David G. *Vietnam 1945: The Quest for Power*. Berkeley, CA: University of California Press, 1995.

Massu, Jacques et Jean Julien Fonde. *L'aventure viet-minh*. Paris: Plon, 1980.

Massu, Jacques. *Sept ans avec Leclerc*. Paris: Plon, 1974.

Massu, Suzanne (Torres). *Quand j'etait Rochambelle*. Paris: Grasset, 1969.

----- . *Un Commandant Pas Comme Les Autres*. Paris: Fayard, 1971.

McAlister, John T., Jr. *Vietnam: The Origins of Revolution*. New York: Knopf, 1969.

McMaster, H. R. *Dereliction of Duty: Lyndon Johnson, Robert McNamara, The Joint Chiefs of Staff and the Lies That Led to Vietnam*. New York: Harper Perennial, 1997.

McNamara, Robert S. *In Retrospect: The Tragedy and Lessons of Vietnam*. New York: Times Books, 1995.

Melson, Charles D. and Curtis G. Arnold. *U.S. Marines in Vietnam: The War That Would Not End 1971-1973*. Washington, DC: U.S. Marine Corps, 1991.

Metzner, Ed̶rd P. *More than a Soldier's War: Pacification in Vietnam.* College Station, TX: ̶s A&M University Press, 1995.

Minorit̶ ̶ups in the Republic of Vietnam. Department of the Army Pamphlet No. 550-̶ ̶Washington, DC: U.S. Government Printing Office, 1967.

̶arold G. and Joseph L. Galloway. *We Were Soldiers Once...and Young: Ia Drang,* Mo̶̶e Battle that Changed the War in Vietnam. New York: Random House, 1992.

̶. *We Are Soldiers Still: A Journey Back to the Battlefields of Vietnam.* New York: HarperCollins, 2008.

̶urphy, Edward F. *Semper Fi, Vietnam: From Da Nang to the DMZ Marine Corps Campaigns, 1965-1975.* New York: Ballantine, 1997.

Navarre, Henri. *Agonie de l'Indochine (1953 – 1954).* Paris: Plon, 1956.

Newman, Bernard. *Background to Vietnam.* New York: New American Library, 1966.

Newton, Jim. *Eisenhower, The White House Years.* New York: Doubleday, 2011.

Ngo Vinh Long. *Before the Revolution: The Vietnamese Peasants Under the French.* New York: Columbia University Press, 1991.

Nguyen Thi Dinh, *No Other Road to Take.* Ithaca, NY: Cornell University Press, 1976.

Nixon, Richard. *Memoirs.* New York: Grosset and Dunlap, 1978

----- . *No More Vietnams.* New York: Arbor House, 1985

Nolan, Keith W. *Search and Destroy: The Story of an Armored Cavalry Squadron in Vietnam: 1-1 Cav, 1967-1968.* Minneapolis, MN: Zenith, 2010.

Nordell, John R. Jr. *The Undetected Enemy: French and American Miscalculations At Dien Bien Phu,1953.* College Station, TX: Texas A&M University Press, 1995.

Olson, James A. and Randy Roberts. *Where the Domino Fell: America and Vietnam, 1945 to 1995,* 2nd ed. New York: St. Martin's Press, 1996.

Palmer, Bruce C., Jr. *The 25-Year War: America's Military Role in Vietnam.* Lexington, KY: University of Kentucky Press, 1984.

Palmer, Dave Richard. *Summons of the Trumpet: U.S. – Vietnam in Perspective.* San Rafael, CA: Presidio, 1978.

Patti, Archimedes L. A. *Why Viet Nam?* Berkeley, CA: University of California Press, 1980.

Pentagon Papers: The Complete Report, Unredacted. CD, BACM Research, no date.

The Pentagon Papers, Gravel Edition. The Defense Department History of United States Decisionmaking on Vietnam. Volume 1. Boston: Beacon, 1971.

Pham, David Lam. *Two Hamlets in Nam Bo: Memoirs of Life in Vietnam through Japanese Occupation, the French and American Wars, and Communist Rule, 1940-1986.* Jefferson, NC: McFarland, 2000.

Pike, Douglas. *History of Vietnamese Communism.* Stanford, CA: Hoover Institution Press, 1978.

----- . *PAVN: People's Army of Vietnam.* Novato, CA: Presidio Press, 1986.

----- . *Viet Cong: The Organization and Techniques of the National Liberation Front South Vietnam.* Cambridge, MA: The M.I.T. Press, 1966.

----- . *Vietnam and the Soviet Union: Anatomy of an Alliance.* Boulder, CO: Westview Press, 1987.

Poole, Peter A. *The United States and Indo-China from FDR to Nixon.* Hinsdale, IL: Dryden Press, 1973.

Prados, John. *Vietnam: The History of An Unwinnable War, 1945-1975.* Lawrence, KS: University of Kansas Press, 2009.

Pribbenow, Merle, trans. of following:

Collected Party Documents. Vol. 29, 1968. Chief Editor, Ha Dang. Hanoi: National Political Publishing House, 2004.

----- . *"The Glorious History of the Heroic Vietnamese People's Security Forces"* [Nhung Trang Su Ve Vang cua Luc Luong Cong An Nhan Dan Anh Hung]. People's Public Security General Department of Security. Hanoi: People's Public Security Publishing House, 2006.

----- . *History of the COSVN Military Command (1961 – 1976) [Lich Sa Bo Chi Huy Mien] (1961-1976).* Colonel Ho Son Dai, editor. Hanoi: National Political Publishing House, 2004.

-----. *History of the Resistance War Against the Americans to Save the Nation, 1954-1975.* Vol.VI. *Defeating the Americans in the Three Nations of Indochina.* Editor, Colonel Ho Khang. Military History Institute of Vietnam. Hanoi: National Political Publishing House, 2003.

----- . *Military Encyclopedia of Vietnam.* Chief editor, Tran Do, Senior Colonel. Hanoi: People's Army Publishing House, 1996

----- . Ministry of Interior, General Department 1, Political Security Department III: *"Anti-Reactionary Forces: Chronology of Events (1954-1975)".* Editorial Supervision: Senior Colonel Nguyen Duc Khiem, Director, PSD III; Colonel

Hoang ~~u~~ Nan, Deputy Director PSD III; Authors: Major Nguyen Hung Linh and L~~ie~~tenant Colonel Hoang Mac. Hanoi: Public Security Publishing House, 199~~7~~

-----. ~~N~~uyen Minh Chau, "Happy and Sad Memories of a Time of War," *KBC Hai ~~N~~ai*, Issue 18, San Jose, CA: June 2003.

-----. ~~9~~th *Division [Su Doan 9]*; Editorial Direction: 9th Infantry Division Command Group and Party Committee; Author: Lieutenant Colonel Nguyen Quoc Dung; Document Research: Major Nguyen Anh Tinh. People's Army Publishing House, Hanoi, 1990.

-----. *The Resistance War in Eastern Cochin China (1945-1975) Vol. I.* Editorial Direction: Military Region 7 Headquarters and Party Committee, Military Region 7 Military Science Council. *Editor, Senior Colonel Nguyen Viet Ta. People's Army Publishing House, Hanoi, 1990.*

-----. *"The Secret Intelligence General and Incredible Spy Missions" [Ong Tuong Tinh Bao Bi An Va Nhung Diep Vu Sieu Hang]* from Nhan Dan newspaper website, 21 February 2004 issue, accessed on 21 February 2004 at *http://www.nhandan.org.vn/vietnamese/chinhtri/210204/sukien_ongtuong.htm*

-----. *7*th *Division: A Record [Su Doan 7: Ky Su]* Editorial Supervision: 7th Division Party Committee and Headquarters, Lt. Gen. Nguyen The Bon et al. Hanoi: People's Army Publishing House, 1986.

-----. *The Ten Thousand Day Journey: A Memoir. [Chặng Đường Mười Nghìn Ngày].* Hoang Cam, Colonel General, as told to Nhat Tien. Hanoi: People's Army Publishing House, 2001.

-----. *Victory in Vietnam: The Official History of the People's Army of Vietnam, 1954-1975.* The Military History Institute of Vietnam. Lawrence, KS: University Press of Kansas, 2002.

Reeves, Richard. *President Kennedy: Profile of Power.* New York: Simon & Schuster, 1993.

Rogers, William B. *Cedar Falls – Junction City: A Turning Point.* Washington, DC: Department of the Army, 1974.

Rostow, W. W. *The Diffusion of Power: An Essay in Recent History.* New York: Macmillan, 1972.

Roy, Jules. *The Battle of Dienbienphu.* New York: Carroll & Graf, 2002.

Rusk, Dean. *As I Saw It.* New York: Norton, 1990.

Sagar, D. J. *Major Political Events in Indo-China 1945 – 1990*. New York: Facts on File, 1991.

Salan, Raoul. *Mémoires: Fin d'un Empire, le sens d'un engagement, Juin 1899 – Septembre 1946*. Vol. 1. Paris: Presses de la Cité, 1970.

----- . Vol. 2. *Le Viet-minh mon adversaire, Octobre 1946-Octobre 1954*.

Schell, Jonathan. *The Village of Ben Suc*. New York: Knopf, 1967.

Schlesinger, Arthur M., Jr. *A Thousand Days: John F. Kennedy in the White House*. Boston: Houghton Mifflin, 1965.

Schoenbrun, David. *As France Goes*. New York: Harper & Brothers, 1957.

Scholl-Latour, Peter. *Death in the Rice Fields: An Eyewitness Account of VN's Three Wars 1945-1979*. New York: Penguin, 1985.

Shaplen, Robert. *The Road from War: Vietnam 1965-1970*. New York: Harper & Row, 1970.

Sharp, U.S.G. *Strategy for Defeat: Vietnam in Retrospect*. Novato, CA: Presidio, 1978.

Sharp, U.S.G. and W.C . Westmoreland. *Report on the War in Vietnam (As of 30 June 1968)*. Washington, DC: U.S. Government Printing Office.

Shawcross, William. *Sideshow: Kissinger, Nixon and the Destruction of Cambodia* rev. ed. New York: Touchstone, 1987.

Sheehan, Neil. *A Bright Shining Lie: John Paul Vann and America in Vietnam*. New York: Random House, 1988.

Sheehan, Susan. *Ten Vietnamese*. New York: Alfred A. Knopf, 1967.

Shelton, James E. *The Beast Was Out There: the 28th Infantry Black Lions and the Battle of Ong Thanh Vietnam October 1967*. Wheaton, IL: Cantigny 1st Division Foundation, 2002.

Shipway, Martin. *The Road to War: France and Vietnam, 1944-1947*. New York: Berghahn, 2003.

Shulimson, Jack. *U.S. Marines in Vietnam: An Expanding War 1966*. Washington, DC: U.S. Marine Corps, 1982.

Shultz, Richard H. Jr. *The Secret War Against Hanoi: Kennedy's and Johnson's Use of Spies, Saboteurs, and Covert Warriors in North Vietnam*. New York: HarperCollins, 1999.

Simon, Guy. *Chroniques de Cochinchine 1951-1956*. Paris: Charles-Lavauzelle, 1995.

Simonin, Paul. *Les Bérets blanc de la Legion en Indochine*. Paris: Éditions Albin Michel, 2002.

Simpson, Howard R. *Dien Bien Phu: The Epic Battle America Forgot*. Washington, DC: Potomac, 2005.

Smith, Charles R. *U.S. Marines in Vietnam: High Mobility and Standdown 1969*. Washington, DC: U.S. Marine Corps, 1988.

Snepp, Frank. *Decent Interval: An Insider's Account of Saigon's Indecent End, Told by the CIA's Chief Strategy Analyst in Vietnam*. Lawrence, KS: UP Kansas, 1977.

Sorensen, Theodore C. *Kennedy*. New York: Konecky & Konecky, 1965.

Sorley, Lewis. *A Better War: The Unexamined Victories and Final Tragedy of America's Last Years in Vietnam*. New York: Harvest, 1999.

----- . *Honorable Warrior: General Harold K. Johnson and the Ethics of Command*. Lawrence, KS: University of Kansas Press, 1998.

----- . *Thunderbolt: From the Battle of the Bulge to Vietnam and Beyond, General Creighton Abrams and the Army of His Times*. New York: Simon and Schuster, 1992.

----- . ed., *Vietnam Chronicles: The Abrams Tapes 1968-1972*. Lubbock, TX: Texas Tech University Press, 2004.

----- . ed., *The Vietnam War: An Assessment by South Vietnam's Generals*. Lubbock, TX: Texas Tech University Press, 2010.

----- . *Westmoreland: The General Who Lost Vietnam*. New York: Houghton Mifflin Harcourt, 2011.

Spector, Ronald H. *Advice and Support: The Early Years of the United States Army in Vietnam 1941 – 1960*. New York: Free Press, 1985.

Starobin, Joseph R. *Eyewitness in Indo-China*. New York: Cameron & Kahn, 1954.

Stone, David. *Dien Bien Phu 1954*. London: Brassey's, 2004.

Sullivan, John F. *Of Spies and Lies: A CIA Lie Detector Remembers Vietnam*. Lawrence, KS: University Press of Kansas, 2002.

Summers, Harry G., Jr. *On Strategy: A Critical Analysis of the Vietnam War*. New York: Presidio, 1982.

Taylor, Jay. *China and Southeast Asia: Peking's Relations with Revolutionary Movements*. New York: Praeger, 1974.

Taylor, Maxwell. *Swords and Plowshares*. New York: Norton, 1972.

Taylor, Telford. *Nuremberg and Vietnam: An American Tragedy*. Chicago, IL: Quadrangle Books, 1970.

The 30-Year War, 1945-1975, Vols. 1 & 2. Hanoi: Gioi, 2002.

Thompson, Robert. *No Exit from Vietnam*. New York: David McKay,

Tonnesson, Stein. *Vietnam 1946: How the War Began*. Berkeley, CA: California Press, 2010. sity of

Tran Tu Binh. *The Red Earth: A Vietnamese Memoir of Life on a Colonial Rubber* as told to Ha An. John Spragens, Jr. trans., David G. Marr, ed. Athens, On, University Center for International Studies, 1985.

Tran Van Don. *Our Endless War: Inside Vietnam*. Novato, CA: Presidio, 1978.

Tran Van Tra, Colonel General. *Vietnam: History of the Bulwark B2 Theatre*. Vol *Concluding the Vietnam War*. Ho Chi Minh City: Van Nghe Publishing House, 1982. (on Internet).

Trinquier, Roger. *Modern Warfare: A French View of Counterinsurgency*. Westport, CT: Praeger Security, 2006.

Truong Nhu Tang. *A Viet Cong Memoir*. San Diego, CA: Harcourt Brace Jovanovich, 1985.

Truman, Harry S. *1945: Year of Decisions*. New York: Konecky & Konecky, 1955.

----- . *1946-1952: Years of Trial and Hope*. New York: Smithmark, 1955.

Turley, William S. *The Second Indochina War: A Short Political and Military History, 1954-1975*. New York: Signet, 1987.

20ᵉ Siecle. *Guerre d'Indochine*. Vol. 1. *De la conquête de l'Indochine à de Lattre*. Paris: Trésor du Patrimonie. no date.

U. S Army Area Handbook for Vietnam. Washington, DC: U.S. Government Printing Office, 1962.

Van Atta, Dale. *With Honor: Melvin Laird in War, Peace, and Politics*. Madison, WI: University of Wisconsin Press, 2008.

VanDeMark, Brian. *Into the Quagmire: Lyndon Johnson and the Escalation of the VN War*. New York: Oxford University Press, 1995.

Van Tien Dung. *Our Great Spring Victory: An Account of the Liberation of South Vietnam*. New York: Monthly Review, 1977.

Veith, George J. and Merle L. Pribbenow II. "'Fighting is an Art': The Army of the Republic of Vietnam's Defense of Xuan Loc, 9-21 April 1975." *The Journal of Military History* 68 (January 2004): 163-214.

Vézinet, Adolphe. *Le général Leclerc*. Paris: J'ai Lu, 1982.

nge War, Strange Strategy: A General's Report on Vietnam. New York:
Walt, Lewi*g*nalls, 1970.

Funk*Village*. New York: Pocketbooks, 1972.

West, B*i*, William C. *A Soldier Reports*. Garden City, NY: Doubleday, 1976.

West*m*es Scott. *The Big Red One: America's Legendary 1st Infantry Division, from
Wh*/ War I to Desert Storm*. Lawrence, KS: University of Kansas Press, 2007.

*i*ks, James H. *The Battle of An Loc*. Bloomington, IN: Indiana University Press,
*0*05.

*id*row, Martin. *The French Indo-China War 1946-54*. Oxford: Osprey, 1998.

--- . *The Last Valley: Dien Bien Phu and the French Defeat in Vietnam*. Cambridge, MA:
Da Capo, 2004.

Young, Marilyn B. *The Vietnam Wars 1945-1990*. New York: Harper Collins, 1991.

Zaffiri, Samuel. *Westmoreland: A Biography of General William C. Westmoreland*. New
York: Morrow, 1994.

Zhai, Qiang. *China & the Vietnam Wars, 1950-1975*. Chapel Hill: University of North
Carolina Press, 2000.

Zumwalt, James G. *Bare Feet, Iron Will: Stories from the Other Side of Vietnam's Battlefields*.
Jacksonville, FL: Fortis, 2010.

INDEX

56014430R10348

Made in the USA
Lexington, KY
09 October 2016